The Truth of *Buffy*

Table of Contents

Preface
   Emily Dial-Driver   1
Introduction
   Jim Ford   5

What's It All About, Buffy? Victor Frankl and *Buffy*
   Emily Dial-Driver   9
Got Myself a Soul? The Puzzling Treatment of the Soul in *Buffy*
   J. Renée Cox   24
Not Just Another Love Song: *Buffy*'s Music as Representation
   of Emerging Adulthood
   Jacqueline Bach   38
Is That Stereotype Dead? Working with and Against "Western"
   Stereotypes in *Buffy*
   Sally Emmons-Featherston   55
Lord Acton Is Alive and Well in Sunnydale: Politics and Power
   in *Buffy*
   Kenneth S. Hicks   67
Willow's Electric Arcs: Moral Choices Sparked by Connections
   Frances E. Morris   83
Is It Art? The Artful "Hush" of St. Francis and the Gentlemen
   Blue Meanies
   Gary Moeller   96
Signs, Signs, Everywhere Signs: Brechtian Techniques in *Buffy*
   David Blakely   107

"The Ants Go Marching": Effective Lyrics in *Buffy* Episodes
  Lori M. Butler   120

"Love the One You're With": Developing Xander
  J. Michael McKeon   131

Texting *Buffy*: Allusions of Many Kinds
  Emily Dial-Driver and Jesse Stallings   142

"What Shall Cordelia Say?" *Buffy* as Morality Play for the
  Twenty-First Century's Therapeutic Ethos
  Gregory J. Thompson and Sally Emmons-Featherston   158

Witchy Women: Witchcraft in *Buffy* and in Contemporary
  African Culture
  Juliet Evusa   173

"I'm Cookie Dough": Exploring *Buffy* Iconography
  Kenneth S. Hicks and Carolyn Anne Taylor   185

A Life Well-Lived: Buffy and the Pursuit of Happiness
  Jim Ford   201

Appendix: *Buffy the Vampire Slayer* Episodes   211
Works Cited   213
About the Contributors   225
Index   229

Preface

EMILY DIAL-DRIVER

I never intended to be a *Buffy* watcher. In fact, not watching much TV and not yet owning a TiVo, I'd never even heard of the series. That changed over one Christmas.

The circumstances: I live in the middle of the USA near an airport, making my house a central location for a widespread and populous family. My side of the family gathers at Christmas: old and young. Every bed and every piece of pullout furniture, every blow-up mattress and every soft surface has an occupant. There are so many people in the house that at night one must step over and around bodies tossing on pallets and slumbering in sleeping bags. It's loud and chaotic and wonderful and wearing. When they all leave, all but my immediate family, the house grows very much bigger.

The Christmas I'm talking about, the day they all left, after many days of that wonderful chaos, with people coming and going and going and coming and making plans and making dinners and yelling for celery and hollering for help in finding pots and pans—only my husband, my son and daughter (both home from college), and I were left. The tree was down, the last leftover was frozen for later consumption, the last lost Game Boy was located, the last lost bag was retrieved, the last car was loaded, the last group was transported to the airport crowded into a small car, and the TV was *not* being commandeered by someone who just *had* to see a program or watch a movie or make everyone watch this wonderful DVD "you all just have to see!"

My son said, "The TV is *mine*," and hit the couch. "Oh, yeah," replied my daughter and landed on the other couch. Trepidation. But, I realized they had the same program in mind, and there would be no dueling remotes. Since they were only at home for a limited period, I couldn't let them watch without me, and we were in for two straight hours of *Buffy* watching, in syndicated rerun, every day, for two weeks.

1

Since they were dedicated watchers—but had not previously introduced me to the pleasures of the Whedon-verses (for which I am thinking about forgiving them), they could catch me up on what had happened previously and what was to come later. For me, that's a very good thing since I always read the end of the book first. (No, that's not weird. The story is important but, for me, it's almost as important to figure out how the story gets to the end—how it works—and knowing the end first lets me do that.)

I had those two weeks of two hours a day of *Buffy*. By the time they went back to college and I went back to work, I was well and truly addicted.

When I came back to Rogers State University, I quietly mentioned to Sally Emmons-Featherston that I had been watching *Buffy*. She exclaimed, "I watch that too." Jim Ford had silently walked up behind us as we were speaking and said, "I watch that too." Suddenly there were three of us. But no. Just then Victor Gischler (who has left for a career as novelist,* but who was then teaching with us) crept up unheard and mentioned that he was also an aficionado, as was his wife, Jacqueline Bach, a doctoral student at Oklahoma State University. Then we discovered that Carole Burrage, the legal assisting program director, was a fan. So we arranged to go to a conference and make a coordinated presentation. We went; Jim drove; we had a good time; we made it back; I bought earrings.

Over the years, we have gathered a number of other *Buffy* scholars (and the university even allowed us to offer a class on *Buffy*). We recruited Lori Butler, Frances E. Morris, and Renée Turk for the next coordinated panel(s). And we added David Blakely, Juliet Evusa, Gregory J. Thompson, J. Michael McKeon, Carolyn Anne Taylor, Gary Moeller, and Kenneth S. Hicks to our cohort. They had endless *Buffy* marathons and became instant watchers. We even added an RSU graduate: Jesse Stallings.

Over the course of the past few years, various groups of us have made several trips to assorted cities. We've had plane delays and cancellations, snow and rain, mosquitoes and fleas. We've taken detours and wrong turns. We've gotten lost in the elevator banks of mega-hotels. We've had hotels charge us for days we never spent there, had the hotels refund our overcharge, and later reapply that charge. During one of our interminable discussions with the hotel management, an experience which was running us very late for our airport shuttle, Sally commented, "I think we've brought the Hellmouth with us." It became a running joke. Every difficulty, every delay, every tiny frustration, someone would say, "See, we did bring the Hellmouth with us."

So the working title for the book became *Sitting on the Hellmouth* (which

---

Victor has five novels out, all wonderful: Gun Monkeys *(nominated for an Edgar Award),* Pistol Poets *(really, it's not set at Rogers State University),* Suicide Squeeze, Shotgun Opera, *and* Go-Go Girls of the Apocalypse. *We miss him. But, as you can see from the Table of Contents, his wife (Jacqueline Bach) is still Buffyized!*

we later changed). Now we don't think we actually work on the Hellmouth. We like our jobs; we love our colleagues; we appreciate our students. We experience all the annoyances that everyone experiences, the aggravations that go with teaching, with working for the state, with life in general; but, when we weigh up our professional lives, the scale definitely tilts toward the positive. *Buffy* watching is part of that positive.

The fact is the work is rewarding, and we've had fun.

It has been such fun, Lori said, "Let's do a book." So we did. Here it is.

Introduction

JIM FORD

In this study we examine the way in which fiction reflects and illuminates reality. Bob Dylan once said that "Popular songs are the only art form that describes the temper of the times." While he's right about popular music, we believe that popular television can be just as illuminating. Joss Whedon's television series *Buffy the Vampire Slayer* is a particularly rich and compelling universe, one in which a number of significant aspects of reality are clearer and sharper. These fifteen essays highlight the way in which *Buffy* meditates on the reality of life outside the box.

Since its conclusion in 2003, *Buffy* has been the focus of a number of interesting studies, from a variety of fields and perspectives, with no signs of the literature abating. From commentaries on particular episodes to philosophical accounts of the entire series, "Slayer Studies" is rapidly becoming its own field. What distinguishes this book, however, is the range of the essays presented and the depth of their analysis. The fifteen authors included hail from a number of disciplines, from literature to the visual arts, philosophy to political science, theatre to cultural studies. The essays themselves share this diversity in topic and approach, but they are also unified by this basic theme, the way in which fiction reflects and illuminates reality.

Of course, the power of great fiction to do this has long been recognized. Whether in canonical works of literature by Shakespeare, Jane Austen, James Joyce, or Toni Morrison; in landmark films by Alfred Hitchcock, Orson Welles, Woody Allen, or Spike Lee; or in classic albums by the Beatles, Bob Dylan, R.E.M., or Radiohead, great fiction transcends simple categories. One of the main arguments of this book is that *Buffy the Vampire Slayer* is in fact great fiction. During the course of its seven seasons the series raised a number of significant topics.

The first essay uses the series as a whole to comment on Victor Frankl's account of the "search for meaning" in human lives. In "What's It All About, Buffy? Victor Frankl and *Buffy*," Emily Dial-Driver argues that the "search for meaning" is played out in the plot and character arcs of *Buffy*. What is the meaning that Frankl and the characters of *Buffy* find? Examining the search illustrates one of the series's most basic philosophies.

The relationship between identity, morality, and the soul is a particularly tough one, and, in her essay, "Got Myself a Soul? The Puzzling Treatment of the Soul in *Buffy*," J. Renée Cox highlights some of the problems with the way the soul is portrayed in the series. While many of the characters espouse and embrace a philosophy in which the absence of a soul means a complete lack of conscience and goodness, Cox proves that a close examination of the creatures and events in Buffy's world show that this simple black-and-white philosophy is illogical. In fact, a belief system which supports a "no soul=no good" philosophy echoes some dangerous and illogical ideas of our past, and Cox highlights the danger in such thoughts.

The next essay focuses on the many ways in which music functions in the series. In "Not Just Another Love Song: *Buffy*'s Music as Representation of Emerging Adulthood," Jacqueline Bach demonstrates that the music mirrors the main characters' journey from adolescents to adults. Music itself, she argues, is crucial to the way in which the series depicts that journey. By analyzing a number of important examples from all seven seasons of the series, Bach provides a compelling account of the characters' maturation into adulthood.

The fourth essay, Sally Emmons-Featherston's "Is that Stereotype Dead? Working with and Against 'Western' Stereotypes in *Buffy*" raises another crucial issue. Emmons-Featherston analyzes one episode in particular ("Pangs" from Season Four), highlighting how popular misconceptions and stereotypes of Native Americans recur in Western culture. In some ways the series's attempt to undermine those stereotypes serves only to reinforce them. Through this close examination, Emmons-Featherston is able to make explicit what this episode really suggests about American Indians and the myth of the American West.

A different sort of myth is the focus of the next essay, Kenneth S. Hicks' "Lord Acton Is Alive and Well in Sunnydale: Politics and Power in *Buffy*." Beginning with Frankenstein, the "Modern Prometheus," Hicks explores a number of ways in which the series generates real insights into the nature of politics and the problem of power in modern life. In many ways, the power that enables Buffy to do good threatens to corrupt that very goodness.

That corruption threatens a number of other characters as well, particularly Willow, who is the focus of the sixth essay, "Willow's Electric Arcs: Moral Choices Sparked by Connections," by Frances E. Morris. Willow undergoes a number of dramatic developments over the course of the series, from good girl nerd to archetypal sidekick to alpha female. Morris traces Willow's overall development, highlighting the ways in which Willow's identity is shaped by her quest for power and recognition and by her inclusion and exclusion in the Scoobies.

These considerations of power and identity are followed by a number of essays dealing with aesthetic considerations, and more specifically, *how* it is that the series is able to reflect and illuminate reality. The first of these is a very different look at the world of *Buffy*. In "Is It Art? The Artful 'Hush' of St. Francis and the Gentlemen Blue Meanies," Gary Moeller considers the artistic qualities of one crucial episode in particular, Season Four's Emmy-nominated "Hush." Moeller identifies a number of surprising artistic resonances in the episode and explains why a casual viewer should take a deeper look at the series as a whole.

The border between fiction and reality is further blurred by the use of certain Brechtian techniques in the series, as David Blakely argues in "Signs, Signs, Everywhere Signs: Brechtian Techniques in *Buffy*." Focusing on a number of specific examples, Blakely points to the ways in which explicit signs create meaning in *Buffy*. In light of Brecht's ideas on alienation, such signs contribute to a more complex interaction between art and audience.

The aesthetic examination continues in Lori M. Butler's essay "'The Ants Go Marching': Effective Lyrics in *Buffy* Episodes," which highlights the way in which the lyrics in each episode enrich the viewing experience. Music is prevalent in the *Buffy* universe, and Butler argues that the song lyrics are integral to the plot and character development of particular episodes. Analyzing how the lyrics function helps Butler examine how the series mimics reality or, perhaps, how reality mimics fiction.

The next essay in this collection traces the development of Xander, one of Buffy's constant companions, by focusing on "Teacher's Pet," an episode from Season One. J. Michael McKeon's "'Love the One You're With': Developing Xander" is intriguing in two respects: first, because it shows how the series develops a number of important characters, not just Buffy, and, second, because "Teacher's Pet" is far from being one of the series' best episodes. McKeon's essay demonstrates how even an average episode of *Buffy* can deepen one's understanding of real human issues.

Another way in which *Buffy* plays with reality is through its vast number and range of allusions, as Emily Dial-Driver and Jesse Stallings argue in their essay "Texting Buffy: Allusions of Many Kinds." By tracking allusions, scholars and fans can come to a better understanding of the often all-too-subtle nuances of this intricate series. *Buffy* is replete with allusions from pop culture, from literature, from film, and even from the series itself. Going beyond a simple "episode guide," this essay analyzes how the series is enhanced by works that surround the audience.

Gregory J. Thompson and Sally Emmons-Featherston then look closely at *why* the creators of *Buffy* would engage in this kind of cultural pastiche, this range and wealth of allusions. In their essay, "'What Shall Cordelia Say?' *Buffy the Vampire Slayer* as Morality Play for the Twenty-First Century's Therapeutic Ethos," Thompson and Emmons-Featherston explain that Shakespeare used this very same technique to hit on points that would be easily recognized by his audiences so that the more profound meanings of his plays could be understood, without the need for lengthy exposition. Similarly, the use of pastiche in Buffy takes well-known motifs and cultural references, while creating new meaning for those references. In particular, the authors compare the *Buffy* character Cordelia to *King Lear's* Cordelia, exploring how the use of these cultural markers create a deeper meaning within the context of the show.

The thirteenth essay is an outsider's view of the series. A native Kenyan, Juliet Evusa discusses witchcraft in American media and in Africa in "Witchy Women: Witchcraft in *Buffy* and in Contemporary African Culture." To what extent is the reality reflected in *Buffy* thoroughly American? Evusa's essay is another meditation on the various uses and forms of power in different contexts.

This is followed by an extended treatment of the various ways Buffy herself is presented in the series. In "'I'm Cookie Dough': Exploring *Buffy* Iconography," Kenneth S. Hicks and Carolyn Anne Taylor consider whether it makes sense to describe Buffy as a feminist icon. Their essay articulates some of Buffy's clearest roles, from savior to oppressed other, and argues that in the final analysis Buffy's rich and complex identity shatters a number of long-held stereotypes.

Sure, Buffy's an icon, but is it all worth it? Jim Ford faces this question in the final essay, "A Life Well-Lived: Buffy and the Pursuit of Happiness." Would anyone really want to be the Slayer? Buffy's struggles throughout the series may make her life seem less than desirable, but she displays real virtues throughout that struggle. Her plight illuminates how complex human happiness really is, in fiction and in the world outside. In the end, Ford contends, Buffy's is a life well-lived.

Ultimately, in these fifteen essays, we argue that *Buffy the Vampire Slayer* is great fiction. In it we can see some of the myriad ways that great fiction reflects and reveals the world in which we live. We hope that this book deepens your appreciation and understanding for the series, as well as of the particular topics treated herein.

What's It All About, Buffy?

Victor Frankl and Buffy

—✎—

EMILY DIAL-DRIVER

Sitting on the couch, feet on the coffee table, soda at hand, staring, mouth slightly open, minimal drool (we hope).

Explosions and car crashes. Dripping knives and maniacal laughter. Flying balls and waving pompoms. Aspiring singers and doughty ventriloquists. Women who sleep with their husbands' sons and men who want to get pregnant. Racing dogs and jumping horses.

People watch television for a variety of reasons: entertainment is at the top. Other motives might range from enjoying mindlessness to garnering information about the world around us. Well, maybe.

Ideally, entertainment is not only designed for mindless staring but comes packaged with information also, information that opens our worldviews, that makes us more aware of others or our environs, that gives us something we might need. Of course, if shows carry messages/information beyond the entertainment value, sometimes that means they are preachy. Mostly that means they fail—critically and financially.

Sometimes we find a program that has great entertainment value while still conveying layers of meaning, leading to critical and financial success. We find a series that comments on "real life." *Buffy the Vampire Slayer* is one of those programs. *Buffy* reflects the same lessons as Victor Frankl's philosophy, which is very much grounded in how life is lived.[1] Since Frankl, along with a number of other philosophers, deals with choice, it seemed using Frankl would be appropriate to illuminate issues in *Buffy*.

I started this process thinking that the main relevance of Frankl to *Buffy* is his emphasis on choice. We know from Joss Whedon's own words that Whedon finds choice an important part of consciousness.

Frankl maintains in *Man's Search for Meaning* that people are not "things" because "*Things* determine each other, but *man*[2] is ultimately self-determining. What he becomes—within the limits of endowment and environment—he has made out of himself" (157). He continues from his own experience, "In the concentration camps, for example, in this living laboratory and on this testing ground, we watched and witnessed some of our comrades behave like swine while others behaved like saints. Man has both potentialities within himself; which one is actualized depends on decisions but not on conditions" (157).

Even this short selection from Frankl illustrates that more than the idea of choice relates to the series. Here he addresses the dual nature of all humanity. Other passages evoke other themes in *Buffy*. In fact, if Joss Whedon had set out to illustrate *Man's Search for Meaning*, he would have developed *Buffy*.

Who *is* Victor Frankl? Frankl was a philosopher and a psychologist, the developer of one of the three main psychotherapies. Freud, Adler, and Frankl are the psychotherapy triumvirate. However, Frankl's experiences in life were far different from those of Freud and Adler. Victor Frankl forged many of his concepts in the depths of the concentration camps, at Auschwitz and later at Dachau. From those and other experiences, he developed a philosophy and a psychotherapy, which are interrelated. It is the philosophy that is reflected in *Buffy*, a philosophy that includes commentary on suffering, identity, duality, morality, and the search for life's personal and universal meaning.

Man's Search for Meaning is divided into four parts: a preface and foreword for various editions; a first section on Frankl's experiences in the concentration camps; a discussion of logotheraphy, Frankl's contribution to psychotherapy based on each person's search for meaning in life; and one or more afterwords which deal with hope and the search for meaning. That search involves various elements: suffering and its relation to life's meaning, choice, and meaning itself.

Suffering is an inevitable part of life, but if "one cannot change a situation that causes his suffering, he can still choose his attitude" (Frankl 172).[3] Most of us have trouble with this, preferring to rail at the situation instead of amending our own attitudes to that situation. Willow is the most pertinent illustration of how important the distinction between situation and attitude is. Willow grieves over Oz's final departure from Sunnydale and does a spell which makes Giles blind and Buffy and Spike plan marriage ("Something Blue"). She grieves for Buffy after Buffy's sacrificial death at the end of Season Five; she deals with her grief by raising Buffy in a hazardous act, the magnitude of which she does not admit; her action damages the cosmological balance ("Bargaining"). Willow does not accept that she has erred until she is forced into the realization she has yanked Buffy out of heaven. Then she realizes non-action — and change of attitude — would have been more useful (but not to the series).

Willow continues to deal with grief in dangerous ways in Season Six. When she loses Tara to Warren's stray bullet ("Seeing Red"), she kills Warren, losing her humanity ("Villains"). She only regains sanity and humanity — and tears — when, taking "humanity-tainted" magic from Giles, she can "hear" Xander tell her he loves her, even as she attacks him. She accepts her grief, mourning Tara, realizing she cannot change her loss and she cannot alleviate her sorrow, but she can react to it more positively and less destructively. At last she chooses an attitude with which she and others can live — literally ("Grave").

Her suffering and her reactions to suffering, however, have taught her humility, almost to the point that she fears to help her friends in their trials with the First Evil in Season Seven, but "meaning is available in spite of — nay, even through — suffering" (Frankl 172). Willow finds that meaning in increased connectedness with her friends (despite early doubts in "Same Time Same Place") and in her willingness to help Buffy "share" power with all potential Slayers in the Season Seven climax.

The past haunts Willow but ultimately supports her: "In the past, nothing is irretrievably lost, but rather, on the contrary, everything is irrevocably stored and treasured" (Frankl 175). When the First Evil visits Willow in the library, telling her that Tara "still sings," Willow at first accepts all that the imposter says. It is only when the First tells her that the world would be better off without her that Willow realizes Tara would never say that: the past supports Willow and she rejects the First ("Conversations with Dead People"). The past, her past, her errors, her mistakes, make Willow a stronger person able to handle stronger power and help Buffy save the world once more.

Buffy has also suffered and made some bad choices. Pulled from heaven in Season Six by friends who think she is in a hell dimension (although why a person who saves the world "a lot" would be in a hell dimension is never satisfactorily explained), she thinks she has "come back different" because Spike can hit her or that she "left something" of herself in the grave because she feels so empty. She chooses a physical relationship with Spike both to punish herself and to make herself "feel something" ("Smashed"). She chooses to ignore Dawn, to use Giles as a teenager uses an indulgent parent, and to deceive her friends.

It's understandable that someone dragged from warm acceptance and completeness into a place that is "hard" and "bright" would be disconcerted and distressed. Buffy spends Season Six recovering her interest in the world and in others, once again leaving her self-centeredness and using her past to give her the strength in the final season to turn down demon power offered to her to make her stronger ("Get It Done"), to accept and overlook her banishment as leader ("Empty Places"), to accept that leadership position again ("End of Days"), and to plan and carry out the victory over the First Evil by potentiating all the "Potentials" ("Chosen").

This is a sharing of power, a giving up of the unique position that Buffy has held. Yes, it is a burden: "While Buffy has exercised social heroism, she has absolutely no desire to be a superhero" (Wilcox 19). Burdens are burdensome (by definition). One is "alone in all the world." But to be unique is also to be special. And being special, being "the one" is perhaps hard to give up. We all want to be special. Buffy gives up what some, including perhaps her, might see as her only special quality (it's not) to become just one of the girls. This could be a hard choice. Her suffering, her past allows her to make this choice. In fact, she learns much about sharing in her relationships with her family, her community (AKA her "Scoobies"). She also learns about suffering and sharing through the second half of Season Seven, especially as she sleeps in Spike's arms, sharing space and faith ("Touched").

Dawn also suffers. She suffers from Buffy's inattention after Buffy returns from her sacrifice of her own life in place of Dawn's ("The Gift"). However, Dawn sees the sacrifice as desertion and sees Buffy's inability to connect after Buffy's resurrection as rejection. Perception of desertion and rejection isn't of the same magnitude as losing heaven or losing a loved one, but "suffering completely fills the human soul and conscious mind, no matter whether the suffering is great or little. Therefore the 'size' of human suffering is absolutely relative" (Frankl 64). Dawn, in the face of her suffering, makes bad choices, among them theft and making a wish that doesn't turn out well. She too learns from her actions—to make reparations and not to use words ill-advisedly ("Older and Far Away").

Suffering,[4] which in no case should be courted, but which, when it comes, big or small, can be endured with grace, can become a lesson. Buffy's characters suffer and learn, just as we all do. Thus, we become who we are.

Becoming ourselves is a function of what we choose, according to the existentialist. Frankl says the word "'existential' may be used in three ways: to refer to (1) *existence* itself, i.e., the specifically human mode of being; (2) the *meaning* of existence; and (3) the striving to find a concrete meaning in personal existence, that is to say, the *will* to meaning" (123). Thus, each person lives, i.e., exists; each person has an existence, i.e., a meaning; and each person seeks to find and understand that meaning, i.e., seeks to find the reason for him/her self to exist. Some philosophers, Adler in particular, say that meaning is gained and lost in the accumulation and loss of power. Some philosophers maintain that meaning is gained — and lost — in urges or desires. For example, Freud says that in the face of desire, in the midst of impulses, people's individualities diminish, they become more identical, in the "uniform expression of the one unstilled urge" (Frankl 178) but, Frankl says, of his experiences in Auschwitz, "*There*, the 'individual differences' did *not* 'blur' but, on the contrary, people became more different; people unmasked themselves, both the swine and the saints" (178).

Those same kinds of experiences did not end at Auschwitz or Dachau. They continue today, not in a Holocaust, but in experiments, in prisons, and in living. Editorialist Shermer, in "Skeptic: Bad Apples and Good Apples," discusses whether people choose their actions or are moved into action by situation. Philip Zimbardo's important Stanford prison experiment concluded early, placed into "roles" of prisoner and guard, healthy, psychologically-normal college students took on those "roles" and acted submissive and/or defiant as prisoners and cruel and/or spiteful as guards. Because the subjects took on the assigned roles, we must "first find out what situations they were in that might have provoked this evil behavior. Why not assume that these are good apples in a bad barrel, rather than bad apples in a good barrel?" (Shermer 35). Shermer asserts that the guards who acted as tormentors and torturers at Abu Ghraib were originally "good apples" placed in a "bad barrel." However, he continues, "we have the capacity for good and evil, with the behavioral expression of them dependent on the situation and *whether we choose to act*" (emphasis mine) (36). Frankl, as we have already seen, says, "Man has both potentialities within himself; which one is actualized depends on decisions but not on conditions" (157). He maintains that it is not the role that causes our actions but our own choice.

So our capacity for being swine exists, just as our capacity for being saints exists. Is this capacity based in situation? Perhaps in part it is, but ultimately, according to Frankl *and* to Shermer, each of us must use our capacity to choose to determine what that self will be. Choices are hard and have consequences—sometimes consequences with which we have to live and suffer — or die, but they are ultimately our choices. We choose whether to turn in the Jew in our apartment; we choose whether to torture the prisoner.

Each of the major characters in *Buffy* determines his/her "self," sometimes acting as "swine," other times as "saints." At each moment, who they are is in a state of determination: "Man does not simply exist but always decides what his existence will be, what he will become in the next moment" (Frankl 154). *Buffy* critic Ian Shuttleworth says *Buffy* has "a deep and abiding preoccupation with senses of identity and role playing as everyday parts of personality in all its forms..." (213–14). Actually, "identity is a matter both of person and of role" (Shuttleworth 228). Buffy is Slayer, the Slayer is Buffy, even as she wishes to be "just another girl." The "other" Slayer, Faith, however, accepts her role as Slayer with vigor and vehemence, to the extent that she sees herself above rule and law until she changes bodies with Buffy and takes her place. Faith, in Buffy's body and in her place, realizes what being a Slayer, with its responsibilities, entails. Her burgeoning realization that not going to rescue the people in danger in the church would "be wrong" compels her to stop her flight from Sunnydale in order to fight vampires ("Who Are You?"). Faith staying to fight vampires is "clearly not in Faith's best interest, but the desire for combat, the call of fate and her own nihilism, override all else" (West 177). More than nihilism is at work here. Faith chooses to act as Buffy would act. She chooses to fight. She also chooses to beat up her body, in which "Buffy" resides, telling "herself" that she is bad, bad, bad. When she is returned to her own body, she flees to Los Angeles where she tortures Wesley and taunts Angel, asking not for "suicide by cop," but "suicide by Angel," who refuses to comply (*Angel*, "Five by Five"). She accepts her punishment for killing a human, staying in prison until she is needed in *Angel* to fight evil in that series or needed in *Buffy* for the final fight in Sunnydale ("Dirty Girls"). From "swine" to "saint," Faith illustrates the maximum swing.

As Faith illustrates the swing from "swine" to "saint," she also illustrates the evolution of character. Living involves change, change in circumstance and change in self: "Man is capable of changing the world for the better if possible, and of changing himself for the better if necessary" (Frankl 154). And change is a constant in *Buffy*: "The real meat in the case of *Buffy the Vampire Slayer* is character, or, more to the point, character change" (Billson 48). In fact, "the evolution of its hero ... make[s] Buffy's story worthy of being sung by the *scop* [bard] in the mead hall" (Fritts).

The creator of *Buffy*, Joss Whedon, says the series is supposed to function "ultimately on the level of message" (Kirkland 67)—and it does just that. It functions on the level of Frankl's messages to the world, one of which is that one must choose who one is. At each moment, one chooses which path one takes: "The show affirms time and again the processes of *becoming* rather than the state of *being* an individual" (Pateman 194), just as salvation and redemption are constant choices: "On *Buffy*, redemption is more of a process than an act" (Stevenson 254).

Recognizing the dual nature of humanity — and choosing the good part — is a part of learning who we are. We have the potential to act in an evil way or a good way. Which way we act depends on us. In *Buffy*, dual natures abound; they are necessary to reflect the potential of good and evil action: "a moral system that fails to account for the dark impulses of humanity and face them is ultimately ineffectual because it embraces a pristine vision of the world that is illusory" (Stevenson 19).

From Willow to Spike, from Oz to Anya, explorations of duality transpire: all the characters "manifest both qualities— good and evil, bright and dark, cruelty and compassion. In doing so, they continue to surprise us, as real people do throughout our lives; and they thereby accurately reflect the confusing ambiguity of life in our own world, thus making the supernatural *Buffy*verse compelling and seemingly real because of its visceral truths" (Resnick 56); "Many of the individuals in *BtVS* are caught in the struggle that Kant finds intrinsic to human nature — that of the 'good' side battling for control against their 'bad' side" (Stroud 180); and "good and bad are not so far apart and that 'bad' is not simply the domain of the 'othered' bad guys but is, instead, the 'other' within" (Krzywinska 183). Since "you can't think of things as bad without relating them to good" (South), the bad actions of characters contrast more brightly the good choices that they make.

Most of the characters have to deal with the "dark side." Oz, for example, plays his darkness out as a werewolf that must be locked up for three days a month ("Phases"). Other dualities are not so metaphorical. Willow, who is "beneath the amicable façade ... an ambivalent, dangerous character" (Battis 32), is like "most dangerous people ... who are totally unaware of their dark sides" (Reiss 114). She denies her most difficult impulses, telling Buffy she does not mind talking about Faith, whom she sees as a rival, but losing enough control to impale a tree with a pencil ("Doppleganland"). Her inability to recognize her own dual nature makes her easy prey to it, enabling her to supplant the Evil Trio as Buffy's major opponent in Season Six.

Anya is a character who does the most waffling between light and dark. Her dark side is both metaphoric (as a demon) and actual. (Even Spike does not go back and forth, swinging from one side to the other, as often as Anya.) She is "'converted' to human ideas such as romance and morality, but this only complicates her identity as a daemon[5], and Anya is now reluctant to exact the gory vengeances she once enjoyed" (Jowett 36). Anya, who originates as Aud, "punishes" her errant husband with a curse that turns him to a troll. She is "rewarded" by being made Anyanka, a vengeance demon who can live forever ("Selfless"). She accidentally becomes human ("The Wish"), and, with the new name Anya, learns how to experience life in the twentieth century as a teen — complete culture shock. After being jilted at the altar — and feeling that same vengefulness and unhappiness at the betrayal that she once felt for her barmaid-loving husband — she once again becomes a vengeance demon ("Hells Bells"/"Entropy").

Anya's character is immature and erratic, happiness making her act in mostly positive ways and unhappiness making her act in very negative ways (like turning a man to a worm in "Beneath You"). She is the apple in a barrel, but it is her choices that make her actions. It is only through her years as human and *centuries* as demon that she learns anything. Both as a demon and as a human, she learns of her own dark side and finally rejects it, willing to give up her life to "take back" the vengeance she has wreaked on a fraternity. At that point she learns a lesson many of us miss, that the consequences of one's action may cost others more than oneself ("Selfless"). Finally, she accepts that she will not sit out the final Season Seven apocalypse because she sees (more or less) the necessity to stand and fight.

Other characters act in the shadows. Giles has his dark moments as well. He kills Ben (who is the human face of Glory, the hellgod) because, as Giles admits to Ben, Buffy is the hero, Giles is not. But he chooses to kill Ben to spare Buffy a later confrontation with Ben's alter-person Glory ("The Gift"). Andrew kills his friend Jonathan ("Conversations with Dead People"), at first wailing that it was all Warren's fault, but finally admitting that he himself committed that horrendous deed and was indeed sorry for his action ("Storyteller"). Never changing his basic personality, he then becomes one of the white hats, fighting on the side of Buffy and the Scoobies ("Chosen"), and later, in *Angel*, becoming a Watcher ("Damage," "The Girl in Question"). Of all the characters, Andrew is the most like Zimbardo and Shermer's examples of apples in a barrel, changing his loyalty and action, depending on the group in which he is placed. I would not trust Andrew at any point, as a member of the Trio, as a Watcher, as a person. If he were in a bad barrel again, he would be a bad apple. It is only when he is surrounded by people acting morally and expecting moral actions that he acts morally.[6] He does not seem capable of independent moral decisions.

Angel/Angelus is the most obvious example of the light/dark dichotomy, acting as the light Angel and the dark Angelus, depending on how ensouled he is at the moment. In Season One, he is good. In Season Two he is evil Angelus and Buffy kills him (even as he has turned to Angel again) ("Becoming, Part Two"). In the *Angel* series, he is generally Angel, but occasionally becomes Angelus, either through accident or his own choice in order to solve a problem and thus save the day after someone, "his people" usually, turn him back to Angel. (Okay, this is complicated, but that's what he does.)

Spike, of course, *is* the dark side through Seasons Two to Four (most of it). He illustrates the duality of human nature through his inhumanity as a vampire: "Acting upon life without a soul, Spike is ultimately capable of horrifying even himself" (Resnick 62), as he attempts to take Buffy sexually by force ("Seeing Red").[7] However, DeKelf-Rittenhouse asks if "the one element that ensured Spike's damnation — his ability to love completely and selflessly — will ultimately pave the way for his redemption?" (151). The answer is yes: "When he [Spike] cannot reach his desired goal through the darkness of the sewers, this vampire will dare the daylight" (Wilcox, *Why* 33).

Love makes one able to face tests of weakness and impulse: "The truth [is] that love is the ultimate and the highest goal to which man can aspire.... . *The salvation of man is through love and in love*" (Frankl 57). The abject sadness of rejected love first turns Spike to Drusilla, who turns him — to a vampire ("Fool for Love"). Out of love, he turns his mother to a vampire, who, as the demon, scorns and rejects him. Out of love and pain, he stakes her ("Lies My Parents Told Me"). Out of love for Buffy, he resists Glory's torture ("Intervention"). Out of love, he seeks — and finds — a soul ("Grave"). In none of these examples is he in a "good barrel"; he is simply acting as a "good apple." Moreover, "Love goes very far beyond the physical person of the beloved" (Frankl 58). Spike illustrates this, as he is content to hold Buffy on the night that she is ousted from leadership of the group in Season Seven ("Empty Places"). He loves her and makes the best choice, exhibiting respect, affection, and support. During Season Seven, he acts as a pawn of the dark, but finally dies as the light ("Chosen"). Through love, he overcomes his past and his weakness to shine as a champion.

Faith tells Buffy, "Human weakness. It never goes away" ("Graduation Day"). Day after day, episode after episode, year after year, season after season, each person must recognize and deal with the impulses of the human psyche: "The scars, the pain, can be lived through and if one accepts one's human weakness— one's dark side — one will be ready to face the test" (Wilcox, *Why* 42). Faith has "completed the leap from Nietzsche to Socrates, accepting the Socratic dictum that 'a man who acts unjustly, a man who is unjust, is thoroughly miserable, the more so if he doesn't get his due punishment for the wrongdoing he commits'" (Schudt 33). Faith must discover for herself that a "morally good life is also the happiest life" (Pateman 87). She does so after reaching *Angel*. Her unhappiness and anger in her first appearances in *Buffy* make her act in irresponsible, criminal, and even murderous ways. She doesn't like herself and compensates by beating on vampires (excessively) ("Faith, Hope, and Trick"), breaking into weapons stores ("Bad Girls"), and killing the mayor's aide (even if by accident: she is overly "amped" and slow to respond to Buffy's pleas to halt the killing stroke since that killing stroke is aimed at a human) ("Bad Girls"). She likes herself so little she accepts her magical change into Buffy's body, at which time she begins to feel what it might be like to be loved — by Joyce, the Scoobies, and Riley. She finds this so hard to accept that she wants to beat "herself" (Faith's body) into oblivion ("Who Are You?"). When conquered and returned to her own body, she runs to the *Angel* series and, as a result of Angel's acceptance of her dark side and his recognition that contrition and penitence can lead to redemption, she begins to accept herself and the love in the world (*Angel*, "Sanctuary").

Making good choices means morality. We know what is right and wrong: "Any being with a soul has the ability to tap into this knowledge of essential right and wrong" (Sutherland and Swan 142). Knowledge must be acted upon: "Buffy does not slay because she has to, but because she chooses to. The moral code that Buffy follows is not inherent in the persona of the Slayer; it is inherent in the person of Buffy. She chooses a life of sacrifice" (Stevenson 109). Her choice and Spike's choice lead to saving the world. Saving the world is only part of the story. Buffy has "mundane responsibilities even in times of mortal misery" (Wilcox, *Why* 187), having to deal with broken pipes and lack of money ("Flooded") when she has been jerked out of heaven ("Bargaining, Part 1"). Just as we are, her friends are "unaware of the effects of bad decisions until it is too late" (Stevenson 199), learning that bringing Buffy back magically leads to invisible spirits taking over their bodies and that the bad decision itself causes discomfort in the cosmology ("Afterlife"). Willow is convinced that her use of bad magic (killing the fawn, for example, in "Bargaining") is for the ultimate good. She assumes that she will give herself a moral pass for killing and that others will grant her a "moral evaluation given to that action depending on context" (Stevenson 177), which may be true, but her moral evaluation stops too soon, since she does not understand what she has actually done. She has not accepted the "commonplace truth that no one has the right to do wrong, not even if wrong has been done to them" (Frankl 113). She plays out this tension. Willow, faced with Tara's murder by Warren, sees Tara's murder as a wrong done to her (not recognizing the wrong was done even more to Tara). She seeks vengeance and revenge, reaching depths of misery and anger — and evil. She turns to wrong, becoming Season Six's ultimate evil.

Willow's face is a graphic representation of every moral/personality change she makes,. As she becomes the opponent in Season Six, she changes from "regular" Willow to "veiny" Willow. Just as seeing the snarly vampire faces says that we're looking at something "bad," her face says Willow has left the path of light. However, it is not so easy in reality to recognize the evil in others. Stevenson says, "true evil often wears a human face" (254), and this is true in *Buffy*. Evil becomes less and less easy to point to, less and less easy to evaluate. Ford, who knew Buffy before her stint in Sunnydale and who suddenly appears at Sunnydale High, was Buffy's friend — and pretends still to be — but he's willing to arrange for her death in the face of his own death sentence from illness so he can "live" as a vampire ("Lie to Me"). Glory, the Exuberant Evil of Season Five, also looks human. She may be a hell god, and looks pretty good as one, but her "human" face is Ben ("Crush"), initially kind when it causes him little effort. However, when the stakes increase in magnitude, he plummets into self-interest and is willing to sacrifice Dawn for his own reward ("The Weight of the World").

The most "banal" of evil (re Hannah Arendt[8]) is the Trio of Season Six. Warren wears a human face, but he is as self-serving, small-minded, and little-souled as any vampire. He makes himself a robot girlfriend which he rejects because she is so predictable ("I Was Made to Love You"). Out of pride and anger, he kills an old girlfriend and blames it on others ("Dead Things"). He steals and kills and exults in both ("Villains"). He has no compunction, no regret, no remorse. He has chosen deliberately to be the "swine." And his nature (his personhood) is very, very small and "icky"; at the same time he is a very, very nasty character.

The characters in the *Buffy* series reflect "the complexity of the moral world in which we live" (Greene and Yuen 275). The world of *Buffy* is almost as complicated as the "real" world in which one must make decisions and in which one is compelled to moral choice on a daily basis. Just as it is a "distinct element of the heroism of *Buffy*'s teen protagonists that they will *not* go to any lengths to avoid 'loser' status" (Wilcox, *Why* 21), we also must make those choices day by day to become part of the mass or to become individual: "it is the individual's performative expressions rather than his or her supposed nature that grounds Buffy and her friends' ethical choices" (Pateman 48). As individual characters and as the Scoobies, the members of the *Buffy* gang face their dual natures and (generally) make the "right" decisions, acting as decent people.

One of the most important statements that Frankl makes is that two "races" exist: "the 'race' of the decent man and the 'race' of the indecent man. Both are found everywhere; they penetrate into all groups of society. No group consists entirely of decent or indecent people..." (108). He then asks, speaking of his experiences in the concentration camps, "Is it surprising that in these depths we again found only human qualities which in their very nature were a mixture of good and evil? The rift dividing good from evil, which goes through all human beings, reaches into the lowest depths and becomes apparent even on the bottom of the abyss which is laid open by the concentration camp" (108). He maintains that "Human kindness can be found in all groups, even those which as a whole it would be easy to condemn. The boundaries between groups overlapped and we must not try to simplify matters by saying that these men were angels and those were devils" (107). *Buffy* shows this: Angel is a vampire with a soul, dedicated (when not Angelus) to helping Buffy and later to "helping the helpless"; Whistler, the demon, calls Angel to his destiny, first as a help to Buffy and then as an aid to any helpless person — or demon; Clem is a harmless demon and, because he is harmless, he is unharmed by the Scoobies; Spike is first evil, then harmless — and unharmed — evil, then in the process of searching for good, and finally souled, redeemed, and willing to sacrifice all, not to impress Buffy, but to "see how it all turns out" ("Chosen").

Ultimately, of course, Frankl is about a person's search for the meaning in life because, he says, "striving to find a meaning in one's life is the primary motivational force in man. That is why I speak of a *will to meaning* in contrast to the pleasure principle (or, as we could also term it, *the will to pleasure*) on which Freudian psychoanalysis is centered, as well as in contrast to the *will to power* on which Adlerian psychology, using the term 'striving for superiority,' is focused" (121). The "will to meaning" is so strong that, if one does not find meaning one way, one will find it in another: "The quest for spiritual meaning is typically a personal matter in the West. In the Islamic world, it often leads the seeker into some kind of collective action, informed by utopian aspiration, that admits no distinction between proselytizing, social reform, and politics" (Packer 61). Thus, if a person cannot find meaning in his/her self, that person will seek meaning outside the self and turn to a "community" which instructs that person in how to think and feel and act. Islamic terrorists have found meaning in destruction, their own and other's. Some people have found meaning through accepting the influence of Jim Jones or becoming a member of the Moonies or joining Heaven's Gate in leaving the world at the approach of the Hale-Bopp comet. It is easy to turn the self over to someone else to direct if one has not found value in existence, if one has not found *meaning* in existence.

Frankl maintains that one may find meaning in three ways: "The first is by creating a work or by doing a deed. The second is by experiencing something or encountering someone" (70). The third way to find meaning is by choice: "even the helpless victim of a hopeless situation, facing a fate he cannot change, may rise above himself, may grow beyond himself, and by so doing change himself. He may turn a personal tragedy into a triumph" (170).

The first way to find meaning, "creating a work or doing a deed" (Frankl 70), resonates throughout *Buffy*. Buffy does her work of Slaying vampires; Giles does his library work and functions as her trainer; the Scoobies work to aid her in her pursuit to diminish evil. Each of the main characters finds a purpose, a meaning, in their battle against evil. The second, "experiencing something or encountering someone" (Frankl 70), over the seven seasons occurs multiple times. Buffy, Amy, and Willow experience the evil of preconception and stereotypes in "Gingerbread," leading Amy to find meaning, first as a rat, and then as an actively malicious witch, harming Willow and others ("Smashed," "Doublemeat Palace") because she has been harmed and because love and forgiveness are not in her — yet. (In *Buffy*, as in life, there's always a possibility.) Buffy becomes a Slayer, not initially her choice, but she accepts her role, sometimes whining, sometimes glorying, but always (mostly) effectively. Xander and Willow encounter Buffy and become the Scooby support, as does Cordelia. Cordelia's encounter with the Scoobies, and experiencing their loyalty and support of each other, lead her from shallow, fashion- and popularity-obsessed teen to a being of light (in *Angel*) without her losing her basic cutting edge. Not only Cordelia, Buffy, and the Scoobies are affected by others and events. Each character, each episode, is an experience and/or an encounter.

The experiences of fighting evil, and the experiences of simply living, lead them, especially Buffy, to acknowledge how difficult life is. In "Amends," Angel wishes immolation to remove himself from pain — and life. Buffy responds, "Strong is fighting! It's hard, and it's painful." She exhorts him not to give up; and, in a miraculous occurrence, the sun does not shine in Sunnydale that day, and Angel does not disappear in fire. In "The Gift," she tells Dawn, "the hardest thing in this world ... is to live in it." Here she sacrifices herself to spare Dawn. Is this such a hard decision for her? Perhaps not. By her sacrifice, she will not have to lose Dawn and experience the grief she has already felt on the death of her mother. She will not have to face having to sacrifice anyone else as she had sacrificed her love, Angel ("Becoming, Part 2"). She will not have to face living without her mother — and growing up. Perhaps here at her jump into the gate, she gives up, not as a sacrifice but because she is tired. She is returned to the world after her sacrifice ("Bargaining") and finds it hard to live in the hard brightness. By the end of Season Six, however, she has reconciled herself to life and greets it with gladness, despite the pain of existence. Each major character in *Buffy* overcomes that pain, leading to the third way to find meaning.

That third way, to "turn personal tragedy into triumph" (Frankl 170) is a central theme of *Buffy*. To name only a few instances of turning tragedy on end, Buffy is jerked from heaven ("Bargaining"), and suffers and sulks through Season Six, but rises to share power with all the Potentials in Season Seven. Xander loses an eye, but fights as a knight for good ("Dirty Girls"). Spike "sees dead people"—and live ones—and becomes mad after gaining his soul, but works through that madness throughout Season Seven to make his sacrifice in saving the world.

It is not only the characters on *Buffy* who search for meaning in the midst of struggle, turmoil, madness, stress. *Buffy* fans search as well: "They want more than how they're being treated by modern society, and so they look to cultural appropriation and communication for something more meaningful than what they're getting in their everyday workaday lives" (Ali). Fans turn to websites (such as the Bronze) for affirmation, for community, for connection, for validation. Other people seek other answers. We all search for our meaning, and if we do not find meaning in who we are or what we do, we often search outside ourselves for someone to tell us both, sometimes to the detriment of ourselves and the larger society when we turn to radicalism or cults of various forms. The *Buffy* characters find their meaning in magic and in power, but ultimately reject those as "meaning makers" and turn to finding meaning in what they do (Buffy), in doing good (Spike), in saving the world—and their loved ones (Xander), and in becoming more themselves (pretty much everyone).

While Buffy generally deals with themes of "issues of power, issues of connectedness (or the lack thereof), and issues of self-identity" (South), "Another recurring theme, says Whedon, is 'the heroism of tiny people'" (Kirkland 67). Anyone can be a hero; anyone can be a saint or an angel: "The show offers a deep spiritual core that is based in ethical behavior" (Reiss xiii). Ethical behavior is rewarded with redemption, but "redemption is hard work, and it is up to us" (Reiss 120). In fact, redemption is such hard work that, like kicking the cigarette habit, it may take more than one attempt. It is good that "second chances, fundamentally, are what redemption is all about" (Reiss 120). According to Stevenson, the series is an "exhortation to make better moral choices" (260), to choose what is right rather than what is expedient. For example, Xander decides to help Buffy find Jesse, who has been captured by vampires, even though Xander is not a Slayer, because Xander is Jesse's friend and feels a responsibility towards him ("Welcome to the Hellmouth," "The Harvest"). After the murder of Tara, Willow has to choose hard life rather than easy death and destruction ("Grave"). And, of course, time after time, Buffy has to choose sacrifice (acting as a Slayer, saving the world) rather than selfishness (dating, parties) ("Never Kill a Boy on the First Date").

How do we choose? On what basis is choice made? Frankl asserts that "being human always points, and is directed, to something, or someone, other than oneself—be it a meaning to fulfill or another human being to encounter. The more one forgets himself—by giving himself to a cause to serve or another person to love—the more human he is and the more he actualizes himself" (133). Maslow's Hierarchy of Needs lists self-actualization as the top of the pyramid, the last "need" for which people strive (Maslow 1–4). According to Frankl, "What is called self-actualization is not an attainable aim at all, for the simple reason that the more one would strive for it, the more he would miss it. In other words, self-actualization is possible only as a side-effect of self-tran-scendence" (133).

Thus, one cannot seek actualization, it comes when one is not focused on self—and selfishness. Buffy, Angel, Spike, and Willow all learn this lesson. Buffy gives up her "only one in all the world" uniqueness to become just one of the Slayers, serving a great cause ("Chosen"). Angel gives up score-keeping all the good he does (hoping the point spread in his favor will allow him to become human) and just does the good; Spike gives his evil up to regain a soul and fight on the side of right in Season Seven of *Buffy* and in subsequent sea-sons of *Angel*; Willow realizes that becoming the baddest witch in the world is just that, bad, and falls into Xander's arms of loving embrace as the sun returns ("Grave").

On seeing the morning sunrise from the inside of a concentration camp, Frankl comments, "'*Et lux in tenebris lucet*'—and the light shineth in the dark-ness" (Frankl 60). This is a line from the Gospel According to John 1:5: "*et lux in tenebris lucet et tenebrae eam non conprehenderunt* (And the light shineth in darkness; and the darkness comprehended it not)" ("Secundum"). Frankl com-ments that one can appreciate beauty in the worst of circumstances. One can find love; one can become a better person; one can reach self-transcendence; one can keep doing the job.

What is our job, then, according to *Buffy*? One reading of Voltaire's *Can-dide* has Candide eventually decide that the meaning in his life is non-existent and irrelevant and that he is to "go and work in the garden" (Voltaire 144); that is, he is to keep to himself and to provide for himself by tilling the land. A more positive reading of *Candide* says that Candide can find meaning by going to "work in the garden" (Voltaire 144), that is, he can make meaning in his life through work.

Buffy is more outer-directed; *Buffy* tells us that our job is to do what is right, to keep on working: "Within early Christianity, for instance, redemp-tion had as much to do with how one lives one's life morally in this world as it does gaining spiritual access to another world" (Stevenson 235). *Buffy* says Slaying (fighting evil) is hard, but, with a little help from friends, it is possible to continue and possibly to prevail, even if triumph is not definitive or final. In the face of overwhelming odds and certain destruction at the end of the *Angel* series, Angel could choose to do nothing; he could choose to run and hide. However, Angel's last words at the end of the series are "Let's go to work"

(*Angel*, "Not Fade Away"). Buffy and her friends have lived by that exhortation for seven seasons, Angel (in a spin-off) for five. The struggle is immense and the fight is never finished ("How many apocalypses is this?" "What's the plural of apocalypse?"): "triumph is only ever temporary" (Saxey 193). Still, the struggle, the job, the unceasing "responsibleness" which is "the very essence of human existence" (Frankl 131) is vital to the series, to each character and to each one of us: the "hopelessness of our struggle did not detract from its dignity and its meaning" (Frankl 104). In fact, "everything will become still worse unless each of us does his best" (Frankl 179) because

> Since Auschwitz we know what man is capable of.
> And since Hiroshima we know what is at stake [Frankl 179].

Buffy and her friends "never cease to do their job" (Reiss xiii) and this is the exhortation to us all.

Notes

1. I'm not going to maintain that Joss Whedon deliberately evokes Frankl because it's fairly irrelevant. The series speaks for itself.

2. Frankl, writing originally in 1946, and translated in 1959, must be forgiven for the usage of *man* for *humans* or *humanity*. I'm sure that if he were writing today, being an astute observer and politically conscious, he'd use inclusive rather than sexist language.

3. The Stoics, of course, said this long, long ago.

4. Philosophers deal with suffering and its effects: "Dostoevsky said once, 'There is only one thing that I dread: not to be worthy of my sufferings'" (Frankl 87); Spinoza says, "Emotion, which is suffering, ceases to be suffering as soon as we form a clear and precise picture of it" (Frankl 95); and Nietzsche says, "He who has a *why* to live for can bear with almost any *how*" (Frankl 97).

5. This, of course, is the spelling in Jowett's text. However, I have chosen to use the boring American "demon" spelling in the remainder of this chapter.

6. See Frances E. Morris's chapter on Willow.

7. Oh, sad. I find Spike such a sympathetic character because of some — many — of his actions, such as his affection for Joyce, his kindness to the frightened and grieving Buffy, his support and care for Dawn, and more — while ignoring others — that I'm reluctant to use the word "rape" in this context, although that's what it was. Audience sympathy is probably the reason the writers had Spike show his dark side so graphically. How could Buffy trust him without a soul? How could she accept his good actions without the positive reinforcement of knowing he had a soul? (See J. Renée Cox's chapter.)

8. Hannah Arendt was a philosopher who wrote *Eichmann in Jerusalem: A Report on the Banality of Evil*, in which she maintains that people who do evil acts are not necessarily insane, but ordinary people. She further maintains that those people are acting within a bureaucracy in a bureaucratic manner. The Trio is not a bureaucracy, but it is a group, with all the pressures and motives of a group.

Got Myself a Soul?

The Puzzling Treatment of the Soul in Buffy

——————

J. Renée Cox

On May 7, 2002, the *Buffy* episode titled "Seeing Red" aired on the UPN network. In this episode — as anyone familiar with the *Buffy* series will certainly recall — Spike attempted to rape Buffy on the floor of her bathroom. The reaction among viewers was immediate and (rightfully) intense; fans discussed the episode on-line at length, voicing opinions and reactions which ran the gamut from absolute condemnation of Spike to sympathetic defense of him, with some surprisingly harsh criticisms of the Slayer herself sprinkled in as well.

The episode hit a nerve with viewers and fans. It hit a nerve with the series creator and the series writers too; reflecting on the episode and on the story-line which continued after Spike's attempted rape of Buffy, series writers Jane Espenson and David Fury voiced their views. Espenson said she was concerned about the sexual assault scene because it would be "very hard to come back from" for Spike, who was one of her favorite characters. David Fury was vocal in his strong reservations about the relationship between Buffy and Spike after Spike's assault on her. Fury also appeared a bit disgusted with fans who wished to see Buffy and Spike reconcile: "Never trust your attempted rapist," he stated in 2003 on DavidFury.net (Espenson and Fury, quoted in Fowler).

The episode aired several years ago, but it continues to generate pages of discussion (on-line and in books), centering around the questions raised by Spike's assault. Many of those questions address the soul,[1] especially Spike's lack of one and his gaining of one after the rape attempt. Did the rape attempt "prove" that Spike was *evil* at that point? Did Spike attempt this horrific act

24

because he lacked a soul? "Seeing Red" brought the question of the soul in *Buffy* to the forefront in a way that had not been achieved on the show prior.

Obviously, in the *Buffy* series, concepts like *good* and *evil* are intentionally blurred and intentionally ambiguous—even inconsistent. What is consistent and linear in the series, though, is that these concepts—good, evil, right, wrong, morality, immorality, damnation, redemption — are all irrevocably connected to the soul. This connection first appears in the series in the story of Angel (in his good configuration)/Angelus (same guy, in his evil personality), but the concept of the soul and its role in morality/immorality and damnation/redemption becomes most prominent and most revealing in the story of Spike. It is his character and his story arc which reveals the most, in my opinion, about what *Buffy* writers and *Buffy* characters think about the soul and its (supposed) impact on a being's morality, worth, and potential for redemption — social and divine.

There is no question that Whedon and staff make tremendously powerful statements about the power of the soul in the series. In 2003, Gregory Stevenson wrote and published *Televised Morality: The Case of* Buffy the Vampire Slayer; it is one of the most impressive and most enjoyable *Buffy* discussions in print today. Stevenson discusses the soul in *Buffy* in ways similar to how Whedon — and many viewers— seem to perceive it. However, on many levels, the treatment of the soul concept in *Buffy* is problematic, at least for me. By "problematic" I do not mean that Whedon and crew have done something "wrong" in their treatment of the soul in the series. I mean that the ideas and philosophies about the soul which are embraced by the characters are problematic, as are some comments made by Stevenson in *Televised Morality* regarding the soul's part in morality, in moral choices, and in redemption on *Buffy*.

Is the soul ever explicitly defined by any character in seven seasons of Buffy? In other words, does any character in the series specifically say, "A soul is _____"? Not that I remember. Creatively, I think, a concrete definition would have limited the concept and would thus have limited the manner in which it was handled artistically.

Does Joss Whedon embrace any specific definition of the soul? As far as I know, he does not. Whedon is quoted in *Televised Morality* as saying that "with a soul comes a more adult understanding.... Can I say that I believe in the soul? I don't know that I can. It's a beautiful concept, as is resurrection and a lot of other things we have on the show that I'm not really sure I can explain and I certainly don't believe in" (Stevenson 89).

Still, it may not be very difficult to define what a "soul" is to the great majority of *Buffy* watchers who are believers in the concept of the soul. In American culture, generally, we could define it as the "spirit," the entity within a person, which is in fact the true living essence of that person. Where does a soul come from? That depends on whom we ask. Many might answer that the soul is bestowed by God — or at the very least, by a creator, whatever and whoever he/she may be. How, when, and why is the soul taken away? Generally, the philosophy embraced by western culture is that the soul departs from the body at the moment of death, and from that point is sent — by something, usually by God, according to his judgment — either into heaven or into hell.

What purpose does the soul serve? Again, generally in the broad view, it serves several purposes. One is that its presence separates humans from animals: humans have souls; animals do not, according to the most widely-accepted belief. Also, the soul is something to be "taken care of," in the sense that it is the condition of the soul which will largely determine, after death, whether the entity will be admitted into heaven or cast into hell. This is a concept that drives us, many would say, not only to behave a certain way, but also to believe a certain way. More specifically, our belief that we have a soul prevents us (ideally) from engaging in an act that is "evil," because doing so will compromise our soul by putting it in danger of damnation.

A key concept surrounding the soul is therefore linked to reward and punishment. This is powerful to many, because it is comforting; the idea that, after death, the soul can be rewarded with admittance into heaven is comforting. The idea that a soul can be punished with banishment into hell is also comforting; not comforting in the sense of our *own* soul being punished in hell — but in the sense of other people's souls being sent to hell. Case in point: a child is abducted, raped, and murdered. The killer is never found and never brought to human justice. It's comforting to believe that the killer will someday die and be punished for eternity — that he did not, in the end, get away with it. Adolf Hitler escaped justice on earth. It's comforting to believe that Hitler is burning in hell and being tortured this very second. The alternative belief — that there is no divine justice and no such thing as divine punishment — would mean Hitler "got away with" all of it. This is too monstrous a concept to entertain — this is too uncomfortable to embrace.

If a being has a soul, it is subject to divine reward and punishment. I find the first curious snag in the philosophy of the soul in *Buffy* on the flip side of this statement. If a being does *not* have a soul, it is cut off from divine reward — but *it is also exempt from punishment.* In *Buffy*, vampires and demons have no souls; therefore, vampires and demons are exempt from punishment. At the moment of the monster's death, the demon-being is simply snuffed out. There is no soul to go on to some other dimension for punishment. The killer has gotten away with it. At first glance, the idea that a vampire or demon has no soul may go a long way towards explaining its evil behavior — and that helps us be satisfied. We can say, "The killer has no soul. It can't be redeemed. It has no chance of being rewarded in heaven. I'm comfortable with that." But the soulless monster is also escaping punishment. Not so comfortable, that one.

Stevenson writes that, on *Buffy,* "the soul functions as a moral compass, allowing one to discern the difference between right and wrong and thus facilitating a choice between the two" (88). The presence of a soul makes free will possible, essentially. He goes on to say that "a moral choice is one that sacrifices self-desire for service" to another, and a choice which contributes to the good of the community is a moral choice as well (166).

By this description, then, every vampire and demon lacks a moral compass—no vampire or demon has the ability to discern right from wrong. What's more, the lack of a soul means the vampire or demon has no free will to choose between a moral act and an immoral act. In essence, in Stevenson's philosophy, the vampires and demons cannot make selfless decisions or make any decisions which contribute to the good of the community. They simply are not capable of it. If a vampire or demon appears to make a conscious decision which contributes to the overall good of the community, it must be by accident only and nothing more.

But there are at least three beings in the *Buffy* series which appear to defy this philosophy of *no soul = no morality*. The beings are all demons, and the first is Whistler. He describes himself as a demon; he has no soul, then. And yet, we see him make choices which are moral, selfless, and which contribute to the larger good. The most striking thing we see Whistler do comes in Season Two, when he finds Buffy, tells her why it is imperative that she destroy Angelus, and tells her how to destroy him ("Becoming: Part II"). It's intriguing that Stevenson avoids any discussion of Whistler's existence, his decisions, or his morality. I can only conclude that this is because Whistler is difficult— Whistler can't be explained in the *Buffy*verse philosophy, or in Stevenson's philosophy of *no soul = no morality*.

The second being which doesn't fit comfortably into the philosophy of *no soul = no morality* is Clem. The only discussion Clem receives appears in a single paragraph in *Televised Morality*, in which Stevenson makes the comment that Clem's choices in life are "not based upon moral reasoning but upon pure pragmatism" (90). Stevenson is specifically referring to Clem's dialogue with Buffy towards the end of Season Seven, when Clem is leaving Sunnydale to escape the First. At an earlier point in the series, we have seen that Clem and many of his fellow demons enjoy playing poker; and when they ante up, instead of placing chips on the table, they bet live kittens—which they enjoy eating. In Season Seven, in "Empty Places," Clem is fleeing Sunnydale (along with thousands of others) to escape the chaos that is accompanying the arrival of the First Evil. He says to Buffy, "You can't swing a cat without hitting some kind of demonic activity. Not that I swing cats, or eat—nope. Heh. Cuttin' way back. Cholesterol. Morals! I mean morals!" According to Stevenson, Clem is still in fact immoral, in spite of this comment he makes to Buffy. Whedon makes a comment along the same lines regarding Clem, that Clem is pragmatic, not moral, and this distinction is essential, according to Whedon, because the "soul marks the real difference between somebody with a complex moral structure and someone who may be affable and even likeable, but ultimately eats kittens" (Stevenson 90). Clem, adds Stevenson, demonstrates that the lack of a soul hinders the ability to make profound moral judgments (90).

Stevenson's and Whedon's comments about Clem are problematic for a few reasons, the first of which is that we don't quite see enough of Clem to make a solid judgment about the complexity of his moral structure. Clem is on screen for less than fifteen minutes throughout the entire series; this isn't time enough to reveal much about a character. We also see Clem in only a few, very limited situations. There isn't much opportunity for him to demonstrate his own moral structure, complex or otherwise (and we could certainly point to the character Forrest Gump as an example of a moral structure which does not need to be complex in order to be profound).

In addition, the few decisions that we *do* see Clem make are kind and selfless, and do contribute to the general good of the community. For example, he makes the choice to watch over Dawn, he does what he can to help her enjoy herself and be comfortable, and, in taking her in, he is consciously contributing to the general good of the community. He is a minor character with minor impact on the story, but I'm not quite sure I could justify condemning him for no other reason than that he is said to lack a soul.

Lastly, Stevenson and Whedon both offer only one "proof" that Clem is immoral, and that is that Clem eats kittens. Eating kittens, according to Whedon and Stevenson, demonstrates an inability to make profound moral judgments. The hypocrisy in this argument is striking, to say the least. Killing and eating an animal is proof that one has no morality? If the worst that Stevenson and Whedon can say about Clem to convince us that he's immoral is that he eats animals for pleasure, we're all in trouble — with the exception of vegans, possibly. Not only do we kill animals and eat them — we slaughter them simply for bragging rights; we hack them up, stuff them, and bolt them to our walls so we can demonstrate how superior we are to them. Who is lacking a moral compass?

At this point, it's tempting to look for a substitute concept for the "soul," for no other reason than that so far in the series, what the soul "is" and "is not" doesn't quite pan out consistently. If we were to give it another name, an obvious choice could be the term *conscience*. Is a *conscience* what was forced upon Angelus so that he became the tortured Angel? Is a *conscience* what was bestowed upon Spike at the end of his trials? This may be the closest we can come to renaming the soul and having it work in every instance. It doesn't work perfectly, however, since (obviously) having a conscience does not necessarily guarantee the making of a moral choice.

Perhaps Freudian terms[2] can help us find a substitute concept for the soul. Does the absence of a soul act, in essence, like alcohol — does it mean that the conscience is diminished and the id takes over? In other words, when a person becomes a demon and the person's soul flies away in the very instance of becoming a monster, then is what we have left the person who *was*— but now without the superego which was formerly present and which was acting as the social filter? If this is the case, then how do we explain Clem's remark to Buffy? If the lack of a soul reveals to us the true nature of a being, this idea may work by way of explaining Angelus—but then that also makes Angel extremely unlikable, and makes the soul appear as nothing more than that which simply masks and controls a person's true impulses (Freud's superego) (Freud, *The Ego*).

Is the soul in the *Buffy*verse standing in for accountability? This seems promising. Vampires "murder," and we believe this is wrong. But we've already examined this concept earlier in this discussion. The whole doctrine of the *soul = accountability* implodes on this notion and nullifies itself because the most "evil" things have no soul, and therefore no accountability and no punishment. We should also remember that vampires and demons are essentially animals in view of the *Buffy*verse characters. Characters in the series make references to vampire/demon status as animals—or worse. In "Angel," as Buffy gears up to fight him, Angel says, "I'm just an animal, right?" To which, Buffy replies, "Animals I like."

The vampires also kill for food — they kill to eat, to survive. We viewers walk amongst animals without souls every day (according to a sizeable number of humans, our cats, dogs, hamsters, elephants, have no souls, etc.); the orca whales that beach themselves to kill and eat seals are animals without souls. However, we do not *blame* the mountain lions and the orcas for having no souls, nor do we recoil in horror and accuse them of "murder" when they kill living things and eat them. What logical — or even theological — defense do we have for condemning cats for eating mice? We have none, and it makes little sense to condemn an animal with no soul — a vampire — for eating the "Happy Meals on legs," as Spike gleefully refers to them ("Becoming, Part II").

So then, back to Clem: how could we explain Clem's comment to Buffy about cutting back on kittens? When Clem stumbles and stutters, "Been cuttin' way back. Cholesterol. I mean morals! Morals!" we may actually be seeing a being who is fully aware that he is an "other" and who is making an effort to fit into the dominant culture. He knows that in the society and culture which he now resides, eating kittens is not acceptable, so he says he doesn't. This is pragmatic to a certain extent, but it's not necessarily manipulatively or evilly pragmatic. Clem may also simply be making an effort to be polite, much as a Christian who finds himself at a Hanukkah party might, out of a desire to be polite, refrain from saying aloud that he had sausage patties for breakfast.

The third and most important demon that doesn't fit comfortably into the *no soul = no moral choices* philosophy is Spike. In spite of the obvious contradictions between the philosophy and the reality, which I will discuss shortly, I have little doubt that Stevenson, Whedon, many of the *Buffy*verse writers, and certainly Buffy, Giles and the Scooby Gang appear to be embracing a philosophy of "*Spike no soul; Spike no good.*"

Giles, as an authority figure to the Scooby Gang, is instrumental in the passing on of this philosophy to Buffy and friends. Giles's position is first revealed to us in the first-season episode titled "Angel": in response to Buffy's question whether it is possible for a vampire to be a good person, he emphatically responds in the negative, telling Buffy that since the person is gone, the soul is gone as well. In the fourth season, Giles becomes a demon for a short time during the episode titled "A New Man," and we again get to hear Giles's position on monsters and souls. As Spike drives Giles around in his car, Giles insists that he refuses to become a monster simply because he looks like a monster: "I have a soul. I have a conscience. I am a human being," he yells. Giles's position is clear in just these two instances. Xander, too, is fully accepting of the idea, that without a soul, a being can come to (and do no) good. Voicing his reasons to Buffy why she should never trust Spike, Xander tells her, "He doesn't have a soul, Buffy" ("Seeing Red"). Jane Espenson is quoted in *Televised Morality* as saying that "As long as Spike doesn't have a soul, he cannot be redeemed" (87).

We recall also Stevenson's comment, presented earlier in this discussion, that "the soul functions as a moral compass, allowing one to discern the difference between right and wrong and thus facilitating a choice between the two" (88) and his comment that moral choices are those which place self-sacrifice higher than self-service and which contribute to the good of the community (166). Stevenson's philosophy appears to line up with that of Giles, the Scooby Gang, and Whedon and crew: Spike, as long as he has no soul, is not capable of selflessness, goodness, moral choices, or redemption.

However, Spike actively makes decisions which are selfless and which contribute to the larger good of the community *before* he "regains" his soul. He engages in actions which are kind, respectful, affectionate, and compassionate. To name a few instances: repeatedly through Seasons Five and Six, he watches over Dawn. He protects her at the risk (and eventually the realization) of harm to himself. He doesn't follow through on his impulse to shoot Buffy as she's sitting on her back porch crying about her dying mother — instead, he makes a choice to put the gun down and speak gently and compassionately to her, asking if there is anything he can do for her ("Fool for Love"). This is especially powerful, considering Buffy's very recent treatment of Spike in the same episode — she has been so arrogant and vicious towards Spike that he has wept with frustration and humiliation. After the death of Joyce (Buffy's mother), Spike brings flowers as a mark of his respect for Joyce; as Willow points out, he does not include a card with the flowers. His action cannot be manipulative or selfish, for it is anonymous and gains him nothing. It is also interesting to note how Spike responds to Xander's accusation in this scene: Xander accuses Spike of being pragmatic, to which Spike replies, "Joyce didn't treat me like I was a freak" ("Forever"). This is a telling remark for Spike to make, and we will pursue it further later.

One of the most impressive moral decisions and actions of Spike's takes place when he suffers torture at the hands of Glory, but still does not tell her that Dawn is the "key." This is an active choice on Spike's part. He later explains his actions to a creature which he believes is a robot (and so again, he stands to gain nothing)—he explains to the robot that he would not put Dawn in danger and that he would not allow Buffy to suffer pain at the loss of her sister. He is also making a decision for the common good of the community—he is not going to allow Glory to discover Dawn's identity and then destroy the world ("Intervention"). Lastly, at the end of Season Five, Spike makes the choice to protect Dawn with his own life on the tower. This is a choice, and it is a selfless one ("The Gift"). We have to remember that every one of the instances mentioned in the paragraphs above take place before Spike gets his "soul" back; these are actions of the "soulless" Spike.

But it seems these choices and actions of Spike do not matter, and they will not matter to Buffy and the Scooby Gang, because they have embraced a belief that *no soul = no good*. As Stevenson writes, "goodness on Buffy is not defined as the mere absence of evil. Rather, it is intrinsically tied to the presence of the soul" (87). One wonders if Spike would *ever* have achieved true decency or validity in their eyes, no matter what he did, as long as he was missing the thing which they believed makes a being valid, worthy, moral, and redeemable—a *soul*.

This is where I come to the biggest problem I have with the *no soul = no morality* philosophy. As I watched the series for the first time, I became increasingly disturbed by the treatment of the soul in the *Buffy* episodes, but couldn't quite put my finger on why I was disturbed. Then I realized that the concept of the soul was being used to incite a philosophical relationship to a "We are superior, you are inferior" world view. It was also being used to drive—and maintain—a wedge between two groups: we could call them the *haves* and the *have-nots*.

Before moving on in this discussion, it is helpful to keep in mind a concept credited to Elias Canetti in *Crowds and Power*: "the identification with the crowd is a social instinct that involves pleasure, emotional release, and a sense of equality. In the physical contact and sense of solidarity with the mass, the individual finds relief from the burden of 'stings' passed down through social authority" (Folks). In the case of *Buffy*, we have two crowds: the beings *with* souls and the beings with*out* souls. For each group, identification with a crowd is a way to maintain a sense of inclusion—and in many cases, to maintain a sense of superiority over the "other" crowd. For a being who wishes to move from one crowd to another, a sense of inferiority may be relieved through that shift—in leaving one crowd and joining the other, one may find, as Canetti puts it, relief from "stings" which have been inflicted by society.

Herein lies the malignancy in the manner in which the *Buffy* creators and characters (and Stevenson) use the *soul* in *Buffy*: a personal or cultural belief which is blind to all else, which refuses to acknowledge gray area and insists on its own infallibility, as we've seen in our own history, is dangerous and detrimental. The "you don't have _____, so you are therefore inferior" philosophy has been sprinkled throughout our entire known existence as humans, but its repetition does not dampen its danger. We have seen the tragic results of "You don't have *the proper ancestry*, so you are therefore inferior." "You don't have *the best education*, so you are therefore inferior." "You don't have the *desirable skin color*...." "You don't practice the *right religion*...." "You don't practice the *correct sexuality*." This is the language of the *haves* and the *have-nots*, and the *haves* use it to prop up and maintain an imaginary superiority. It appears that this is how the *no soul = no morality* philosophy is used in the *Buffy*-verse.

There are two very dramatic instances in which two females—Cecily first and then Buffy—use a language of superiority when speaking to Spike. Cecily, when William (the human who becomes the vampire Spike) offers his love to her, coldly rejects him because he has no money and no social status: "You're beneath me," Cecily sneers ("Fool for Love"). Later, Buffy rejects Spike just as brutally—using the exact same words: "You're beneath me"—and it is her possession of a soul and his lack of one that drives her remark.

Giles and Xander cling to this difference between themselves and Spike as well. They take every opportunity to remind Spike that he has no soul, so Spike cannot be good or moral. Giles and Xander use Spike's lack of a soul as a club with which to repeatedly knock him down and remind him that he will never be acceptable. Just one example comes in the episode titled "Smashed." Spike says to Giles, "A man can change," to which Giles replies, "You're not a man — you're a thing. An evil, disgusting thing."

Language, points out Geert Hofstede, "plays a crucial role in intercultural interactions" (425). We could consider these two groups—the beings with souls and the beings with no souls—as two intercultural groups which are indeed speaking to each other using very specific modes of discourse. Language is extremely powerful and extremely revealing when we are observing how these two groups in *Buffy* speak to each other. Hofstede goes on to point out that "we use verbal clues to attach identities to members of our own and other groups, to express feelings of inclusion and exclusion, superiority and inferiority, tolerance and racism" (425). It becomes quite obvious that language is being employed in this very manner in the *Buffy*verse, and this disturbing use of language makes it difficult for me to view the presentation and use of the *soul* concept in this series as a completely benign element.

Buffy clings most desperately to the idea of the soul as the "thing" which keeps her superior and Spike inferior. She tells him he is beneath her ("Fool for Love"). She repeatedly makes references to his lack of a soul and the fact that this failure places her out of his league. In "Dead Things," Buffy tells Spike, "I am not your girl. You don't have a soul. There is nothing good or clean in you. You are dead inside. You can't feel anything real. I could never be your girl" (after which, she continues to beat him bloody. He never strikes back. She leaves him in the street). In spite of selfless, apparently moral, choices and behavior exhibited by Spike, Buffy continues to berate him and discredit him for his lack of a soul, and reminding him that he is "not a part of [her] life" — in spite of the fact that she has become involved in an intense sexual relationship with him ("Normal Again").

To Spike's face, at least, Buffy stubbornly adheres to the *Spike no soul; Spike no good* philosophy. I find this surprising because this "Demons bad. People good" world view is exactly what Buffy criticizes Riley for in Season Four ("New Moon Rising"). Buffy says to Riley, "You sounded like Mr. Initiative. 'Demons bad. People good.'" Riley replies, "Something wrong with that theorem?" to which Buffy answers that there are "different degrees [of] evil"; and she expands her explanation by stating that evil is different, depending on the demon. There are creatures, Buffy tells Riley, which "aren't evil at all."

But Buffy has pointed out the splinter in Riley's eye while she has a plank in her own. She behaves often through the series as many others who adopt an absolute moralistic philosophy of life — when confronted with the fact that this absolute philosophy of morality is illogical and doesn't "work" in every single instance, she becomes agitated and belligerent. However, when it happens that this absolute philosophy will suit her own purpose, she clings to it unequivocally, and uses it against Spike, despite her earlier declaration to Riley about the potential for demons to be "good."

When Spike realizes that he'll never be accepted or forgiven or enfolded into Buffy's world until he has this *thing* that he is lacking, he goes out and gets it. I get the impression that Spike himself, in order to evaluate himself justly, does not believe that he needs this thing, this *soul*. We could argue that he seeks to obtain one in the same way that any marginalized "other" might go out and obtain whatever it is that will make his fellow beings accept him as valid. The dialogue which follows comes from the episode titled "Beneath You," when Spike first returns from the trials that return his soul to him. Spike says, "I tried to find it, of course," to which Buffy asks, "Find what?" and Spike replies, "The spark. The *missing*— the *piece*. That *thing* that would *make me fit* [emphasis added]."

We could also argue that Spike has made an attempt to move from one crowd (perceived as the "inferior") to another crowd (perceived as the "superior"), but Spike himself isn't clear on whether or not he has successfully made that move. It is interesting to note that Spike, when he first comes back, does *not* use the word "soul" in reference to the change that has come upon him. Buffy is the first to use it ("Beneath You").[3] It seems Spike is not quite sure what has happened to him, and he obviously views the word "soul" with some suspicion and confusion. Later in the same season, when Principal Robin Wood jeers at Spike, "Oh, what, you're a good guy now?" Spike responds with words which perfectly capture my own perturbation with the ideas surrounding the "soul" in Buffy's world. Spike replies, "Yeah. Got myself a soul. Whatever that means" ("Get It Done").

Am I suggesting that there is in fact no such thing as a soul in the *Buffy*-verse? Yes and no. *Yes*, in the sense that I don't accept Whedon's, Stevenson's, or the Scooby Gang's claims that the presence of this thing called a soul, and only this thing called a soul, makes a being in the *Buffy*verse capable of choosing to behave in a profoundly moral way or makes a being capable of redemption. Neither do I accept that the possession of a soul makes one "better" than one who has no soul. The validity of "I have a soul, so I am superior — you don't have a soul, so you are inferior" crumbles under close scrutiny, as has every other philosophy which has been created in order to maintain the unjustified and inexcusable treatment of one group of people by another.

It is especially puzzling that Whedon, many of his writers, and Stevenson believe that Spike's attempted rape of Buffy spurs him to go out and seek a soul. Stevenson's remarks are especially intriguing: he states in Chapter 6 that "after the rape attempt, Spike is torn between the monster and the man within him" (88) and in Chapter 14 writes that "Spike's attempted rape of Buffy is the catalyst for his quest to reclaim his soul" (209). My question is, how and why would a being who has no soul, and no conscience, and no ability to judge between morality and immorality, suddenly become capable of perceiving this lack, in the first place, and then also become capable of perceiving it as a "wrong" which needs to be "righted"? The logical leap cannot be made. It is akin to claiming that a completely color-blind person can suddenly become capable of comprehending that chocolate brown is being worn by everyone and that chocolate brown would be flattering to his own complexion too. In regards to Spike's action after the attempted rape, I believe Spike already had a conscience (small, and by no means flawless, but definitely there), and he already had the ability to judge between morality and immorality. If he had not had this ability already, he would not have considered it necessary to seek redemption for his actions. And as a viewer, I am by no means convinced that Spike went to Africa specifically to seek a soul.

It is tempting to suggest that the *soul* is largely in the *Buffy*verse characters' imaginations— and possibly, only in *our* imaginations. The objection from those who are familiar with the series might obviously fall along the lines that there is *something*, and, if it is not entirely tangible, it at least certainly has an impact on some characters, such as Angel/Angelus. I would agree, to a certain extent. There is no question that there is *something* which is forced upon Angelus, and this something makes him now Angel. Without this something, Angelus becomes one of the most frightening characters in the entire seven seasons (more frightening, and without question far more "evil" than Spike. Recall the episode titled "Lies My Parents Told Me," during which a character asks Spike, since he got his soul back, if he is therefore just like Angel. Spike replies vehemently, "I'm *nothing* like Angel").

There indeed seems to be something tangible that is called a "soul," and we can't help but refer as a case in point to Spike's experience in the caves of Africa. After Spike undergoes torture, the demon, who asks Spike if he wishes to be his "former self," bestows *something* upon Spike, and it changes him radically; the demon obviously does something very powerful to Spike — it appears, especially visually, that the demon "gives" something to Spike, and whatever it is, Spike has an undeniable, immediate physical reaction to it ("Grave").

This scene strikes me as an echo of the scene in which the Wizard of Oz "gives" a "heart" to the Tin Man, a "brain" to the Scarecrow, and "courage" to the Cowardly Lion. We know that, in fact, all the Wizard gives them are useless trinkets (we do not forget that the Wizard himself is a fraud). But the useless objects, once bestowed, have the power to convince the Tin Man that he now has a *heart* (which he has shown he had all along), to convince the Scarecrow that he now has a *brain* (which he has shown he had all along), to convince the Lion that he now has *courage* (which he has shown he had all along). We, the audience, know the trinkets aren't remotely necessary. But the Tin Man, the Scarecrow, and the Lion came to the Wizard absolutely convinced that they needed some *thing* — some*thing* which they felt they were lacking, and that lack was keeping them in the margins. Once they had this *thing* (they believed), they would be fully valuable and legitimate in their own eyes, as well as in the eyes of their companions and in their larger society. And so, each joined in on a quest to obtain that thing.

This, too, is Spike's story. He has already demonstrated a capacity to love, already demonstrated a capacity to be selfless, and, possibly most importantly, has demonstrated that he has a conscience — this is why he goes on the quest to begin with. He is racked with self-loathing and guilt after his assault on Buffy. He leaves Sunnydale and voluntarily subjects himself to horrific tortures and punishments (again, I must ask the question of Stevenson — why would a being who has no sense of morality suddenly decide he deserves punishment? On what basis would he decide that, unless he already had that conscience to begin with?).

I see the demon who "bestows" a "soul" on Spike in the same light as I see the Wizard. The Wizard, being a wise man, knows there is no such thing as a "heart," a "brain," or "courage" that could be bestowed and have any impact on the receiver. These are concepts only — not tangible things. But the Wizard, being a wise man, also knows he cannot explain this to any of the three — they have their hearts set on receiving *something* from him. Like the Wizard, the demon is older, wiser (possibly), more powerful, and certainly an authority figure in Spike's perception. The demon simply says, in essence, "I have just given you a soul. You now have one," and *Spike believes it* — that is all that matters. Just as the Scarecrow leaves the Wizard's chambers fully convinced that he now has a "brain" whereas before he did not, and, as the Scarecrow from that moment begins to actively engage and use his new "brain," Spike leaves the demon's chamber fully convinced that he now has a "soul" whereas before he did not, and Spike from that moment begins to actively engage and use his new "soul." To put this claim in its simplest form, it may all be in Spike's head. It may be pure psychology. However, the psychic realization that he has a soul leads him to sorrow over the evil he has committed.

Entertaining the idea for a moment that it *is* pure psychology, that the "soul" is a concept in the imagination and nothing more, what can we determine? Also for a moment, completely rejecting the treatment and use of the *soul* concept in the Buffy series because of its contradictory presentation and because of its negative potential, the question then becomes, if there is no such thing as a soul, then what about redemption? Is it possible in the *Buffy* worldview, or in Stevenson's view, for any being to be redeemed without a soul? Jane Espenson's quote regarding Spike, presented earlier in this discussion, would indicate that the answer is no: "As long as Spike hasn't a soul, he cannot be redeemed," Espenson says (Fowler). Stevenson agrees, writing that Spike needs a soul to overcome his monstrous nature; without that soul, redemption is impossible (88). The answer to the question of whether redemption is possible without a soul then appears to be an unequivocal, resounding "absolutely not." I am reminded of Caleb's line in "Dirty Girls": "I like to keep things simple: good folk, bad folk, clean folk, dirty folk," he says. Some of the *Buffy* writers, the *Buffy* characters, and even Stevenson appear guilty of drawing the same unforgiving line. This is disappointing.

We should find that an absolute philosophy which rules redemption out for any being, for any reason, is unacceptable. The ideal situation — and the one I hope we would all wish for — is one in which redemption is never impossible. The very word itself — redemption — seems to promise that it is available to all, regardless of prior or present circumstances. The *Buffy* series is a case in which the work itself may have transcended the wishes and intentions of its creators. Even as the writers and characters embrace an unduly limited notion of the soul, a more noble conception emerges through the story of Spike. Redemption becomes possible when we strive to find selflessness, conscience, and a capacity to love within ourselves where before there was none. Buffy's comment to Spike in Season Seven drives home this point: she tells him, "You faced the monster inside of you and you fought back" ("Never Leave Me"). Spike's story therefore illuminates two possibilities: that morality requires only what is already within us and that redemption is something we can bring about for ourselves — perhaps there need be nothing supernatural about it.

Notes

1. See also Scott McLaren, "The Evolution of Joss Whedon's Vampire Mythology and the Ontology of the Soul." *Slayage: The Online International Journal of Buffy Studies 18*

5.2 (2005). 8 September 2007 <http://www.slayageonline.com/essays/slayage18/McLaren. htm>.

2. Freud divides the mind into id (impulse), ego (intellect), and superego (conscience).

3. Anya notices that Spike has changed and recognizes what makes him different, but does not use the word "soul."

Not Just Another Love Song

Buffy's *Music as Representation of Emerging Adulthood*

———⟳———

JACQUELINE BACH

In the popular show *Buffy the Vampire Slayer*, the influence of music is too significant to ignore. It plays in the background; characters listen to it and use it to comfort, seduce, differentiate, and celebrate; in conversation, they refer to lyrics, bands, and notable historical events, such as the breaking up of the Beatles. Many episode titles are song titles or references to them. When music takes over or is completely absent from a scene or episode, fans and scholars notice. Furthermore, music acts as a narrator, helping to connect past, present, and future events.

Music follows the main characters throughout seven seasons, and music reflects their journeys from adolescents to adults. Since much of what *Buffy's* music does is so closely related to the overall narrative of Buffy's "growing up," it seems only natural that the show's music would demonstrate a similar experience. *Buffy's* background music is an important part of that complicated narrative, and those who write, find, or edit music for the series tackle the issues of becoming an adult. Like many of the show's devices, *Buffy's* music reinforces the main characters' experience of what sociologist Jeffrey Arnett calls "emerging adulthood" or the period of time between adolescence and adulthood (*Emerging*).

Many elements work together to produce this emergence experience — the sets change; clothing changes; the language the characters speak changes as well. *Buffy's* music finds itself having to play a role in this change in addition to the many other roles it plays. Music not only communicates the mood of a scene or illuminates a character but also provides commentary on the plot and contributes to the show's postmodern qualities.

When scholars turn to the experimental use of music in *Buffy*, they often reference three particular episodes: "Hush," "The Body," and "Once More with Feeling." These three episodes occur in three consecutive seasons (Four, Five, and Six) and their use of sound and silence demonstrates the evolution of *Buffy's* music. Wilcox (*Why Buffy Matters*), Hill, Dechert, and Knights, in particular, articulate the complicated relationship of music with the series's narrative, characters, and fan community. Through various approaches, they explore how *Buffy's* music grows from a more traditional role as background commentator to a more active participant in the forwarding of plotlines and development of characters.

While *Buffy's* music fulfils a variety of functions, there remains a consensus among scholars that it primarily works to further the series narrative and to comment on characters' identities. In "My Boyfriend's in the Band," Dechert sorts *Buffy's* music into three categories: contributing to the mood and theme of a scene, establishing and tracing the growth of characters' personalities, and building community among fans (219). She explores the on-line fan communities and the connections between characters forged within the show as a result of the eclectic musical mix.[1]

In addition to charting the growth of characters and contributing to the mood of scene, *Buffy's* music often assumes the role of narrator/commentator and indicates when a scene occurs in another time or place. For example, one of Franz Joseph Haydn's string quartets plays during a flashback to Anya and Halfrek's conversation, post-destruction of St. Petersburg, Russia, in the early 1900s. In this way, music works much like a costume or a set to transport the action to another time or place. Examining how music functions in the series helps convey the multiple ways it also reflects the main characters' growth.

Because of its many forms, scholars note that it is difficult to discuss *Buffy's* music; in fact, they disagree as to how to use the traditional terms which refer to the narrative function of music. In *Why Buffy Matters*, Wilcox frequently refers to instances when *Buffy's* music assumes different roles: diegetic and non-diegetic (or extra-diegetic). According to Claudia Gorbman, diegetic music refers to instances when the music comes from a source on screen (3), for example, when Xander listens to Pasty Cline on his stereo after Buffy rejects him. Non-diegetic music, on the other hand, is music and/or sounds which originate "off screen," for example, much of the background music which the characters cannot hear but the audience can (Gorbman 3). Gorbman uses the term metadiegetic to describe music that is referential to music used in a previous scene and then again to remind viewers of earlier events (22–23), such as the repetition of Cordelia's and Xander's melodramatic love theme.

Knights, on the other hand, chooses to use the film and television industry's terms "scoring" and "source music" instead of narrative terms because, she argues, non-diegetic and diegetic music both contribute to "narrative function" (6). Scoring, which combines the music which originates on-screen and off-screen, she explains, takes on a "closer relationship" with a scene than just source music (music/sounds originating solely from the characters) typically does. Since characters either choose source music or it comes from bands or musical devices, like radios, this music is restricted in what it can do. Therefore, Cordelia and Xander's kissing melody is not only scoring because it reflects the character of their relationship, but also metadiegetic (referential) because it comments, reminds, and contrasts their and other relationships in the show.

It is scoring that gives *Buffy's* music the opportunity not only to grow with the characters but also to grow as a character itself. The show's musical supervisor, Johnathan King believes that the show's popular (contemporary) music "has become another character" because of its own fan base (Hill). When all the various musical pieces are considered, the show's music gains a particular identity, which is closely linked to an adolescent's journey to adulthood. However, while noting the connection of source music with narrative, Hill points out that sometimes even the viewer is unaware of the significance. Indeed, viewers might become so involved in the dialogue or fantastic fight choreography that they miss the significance of a particular piece of music or its lyrics.

In addition to those authors who consider the narrative aspects of *Buffy's* music, several others pay attention to how characters' identities are intrinsically linked with music. Pateman notes how *Buffy's* music instructs viewers to interpret certain characters' personalities, and, in particular, how Giles's musical tastes emphasize his distance from the rest of the Scooby Gang (178).

The show's theme song, in particular, introduces the idea that this show will detour from the typical damsel-in-distress horror story. Using Philip Tag's study of male and female codes in music, Halfyard argues that the show's theme music, which is "rhythmically irregular" and "at the same volume [loud] throughout," exhibits the characteristics of male coding ("Love," 2). In this way, Nerf Herder's theme song, with its driving melody and aural references to horror films (like a wolf howling and a cauldron bubbling), subverts what is to come. In this way and other ways, *Buffy's* music continually undermines the horror film tradition and gender expectations.

The uses of music in *Buffy* are just as postmodern as the show's other elements: it is repetitious, recursive, self-conscious, ironic, and "delights in ... baffling the binary" (Pender). In *Buffy*, musical allusions recur in language and in music in such a way that devoted viewers delight. For example, in Season Two, Oz, when asked what a girl would have to do to impress him, responds she would need a "feather boa and the theme from *A Summer Place.*" In Season Seven, the theme music from *A Summer Place* plays as Sunnydale's females pursue the teenage football hunk R.J., who is wearing his father's letterman jacket enchanted with a powerful love spell.

Able to insert itself into the series in multiple ways, music not only entertains but also serves as a vehicle for emphasizing relationships among the various characters and plotlines. Music, like the show's use of language, also serves to comment on one of the series's main narrative arcs — the relationship between adolescence, adulthood, and the in-between.

In his DVD commentary to "Hush," Joss Whedon refers to the recurring tensions within language, sexuality, and normality that pervade the series and how spoken language often gets in the way of communication. According to Whedon and further explored by Wilcox, *Buffy* uses language to emphasize the difference between the adolescent and adult worlds ("There Will").

Finding an identity and identification with others shape adolescents' experiences. Erik Erikson characterizes adolescents as being between identity and identity confusion (*Identity* 55). This tension between stability and instability exists in the term's etymology. The term *adolescent* comes from the Latin word *adolēscene* which means "to grow up." Its present participle form means "growing up," and its past participle *adultus* means "grown up" ("Adolescent"). The overlapping of these terms hints at the desire of adolescents to gain adulthood and adults to regain their adolescence.

For Erikson (*Identity*), adolescence is an important stage when youth seek to bring together various facets of their identities into a coherent whole (Miller 187). *Buffy*'s music also displays this desire, and this desire works through the various roles music plays in the show's narrative. Buffy longs to be normal but resists normality each time she experiences it. (For example, she wants her powers to return in "Helpless"). Buffy's music serves as a way for her to express something she cannot or does not want (at least consciously) to acknowledge — the pull of adulthood and her desire to experience a conventional adolescence.

During the adolescent years, psychologist Mary Pipher writes, girls lose themselves (19–20). Jan Jagodzinkski, working through a Lacanian[2] lens to explain how one can never obtain his or her desire, attributes this loss to girls being unable to identify with the societal depiction of an "ideal woman," which is why Pipher's patients had to seek help to "reidentify" with "what it means to be a 'young woman' in the social order" (224).

A clear example of this is Buffy's younger sister Dawn, who, first, is not human and, second, remains an adolescent in series chronology for the remainder of the series. Dawn continually either has her music selected for her or is associated with stereotypical early adolescence music. For example, in "I Was Made to Love You," Giles refers to fourteen-year-old Dawn's music as "aggressively cheerful." However, because of entering the series in Season Five, Dawn really is not given a chance to have her character developed through music as the other characters have in the first four seasons of the series. In Season Seven's "Conversations with Dead People," Dawn turns on the radio and dances to Los Cubaztecas's "Nicolito"; the radio has remained on the same station since Season's Five "Listening to Fear," when Buffy uses Latin music to cover her sobs. Dawn leaves the series on the cusp of an emerging adulthood, and viewers can never be sure what type of music would have defined the confident, compassionate young adult of the last episode.

Adolescence is often referred to as a period of "storm and stress," and at times *Buffy's* music reflects those themes. But, like most qualities appearing in *Buffy* characters, adolescence resists dichotomies. Exploring the characteristics of contemporary society, Jeffrey Arnett reconsiders G.S. Hall's 1904 use of these two descriptors ("storm and stress") and calls for a modified view of adolescence based on cultural and individual variations of the three characteristics which typically shape this period[3] ("Adolescent"). As I said, in later work, Arnett goes on to name the period of time between eighteen and twenty-five as "emerging adulthood," and proceeds to outline the characteristics of this transitional period. His research with college-age students suggests that they do not define adulthood as beginning with "distinct events," such as finishing education, getting married, or working full time, but more in terms of a gradual "accepting responsibility for one's actions, making independent decisions, and becoming financially responsible" (*Emerging* 15).

Beginning with Season Four, many of the characters in *Buffy* undergo similar experiences and the series becomes even more marked by Buffy's accepting and identifying with her role and responsibilities as the Slayer, or in other words, the adult. When examined season by season, in a linear fashion, *Buffy's* music contributes not only to the narrative arc of each season but to the series's overall commentary on the main characters' journeys from adolescence to adulthood.

Age of Identity Exploration:
Seasons One and Two

From the first season, the background music accompanying each episode establishes itself in particular roles which will continue for the next six seasons. The music in these first twelve episodes, influenced in part by Whedon's confession of his fascination with horror films, comes from two main sources: Christopher Beck's score and the various bands which play at the Bronze. Just as adolescents need their own place to express their identity, these bands provide essential commentary on characters' entrances into the later years of adolescence. In the beginning, music frequently acts in non-diegetic ways in the show as certain lyrics accompany/enhance the main characters' actions and emotions. For example, as Buffy prepares for her first night at the Bronze, Sprung Monkey's "Saturated," a song about how young people's minds are impressionable, plays as she tries to find something to wear. While music frequently foreshadows events or comments on what's occurring on the screen, it never seems didactic.

More noticeable, however, is the background music which accompanies the appearance of the non-vampire villains in the series. In fact, for the first two seasons, individual villains are paired with distinctive music cues, as well as songs by bands, more than Buffy and her allies are.[4] Since many of the villains in these early seasons die by the end of the episode, background music fills up the narrative gaps and summarizes the particular background of each monster. While each vampire attack is usually paired with the traditional violin strains of many past horror films, each non-vampire villain receives his or her own particular twist to this staple of scary cinema.

For example, with the first appearance of the bounty hunter/warrior team, the Three, who are out to kill Buffy and Faith (only to mistake Cordelia for Faith), comes a brief militaristic melody, paired with the clanging of their armor ("Homecoming"). In the episode in which hyenas imported from Africa possess Xander and a group of Sunnydale students ("The Pack"), the music consists mainly of tribal drums. In the "Out of Mind" episode, there is a direct connection to the villain (a girl who turns invisible because she had been ignored by everyone at school) and the flute she played in the band. Because the audience will spend more time with the main characters, their music, at first, is not as overt in their characterization.

In the second season, character-enhancing music accompanies the three vampires which dominate this season (and several seasons thereafter)—Angel, Spike, and Drusilla. At this point, the background music still assumes the role of explicator and narrator and remains at a distance from the characters and their struggles, including the reappearance of the soulless Angel and Buffy's struggle to "just be normal." With the appearance of Spike in "School Hard," the audience first hears the punk-inspired, Johnny Rottenish soundtrack which defines his personality throughout the show and does not change for many seasons. Drusilla's appearances are filled with the tinkling of a little girl's jewelry box. The eeriness of the music, paired with the shots of her dolls, emphasizes the insanity of her character and seems typical of psychological horror films. Her music completes the little girl aspect of her personality and makes her cruelty even more disturbing.

In "The Dark Age," Buffy and Giles connect through their different musical choices, and the audience begins to understand these characters' identities better through their tastes in music. Giles's personality and his own adolescence, for example, is tied to seventies rock music. Buffy, like many adolescents, is still experimenting with her tastes in music and has tried to assert her independence with Giles by convincing him that she should be allowed to pick her own workout music. Her workout music, which Giles calls "meaningless sounds," does not convey her character's complexities. (Buffy seems to sense that this music might not truly convey who she will become; in fact her workout music changes in several future episodes.) Knowing of Giles's distaste of her music, Buffy reminds him of their different tastes in music in order to distract him from thinking about his disastrous relationship with his girlfriend Jenny.

As Knights explains, Buffy tries to connect with Giles by acknowledging his distaste of her music. In this conversation, she reenacts the assumptions often made by adolescents about adults' tastes because of adolescents' inability to create an entire picture of their parents' experiences. In fact, as adolescents, these adults may have once liked music of which their parents might not have approved. Incomplete perceptions of adults by adolescents often cause conflicts (Head). What is important about this scene is that Buffy and Giles actually connect and are comforted through their distaste for each other's music — music associated with their decades-apart adolescences.

By the end of the second season, just as the characters grow into their late adolescence and become more confident in their roles, so too does the background music grow out of its role as merely enhancing what is happening in each scene. Angel's flashbacks to his life in Ireland are set to period music. By the last episode, "Becoming, Part Two," Buffy earns her own distinctive music — Sarah McLachlan's "Full of Grace," which "plays as an older, wiser Buffy leaves Sunnydale" (Dechert 220).

Age of Identity: Season Three

By the time she comes back in Season Three, Buffy fulfils McLachlan's lyrics from Season Two. She comes to understand her destiny, accept it somewhat, and know it's time to go home. The lines about knowing that one could do better from McLachlan's song "Full of Grace," which played during the last episode of Season Two, foreshadow the growing up which will occur in Season Three when Buffy and the Scoobies turn eighteen. The members of the Scooby Gang are seniors, preparing to leave high school behind. As they do so, they exhibit bouts of independence and confidence but those instances remain somewhat awkward and immature, as suggested by the music which accompanies these scenes.

Xander, one of the main characters, exhibits a growth of his role in the evil-fighting business during the season. In "The Zeppo," he attempts to stop a group of demon/vampire former-high-school males, and his background music is ironic, playful, and recursive. This light, fast-paced music is juxtaposed with the dramatic strains of Buffy's music. Buffy is, at the same time, "really" saving the world; however, it is Xander's fight which seems more important in the episode even as the music seems to play into that irony and diminish its importance.

According to Halfyard, the music performed at the Bronze serves as a way for music to create a youth sub-culture which prohibits adults like Giles ("Singing"). However, in Season Three it is the adults' adolescent sub-cultures that are revealed through music performed at the Bronze. In "Band Candy," when the adults acquire teen-age-like behavior, four "grownup" men sing "Louie Louie" on the stage of the Bronze, thereby subverting the "coolness" of the previous bands which performed there. Furthermore, their song choice refers to their own adolescent sub-culture which Willow, unlike Buffy who seems to be more familiar with Giles's taste, does not seem to get.

Buffy responds to the adults' regressive behavior by asking if there is a Billy Joel concert in town. She tries to understand their behavior by associating it with the music she assumes they listen to, although the Kingsmen's popularity predates Billy Joel's by a decade. Even the adolescent Joyce and Giles experience a musical misconnection, with Giles preferring Cream's "Tales of Brave Ulysses" and Joyce preferring Seals and Croft.[5] Adolescents and adults often claim not to understand each other's music, making statements which help them keep distance from each other; this seems to underscore the point of this episode, unlike in "The Dark Age" when music bridges teen and adult experiences.

Music continues its association with sex during this season, but it lacks the sophistication it will gain in the later seasons. Some romantic music is carried over from the second season, indicating that those relationships may be stagnant. Xander and Cordelia's kissing music from Season Two, for example, is heard again ("Anne"), as is much of Buffy and Angel's music. The music playing at Buffy's and Angel's wedding, of which Angel dreams, features a lovely harp melody which continues to play during their breakup. This continuation of music from one happy scene to one tragic scene stresses the impossibility of their relationship growing.

Heavy guitar music and the singing of Barry White accompany Cordelia's and Willow's growing sexual identities respectively. As for the villains, Spike returns to Sunnydale barely able to croak out the lyrics to "My Way." Drusilla has dumped him and all of his confidence from the second season is lost. By the end of the episode as he drives off into the sunset, Sid Vicious's version of "My Way" remains his anthem, and the passion with which he now sings mirrors his regained confidence ("Lover's Walk").

In keeping with the themes of the season's narrative arc, the music by the end of the season complements the theme of the high school community putting aside their differences and coming together to fight the mayor. The music at the prom is unlike the music the characters usually dance to at the Bronze. First, there is no live band, and the DJ's music seems childish and unsophisticated when compared to the rest of the series' music.

However, the music mirrors Sunnydale's seniors' realization that they are about to graduate and pursue their own interests. Even Oz "tears up" when they hear "We Are Family." Furthermore, the music which ends "Graduation, Part One," briefly continues in the opening to "Graduation, Part Two." "Part Two" begins exactly where "Part One" ends—with Buffy stabbing Faith and watching Faith fall off the building. The mourning strains of what sounds like a cello play during this scene and connect the two episodes. This music is important in Buffy's journey because it reminds the viewer of the two Slayers's complicated relationship. Buffy needs Faith's blood to save Angel and is willing to kill her to get it, yet they were once allies. The music underscores this relationship and pays tribute to Faith's exodus from the show.

Age of Self-Focusing: Season Four

Finally in Season Four, as Buffy and her Scooby Gang leave high school and enter a larger world, the background music must transform to match this period of self-focus. During this time of "self-focus," emerging adults make decisions that will help them understand who they are and what they want from life in order to gain self-sufficiency (Arnett, *Emerging* 11–12). Once again, music helps *Buffy's* characters define who they are or wish to be.

During their initiation into college, many of the characters also experience bouts of isolation and of intimacy as well, which are both expressed through music. By playing at various parties with his band, the Dingoes Ate My Baby, Oz has already gained entrance into this world through his music. For Buffy, one of her early confrontations begins in her dorm room with her new demon roommate Kathy. Kathy plays Cher's "Do You Believe in Love?" incessantly. It is not the fact that Kathy plays the same song over and over that bothers Buffy so much but the fact that Cher's lyrics about not needing someone and being strong enough remind Buffy of her relationship with Angel.

Buffy's own soundtrack changes as well. In the opening teaser (the usual Buffy/vampire fight) of "Beer Bad," the usual fight scene music is replaced with techno music as a leather-clad Buffy pummels a vampire. (Is this the music she usually plays in her head as she is fighting? Is this music commenting on the usual music which accompanies these scenes?) Awakening from her daydream into a large lecture hall, Buffy listens to Professor Walsh ask, "What do we do when we can't have what we want?" before returning to her fantasy world. After spending several seasons with Buffy, the viewer is beginning to realize that she has yet to really define herself through music, especially in regards to her training and fighting. North and Hargreaves' study demonstrates that adolescents not only define their own identities through [pop] music but also that "preference for a particular style [of music] may carry an implicit message to other adolescence regarding a range of attitudes and values" (76).

Music grows in its role as storyteller this season. The episode "Hush," during which all the characters are rendered speechless, relies on music and pictures to tell the story of floating morticians/surgeons who extract all sound from Sunnydale in order to perform their heart-collecting quest.

This episode is by far one of the more terrifying as viewers can only imagine what the screams of those slaughtered must sound like. This episode uses not only Beck's musical score but also Saint-Saens's *Danse Macabre* to emphasize the fairy-tale like quality of the plot. Here, the music nearly dominates each scene and becomes the voice which guides Buffy to her future endeavor. This episode serves as a precursor to (or younger version of) the musical episode of Season Six by providing a model in which music not only sets the scene but takes over the narrative from the characters. The difference is that in "Hush" Giles is able to choose the music to accompany his explication, a choice he is not given in "Once More with Feeling" or during his dream sequence in "Restless," in which he must sing instructions to the Scoobies rather than tell them. In "Once More with Feeling," a demon's spell makes him sing; in "Restless" it is his subconscious.

Another quality of emerging adulthood is that by the end of it "many individuals have incorporated sexuality into their self concept" (Lefkowitz and Gillen 250). This formation begins for many of Buffy's characters in Season Four, and continues for Buffy — who is dumped by Parker, then finds Riley — and Willow, who will begin a lasting relationship with Tara. The characters express their increasing knowledge of and experience with sex and sexuality through music. Xander, for example, entwines Buffy's emerging adulthood with a singer/songwriter when he describes a type of sex as "tender Sarah McLachlan sex." Also, this season introduces Christopher Beck's interpretation of the Buffy/Riley relationship with music, which Whedon describes as being "bluer and stranger" and more adult than the Buffy/Angel theme ("Commentary: 'Hush'"). In addition, Willow, having discovered her love for Tara, does not need Barry White to speak her affection.

Finally, two characters sing during this season, one as a way of trying to connect with adults and another as a way of expressing his experience as an emerging adult. In "Superstar," troubled adolescent Jonathan sings swing music on the Bronze's stage and delivers a very grownup performance; however, instead of reality, it is his fantasy of what he would like to be as an adult.

Unlike in "Restless" when Giles appears in Xander's dream and badly sings directions from the Bronze's stage (a place where he doesn't belong), Giles surprises the group (and some of the show's audience) with his own singing. Early in "Where the Wild Things Are," Giles tells Willow that he is going to attend a meeting for grown-ups. When they show up at the coffee shop to get him, they find Giles accompanying himself on the guitar and singing the Who's

"Behind Blue Eyes." Willow responds to this performance: "Now I remember why I used to have a crush on him," and Xander describes him later as a "god of acoustic rock."

In "The Yoko Factor," Spike sneaks up on Giles playing Lynyrd Skynyrd's "Free Bird" and proceeds to remind Giles that Buffy has not needed Giles's help lately and that Giles is unemployed. Thrust back into his own emerging adulthood, Giles seeks the music of his youth to distract and comfort him. These performances simultaneously separate Giles from and connect him with the rest of the emerging adults in the series because those emerging adults are confronted with the thoughts that Giles was once like they, yet they are uncomfortable with his public displays of his youth.

Age of Instability: Season Five

In Season Five, Buffy assumes new responsibilities as Dawn's big sister. The first new type of music which appears in Season Five is Buffy's new workout music. As she balances in a handstand on a wooden block and Giles instructs her in a Yoda-like voice, New Age music plays in the background instead of her usual "music with a beat." A similar type of music occurs in the fifth episode, "No Place like Home," during Buffy's trance. It is in this episode when Joyce tells Buffy that she has grown up, contrasting with Joyce's observation in Season Two when she is unsure of Buffy's demeanor after Buffy has made love with Angel. Having sex does not equate to growing up; and, according to Pipher "most early sexual activity tends to be harmful to girls" (208). Spike, on the other hand, sings the Ramones's "I Wanna be Sedated" ("Blood Ties"), keeping him connecting with his signature punk rock music.

Music not only comforts but helps block out the tragedies characters face in this season. Believing that her mother is cured and that all is right with her relationship with Riley, Buffy asks him if they can put Emiliana Torrin's "Summerbreeze" on "repeat all night" so they can dance to it. In doing so, she suspends the onset of adult experiences which are to come.

Season Five, the season following the episode in which background music functions as the only voice ("Hush"), includes an episode in which the background music is *completely* absent from an episode. Its absence acts as what Gorbman calls a "*diegetic musical silence* [her emphasis]" and its silence should be paired with events whose emotional content are explicit. In "The Body," music's refusal to comment on events actually acknowledges that sometimes it is important for music *not* to comment. Writers and directors of the episode "The Body" reject the notion of using music to tell the story of Joyce, Buffy's mother, dying and the events which occur afterward. Unlike during music-heavy "Hush," the viewer of "The Body" listens only to voices and sounds throughout the episode.

As Dechert eloquently points out, the absence of music focuses our attention to other sounds; ordinary background sounds become abnormally louder and the characters' grief is mirrored in the audience's lack of a soundtrack telling them how to feel (220). In an especially poignant moment, Anya exclaims to Xander, Tara, and Willow, "I don't understand how this all happens. How we go through this [mourning Joyce's death] ... no one will explain to me why." Anya's words about her confusion as to how to behave or feel can be applied to the lack of music in this episode. The inclusion of background or even source music might cue the viewer when to cry or when a character has a moment of relief. In "The Body," music becomes a mourner, choosing to lament and show respect by being silent, yet still present, in this scene which is a tribute to Joyce. Music returns in the next episode in Giles's home as he replays "Tales of Brave Ulysses" (Cream), not because Joyce liked it, but because it reminds him of their regression to a happier time, their adolescence, during which they were able to be intimate, an act in which their adult selves would not let them engage. In Season Five and the next, music follows the uneven rate at which some of the characters mature.

The Age of Possibilities: Season Six

Arnett's description of emerging adulthood as a time when people "have a chance to change their lives in profound ways" (*Emerging Adulthood* 17) fits the narrative arc for Season Six and its use of music exceptionally well. In "Wrecked," Willow's experimentation with the darker, addictive side of magic at the warlock Rack's den is accompanied by Laika's song "Black Cat Bone" which is electronic music overlaid with ethereal female vocals. In "Dead Things," Buffy uses music to explain her distance from the contemporary adolescent fads. In a post-coital conversation with Spike about his decorating taste, she shares that the New Kids on the Block posters on her bedroom walls are "beginning to date her." Experimentation, a necessary element in adolescence, contributes once again to the show's emphasis on growing up.

If *Buffy*'s music simultaneously consists of both adolescent and adult qualities, then Season Six's musical episode "Once More with Feeling"[6] actually "silences" the cast. As Clarke contends, this episode's music, written by Whedon and sung by the cast, is enjoyable on its own for most of the episode. Captivated by musical dance numbers, a viewer might be surprised by the serious turn at the end of the episode. Clarke notes that the narrative abruptly interrupts the liveliness of the ending as it "arrest[s] the fun" and informs the audience that "music as utopia" is "anti-narrative" (7). In other words, this episode is not meant to serve as a distraction from the season's narrative arc but is just as important as non-musical episodes. Musical episodes, like the emerging adults in the show, must take on more responsibilities. The music in this episode has outgrown its role as background commentator and directly contributes to the show's narrative in a way that has not been previously explored in the first five seasons.

Taking into account not only Buffy's character development but also the show's emphasis on language getting in the way of communication (which accounts for its removal in Season Four's "Hush"), it is not surprising then in Season Six that music enables Buffy and the rest of the cast to take a larger step in illustrating the significant changes which are about to occur, and the music forces them unwillingly to reveal secrets. Wilcox characterizes these performances as song soliloquies, but the characters before this point have been unable or unwilling to find a way to express their innermost feelings (*Why* 56). Only music, acting in the position of an omnipotent narrator, is able to reveal what the audience (and Spike) has known since the beginning of the season.

The songs are a perfect foreshadowing for the rest of the season's events since each character, as the demon Sweet remarks, reveals his or her innermost secrets— something the characters have been unable — or unwilling — to express in previous episodes. Spike and Buffy are united during one of their most tender moments when they sing to one another at the end of the episode "just before the curtain falls."

But the ending music tells another story: it is the orchestral music which usually plays at the end of a musical. Buffy and Spike are playing adult roles, such as those previously played by adults from well-known musicals. Their budding sexual relationship parallels Dawn's growing sexual identity which began in the episode previous, "All the Way," and is highlighted in her dance number with the demon Sweet. In his DVD commentary to "Once More with Feeling," Whedon explains that Dawn's musical performance with the demon Sweet is a way for Dawn to "show a little more of herself."

Whedon decides to allow the episode's songs to resolve several important plot lines as well. Giles must leave Buffy, and Tara must leave Willow, and so they often share verses to foreshadow upcoming departures. The audience also sees the problems lurking beneath the surface of Xander and Anya's relationship and, most importantly, witnesses the group learn that they extracted Buffy from heaven. The gang's only response is to wonder "Where do we go from here?" as they realize the import of their good intentions. During this period of instability and experience, Arnett notes, emerging adults "learn something about themselves and hopefully take a step toward clarifying the kind of future they want" (*Emerging* 11).

In the final episodes of the season, music enhances the series's message that the challenges of becoming an adult do not have to be supernatural to be devastating. In Season Six, people are shot with guns, Spike nearly rapes Buffy, and Xander leaves Anya at the altar. Yet, these events are coupled with two songs which signify the growth Buffy and Spike will experience in the next season. When Spike is about to fight the demon in Africa and seek to be what he was so the Slayer "can get what she deserves" ("Grave"),[7] he taunts him with the Nirvana song "Smells like Teen Spirit." Is he ready to replace the punk era with grunge? Buffy finally realizes her role as a parent as she reveals to Dawn, "I don't want to protect you from the world; I want to show it to you." In the final tear-jerker scenes of this season, the viewers come to realize that the lesson all along has been that adulthood can be mundane. The message here is quite simply expressed through Sarah McLachlan's version of the "Prayer of St. Francis": do good, do forgive, and do live. In the next season, *Buffy's* music returns to its uses from the first season, but it is clear by the final episode that it has grown up.

Adults at Last: The Final Season

Season Seven marks the return of adolescence to the series as the new young generation of potential Slayers joins the fight and the journey toward adulthood begins for them. Buffy and the Scooby Gang now find themselves acting as adults and caretakers. In ways similar to Erikson's characterization of adulthood (*The Life Cycle Completed: A Review*), they are now sharing their identities with those to whom they are committed—the Potentials. It certainly seems as if the music is geared toward a slightly younger group to match the personalities of these teenage girls who have been called upon to help in the fight against the First. Spike, who is possessed by the First for the first several episodes, sings wisps of folk songs, songs which do not reflect who he is but do reflect who he was and heighten his separation not only from the group but from himself. Buffy also realizes just how alone she is in this fight, and must experience what Arnett calls "learning to stand alone" (Tanner).

In contrast to the other emerging adults in the season, two musical numbers stunt two characters from emerging as adults. Anya continues to identify herself through Xander; and, in "Selfless" (the title certainly reflects the many layers of lack of self), she sings a musical number "I Will be His Missis" which was "left out" of Season Six.[8] During this flashback, Anya, in a Disney *Little Mermaid*-like number, dons her wedding gown and sings of her love for Xander and her wished-for role as his wife. She sings of her lack of even a maiden name and how their union should give her life the purpose she craves. As a human, she literally cannot imagine herself without Xander. In the final episodes, Anya stays to help save Sunnydale and dies in the final battle, presumably still in love with Xander.

Andrew, the last of the evil geek Trio, finds his path; however, he remains tied to his adolescence through music in most of this series. In Season Six, we find Andrew, Jonathan, and Warren, like other villains in the series, with music helping to show their arrested development. (For example, the horn in their van plays the *Star Wars* theme.) In "Storyteller," Andrew creates his own sort of childlike music and lyrics to accompany his vision of the Trio's future in paradise. During this vision, Warren and Andrew hold different instruments—a pan flute (one of the instruments that Andrew uses to summon demons) and a lute, as Andrew sings "We are as gods." Jonathan holds a golden cup and pitcher. This daydream, which occurs in a flashback, furthers the Trio's association with sorcery and male sexuality as well as commenting on future events. Jonathan mimes pouring wine from his pitcher into the cup, foreshadowing the sacrificial role his character will play in the rising of the First (Andrew stabs Jonathan so his blood will spill on the seal and allow the First loose in the world).

Andrew also works with music to reintroduce characters in this season. For Faith, who rejoins the last season to help fight the First, Andrew uses movie trailer music and a voice-over to catch viewers up on her role in the series. It is only during the last moments of "Chosen" that Whedon allows Andrew to recognize his calling—telling stories. With the re-entrance of Faith comes a return to the Bronze, where she takes the Potentials dancing, sensing the ability of youthful music to calm them. In many ways, Faith understands these adolescents and their needs more than Buffy does, and Faith uses music to connect with them.

Another way Arnett characterizes the period he calls "emerging adults" is as an "age of possibilities, when many different futures remain open ..." when young people have "not yet committed to a new network of relationships and obligations" (*Emerging Adulthood* 16). At least twice in the final episode, Whedon expresses this notion that there is "closure—but not a closing" ("Commentary: 'Chosen'"). The first time occurs during Buffy's goodbye speech to Angel in which she describes herself as cookie dough that has not finishing baking.[9] The second time is the shot of the road, along which the school bus has run, meeting the horizon.

In Season Seven, the background music reveals an epic feel: music plays even more of a traditional cinematic role. In his DVD commentary to the final episode, Whedon reveals his desire to create that epic feel for the last episodes and his use of the music works with the other elements to create this experience. Robert Duncan's orchestral soundtrack is dynamic and grand. The music must be as large as the cries from the Turok-han, the super-vampires, who pour out of the Hellmouth into "a stunning battle dance such as the world has never seen" (Whedon, "Commentary: 'Chosen'"). Rather than turn to another classical work, as the show has done in earlier episodes ("Hush" and "Selfless"), Duncan's music, with its symphonic mix of violins, percussion, and winds, makes a strong impact on the final scenes. *Buffy's* music has grown up and we become aware of its potential in the final battle as it matches the final dramatic scenes. However, as Dawn asks, after their epic battle and the awakening of potential Slayers, "what are we gonna do now?" Buffy's music proves it, too, can assume adult responsibilities.

Conclusion

In Season One, a Sunnydale High teacher remarks that his research has led him "to conclude that one of our most fundamental needs after finding shelter is to be heard" ("Nightmares"). As the audience follows each *Buffy* episode, music and ultimately sound creates a history throughout the series and stands as a character, with a past, present, and future, which has undergone as much growth and change as Buffy herself. Even the Nerf Herder theme song echoes the narrative arc from adolescence to adulthood. In Season One, the sound of bubbling accompanies the shot of a cauldron filled with green goo. As the show grows away from its depiction of witches as potion-making caricatures and New Age earthy types, the bubbling cauldron disappears from the opening credits and the music loses the bubbling cauldron sound.

Arnett concludes that "most emerging adults look forward to a future they believe is filled with promises ... [and] they almost unanimously believe that eventually they will be able to create for themselves the kind of life they want" (*Emerging Adulthood* 228). The epic music which accompanies the final episode and the characters' reaching this point is no coincidence, but it takes seven seasons for the narrative arc, its characters, and its music to reach this conclusion, which is an actual beginning to the Scooby Gang's adulthood.

Notes

1. Even today, there are sites devoted to Season Six's episode "Once More with Feeling."

2. Jacques Lacan was a French psychoanalyst and philosopher who re-read Freud, emphasizing how Freud's theories interplay with linguistics. In addition, Lacan maintains that an item loses desirability for a person when other people lose desire for that item. In relation to the Lacanian lens specified, basically, Lacan invented the "mirror stage" in which he proposes that, when infants (six to eighteen months), looking in a mirror, first recognize that they have a self outside of their own self, they will forever seek that unity of self they once had. Before the "mirror moment," infants related identity in the mother; now, identity is related to what the infant sees in the outside world. And, for Lacan, once an infant passes through the mirror stage, that infant can never return to the sense of self as unified and stable.

3. Those three aspects are conflicts with parents, mood disruptions, and risk behavior.

4. In the sixth season, geek villain Andrew plays various wind instruments to call demons.

5. In Season Three's DVD extras actress Kristen Sutherland (who plays Buffy's mother) remembers her teenage years and wanting to connect with men who were more interested in listening to their music than talking.

6. After writing episodes without voices and then without music, there seemed to be only one route left — writing a musical. Whedon wrote the melodies and the lyrics for the groundbreaking episode "Once More with Feeling," a musical episode complete with singing and dancing, performed almost entirely by the cast.

7. He actually succeeds in regaining his soul.

8. In actuality, Whedon wrote her number in one night during this season (Goddard and Solomon).

9. Arnett comments that "Emerging adults believe they *should* explore different love relationships, that such exploration is both normal and necessary" before marriage and that "they are eager for the opportunities that emerging adulthood provides for having a variety of love relationships" (*Emerging Adulthood* 74).

Is That Stereotype Dead?

Working with and Against "Western" Stereotypes in Buffy

———— ⊶⊷ ————

SALLY EMMONS-FEATHERSTON

"You're not the Indian I had in mind."
— Thomas King (32).

In *The White Man's Indian*, scholar Robert Berkhofer asks, "why do [we] think about the Indian the way we do today?" (xiv). The simplistic answer to this question is that American culture teaches us to think of Native Americans as looking, acting, and behaving according to specific patterns. Misconceptions of native people began at First Contact and continue today, even in such popular culture as *Buffy the Vampire Slayer*. Interestingly, although the stereotypes have evolved from generation to generation, remnants of the early stereotypes established in the journal writing of America's first explorers (think Christopher Columbus and Amerigo Vespucci) still exist.

While I simply do not have the room to trace the origin and evolution of these stereotypes, it would be lax of me not to mention that the journal and letter writings of America's early "discoverers" influenced how Americans conceived of Indian people. It is from these writings that two central stereotypes emerged: the "Red Devil" and the "Noble Savage." In short, the red devil is the savage Indian who is blood-thirsty, primitive, and brutal. In Vespucci's writings, the red devil is amoral, sexually over-active, without culture or government, and even cannibalistic. In contrast, the noble savage is the romanticized Indian. He is peaceful, rarely speaks, is enlightened, communes with nature, attempts to befriend immigrants, and is stoic. The stereotype dictates that a noble savage is still a savage; he has the potential for transforming into a red devil if provoked.

55

Over time, additional stereotypes gradually emerged: the idealized Indian maiden/princess (remember Pocahontas?); the vanishing Indian (the idea that the cultures, traditions, languages, and lifeways of all Indian people are slowly disappearing); the drunken, lazy, poverty-stricken and reservation-bound Indian; the mixed-blood Indian who feels trapped between cultures; the warrior Indian; the shaman Indian.

All of these stereotypes remain today in varying degrees. Berkhofer explains that "In spite of centuries of contact and the changed conditions of Native American lives, Whites picture the 'real' Indian as the one before contact or during the early period of that contact" (28). Thomas King, contemporary Cherokee writer, echoes this sentiment when he writes, "In the end, there is no reason for the Indian to be real. The Indian simply has to exist in our imaginations" (54). King further states, "Somewhere along the way, we ceased being people and somehow became performers in an Aboriginal minstrel show for White North America" (68). Andrew Macdonald agrees, stating, "The very word 'Indian' is a conflation of hundreds of tribes, languages, and cultures into one emblematic figure: the Other, the Alien, the generalized Non-European" (Grassian 8).

As more immigrants sought freedom in America, more people began to record contact with Indian people and their impressions of the natives' lifeways (which were foreign and strange — and pagan — when compared to what the Whites were accustomed). These impressions emerged in letters home, newspaper articles, poems, plays, short stories, novels, and art. With the advent of technology, photographs and recordings were added to this mix.

Fast-forward to the late twentieth and early twenty-first centuries and media, such as cinema, advertising, music, and all-things popular culture, entered the picture. The bottom line? Native Americans have been stereotyped since First Contact; these stereotypes affected how people who came to this country perceived of native people, and these stereotypes continue to inform how people today think of American Indians.[1]

An excellent example of this pigeon-holed thinking is found in "Pangs," an episode of *Buffy the Vampire Slayer*, a TV show which experienced unexpected success on a network that was not part of the trio of powerhouse TV networks. As evidenced by the number of academic books springing up about *Buffy the Vampire Slayer* (and, yes, here is yet another), this show about vampires, witches, demons, and magic has more to offer than early critics thought.

Although *Buffy* has very few minority characters (unless one considers the vampires and demons to represent the "minority") and storylines, it gives us the unexpected when it delivered "Pangs" in Season Four. One of a smattering of holiday episodes, the setting in "Pangs" is Thanksgiving. How apropos, then, that Native Americans also appear in this episode. Scholar Dominic Alessio writes that Jane Espenson, the writer of this episode, and Michael Lange, the director, were "only too well aware of postcolonial issues raging in contempo-rary America. The very fact that this issue was even raised in a *BtVS* episode, let alone telecast as a Thanksgiving Special, would indicate that the choice of topic was deliberate" (736–37). How disappointing that a TV show — which is lauded for its smart writing, abundance of intelligent allusions, and ground-breaking depiction of the first loving and realistic homosexual relationship on TV — relies upon stereotypic thinking in its portrayal of the native characters. Even if the episode engages in a debate about the ethics of celebrating Thanks-giving, this does not excuse it from relying on age-old stereotypes.

As a reminder, "Pangs" depicts a construction team beginning work on the new UC–Sunnydale Cultural Partnership Center after the requisite speeches and ground-breaking ceremony of university and museum officials. Suddenly, Xander, one of the construction workers, discovers that the site is actually rest-ing on an old California mission when he falls into a cavernous hole. This dis-ruption of the forgotten mission unleashes a Chumash spirit who has inhabited the mission. The rest of the episode follows the "Scooby Gang," Buffy's circle of friends, as they debate how to deal with this spirit and worry about whether they should celebrate Thanksgiving.

From the opening scene, viewers are immersed in stereotypes. When the Chumash spirit appears, it is a moving green vapor which magically transforms into an Indian warrior, all while the expected mystical flute music is playing in the background. (Oh, how I would like for a TV show to actually feature the music of a native band like Indigenous in its soundtrack, but no, we have to have the expected flute music.) Of course, the warrior is everything that we anticipate: he is wearing buckskin, his hair is long, and his face displays the requisite paint expected from a native warrior. Moreover, he is able to shape shift; after all, that is what a dead Indian warrior should be able to do, right? The next time we see the warrior named Hus, he is standing in a room filled with display cases; inside the display cases are native objects, including weapons.[2] With agility and speed, Hus smashes a display case, gathers up var-ious weapons, and brutally slits the throat of Dr. Gerhardt, future curator of the Cultural Partnership Center.

The basic premise of *Buffy the Vampire Slayer* is that Buffy, supreme pro-ponent of all that is good, confronts evil on a weekly basis. In two short scenes, viewers are told that Hus is the quintessential "bad guy" whom Buffy will van-quish. Hus is savage in appearance and behavior, all befitting the "Red Devil" stereotype that he represents. Showing no regard for the museum's property (he is primitive after all), he destroys display cases and savagely kills a woman by slashing her throat. To add insult to injury, Hus then cruelly cuts off Dr. Gerhardt's ear as a trophy.

In *The Existential Joss Whedon*, J. Michael Richardson and J. Douglas Rabb praise this episode for depicting Hus cutting off Dr. Gerhardt's ear, writ-ing that "Many more people now know about this kind of atrocity" (163). What is missing in Richardson and Rabb's logic is that most viewers will be totally unaware that early settlers were paid by government officials for killing native people and that these settlers proved how many victims they had killed by showing their collection of scalps, skins, and sometimes ears. Instead, what viewers will see is Hus behaving like a blood-thirsty savage who is bent on revenge. Later, viewers will watch as Hus visits a Sunnydale church and — once again (surprise, surprise)— savagely kills another person, this time a priest. Meanwhile, the Scooby Gang realizes that Xander has been infected with malaria, smallpox, and syphilis, all because he fell into the site where the now-rediscovered mission used to be.[3]

Hus is seeking revenge on those who have wronged his people: the curator because she represents archeological and ethno-historical research on native sites; the priest because he symbolizes the destruction of Chumash lifeways in California (keep in mind that the fictional Sunnydale is actually based upon Santa Barbara, an early mission site); and, Xander? Well, poor Xander is guilty by association. Like the curator, Xander — because he is part of the construction company building the new Cultural Partnership Center — represents an archeological violation of native sites. It is no accident that Xander's punishment is to be infected with malaria, smallpox, and syphilis, for these are all diseases that were introduced to the Chumash (and many other tribes) by the mission system, decimating their populations.

Interestingly, Buffy, the "good guy," is featured in the episode's first scene as wearing a black cowboy hat. This complicates everything. If Buffy is the good guy, then why is she wearing the hat that Western mythology tells us is worn only by the bad guy? Does this mean that we should be rooting *against* Buffy and the Scooby Gang in this episode? If so, are we meant to excuse Hus's savagery? For those who are familiar with Joss Whedon's, *Buffy the Vampire Slayer*'s creator, *modus operandi*, this upholding and subverting of stereotypes is typical. In "Pangs," it is "western" mythology and Native American stereotypes that are being upheld and subverted, rather than Whedon's more typical subjects. Buffy *is* the heroine; wearing the black hat, however, symbolizes the ethical quandary that she will soon be debating with herself and her friends. In the teaser to "Pangs," Buffy encounters a vampire who exclaims, "Why don't you just go back where you came from? Things were great before you came." I can't help but think that Joss Whedon's writers, when writing this dialogue, were aware of the bumper sticker that is popular in native communities that depicts Christopher Columbus's arrival on North American soil. Upon witnessing this arrival, an elderly Indian man ironically states, "There goes the neighborhood."[4]

What sets "Pangs" apart from other *Buffy* episodes is that this episode explicitly deals with an issue of race. As such, it raises an interesting ethical dilemma for the Scoobies: if Hus is seeking revenge because of the atrocities committed on his people in the past as a result of the mission system, will it be morally right for Buffy to Slay him? What is their ethical responsibility to the Sunnydale community when it is juxtaposed against their ethical responsibility to the Chumash tribe? Against the backdrop of the Thanksgiving holiday, the characters debate these questions and disagree about what their moral responsibility to Sunnydale is.

According to Matthew Pateman in *The Aesthetics of Culture in Buffy the Vampire Slayer*, it makes sense for Willow to represent the voice of social justice among the Scoobies. Willow's mother is characterized as a liberal-minded activist throughout the series, so Willow has been raised to be cognizant of issues. Moreover, Willow knows what it is like to be marginalized. Not only is she Jewish, she has been cast as an outsider since the beginning of the series. She is the dowdy, book-loving, computer geek without any supernatural power when we first meet her. She is not part of the popular crowd in high school and only "fits in" with the Scooby Gang, also outsiders of sorts. Even when Willow discovers magic and develops a tangible power, she is still part of a group — witches — that has been ostracized and persecuted. Moreover, Willow's (later) homosexuality sets her apart from the largely heterosexual world of Buffy.

Willow is the researcher in the group so, when Hus is unleashed and starts killing people, Willow turns to books to try to learn more about Hus, the Chumash, and what might be motivating Hus's actions. After learning that the Chumash were victims of genocide as a direct result of the California mission system,[5] Willow starts to empathize with Hus and his warriors,[6] and begins to think that Hus's revenge is justified. When Buffy asks Willow what happened to the Chumash, Willow exhorts, "How about imprisonment? Forced labor? Herded like animals into a mission full of bad European diseases. The few Chumash who tried to rebel were hanged, *and,* when a group was accused of stealing cattle, they were killed; men, woman and children, and for proof to bring back to their accusers ... they cut off their ears."

In Buffy's first physical confrontation with Hus — who has very little dialogue in the episode — Hus tells her in clipped, simple English, which affirms the stereotypic portrayal of Indian people in Western movies (the only thing missing is Hus pounding his fist on his chest for dramatic emphasis!), "I am vengeance. I am my people's cry. They call for Hus, for the avenging spirit, to carve out justice. You slaughtered my people." Willow wants to make reparations to Hus and his people by giving back the land that was stolen from them, but Giles points out that the land is not theirs to give. Moreover, this token offering could not possibly make amends for the attempted destruction of the Chumash population and their lifeways.

Buffy is ethically torn. Recognizing this, Giles, the pragmatist among the group, attempts to persuade her that her moral responsibility is to vanquish Hus. Giles understands history and realizes the wrongs that were done to the Chumash, but he also recognizes the threat that Hus represents to Sunnydale; thus, his concern is to keep Hus from harming anyone else. To Willow, who calls Giles "unfeeling guy" because of this viewpoint, Giles says, "I think your sympathy for his plight has blinded you to certain rather urgent facts. We have to stop this thing." Giles's proclamation dehumanizes Hus; he is a thing, not a person, or a spirit. This is typical of the rhetoric surrounding Native Americans, especially in the late nineteenth and early twentieth centuries. If a person is dehumanized, then the guilt associated with decimating that person's culture, traditions, and people is removed.

Spike, perhaps because of his "bad boy" persona in the series, represents the politically incorrect voice of imperialism: "You won, all right? You came in and you killed them and you took their land.... It's what Caesar did, and he's not going around saying, 'I came, I conquered, I felt really bad about it.'... You had better weapons, and you massacred them. End of story." Ironically, Xander, no friend to Spike, finds himself actually agreeing with him.

For perhaps the first time in the *Buffy*verse, Buffy is uncertain whether the "bad" guy really *is* the bad guy. Buffy is the Slayer and her role is to Slay the evil demon. But is Hus truly evil? Buffy waffles on her position, one moment affirming Willow's beliefs, the next, Giles's. She states that she wishes she could find a "non–Slayee way" to stop Hus.

As moral choices often do, the difficult choice divides the group of friends.[7] Recognizing (and disliking) the growing tension developing in the group, Buffy, the group's leader, attempts to reduce the strain whenever the question of how to respond to Hus is raised by redirecting the conversation to the Thanksgiving dinner that she is planning. Willow reminds her that "Thanksgiving isn't about blending cultures, it's about one culture wiping out another," but Buffy remains firm in her belief that, if she can just plan the perfect Thanksgiving dinner, things will somehow work out. To Buffy, whose life is constantly in turmoil, Thanksgiving represents an escape from this chaos and a celebration of family and community — in other words, her group, the Scoobies. Buffy succumbs to the romanticized depiction of Thanksgiving that modern American society celebrates.

Unfortunately, what is unfolding in "Pangs" as an interesting moral debate ultimately collapses into the typical *Buffy* good-guy/bad-guy confrontation that must occur in order for the episode to resolve its plot. When Hus and his warriors attack the Scooby Gang at Giles's apartment (ironically referred to as "Ft. Giles," a nice example of the writers subverting Western mythology), the moral debate ends and Hus becomes the red devil that viewers expect him to be. No longer are we encouraged to sympathize with his people. Hus is trying to kill our beloved Buffy and Giles (and even Spike); he becomes the bloodthirsty and savage demon — the "thing" that Giles once called him — that must be destroyed.

Even Willow, who is riding to Buffy's rescue with Xander (still inflicted with various diseases) and Anya, Xander's girlfriend, all on bicycles — a metaphoric nod to the cavalry rushing in to save the day — does not hesitate to pick up a shovel and begin beating the native warriors that she has sympathized with throughout the episode, saying, "Why ... don't ... you ... die!" with each blow. Later, she confesses, "Two seconds of conflict with an indigenous person, and I turned into General Custer."

This statement is significant. We have to keep in mind that history confirms General George Armstrong Custer's well-known anti–Indian sentiment, though historical renderings also depict him as an example of a great military leader. How easy it is to dismiss that General Custer brutally slaughtered men, women, and children, all because they were members of the wrong race. Even Spike's — who is tied up and immobile in a chair (he is a vampire, after all) — imperialistic rhetoric disappears when Hus's warriors start shooting arrows at him until he resembles a human pin-cushion. "Remember that conquering nation thing?" he yells to Buffy and Giles. "Forget it. Apologize." When facing death, Willow, Spike, and Buffy all change their viewpoints on how to deal with Hus and his warriors.

In "Things Are Different Now?: A Postcolonial Analysis of *Buffy the Vampire Slayer*," Dominic Alessio calls the ending to this episode a "cop out" because the post-colonial debate is just forgotten. Gregory Stevenson disagrees, saying the entire episode's focus is really upon the theme of Thanksgiving, and that Buffy's proclamation that "the whole point of Thanksgiving [is that] Everyone has a place to go" is the episode's moral lesson. Alessio argues that "the issue of race in *BtVS* remains one demon that Buffy can't deal with, one frontier that Buffy is incapable of crossing" (738).

Stevenson counters by saying that "Spike functions in this episode as a demonstration that Buffy has indeed attempted to cross that frontier. Homeless and with no place to belong, Spike knocks on the door of Giles's apartment and Buffy lets him in. Spike has gone to his enemy for help" (234). Stevenson continues, "If the problem has been that the early colonials killed and oppressed their perceived 'enemies' (Chumash), here that past sin is reversed. Their enemy is not killed, but is made a part of the family in a sense. On Thanksgiving Day, Buffy gives Spike a 'home' — he even sits at the table with them during their Thanksgiving meal" (234).

Hold up, whoa, wait a minute. First of all, the atrocities committed against the Chumash cannot be reversed. A population was subjected to near genocide; a tribe was virtually wiped out by various crimes against it. Buffy and the Scoobies do not embrace Spike and welcome him into the proverbial "fold" by giving him entrance to Giles's apartment. Instead, he is tied up — oppressed — and is denied any sustenance at the end of the episode when the rest of the gang enjoys its Thanksgiving meal. Allowing him to sit with them at the table — tied up! — may not be a symbolic acceptance of him; instead, it could be a metaphoric slap-in-the-face, a reminder to him that he is different and that this difference prevents him from being one of them.

Secondly, we should not forget that Hus and his warriors are eventually

"Slayed." Sure, Buffy debates whether she should extinguish him; she even exclaims "you can have casinos now!" to Hus in the hope that it will persuade him to stop his attacks; but Hus must be destroyed because he is the enemy. Although he is seeking retribution for the brutality that his people faced, he remains the savage red devil who cannot be reasoned with. Red devils, according to the stereotype, do not possess the capacity for higher reasoning; they are savage and blood-thirsty.

Buffy's immature thought that casinos will make up for past atrocities underscores what many American people think: that because today's Indian people enjoy federally-funded housing, schooling, and health care—and have casinos!—that all should be forgotten. Some Americans even resent that today's Indian people have access to government support, apparently forgetting that ethnic cleansing occurred right here in the United States, land of justice and liberty for all ... unless you are a member of the wrong race, and your land contains valuable resources like gold and oil, and your religion is deemed "bad" because your beliefs are different.

About this episode, Dr. John Anderson, a specialist on the Chumash people, states in his short Internet article "Television Stereotyping of the Chumash" that the characterization of Chumash people in "Pangs" is "offensive and unfair." The teaser for *Buffy the Vampire Slayer* is that "In every generation, there is a chosen one. She alone will stand against the vampires, the demons, and the forces of darkness; she is the Slayer." According to this logic, Hus must be slain because he is a demon; Buffy, in contrast, must be ethically right because as the Chosen One her moral authority is unquestionable. Anderson writes, "The Chumash people are not a force of darkness, and it seems to me that an apology ... and some positive television coverage of contemporary Chumash life is in order." What do we really learn about the Chumash from "Pangs"? Are we immersed in the Chumash's world view? These are two questions that native scholars like myself ask when we consider how Native Americans are depicted, whether in literature, film, music, or television.

So, for fun, I have an idea. We'll make a list of the things we learn about Indian people from "Pangs": 1) they are savage; 2) they speak very little; 3) they wear buckskin; 4) they are magical; 5) they are scary; 6) they are primitive; 7) they are killers; 8) they must be stopped.

In reality, the Chumash were a thriving people. According to the Santa Ynez Band of Chumash Indians' official website, before the California Mission Period, the Chumash numbered approximately 20,000 people and lived in 150 different villages, some as large as towns. They lived along the coast of California from what is now present-day Malibu to Monterey County, and also on the Northern Channel Islands. Unlike other tribes, the Chumash were not nomadic. They lived in one area in permanent dome-shaped homes. As many as fifty members of a family might live in one home. The Chumash's livelihood depended upon hunting wildlife and, especially, marine life. They possessed their own system of money and enjoyed trading with other tribes and peoples. In general, the Chumash were peaceful ("like fluffy Indigenous kittens," states Willow in this episode), though they did possess weapons like the bow and arrow, the spear, and a harpoon, items that were all used for hunting and fishing. The Chumash were noted for their elaborate rock paintings and intricate basketry. After the California Mission Period, the most devastating period to California Indians, the Chumash's population fell to a shockingly low 250 people. Their way of life was shattered by disease and forced assimilation to another culture's way of living. Their land had been taken away from them and many (to survive) concealed their true identities by speaking English or Spanish (*Santa*).

However, unlike information suggested in "Pangs," Chumash people did not vanish. There are currently approximately 3,500 Chumash living across the United States, some still in California (Sonneborn 49). "The pressure has always existed for us to assimilate and forsake our culture," states the official website of the Santa Ynez Band of Chumash Indians: "Despite the many attempts to eradicate our culture, we maintained our connection to our ancestors and to our core identity of being Chumash. We survived because of our strength as a tribe and our spiritual connection to Chumash heritage."

Although many of today's Chumash people are not federally recognized as card-carrying members of a tribe (an issue to be discussed in another paper), the Chumash who live on the Santa Ynez Reservation in California possess their own constitution and governmental system. They also own and operate the successful Chumash Casino Resort (see, they do have a casino!). Chumash traditional culture, ceremonies, and language are enjoying a renaissance as younger members of the tribe embrace their ancestry. Hus and his warriors would likely be proud to see what modern Chumash people are doing!

Like Buffy, who struggles with her ethical responsibility in this episode, the "Pangs" storyline is complex and contradictory. At various points, it appears to support native people and empathize with their many historical and personal losses; at other times, it relies on typical stereotypic imagery in its characterization. "Pangs" acknowledges American's violent history with Native Americans, but only superficially. Contemporary Coeur d'Alene writer Sherman Alexie states, "If people start dealing with Indian culture and Indian peoples truthfully in this country, we're going to have to start dealing with the genocide that happened here. In order to start dealing truthfully with our cultures, they have to start dealing truthfully with that great sin, the original sin of this country, and that's not going to happen" (Grassian 8).

Once the Scoobies' debate is over and the ultimate battle ends, nothing can change the fact that the dead Chumash that Hus mourns will always be dead. Nothing can possibly compensate him for this loss. While the writer and director of "Pangs" attempted to raise public awareness of a serious racial subject in this episode, the native characters, ultimately, are still viewed as demons (which is typical of red devil rhetoric and imagery) who must be destroyed. Hus and his spirit warriors represent a threat to the Sunnydale community, and so must be eradicated; in the United States, we know that indigenous people at large were also seen as a threat to everything "civilized" so they were displaced, Christianized, "civilized," and terminated.[8]

Contemporary Native American writers, poets, and filmmakers are beginning to respond to the atrocities of history. For example, controversial Menominee prose poet Chrystos writes in her poem "Winter Count" from *Dream On,*

> [....]For every person who came here to find freedom
> there are bones rattling in our Mother
> The ravage of suburbia covers our burial grounds
> our spiritual places, our homes [....]
> Down the long tunnel of death my grandmothers cry   *No*
> *Give no solace to our destroyers* [....]
> *Never forget*
> *america is our Hitler*[9]

Chrystos is radical in her viewpoint and does not reflect the way many native people think about America. In fact, among Native American literature experts, she belongs to a classification of poets known as the "badass" poets. Her poetry is fueled by anger over the destruction that occurred in the past. Nevertheless, like Hus, she is responding in her own way to the atrocities that occurred to her people.

It is easy to understand this anger. Consider, for instance, Deborah A. Miranda's (Esselen and Chumash) experience upon returning home to California to visit family. In a posting to the Study of American Indian Literature discussion group, Miranda describes visiting the Soledad and Carmel Mission sites, locations where some of her ancestors would have been at one time. She writes that her sister warned her she would see actual remains of their ancestors lying on the ground and confesses, "I was so unprepared for what I saw. Bone fragment everwhere [sic], teeth, artifacts.... [We] circled the Mission with sage, mugwort and tobacco, literally picking up the pieces and reclaiming the space. It took most of the day." She continues, "To see those children [some of Miranda's relatives] ... running up to us with their hands full of ancestors ... indescribable, incomprehensible." Does "Pangs" show us this reality of modern Chumash life? Sadly, no. Though the episode hints it will be different from other TV shows by raising important issues about the history of Indian people in America — suggesting that it will transcend traditional stereotypes, the message is ultimately lost when it resorts to typical *Buffy* good guy vs. bad guy antics (and violence) in the episode's conclusion.

"Pangs" is full of dualities. That is what makes it interesting to me. It attempts to do what television shows seldom do: engage in a serious racial discussion, all within the confines of a fantasy show aimed at teenagers. "Pangs" recognizes that the Thanksgiving holiday is a symbolic reminder of the radical changes that many native lifeways underwent as a result of direct contact with other peoples and cultures. Despite this attempt, however, and despite its interesting subversion of elements of Western mythology, it falls back on age-old stereotypes of native people, confirming what some Americans have thought all along: Indian people are trapped in the past; Indian people are primitive and savage; Indian people lack higher reasoning. As in the old black and white cowboy and Indian westerns, Indian people fight but ultimately lose.

In fact, Thomas King argues that these stereotypes cement Indian people in the past (this is certainly true with Hus) and that native writers must contend with this daily. He states that "the North American past, the one that had been created in novels and histories, the one that had been heard on radio and seen on theatre screens and on television, the one that had been part of every school curriculum for the last two hundred years ... was unusable" (106). He contends that the past of which he speaks "not only trapped Native people in a time warp, it also insisted that our past was all we had. No present. No future. And to believe in such a past is to be dead" (106).

Sherman Alexie (Coeur d'Alene) jokes about these stereotypes in his ironic poem "How to Write the Great American Indian Novel," pointing out that "All of the Indians [in modern renderings of Indian people] must have tragic features: tragic noses, eyes, and arms. / Their hands and fingers must be tragic when they reach for tragic food" (Purdy and Ruppert 425). For many contemporary Native American writers, being able to joke about the stereotypes is a way to disarm them. Chrystos takes a different approach to responding to the stereotypes in her poem "I am not your Princess." In this poem, Chrystos situates her readers in the twenty-first century, insisting that they acknowledge that Indian people are the same as any other people: "Look at me / See my confusion loneliness fear worrying about all our / struggles to keep what little is left for us / Look at my heart not your fantasies" (*Not Vanishing* 66). Thomas King painfully questions in *The Truth about Stories*, "What is it about us you don't like?" (147), after explaining that images regarding Native Americans were well-established by the turn of the twentieth century and that today's Indian people must confront this fixed imagery regularly.

It is perhaps because I am a Choctaw that the subject matter in "Pangs" is personal to me. When I watch this show, I focus upon Hus and his warriors. Former Cherokee Chief Chad Smith states in the documentary *Savage Country: American Indian Mascots in Oklahoma High School Football* that portrayals of native people must teach young Indian children something positive about their people and the portrayals must contribute to the tribes' overall cultures, or else the portrayals aren't useful. *Buffy the Vampire Slayer*'s "Pangs" accomplishes neither of these tasks.

Notes

1. One of the best analyses of the origin and evolution of these stereotypes is Robert Berkhofer's *The White Man's Indian*.

2. This scene reminds me of the many native artifacts on display at the Smithsonian and other museums. Displaying the artifacts suggests that the original owners have vanished — another predominant stereotype that Native Americans can't seem to escape — yet such a display also often fails to acknowledge that these "artifacts" belonged to real people who prayed, built homes, and experienced the same worries and joys that all people experience, regardless of when and where they live. Many of the items on display in museums are sacred objects that have been removed from burial grounds; to display them is to undermine the spiritual and personal significance of the people to whom they belonged. For an interesting fictional account of the ethics of displaying traditional tribal and cultural items, readers should refer to Anna Lee Walters's novel *Ghost Singer*. In this novel, the now-deceased humans who once "owned" these artifacts in real life haunt the museum. The act of removing the artifacts from burial grounds "unleashes" the spirits; only through the ceremonies of several medicine people are the spirits finally sent to the next life.

3. It is worth noting that when Spike first seeks help from the Scoobies in "Pangs," he is depicted wearing a tattered blanket. History tells us that many Indian people were deliberately infected by fatal diseases when military personnel gave them blankets infected with smallpox and other illnesses. For more on this controversial issue, see Elizabeth A. Fenn's article "Biological Warfare in Eighteenth Century North America: Beyond Jeffery Amherst" in *The Journal of American History* (March 2000).

4. In *Televised Morality* Gregory Stevenson argues that this "vampire is a metaphorical representation of oppressed Indigenous peoples" (231). I disagree. In Buffy's world, with the exceptions of Angel and Spike, vampires are consistently portrayed as evil. To claim that this *one* vampire represents an oppressed American Indian is illogical.

5. According to *The Chumash*, before the arrival of the Spanish in California there were about 20,000 Chumash people. By 1840, following the California mission system, the population had fallen to a mere 250 people (Sonneborn 39). What accounted for the loss of so many lives? Native historians generally agree that it is the result of a number of factors: forced acculturation to a dominant culture; exposure (sometimes deliberately) to new diseases; forced removal from tribal land; brutal treatment by missionaries attempting to acculturate the Chumash to Christianity; and murder. The story is the same for countless Indian people across the United States. For more information, see Robert F. Heizer's *The Destruction of California Indians*.

6. Naturally, Hus magically raises the spirits of dead Chumash warriors to help him. Non-native viewers expect this; after all, don't Indian people possess magical powers?

7. For an explanation of how our brains make moral decisions see Frances E. Morris's chapter.

8. Native Americans were displaced by the Removal Act of 1830. Pushed through Congress by President Andrew Jackson, this act forcibly relocated thousands of Indian people to Indian Territory (now known as Oklahoma). Most notably, the so-called "five civilized tribes"— Cherokees, Choctaws, Chickasaws, Creeks, and Seminoles— were removed to Indian Territory on the historic march known as the "Trail of Tears" because so many Indian people died on the way. The Termination Act of 1953 terminated federal treaty obligations in the hopes that it would be easier for native people to become acculturated to the dominant society if they no longer were excluded to reservation community. Between 1954 and 1962, Congress "stripped sixty-one tribes of all federal services and protection" (King Thomas 136). Today, there are Indian people who are culturally and genetically Indian but are not recognized as being Indian because their tribes no longer exist due to this racial policy.

9. Reprinted with permission of the author. From Chrystos, *Dream On* (Vancouver, B.C.: Press Gang, 1991).

Lord Acton Is Alive and Well in Sunnydale

Politics and Power in Buffy

⧫

KENNETH S. HICKS

"Power tends to corrupt, and absolute power corrupts absolutely."
—Lord Acton, letter to Bishop Mandell Creighton, 1887 (Dahlberg-Acton)

One of the most prevalent narratives in the horror genre is what might be called the "Modern Prometheus" premise (which is all about power). Within this narrative, the greatest threat to humanity is curiosity unbound by any sense of morality and restraint. One of the original wellsprings of horror, "Modern Prometheus" emerged as an anti–Enlightenment[1] expression of mistrust in the conceit that human progress is inevitable. Much as the Luddites[2] who smashed the machinery of early English factories that they viewed as evil, conservatives like Coleridge warned of mucking about with forces beyond human comprehension, hinting that many of the aspirations of early Enlightenment thinkers was not simply wrong-headed but blasphemous.

The original protagonist of Mary Shelley's seminal novel *Frankenstein, or the Modern Prometheus*, Victor Frankenstein becomes obsessed with discovering a cure for death and, in his genius, succeeds in shattering the barriers between life and death. The resulting horrors are meant as a cautionary tale in which "can" does not always equate with "should." The monster Frankenstein unleashes is uncontrollable and, in seeking to preserve his own life, deliberately lashes out at his creator for rejecting him. The seduction of knowledge, and the power to control others that comes with tinkering with forces beyond one's comprehension, is a powerful source of inspiration for much of what takes place in *Buffy the Vampire Slayer*'s Sunnydale.

67

Power is a central theme of *Buffy*. What is instructive about *Buffy's* treatment of power is that each of the protagonists on the show has moments in which he or she manipulates others for selfish or self-serving reasons or gives in altogether to the dark pleasures of raw power. And while the horror genre often produces cartoonish depictions of politics, *Buffy* occasionally succeeds in generating serious insights into the problem of power.

Power Corrupts: Government and the Powerful as Arbitrary

While the "Modern Prometheus" narrative produces a rich mine of potential political topics, horror narratives can also veer into cartoonish depictions of politics. *Buffy* certainly has its share of outlandishly-evil politicians (e.g., Mayor Wilkins) and ridiculously-incompetent bureaucrats (e.g., the Watcher's Council), but the show also offers a powerful critique of elitism and points out that the best recipe for the responsible use of power is openness and accountability.

The show also seemingly shares with the author of the *Modern Prometheus* an anti-positivist[3] bias. The show's writers appear to agree with Goya's observation that "the sleep of reason brings forth monsters" (Simon). In *Buffy*, reliable information comes from ancient demonology texts and sometimes from dreams and visions akin to revelation. Belief in Enlightenment rationalism — which compels the willful rejection of that which lacks a reasonable explanation — often appears as part of the explanation why the adults of Sunnydale can ignore the horrible events that occur around them.

In Season One's "The Harvest," the gang prevents an apocalypse and, in the process, deals with numerous vampires who were clearly seen by many of Sunnydale High's students. In the aftermath, one student claims to have heard that "it was rival gangs, you know, fighting for turf? But all I can tell you is they were in an ugly way of looking." Giles explains the phenomenon in the following terms: "People have a tendency to rationalize what they can and forget what they can't."

The first appearance of government agents in *Buffy* occurs near the end of Season One in "Out of Mind, Out of Sight," when Sunnydale High School is terrorized by a girl, systematically ignored by teachers and students, who, as a result of this constant disregard, disappears, goes insane, and begins a demented campaign of vengeance. Just as Buffy is confronting the invisible Marcie to prevent her from cutting up Cordelia's face, government agents burst in and whisk Marcie away with officious reassurances about "rehabilitation." At the end of the episode, however, we learn that the government is in the business of teaching invisible people skills like assassination and infiltration. Although the primary lesson of "Out of Mind, Out of Sight" is the importance of dignity and the respect we show in acknowledging one another, the underlying ironic lesson is that the government is exploiting those who have been "disappeared" by societal neglect and using them for nefarious purposes.

Season Four's "The Initiative," a government-funded program which captures and researches vampires and demons, is also emblematic of the show's more caricatured portrayals of government. The program is highly secretive, has deep pockets (hence the labyrinthine bunker beneath UC-Sunnydale), and has clearly been tasked with researching demon's strengths and weaknesses for some secret military project. The Initiative also secretly feeds its soldiers vitamins and chemicals to improve their strength and reflexes. The Initiative's leader, Professor Maggie Walsh, at first attempts to bring Buffy into the Initiative, but, when she realizes that Buffy cannot be easily controlled and knows about "Project 314" (e.g. Adam, who becomes the primary antagonist for Season Four), she decides that Buffy needs to die and sets her up to be killed in a demon ambush. Buffy survives the attack and seeks to confront Dr. Walsh, but Walsh has already been killed by her creation Adam, a Frankenstein-monster of blended human and demon parts tied together with computer technology. Walsh later becomes a zombie-slave to Adam in a fitting *homage* to the horror classic.

The Initiative verges into caricature in part because its incompetence is unexplained. Certainly, government can be incompetent, and its incompetence can often appear unexplainable, but there is a kind of libertarian "government is incompetent because it is incompetent" assumption that seems inconclusive and unsatisfying.

A third exemplar of the show's somewhat jaundiced portrayal of government is the Watcher's Council, a secretive organization that recruits and trains the "Watchers," who then train and guide each Slayer as the old Slayer dies and a new Slayer gains her powers. In Season Three's "Helpless," Buffy learns that part of the Council's tradition is that on a Slayer's eighteenth birthday the Council "tests" her by placing her in a controlled test against a vampire, an incredibly arbitrary test that naturally spins out of control when the vampire escapes and "turns" one of the Council's security personnel.

The Council passes Buffy when she kills the vampire, and, when Buffy protests about the fairness of the test, Council member Quentin evenly remarks, "We're not in the business of being fair. We are fighting a war." The Council then fires Giles on the grounds that he expressed "a father's love for the child and that is useless to the cause" ("Helpless"). That the Council would perceive respect, trust, and care as "useless to the cause" is evocative of the casual inhumanity that inhabits stagnant bureaucratic organizations and which justifies arbitrary conclusions on the grounds of some inappropriate but measurable metric.

The Watcher's Council's secretive and authoritarian tendencies are further revealed in Season Five's "Checkpoint." A Council team descends on

Sunnydale, announcing that they have secret information about the "Big Bad" facing the Scooby Gang; however, before they will share that information, they impose an Inquisition-style "review" of Buffy and her friends, asking leading and arbitrary questions and being generally intrusive. The empty nature of the Council's threats is revealed when Buffy calls their bluff, saying, "Everyone's lining up to tell me how unimportant I am. I just figured out why. Power. I have it. They don't. This bothers them." As Buffy reminds the Council's leader Quentin, "Without a Slayer, you're pretty much just watching *Masterpiece Theater*." The Council is revealed as a bullying-yet-impotent, hidebound organization, too blinded by tradition to recognize when its methods and practices have stopped making sense.

In Season Seven's "Never Leave Me," the Council and most of its secret knowledge is destroyed in a single explosion by minions of the First Evil. The fact that the Council could literally be destroyed and those members not killed, scattered, and rendered impotent in the coming struggle is suggestive of a deeply incompetent organization.

A corollary to the "government is bad" metaphor is "authority figures are bad/incompetent." The first principal of Sunnydale High School is portrayed as a harried and well-meaning buffoon who is literally consumed by a pack of hyena-possessed students in Season One's "The Pack." His successor, Principal Snyder, clearly doesn't like children, bullies teachers and students alike into doing his bidding, and nurses a particular animus toward Buffy. In Season Two's "When She Was Bad," Snyder confesses to Giles[4] his abhorrence of children: "One day the campus is bare. Empty. The next, there are children everywhere. Like locusts. Crawling around, mindless, bent on feeding and mating. Destroying everything in sight in their relentless, pointless desire to exist." In Season Two's "School Hard," Snyder invites Buffy to "Think of me as your judge, jury, and executioner," an announcement to Buffy that she will not get a fair hearing in the event of trouble.

Snyder's snide and mean-spirited observations can be seen as evidence of his willingness to arbitrarily punish students and could further be interpreted alternatively as sadistic enjoyment of abusing power. In Season Two's "Becoming, Part One," Snyder demands to know where Buffy is. When Xander attempts to answer, Snyder snarls, "Whatever comes out of your mouth is a meaningless waste of breath, an airborne toxic event."

Later, in Season Two's "I Only Have Eyes for You," Snyder confronts Buffy, accusing her of committing the near-killing of a student. Buffy defends herself, but Snyder shows how determined he is to pin the event on her: "People can be coerced, Summers. I'm no stranger to conspiracy. I've watched *JFK*. I'm a truth seeker.... I'm gonna look at all the pieces carefully and rationally, and I'm gonna keep looking until I know exactly how this is all your fault."

Snyder, however, is less a villain than an irritant and obstacle to Buffy and the Scooby Gang in their efforts to combat evil. He is a small man with a

Napoleon complex, who judges everyone around him and finds them wanting. When he does find a pretext for expelling Buffy, in Season Two's "Becoming, Part II," Buffy protests her innocence of the crime of which she is accused, saying that "the police will figure it out." Snyder sneers, "In case you haven't noticed, the police of Sunnydale are deeply stupid." In Season Two's "I Only Have Eyes for You," Snyder reveals that he knows about the Hellmouth and is apparently assigned to the school to deal with the problems that naturally follow from placing a public high school directly over a portal to demon dimensions.

By Season Three, Snyder is pretty clearly a *deus ex machina* seeking to isolate and weaken Buffy. In Season Three's "Choices," when the Scooby Gang is caught in a Mexican standoff with the Mayor, Principal Snyder walks in with some police officers, expecting to break up some sort of drug operation. Snyder's unsurprised demeanor at seeing the Mayor surrounded by vampire lackeys suggests that he is clearly compromised. He gives voice to his frustration, plaintively asking, "You. All of you. Why couldn't you be dealing drugs like normal people?" Snyder's end, in Season Three's "Graduation Day," is particularly fitting: he is consumed by the Mayor-turned-demon even as he stupidly demands order and discipline.

In Season Six's "Flooded," Buffy—faced with bankruptcy and unable to meet the financial obligations of keeping her mother's home—proposes burning it. While she's joking, behind the joke lays the kind of resentment that everyone who has been in her situation might feel. "It's bills," Buffy protests, "It's money. It's pieces of paper sent by bureaucrats we've never even met." Buffy is experiencing the impotence people in similar situations feel when confronted with the impersonal workings of a bureaucracy that is tasked with collecting debt and is indifferent to tragic circumstances that leave a family unable to meet obligations. One of the more effective portrayals of power in *Buffy* is the arbitrariness of large-scale bureaucracies in dealing with small-scale tragedies.

Absolute Power Corrupts Absolutely, Part I: The "Deal with the Devil/Demon" Metaphor

Two of the clearest examples of people voluntarily giving in to the temptations of power are Angel and Spike. In the Whedon narrative, vampires are the result of a demon possessing the body of a human, and the purging of human's soul—and with it conscience—from the body. The need of vampires for blood is parasitic; the demon requires blood to maintain the human body unchanged. The show maintains that a person can be killed by draining a victim of blood but that such an event will not necessarily result in the person becoming a vampire. Instead, turning a person into a vampire requires an affirmative act, with the victim — nearly drained of blood — then taking the blood of his/her vampire "sire." For Whedon, lack of a soul corresponds to a lack of conscience, and the need for blood necessarily drives vampires into predation; while any blood will sustain a vampire, the preference is for human blood. Without conscience guiding their superhuman strength, vampires naturally glory in their freedom from conventional human mores.

Both Angel and Spike volunteer for vampirism, albeit for different reasons. From historical flashbacks in Season Two's "Becoming, Part I," we learn that Angel as a human was the somewhat dissolute son of minor Irish nobility whose stern, patrician father disapproved of his son's forays into the taverns of the nearby town. One night in 1753, drunk and upset after a fight with his father, Angel spies a beautiful young woman walking into an alleyway. He follows, thinking to offer her protection and perhaps seduce her, but she turns out to be the vampire Darla, who makes cryptic comments of all the exciting things she has seen and done. With impulsive "I'll try anything once" bravado, Angel says, "Show me your world," and is turned into one of the cruelest vampires of recent history.

Emblematic of his viciousness is the way Angelus turns Spike's sire and paramour Drusilla into a vampire. Darla spots Drusilla, a younger daughter of wealthy English family, and recognizes that Drusilla is clairvoyant. In "Becoming, Part II," Angelus goes to great lengths to drive Drusilla mad, first killing her family, and then mentally torturing her as she resides in a convent. When she goes to confession, Angelus, in the guise of her confessor, tells her that her fate is to be evil: "You're the spawn of Satan. All the Hail Mary's in the world aren't going to help. The Lord will use you and smite you down. He's like that."

Eventually, Angelus proposes turning the now-insane Drusilla into a vampire, suggesting to Darla that eternal torment is a better end to the game than mere killing. Angelus's imaginative cruelty suggests the degree to which he views evil as a game to be played for points. "Am I learning?" Angelus asks Darla, after revealing his plan to turn the now-insane Drusilla into a vampire.

Angel's embrace of evil is ultimately undone by Darla, who in 1898 gives Angel a young gypsy girl as a food gift. However, the gypsies discover who killed the girl, a village favorite, and curse Angel with a soul/conscience, which means an eternity of torment with the knowledge of how many innocent lives he and Darla took over one hundred and forty years of rampages. Interestingly, when Darla discovers that Angelus has been ensorcelled and ensouled, she reacts with disgust, shouting, "A filthy soul," and drives Angelus out by threatening to stake him.

Darla's reaction to Angel's curse demonstrates the problem of making deals with demons. Her fury is akin to that of a co-dependent whose drinking buddy has gone on the wagon; no longer useful as a source of sadomasochistic amusement, Angel is rejected by Darla as no longer worthy of alliance. In this sense, a vampire's conception of love must be purely instrumental, using one another to augment the power and capacity to work evil. In Season Two of the *Buffy* spinoff *Angel*, the viewer learns that Angel recognizes Darla's gift for what it is: a curse. In "Darla," Angel refuses to return the favor of "siring" a resurrected-but-human Darla, recognizing that what Darla did to him was something that a demon might be expected to do to a human, but it was not something that Angel could justify doing in return to Darla, even as punishment.

Spike's turn to vampirism is complicated in a different way. While Angel's decision was mitigated by his drunkenness—and hence incapacity to competently make such a life-altering decision — William's transformation into Spike is that of a frustrated romantic scorned by society turning to a means of escape. In Season Five's "A Fool for Love," viewers are witness to Spike's transformation by the mad Drusilla in London in 1880. Mocked by friends for his hideous poetry and coldly rejected as a suitor, Spike finds himself in an alleyway, tearing up his poetry and crying to himself. Drusilla flatters him, claiming to see what others do not, and offers him "what he wants." Spike does not resist when she bites him and begins the process of turning him into a vampire.

Initially, Spike's transformation can be seen as the act of a selfish man seeking power or at least release. However, it could also be that his primary motivation is to cure his mother's impending death by consumption through his vampire's bite. He tells Drusilla of his desire to sire his mother, which takes even the maddened Drusilla aback. He approaches his mother, saying, "Think of it. No more sickness. No more dying. You'll never age another day.... We'll be together forever." Afterward, the demon in his mother announces her eagerness to cut Spike loose from her apron strings, quoting some of William's bad poetry and derisively snorting, "You honestly thought I could bear an eternity listening to that twaddle?" She derides his transformation, calling him a "limp, sentimental fool." She accuses him of Oedipal desires, "All you ever wanted was to get back inside me. You finally got your wish, didn't you?" Horrified, Spike stakes his mother, managing to sire — and kill — his mother before his career as a vampire has even begun.

Spike's romantic failures and his inability to save his mother explain his almost uncontrollable appetite for violence and ultimately his obsession with killing Slayers: "To most vampires, the Slayer was the subject of cold sweat and frightened whispers. But I never hid. Hell, I sought her out. I mean, if you're looking for fun, there's death, there's glory and sod all else, right? I was young."

Angel's and Spike's excess can be viewed as part of the problem of power. With power comes the capacity to reject the laws and rules that allow communities to survive. Rather than being "upright citizens," vampires virtually always glorify the freedom that comes with repudiating conventional morality. "I was through living by society's rules," Spike tells Buffy in Season Five's "Fool for Love," "Decided to make a few of my own. Of course, in order to do that ... I had to get myself a gang." Suggestive of Spike's logic is that in order to make rules a person needs the kind of power that emanates from violence which breeds a reputation that can be used to provoke fear and intimidation.

The contrast between Spike's glorification of violence and Angelus's glorification of cruelty — depicted in their argument in "Fool for Love" — highlights their fundamentally different paths in the descent into evil. Spike the romanticist rebel wants to take on the world while Angelus the sadist wants to work his cruel stratagems in anonymity. As Angelus's transformation of Drusilla indicates, he always recognizes what he is doing as evil; he just does not care. Spike's rage, in contrast, seems fueled by his sense of rejection of a world that has rejected him; in a cruel, Hobbesian world, where life is "nasty, brutish and short" for everyone but the living dead, justice is nothing more than the will of the strong.

Buffy often presents storylines that give evidence to serious class resentment, and class conflict often yields to some sort of power struggle. Xander acts as a useful channel to develop the thesis that the rich and powerful of society are not playing by the same rules. In Season Two's "Reptile Boy," for example, a high school-aged Xander is drawn to a college fraternity party to defend Buffy — an impulse Willow sees as attempting to prove "that you're just as good as those snotty college guys" and thus worthy of Buffy's affection — and finds himself the object of the fraternity brother's drunken hazing. It turns out that Xander's suspicions of the fraternity boys are born out; for decades, the fraternity has been sacrificing young girls to a reptile-demon in their basement and has been rewarded with wealth and status. Several of Joss Whedon's story arcs in *Buffy* and *Angel* revolve around similar story lines, hinting that the rich and powerful do not play by the same set of rules required of the not-so-rich-and-powerful.[5]

Xander's love life is a tragi-comic rumination on the romantic choices people make. Xander appears at times to vie with Buffy for most unlucky in love. In Season One's "Teacher's Pet," Xander falls under the spell of a substitute teacher who is really a demon that preys on virgin men. In Season Two's "Inca Mummy Girl," a seemingly-beautiful young exchange student with whom Xander shares a mutual attraction is in reality an Incan mummy who must kill people in order to retain her youth. In Season Two's "Bewitched, Bothered, and Bewildered," Xander persuades the witch Amy to cast a spell on Cordelia, who has broken up with Xander on Valentine's Day in the face of peer pressure from her friends. Xander says, "I want, for once, to come out ahead. I want the Hellmouth to be working for me."

Unfortunately, the spell goes awry, causing *every* woman in Sunnydale — including the mad vampire Drusilla — to fall crazy in love with him. When Drusilla asks him, "How do you feel about eternal life?" Xander answers, "We couldn't just start with coffee? A movie?" Xander's seeming inability to attract or keep a woman who is not also a demon — or even keep demon women — may be chalked up to fate (some people are simply unlucky in love), but in Xander's case it is suggestive of the reality that choices have consequences. Xander's decision to be in the Scooby Gang narrows his avenues for romance but broadens his life.

Season Two's "Lie to Me" offers another interesting illustration of how "deals with the devil" rarely turn out the way humans envision. An old school friend of Buffy's named Ford comes to Sunnydale to finish high school. Ford, however, has a secret agenda. He is part of a group described by Xander as "vampire wannabes" and is seeking to persuade the primary bad guy of the season, Spike, to turn him into one. He and his friends romanticize vampires, whom they describe as the "Lonely Ones," and, when Angel, Xander and Willow go to the club, one of the vampire groupies tells them that vampires are misunderstood and that "they who walk with the night are not interested in harming anyone. They are creatures above us. Exalted."

Ford's intention is to betray Buffy, luring her into a secret club that used to be a bomb shelter devoid of exits; in exchange for the Slayer's death and a buffet of vampire groupies, Ford hopes that Spike will agree to sire him and make him a vampire. Buffy discovers his treachery and confronts him at the club, challenging him to justify the deaths of all the other humans in the club so that he can become a vampire. Ford then reveals that he has brain cancer and is dying, shouting, "I've got maybe six months left, and by then what they bury won't even look like me. I'll be bald and shriveled and I'll smell bad. No, I'm not going out that way." Buffy reminds Ford, "You have a choice. You don't have a good choice, but you have a choice. You're opting for mass murder ... and nothing you say is gonna make that OK."

Buffy is able to foil the plot by capturing Spike's paramour, Drusilla, threatening to kill her unless Spike and his vampire gang free the humans. However, Ford stays behind, demanding that Spike transform him. Unfortunately for Ford, he gets his wish, rises from the grave, and is promptly staked by Buffy.

The idea that disease can breed desperation and can cause a person to become callous of the feelings and rights of others is an important source of motivation for Ford and causes Buffy a great deal of trouble. "I wish I could just hate him," Buffy confides to Giles after the ordeal. Giles responds to Buffy's complaint about the complexities of knowing whom to trust with the observation, "I believe that is called growing up." Buffy nonetheless understands the motivation behind Ford's calumny — fear, and the uncertainty that death presents — which so often appears to be the motivation for evil.

Sunnydale's mayor, the primary villain of Season Three, best illustrates the "deal with the devil" metaphor. Rumors about Mayor Richard Wilkins go back to Season Two, but we are really introduced to the character as he is recruiting the vampire Trick onto his staff in Season Three's "Homecoming." The Mayor applauds Trick's attempt to ambush Buffy and Faith by turning Sunnydale's Homecoming Dance into "Slayerfest." The major season plot is

Mayor Wilkins's ambition to be translated into a huge and ancient demon known as an Olvikon, a huge, worm-like creature with immense power (Whedon).

Wilkins captures the Janus-faced duplicity that so many Americans suspect about their public servants—people who speak in a folksy style but who cynically make corrupt deals. As Harry Groener, the actor who played Wilkins, has suggested, the closer the Mayor comes to power the less frightened he becomes of potential threats: "the closer we get to absolute power, the closer we get to the parts that corrupt" (Stokes). The Mayor routinely employs vampires and assassins to do his bidding, but offers Faith a glass of milk to relieve her concerns over getting to the Books of Ascension before Buffy (while implicitly threatening to kill Faith if she fails him). When Faith brings the report of her successful assassination of a professor whose research was bringing him closer to the Mayor's secret ambitions, the Mayor beams, "No father could be prouder" ("Graduation Day, Part One"). Wilkin's ruthlessness is hidden behind a carefully-cultivated façade of hokey charm.

Another important metaphor is the Mayor's imperviousness to physical harm in the final one hundred days before his ascension. Like real life politicians who use their positions to enrich themselves and their supporters and whose connections shield them from public scrutiny—and harm, the Mayor cannot be touched by any weapon. When the Mayor confronts the Scooby Gang in "Graduation Day, Part I," Giles stabs him through the heart with a sword, an action which the Mayor uses as an opportunity to gloat over his invulnerability, chiding Giles for his "thoughtlessness," and asking him what kind of role model he is being for the children. "They look to you to see how to behave," Wilkins mockingly admonishes.

When Buffy and Faith both arrive at the hospital needing emergency care—Faith after having been stabbed by Buffy, and Buffy having been drained by Angel to save his life—the Mayor attempts to smother Buffy in revenge, which lends insight into his depth of attachment to Faith. When Angel stops him, Wilkins vows revenge, "Get set for a world of pain! Misery loves company, young man, and I'm looking to share that with you and your whore!"

The Mayor's own sense of invulnerability is his ruin. The Scooby Gang realizes they cannot stop his Ascension but through research discover that in demon form the Mayor will be vulnerable, although difficult to kill. The Mayor's end is suggestive of a couple of important lessons regarding power. First, immunity from accountability can breed arrogance, which leads to hubris. Most politicians imbued with a sense of their own invulnerability sow the seeds of their own destruction. Second, even seemingly all-powerful forces can be defeated by superior planning. The Scooby Gang uses organization and tactics to counter the Mayor's forces and to lure the now-monstrous demon–Mayor into the high school, where he can be trapped and destroyed in a huge explosion.

In each instance, characters are drawn to power for different reasons. Whether they desire to escape the confines of a too-narrow life or to escape a premature death or whether they simply want to be loved and respected, Angel and Spike present believable depictions of how a person can be tempted to pursue power regardless of the cost. Likewise, Mayor Wilkins's "deal with the devil" is a good metaphor for those drawn into politics by the allure of absolute power and who compromise themselves in its pursuit.

Absolute Power Corrupts Absolutely, Part II: Going Over to "The Dark Side"

The idea that some people are simply better than others, and therefore can act with impunity, is another important source of bad deeds in *Buffy* and provides another kind of cautionary tale. The danger of thinking one is above the law is what characterizes most of the "Big Bads." However, the temptations of power also frequently draw people into bad actions, which is another aspect of *Buffy's* complex moral narrative.

One illustration is the character Veruca in Season Four's "Wild at Heart." Oz, a werewolf, breaks out of his cage and goes for a romp with a female werewolf, which turns out to be Veruca, a fellow musician and singer in another band and a person to whom Oz appears to be powerfully attracted. The idea of wild abandonment at the heart of the werewolf myth is captured in Veruca, whose stage presence and songs seem to glorify the idea of giving in to passion. When Oz, mortified at having cheated on Willow, tells Veruca he needs to figure out how he broke out of his cage, Veruca laughs, "God! Somebody's domesticated the hell out of you."

Oz voluntarily cages himself to prevent himself from hurting others, but Veruca glorifies her three nights a month of freedom from the conventions of civilization, saying to Oz, "Soon, you start to feel sorry for everybody else because they don't know what it's like to be as alive as we are. As free." Later, when Veruca traps Willow[6] with the intent of killing her and Oz interposes himself, she argues that Willow "is the one keeping you in a cage.... You're an animal. Animals kill." However, when they change into werewolf form, it's Veruca that Oz attacks first, tearing her throat out. After Buffy tranquilizes him and he returns to normal, Oz realizes he must leave Sunnydale, telling Willow that "Veruca was right about one thing. The wolf is inside of me all the time, and I don't know where that line is between me and it."

The contrast between Oz's and Veruca's attitudes toward their curse is telling. The origin of Oz's curse is known; in Season Two's "Phases," Oz discovers that his infant cousin Jordy is a werewolf, after Jordy has bitten and transformed him. Oz does not know he is a werewolf until after he has transformed several times, but, once he discovers his curse, he takes steps to prevent it from causing harm to innocent people. We do not know how Veruca comes to be a werewolf, but she appears to have been cursed much longer and is indifferent to the fate of anyone who gets in her way when she is in her werewolf form because she believes that she is better than they. The contrast between the two is similar to the comparison of a repentant alcoholic aware of addiction and fighting it and the determined drunk who pursues whatever lifestyle enables the addiction to continue — no matter whom it hurts. Veruca's unwillingness to restrain her werewolf powers marks her as evil.

Faith's storyline also illustrates the temptations of power from a number of perspectives. Initially, Faith is a Slayer like Buffy, but over the course of Season Four she increasingly begins to display erratic behavior. Where Buffy is decisive, Faith is impulsive. The first hint that Faith is emotionally on edge comes in "Faith, Hope, and Trick" when she uses excessive force in killing a vampire and Buffy questions whether she has the right make up to be a Slayer. In "The Zeppo," after Xander saves Faith from a demon, she seduces him, saying, "A fight like that ... and no kill.... I'm ready to pop." Afterward, she ushers him out the door, saying, "That was great. Gotta shower." Throughout, Faith is portrayed as sexually promiscuous and emotionally volatile, two important precipitates in her slide toward evil.

Faith's turn to the dark side begins in "Bad Girls." As the two Slayers battle a demon that bears a disturbing resemblance to "Jabba the Hut," Faith explains her philosophy as "Want. Take. Have." She gets herself and Buffy arrested for breaking into a sporting goods store looking for weapons to fight the Jabba-ish demon Balthazar and his horde of vampires. When Buffy and Faith cause an accident escaping from the cops, Buffy wants to call an ambulance, but Faith dismisses her concerns: "Five people already have.... Let's get out of here." When Faith accidentally kills Allan, one of the Mayor's human employees (and seemingly an innocent), and then feigns indifference and attempts to evade responsibility, Buffy realizes that Faith is truly out of control and is increasingly becoming dangerous. Faith rejects Buffy's protest that being "a Slayer is not the same as being a killer." Recognizing that Buffy won't agree to suppress evidence about the murder, Faith then attempts to shift the blame to Buffy, highlighting the lengths to which Faith will go to avoid responsibility.

When Buffy enlists Angel's aid to try to reach Faith, Faith's resistance to any form of intervention is absolute. "You gonna shrink me, now?" she challenges Angel. When Angel talks about his past, and how god-like killing made him feel, and how going down the path Faith is headed will ruin her, Faith jokes, "I hope evil takes MasterCard." In her next confrontation with Buffy, Faith once more tries to persuade Buffy that Faith is right about the "live on the edge" philosophy. "You've got the lust," she says, "And I'm not just talking about screwing vampires." Faith clearly thinks that she and Buffy are better than "normal people," evidenced by her claim to Buffy that "in your gut you know we don't need the law. We are the law." Later, Faith kills the Mayor's vampire henchman Trick as he is about to kill Buffy, but her good deed is deceptive; instead of seeking forgiveness and redemption, she throws in her lot with the Mayor and becomes his Slayer-assassin.

A major source of Faith's turn to evil is her emerging resentment of Buffy. Early in her tenure as the Mayor's henchman, she attempts to seduce Angel, hoping that a sexual encounter will release his soul and turn him back to evil, thus distracting Buffy while the Mayor completes his transformation to demon. The seduction ploy not working, she next attempts to purge Angel of his soul through a magic spell. As she approaches Angel, she conceals her intentions with a superficial non-apology: "I'm not so good at apologies. Mostly I think the world's out to screw me so I'm generally more owed than owing." When she and the seemingly-transformed "Angelus" capture Buffy, her resentment toward Buffy comes out at confessional length: "Everybody asks, 'Why can't you be more like Buffy?' ... You get the Watcher. You get the Mom. You get the little Scooby Gang. What do I get? Jack squat. This is supposed to be my town!" And she is certain that serving as the right hand of Mayor Wilkins will get her all the power she feels is rightfully hers and is denied because of Buffy.

Faith is representative of a fall into evil, but Willow is also prey to that impulse. Willow's descent into addiction to dark magic in Season Six, culminating in her break with sanity following Tara's death, is possibly the best example in *Buffy* that "sometimes good people do bad things." Initially, Willow's experience with magic is small-scale and occasionally helpful to the Scooby Gang in their fight against evil. Her spells in the early seasons often go comically awry, but, in Season Three's "Choices," she manages to stake a vampire with a levitating pencil. By Season Six, however, Willow is becoming an increasingly-powerful witch in her own right. At various points in earlier seasons she toys with dark magic, causing her then-boyfriend Oz to warn her that the magic she is practicing is "touching something — deep — dark. It's not fun" ("Fear Itself").

After Oz leaves to find a way of controlling his own demons, Willow enters into a romantic relationship with Tara, and her confidence blossoms as her powers grow to the point that she is the most powerful person in the Scooby Gang, aside from Buffy. Increasingly, Willow's feelings of insecurity are replaced by the desire for power and respect. She sees magic as an easy pathway to both, not recognizing the price it will exact. She uses increasingly-manipulative dark magic without thinking through the consequences and finds herself enthralled by its power.

An illustration of Willow's degeneration occurs in Season Six's "Wrecked." Willow, having lost Tara due to her increasing addiction to manipulative dark magic, finds a way to return Amy — who has for several years been trapped in rat form[7] — to human form. She and Willow begin to party, using magic to control people in the Bronze for their amusement. When that gets boring, Amy takes Willow to a kind of "magic shooting gallery," where a particularly nasty warlock named Rack sells powerful spells that "last for days, and the burnout factor is, like, nothing." Willow succumbs to the temptation, and Rack "takes her on a little tour," which is portrayed as a kind of magical heroin trip, in which the warlock exploits Willow's need for dark power the way a dealer might exchange drugs for sex with desirable junkies.

Season Six follows a narrative of Willow's descent into dark magic. Season Six's "Bargaining, Part One" sees Willow brutally killing a fawn for its blood in order to work a powerful spell to bring Buffy back to life. Over the course of the season, Willow descends into a very realistic cycle of sobriety and backsliding. The season culminates in the traumatic killing of her lover Tara by one of the evil Trio, Warren. Still splattered with Tara's blood, Willow goes into full vengeance mode, killing the dark magician Rack for his powers and tossing the Magic Box for dark spells. She then searches out and mercilessly tortures Warren. After explaining to Warren why she is torturing him, she reverts to "Evil Willow" mode, murmuring "Bored now," and magically, gruesomely, and instantaneously flaying him alive.

Later, she confronts Buffy and the other Scooby Gang members, who are trying to prevent her from killing the rest of the evil Trio. Giles returns to Sunnydale with powerful magic borrowed from a coven of witches in Devonshire, England, and manages to contain her for a time, but she overcomes him and is contemptuous of the idea that she ever thought that Giles had anything to teach her. "You're such a hypocrite," she rages, "Waltzing in here with your borrowed magic ... to tell me what? That magic is bad? I don't think you're in any position to be telling me what to do." Then she drains Giles of his magic energy, exposing her to all of the suffering in the world, which in her deranged state leads her to attempt to destroy the world.

She is prevented from destroying the world by Xander, her oldest friend, whose repeated statement, "I love crayon-breaky Willow and I love scary, veiny Willow," causes the dark magic to burn out before she can finish the spell. Giles later reveals that dark magic originates in emotions like rage and the thirst for power and revenge and that good magic springs forth from emotions like empathy and love. Willow is saved by Giles giving her white magic and by Xander reminding her of her essential humanity.

Oz, Veruca, Faith, and Willow each find themselves dealing with power beyond their control. Oz's struggle with power makes a useful contrast with Veruca's irresponsible embrace of the same curse. In contrast, Faith's resentment for Buffy pulls her already-impulsive nature down a dangerous path. Her "tough girl" attitude makes it more difficult for her to turn back from the brink, and so she embraces evil rather than admit to her wrong-doing. Willow's descent into madness is all the more poignant, considering her sweet nature in Season One. Anyone who has had a family member — sweet and innocent as a child — who succumbs to addiction later in life can identify with Willow's path toward evil.

In Season Two's "Ted," after Buffy has apparently killed her mother's new boyfriend Ted, Cordelia suggests that perhaps Buffy should not be bound by the rules of normal humanity. "I don't get it," Cordelia says, "Buffy's the Slayer.... She's like this superman. Shouldn't there be different rules for her?" Willow responds, "Sure, in a fascist society." While the Scooby Gang worries about what the police will do to her, Giles observes that whatever "the authorities have planned for her, it can't be much worse than what she's doing to herself. She's taken an innocent life. The guilt; it's pretty hard to bear, and it won't go away soon." Guilt, fueled by conscience, is typically what is suspended in the process of succumbing to the temptations of power. What separates Buffy from the other characters explored in the series is that she is aware of the essential connection between power and responsibility, and, while she longs to set her Slayer powers down, she very rarely steps over the line in using those powers.

Transcending Power: Politics and the Power of Redemption

In Season Two's "I Only Have Eyes for You," the students at Sunnydale are haunted by a ghost caught in purgatory who is compelled to possess individual students, teachers, and staff workers. Those possessed are forced to relive the horrible night decades ago when the ghost, then a young man, kills his lover-teacher. Giles is able to piece together what is happening, recognizing that the ghost is trying to "resolve whatever issues are keeping him in limbo." Giles explains that the ghost is doomed to kill his lover over and over again and that "forgiveness is impossible," Buffy says, "Good. He doesn't deserve it."

Giles, however, recognizes the essential power of forgiveness: "To forgive is an act of compassion, Buffy. It's not done because people deserve it. It's done because they need it." When Buffy disagrees, saying that what the ghost did was unforgivable and that no amount of remorse can take it back, and that "he's gonna have to live with it," Giles replies, "He can't live with it, Buff. He's dead."

As much as *Buffy* is a show about power, the realities of power require that the show also be about redemption. So often, what separates the good from the evil on *Buffy* is that the good recognize the wrong they have done and seek to reconcile themselves to the people they have hurt. In the vampires' cases, the show demonstrates that guilt produces a kind of madness that can last for decades. In Faith's and Willow's cases, redemption comes with rehabilitation.

Lord Acton's dictum emerged from the enormous controversy among Roman Catholics when Pope Pius IX asserted the dogma of papal infallibility. Acton, a Catholic, was opposed to the decree; and the dictum, offered in a letter in 1887 to Bishop Mandell Creighton, justified his opposition to the view that anyone could be infallible. The phrase he used, however, contains a third verse, which could be paraphrased "the great are almost always bad" (Dahlberg-Acton). Power, and the things that we must do to keep and hold power, covers us with its taint. Buffy "saved the world. A lot" ("The Gift"). She also was required to kill. A lot. Regardless of whether the dead were undead, the act of killing carries a price, and Buffy repeatedly pays that price. Throughout the seven seasons of *Buffy*, she is often portrayed as experiencing a kind of psychic shell shock at the things she has seen and done. Like the scarred war veteran who refuses to revel in stories of war, Buffy is affected by what she has had to do in the service of humanity — or in the service of some greater good. In the end, in Season Seven, Buffy transcends power, not by surrendering power, but by sharing power with all the other Potential Slayers throughout the world. One might suspect that such a resolution to the problem of power and the resistance to evil would have met with Lord Acton's approval.

Notes

1. The Enlightenment was a period in the 1800s in which reason was considered the most important element in decisions. Thus, the anti–Enlightenment position was that reason is not sufficient to make decisions.
2. The Luddites of the 1800s were against the progress (mechanization, etc.) brought about by the Industrial Revolution.
3. Anti-positivists believed that human society and science must be studied using different methods.
4. Giles is an exception to the "bad" authority figure in that he has some authority over Buffy — even as she tries to, and often succeeds in, defying it. She turns to him as an authority figure in trying to deal with Dawn, for example ("Tough Love").
5. Season Four's "Beer Bad" has a similar class resentment ring to it, with a twist. There, Xander tends bar while Buffy and Willow go off to college. Xander attempts to make time with a college girl but is patronized by a wealthy college guy who smirks, "We are the future of the country, and you keep our bowl of peanuts full." The shoe is on the other foot, however, when the "future of the country" — and Buffy — drink beer cursed by the bartender's brother-in-law and turn into people of a Neanderthal persuasion.
   In addition to "Reptile Boy," in the opening episode of *Angel*'s first season, Angel is confronted with an antagonist in the form of a millionaire vampire preying on helpless young women newly arrived in Los Angeles. He has wealth — and the services of the ruthless law firm Wolfram and Hart — to shield him from justice. This sort of story arc is more prevalent in *Angel* than *Buffy*.
6. To be fair, Willow appeared to be in the process of whipping up a pretty dark spell that was aimed at both Oz and Veruca. While she stops the spell on her own before Veruca interrupts her, her impulse to use magic to punish foreshadows her later, more profligate use of magic.
7. In Season Three's "Gingerbread" she turns herself into a rat to escape a crowd of demon-influenced adults who are determined to burn all the witches of Sunnydale.

Willow's Electric Arcs

Moral Choices Sparked by Connections

———∞———

FRANCES E. MORRIS

It is curious — curious that physical courage should be so common in the world, and moral courage so rare.

—Mark Twain

Moral choices: "bored now" ("Doppelgangland").

Discussions concerning moral choices often elicit droopy eyelids or, worse, righteous indignation. Yet, who could not argue that a better understanding of why humans make the moral choices they make would be beneficial? The character Willow, in Joss Whedon's *Buffy the Vampire Slayer*, made "bored now" part of the pop-culture lexicon; indeed, Willow's simple, two-word phrase exemplifies the lack of interest in others that is so often a precursor to making poor moral choices.

Fortunately, the character Willow is not boring; in fact, Willow provides good, unambiguous (and non-boring) examples of both positive and negative moral choices. Casual viewers and some critics of *Buffy* may be quick to identify Willow's negative moral choices with her connection to magic. However, a careful delineation of Willow's moral choices demonstrates that Willow's magic magnifies her moral choices, both the positive ones and the negative ones, but magic does not control Willow's moral choices. Willow's moral choices reflect the strength of her connection to the "Scooby Gang." Willow has what Mark Twain called "moral courage" when she has a strong connection to the "Scooby Gang," but when her ties to the group are compromised, so are Willow's moral choices.

Where Willow, or anyone, finds the moral courage to make positive moral choices has continually vexed humanity. Indeed, Socrates and Aristotle had opposing views on many aspects of moral choices. Socrates (a very intelligent, moral, and idealistic man) believed that, if an individual knew the right and just way, the individual would always strive to choose the moral pathway. Essentially, Socrates perceived the discovery of the right or moral way problematic. He posited that once an individual determined the moral answer, which would be the hard part, the individual would make the virtuous choice (Plato).

Aristotle (a very intelligent, moral, and pragmatic man) disagreed. According to Dr. Garth Kemerling, Aristotle believed that "The great enemy of moral conduct ... is precisely the failure to behave well even on those occasions when one's deliberation has resulted in clear knowledge of what is right." In light of humankind's violent history (think the twentieth century — and the nineteenth, oh, and the eighteenth and the seventeenth — okay, think human history), Aristotle's words clearly pass the test of time. What is not so clear is why we often tragically fall into league with Aristotle's "great enemy of moral conduct" (Kemerling). To assist in understanding "why" individuals sometimes make positive and sometimes make negative moral choices, perhaps it would be beneficial to begin with a query on "how" humans physically make moral choices. "How" moral choices are made, for our purposes, refers to the section of the brain that is most involved in making moral choices.

To help discover how individuals make moral choices, modern researchers have a source that was unavailable to Socrates and Aristotle: twenty-first century science. To be more precise, scientists can study how the brain functions through neuroimaging by using a test called functional MRI (fMRI). In *Hard-wired Behavior: What Neuroscience Reveals about Morality*, Laurence Tancredi, a lawyer and clinical professor of psychiatry at New York University School of Medicine, defines fMRI as "An MRI technique modified to show the relative activation of areas of the brain when a particular activity is being performed" (213). For example, if a subject were making a moral decision while undergoing an fMRI, the test could identify which section of the individual's brain was the most active while the individual was making this decision.

A study in 2001 headed by Dr. Joshua Greene, a cognitive neuroscientist and philosopher, used fMRI to study the pathways in the brain involved (i.e., active parts of the brain light up) when the tests subjects were asked to answer questions concerning moral choices on both personal and non-personal moral dilemmas.

For example, in one thought experiment, an out-of-control train rushes down a track, destined to kill five people; the test subject's challenge is whether or not to pull the lever that would send the train down a different track which would result in saving the original five people but killing one other person. The test subject must make the choice. The question is followed by a scenario that increases the personal involvement of the test subject: the subject is faced with the same runaway train with five people facing imminent death, but this time the resolution of the situation is more personal because the subject is one of two people on a footbridge above the train tracks, and "the only way to save the five people is for one bystander to push the other in front of the train, killing the fallen bystander" ("Brain"). Joshua Greene, the Princeton scientist that conducted the study, reported the following: "we found that judgements in response to 'personal' moral dilemmas, compared with 'impersonal' ones, involved greater activity in brain areas that are associated with emotion and social cognition" (848). The study demonstrated that the more personal involvement of the subject (similar to the second scenario) in the resolution of the problem the more the emotional structures of the brain control the response. *Science Daily* went on to report that in this same study the "areas associated with working memory, which has been linked to ordinary manipulation of information, were considerably less active during the personal moral questions than during the others" ("Brain"). In other words, the fMRI showed the emotional section of the brain to be very active and the cognitive portion of the brain to be much less active while individuals were making personal moral choices—and the brain activity became more emotional the more personal the decision became.

The Princeton researchers are not alone in their findings. A number of recent studies have used brain scans to discover how the brain functions during moral decision making: "Moral decisions can often feel like abstract intellectual challenges, but a number of experiments ... have shown that emotions are central to moral thinking" (Vedantam).

When it comes to making moral choices, the practical Aristotle and many modern scientists would probably agree that Mr. Spock we are not. Even though brain imaging denotes the emotional portion of the brain engaging when an individual makes personal moral choices, it remains beyond the capacity of any brain scan to determine the validity of an individual's moral choice. Modern science has provided a vital and universal (and possibly frightening) clue on how moral choices are made, but for our purposes of answering "why" a positive or negative moral choice is made, the gray matter, albeit lighted and emotionally-charged, remains gray.

To shed light on why some individuals use emotions to make positive moral choices and others allow emotionally-charged decisions to lead them to poor moral choices, we could look to the modern physical world, but such an endeavor would require a deciphering of all the contemporary bickering concerning values and moral choices: Democrats, Republicans, Christians, Jews, Muslims, agnostics, atheists—too large—too confusing—too loud—too "Bored now" ("Doppelgangland"). Obviously, it would be beneficial to study "why" moral choices are made in a less hostile, less active, and less complicated atmosphere. What is desirable in the study of morality is a modern arena that facilitates defining a positive moral choice and the setting of parameters.

From the information gleaned from such a forum, it might be possible to determine a pattern or to observe a connection present when an individual chooses ethical as opposed to corrupt moral choices. Fortunately, there exists such a forum, for, since early humans have gathered around a campfire to share sustenance, the human clan has tried to sustain its moral courage and ethical awareness through storytelling: Homer, Jesus, Charles Dickens, Harriet Beecher Stowe, Kate Chopin, Barbara Kingsolver, and so many others have shared with us the benefit of stories with morals.

As recently as 2006, Harvard Business School taught ethics and endeavored to foster good leadership qualities in students by discussing the leadership problems and ethical or not-so-ethical choices made by fictional characters. Joseph L. Badaracco, Jr., professor of business ethics at Harvard, claims that "In the best stories, literature and life converge. The characters come across as real people, not puppets or specimens in lab dishes" (4). Badaracco goes on to say that "as we look closely at these men and women, we confront a series of challenging questions— about the individuals in the stories and about ourselves" (4). One character that Badaracco's students study is Chinua Achebe's character Okonkwo from the novel *Things Fall Apart*. Okonkwo is a character who possesses a strong moral code, which in the end proves not to be flexible enough to meet the changing needs of his people. When the British arrive bringing Christianity and the seductive trappings of the West to his Nigerian village, Okonkwo knows that the Ibo village's "way of life is in peril" so he "tries to rouse his clan in opposition, but no one follows him" (Badaracco 32). Dismissed by his followers, this strong leader commits suicide, an act that his people believe not only "makes a person's body evil, so no tribe member can touch the body," but also requires the village to make sacrifices to make up for the "desecration" (Badaracco 35).

Badaracco asks his students to ponder questions about how this once powerful leader could "fail to understand what his fellow tribesmen would and would not do? And why did he choose to violate a fundamental ethical principle of his community?"(36). Badaracco uses Okonkwo to demonstrate that a good moral code needs to be more than a set of strong personal convictions. Badaracco points out to his students that "personal convictions must be deeply melded with the convictions and concerns of others" (50–51). Thus, engaging with compelling fictional stories can lead to a meaningful examination on a personal level of why individuals respond to moral challenges the way they do.

Auspiciously, the world of popular television provides a compelling fictional show, Joss Whedon's *Buffy the Vampire Slayer,* that a multitude of fans and esteemed academics, such as Gregory Stevenson, J. Michael Richardson, and J. Douglas Rabb, agree concerns itself with moral choices. In fact, Gregory Stevenson, a professor of religion at Rochester College, has written a scholarly text, *Televised Morality: The Case of* Buffy the Vampire Slayer, as a case study for evaluating televised morality. In addition, two Canadian scholars, J. Michael Richardson and J. Douglas Rabb, one a professor of philosophy and one a professor of literature, in *The Existential Joss Whedon*, "regard Whedon's entire corpus as a single moral argument which represents and examines ethical thinking as narrative and metaphor rather than as grounded in axioms, moral principles, or rules of behavior"(4).

Gregory Stevenson says that making moral decisions on *Buffy* has little to do with religious dogma or concerns over heaven and hell: "what distinguishes moral choices on *Buffy* is the value placed upon human life. An immoral choice is one that is self-centered with no regard for others.... A moral choice is one that sacrifices self-desire for service to others" (166). Stevenson's definition, considering the gray area involved in defining a moral choice, provides a surprisingly simple and workable measure of what we will consider here a moral choice: The first tenet is that human life is inviolable, and the second tenet is that an individual is willing to risk his or her own aspirations for the betterment of others.

Now that we have a working definition of a moral choice, we need to make a difficult choice. In Joss Whedon's *Buffy the Vampire Slayer,* all the protagonists find themselves embroiled in making moral choices. Often these choices deal with life, death, and immortality. With so much at stake, each episode tests the moral fortitude of the characters, so the challenge is to choose one character who makes a plethora of both positive and negative moral choices. This challenge requires very little trepidation because arguably no character in *Buffy* struggles more with the emotional power that drives moral choices than Willow Rosenberg.

Amazingly, Willow's clothing hints at Willow's ethical status, for she transforms from the geeky girl dressed in "the softer side of Sears" ("Welcome to the Hellmouth") and a voyeur of life; to blossoming and stylishly-dressed "seeker of knowledge" Willow ("The Dark Age"); to "scary veiny [black] Willow," symbolizing poor moral choices ("Grave"); and finally in the final episode, "Chosen," to the glowing, white-haired "goddess," symbolizing positive moral choices, who is willing to risk perpetual black veinyness to help save the world. Since this discussion centers on choice, Willow, like many in the real world, and unlike Buffy, the Chosen One, has to choose to be the one who must navigate a labyrinth of moral choices, and Willow's choices range from good, to difficult, to tragic, and in the end to spectacularly good.

Finally, to ensure that the "why" of moral choices retains the measure of universality contained in the earlier cited scientific evidence, we need to address the issue of moral relativism. Simon Blackburn, Cambridge University philosophy professor, defines moral relativism: "Relativism is 'Different opinions, no one authority, and as many 'truths' as there are people or societies or cultures advancing different ways of doing things'" ("What"). So, the unadulterated Stevenson definition of a moral choice escapes the moral relativism charge because it transcends the contingencies of ethnicity, religion, culture, and time. Also, *Buffy* is a fictional venue that employs the same ever-effective literary device also used by those early storytellers gathered around the fire, and by

Homer, Jesus, Dickens, Chopin, Stowe, Kingsolver, and now Whedon: moral metaphors.

According to Richardson and Rabb, "Whedon's treatment of morality as metaphor avoids the charge of ethical relativism, because ... his moral metaphors themselves are grounded in Sartrean[1] corporeal consciousness, in shared experiences as embodied beings" (5). Essentially, Whedon's moral metaphors provide examples of the Scoobies learning to trust and rely on each other time and again. Indeed, the "shared experiences" in *Buffy* become a vital component behind the emotional power that drives individuals to make either positive or negative moral choices. Identifying and examining the emotional power behind Willow's moral choices leads us to understand "why" Willow sometimes makes positive ones and sometimes makes poor ones.

So what is the power that changes the mousy, jumper-clad, disconnected Willow in the first season, to stylishly-dressed guru (teacher/researcher)Willow in subsequent seasons, to the dangerous "black Willow" in the sixth season, then back to a frightened Willow who finally transforms to "goddess" bright white Willow in the last episode of *Buffy*? Willow's transformations are in direct correlation to a meaningful connection to the Scooby Gang. When Willow loses her connection to the gang, she makes poor and dangerous moral choices; when positive *emotions* are revisited by the reattachment to the gang and a reconnection to the shared experiences of the group is reestablished, Willow is able to sacrifice "self-desire for service to others" (Stevenson 166). Willow finds the connection needed to make difficult but positive moral choices.

The awakening of Willow's power to make positive moral choices stems from Buffy's offer of friendship and belonging. Buffy chooses the nerdy Willow and the shallow ("looking at linoleum makes me wanna have sex" ["Innocence"]) Xander (Willow's only friend) over the cooler, yet superficial, in-crowd led by Cordelia. In the very first episode, Buffy's friendship helps the boy-shy Willow find the strength to talk with a stranger, Thomas, at the local teen hangout, the Bronze. Unfortunately for Willow, Thomas is a vampire. When Willow leaves the Bronze with him to go "get some ice cream" and ends up as potential fodder for the ensuing Hellmouth harvest, Buffy and Xander arrive just in time to save Willow ("Welcome to the Hellmouth").

It is from Buffy's friendship that Willow feels for the first time the emotionally-engaging power of being connected to a morally-driven group. Instead of being frightened back into a voyeur status by having her first real date turn out to be a blood-sucking killer, we witness a braver Willow, one willing to help Buffy fight the "forces of evil." Lorna Jowett in *Sex and the Slayer* makes the following observation about the early Willow: "Willow is ... shown initially to lack female friendship structures (her best friend is male), but she is empowered by her new relationship with Buffy and her inclusion in the Scooby Gang" (37). Jowett goes on to say that "Willow is further empowered by the acceptance and value placed on her special talents as they contribute to the group effort" (37). The power of acceptance and the ensuing stronger self-esteem gives Willow the emotional connection to make a positive moral choice. She leaves her heretofore voyeur state, which is, if not a morally negative state then certainly a morally neutral state, for the next stage of her development. She becomes the very engaged researcher/teacher for the Scooby Gang.

By the second episode, "The Harvest," Willow's role as researcher/teacher demonstrates how the emotional connection to the Scooby Gang has helped her find the opportunities to make positive moral choices. At the beginning of this episode, Willow volunteers to use her computer skills to hack into and decrypt the city's diagram of the electrical tunnel system where the vampires have been hiding. Obviously, this is an illegal action, but Willow is on the moral high ground because she is willing to risk the penalties of computer hacking to help stop the first (and there are many, many more) apocalypse.

Later in this same episode, Willow admits that she is afraid to physically go back into the dark tunnels to fight the evil that is there; however, she says that not only does she want to help, but she also needs to be part of the ensuing fight. She is frightened, yet she is willing to take whatever risks are necessary to help the group destroy the evil harvest growing under Sunnydale. Even though Willow's research help typically begins in the library, she overcomes the fear of the "dark tunnels" and fights in the scary physical battles with the monsters of the dark ("The Harvest"). As the early shows progress and her connection to the group and its moral code grows, Willow (even before she becomes a witch) demonstrates the courage to make positive moral choices because, time after time, she is willing to risk getting in trouble in school, getting in trouble with the law, and, well, getting killed to help defeat the evil that attacks Sunnydale.

In fact, all members of the Scooby Gang draw strength from the group. In Season Four, the importance of the group's dynamics is explored in "The Yoko Factor" and in "Primeval." In "The Yoko Factor" the conglomerate of evil, Adam, realizes the strength of the Scooby Gang, so he commandeers Spike (who at this point in the show is still a morally-challenged vampire) to spread discord in the group by planting seeds of doubt in each member's mind about how the group perceives him or her. The group is for a while dysfunctional, which puts not only the group but all of Sunnydale in grave danger of succumbing to a world ruled by the technologically-enhanced demon-human combination that is Adam. In the next episode "Primeval," the group must unite to defeat Adam. Willow, proficient in the use of magic, is able to combine the group's attributes: Buffy's Watcher Giles's mind, Xander's heart, Buffy's strength, and her own spirit (Stevenson 147). Stevenson says of this event that "Through the sharing of their strength, Buffy and her friends wield a power that the solitary Adam cannot comprehend" (147). Willow's connection to the group power gives her a tempting taste of mystical power. Because Willow's use of power leads to a positive moral outcome — the Scooby Gang once again saves the world — this experience surely builds in Willow the false confidence that her use of power will always be for the greater good.

However, in Season Six, the loss of Buffy shatters the protective force of the Scooby Gang, which causes Willow to experience the frightening yet seductive power of the dangerous black Willow for the first time. Willow and the grieving, Watcherless gang decide to bring Buffy back from the dead: a poor moral decision that a fully-functioning and a fully-informed group would never have made. In these episodes, "Bargaining, Part One and Two," Willow flirts with an addictive evil power; her resurrection spell, as poor moral choices so often do, has negative repercussions because, along with bringing back Buffy, the spell also brings back a demon ghost. Also, we learn from Spike that Willow knew that the resurrection spell could have brought Buffy back "wrong," wrong enough that Willow would have had to destroy the Buffy she resurrected ("After Life"). When Giles learns what Willow has done, he calls her a "rank, arrogant amateur" and "a very stupid girl" ("Flooded"). Even the still morally challenged Spike seems to understand that Willow has made a poor moral choice. He says "Willow knows that there were risks in bringing Buffy back. That's the thing about magic. There are always consequences" ("After Life").

With little regard for the good of the group, Willow does not clue the Scooby Gang in on the possible disastrous consequences of bringing Buffy back. Even though the resurrected Buffy appears distant and miserable, Willow remains arrogant, for she responds to Giles's chastisement by assuring Giles that she and her powers are indeed amazing; when Giles reminds her of the danger of the magic she used, she replies, "It's not a good idea to piss me off" ("Flooded"). Willow's dismissive attitude toward Giles and her use of scatological terminology demonstrate how disassociated she is from the Scooby Gang and its core principles. (She is also, metaphorically, "marking her territory" and warning Giles off.) Willow seems to be so infatuated with her dominion of magic that she is unaware that her power has a dark side, unaware that all power needs to be connected, unaware that power corrupts, unaware that she deceived the Scooby Gang, unaware that Buffy is in pain, unaware that she has made a very poor moral choice.

Later in Season Six, Willow's continuing obsession with magic causes an alienation from the Scooby Gang and her breakup of Tara (Willow's significant other). Tara warns the arrogant Willow that Willow is in danger of losing herself to the dark side of her magical powers. Ever since Willow cheated death (and Buffy) by bringing Buffy back from heaven, Willow has been in the morally compromised "all-about-me-and-my-power" mode. She seems to be incapable of noticing the pain of others. She dismisses Tara's concerns over Willow's over-reliance on magic. And when Tara is angry at her lover's attitude, Willow slips deeper into a morally-challenged state and casts a forgetting spell on Tara ("All the Way"). The spell works for a time, and all is well between Tara and the smug Willow until the truth is revealed, and Tara breaks up with Willow. She makes it clear that the only way to repair the relationship is for Willow to stop all use of magic ("Tabula Rasa").

The loss of Tara, as such losses often do, awakens Willow's desire to reconnect with her lover, with the Scooby Gang, and with her moral self. The Scooby Gang gathers around and helps Willow find the strength to become magic-free ("Wrecked"). Willow's resolve to leave the power of magic alone is evident in the episode "Normal Again" when she uses the slower scientific method to develop the antidote to cure the dying Buffy from the venom of the Glarghk Guhl Kushmans'nik (the demon summoned by the Trio in one of their many attempts to hamstring Buffy). Tara witnesses the magic-free Willow, and by the next episode Willow and Tara have reunited ("Entropy"). All is well until Tara's murder shatters Willow's world: "Grief is the gateway to despair" (Korsmeyer 167). The despair or hopelessness that Willow feels severs her connection to the group and to the world.

Willow's isolation becomes evident when the former sharer-of-knowledge Willow enters the Magic Shop and instead of using the "Evelyn Wood on amphetamine" speed-reading techniques that she used to learn the magic needed to bring Buffy back from heaven, she uses magic to march the printed words up her arms and into her body — she, the teacher, steals the knowledge and leaves the books blank: a shockingly selfish choice ("Villains"). Willow's pain can only be assuaged through revenge. Enter "scary-veiny Willow." Willow's solitude of rage leads her to kill Warren ("Villains"). Arguably, Warren is a despicable murderer, but he is a *flesh* and blood human, that is, until Willow skins him. Willow has broken the first and most important tenet of the *Buffy's* moral code: she has taken a human life. It is evident from Willow's own words that she has severed all ties to herself and to the group. She tells Giles, "Willow doesn't live here anymore" ("Grave").

Willow seems completely alienated from the group, and from her original self-deprecation, when she says, "let me tell you something about Willow. She's a loser. And she always has been. People picked on Willow in junior high school, high school, up until college. With her stupid mousy ways. And now? Willow's a junkie" ("Grave"). Stevenson discusses this same quote, and he points out that "Willow's insistence on referring to herself in the third person shows the extent to which she has disowned the real Willow" (242). The use of third person also distances Willow from the Scooby Gang. Willow appears to be unstoppable on her quest to end her suffering; and, according to her, all the pain in the world, for she tells Giles that she has so much power that she can feel everyone's pain ("Grave"). She claims that by ending the world she will not only stop her own pain, but she will also stop the suffering of the world and of all the "poor bastards" ("Grave"). Willow has chosen to allow her pain to isolate her from a connection to the Scooby Gang, and its moral code, so it becomes easy for her to rationalize that destroying the world is a *good idea*.

However, the Scooby Gang is not ready to disconnect from Willow, for it is the connection to the gang, this time through Giles and Xander, that brings Willow back from this self-directed apocalypse. Near the end of "Grave," Giles, at great risk to his own life, finesses Willow into stealing the Coven's power from him so that the pure magic from the Coven can provide the conduit needed for Xander to reconnect with the "spark of humanity" remaining in Willow ("Grave"). Xander races to the bluff where Willow is busily preparing to destroy the world. He tells Willow that if she is indeed going to destroy the world that he wants to die with his best friend, Willow. He tells her that he loves her and reminds her that he has loved her since she cried in kindergarten because she was afraid to tell anyone that she broke her yellow crayon: "I love you. I loved crayon-breaky Willow and I love ... scary veiny Willow" ("Grave"). Xander tells Willow that even if she kills him he will still love her.

Willow responds with a slashing gesture that knocks Xander down and puts three bleeding gashes on his face. Action similar to this is repeated three more times. Each time Willow knocks him down, the wounded Xander gets up and repeats "I love you." With each "I love you," "scary veiny Willow" is visibly weakened. Finally, Willow begins to cry. Xander walks up to Willow; and, with her magic spent, Willow begins to hit Xander with her non-magical fists; then, she falls to her knees, and Xander kneels next to her and wraps his arms around her. One more time he says, "I love you." While sobbing in Xander's arms, "scary veiny Willow" fades and redheaded Willow returns ("Grave"). It is the connection to humanity through Xander that brings Willow back to Willow and to the Scooby Gang: the reconnection to positive emotions initiated by Xander's love allows her to decide to not destroy the world — a very good moral choice, indeed.

The opening of the final season finds Willow frightened of her powers, frightened of the emerging Hellmouth, frightened of her control over her powers, and frightened of being rejected by the Scooby Gang ("Lessons"). During this first episode of Season Seven, we learn that Giles has sent Willow to recuperate in the English countryside under the care of that influential Coven, but the rehab has been cut short because Sunnydale's Hellmouth is rumbling and will soon open. In "Lessons," Willow learns that even the members of the powerful British Coven are afraid of her powers. Willow tries to argue with Giles that she is not so powerful that the Coven should fear her. Giles replies, "You're connected to a great power, whether you feel it or not," and he assures her that even though she wants him to take her power away that her power cannot be taken from her, for he says that magic power resides deep inside Willow, and that she is the one responsible for this power ("Lessons").

Willow informs Giles that she has seen the Hellmouth and that "it's got teeth" ("Beneath You"). Willow also tells Giles that she does not know if she is strong enough to destroy this fanged Hellmouth without becoming "all veiny and homicidal again" ("Beneath You"). But mostly Willow is afraid that she will not be able to reconnect to the Scooby Gang. She seems to want Giles to tell her that that she will be wanted back by the group; however, Giles does not know how the Scoobies will react to Willow, so in true Watcher style he reminds her that "you may not be wanted but you will be needed" ("Beneath You"). Armed with the knowledge that the Scooby Gang may not want her back but they will need her, she makes a positive moral choice to return to Sunnydale because her friends are going to need her.

And she is needed because the most powerful apocalypse yet, a "bidet of evil," is brewing under Sunnydale ("First Date"). When Willow returns to Sunnydale, her fears magically make it impossible for Willow and the gang to see each other. Once again Willow's appearance, or in this case her invisible status, corresponds to her ethical state: Willow's guilt over "skinning" Warren and her previous quest to destroy the world and its pain has created an "invisible" dilemma. Only when the group realizes that they cannot see each other and Buffy says how glad she is that Willow has returned is the spell broken, and the gang is able to save Willow from a flesh-eating (major irony there) monster ("Same Time, Same Place"). The Scooby strength has once again embraced Willow. Later when Willow, weakened by the flesh eating monster, is trying to connect with the earth to heal herself, Buffy takes Willow's wounded hands and says, "I have so much strength I'm giving it away" ("Same Time, Same Place"). With the tether to the gang restored, Willow begins to heal physically and emotionally.

However, later in the season Willow is afraid to be intimate with Kennedy (her new love interest), and for good reason because when she gives in to the relationship, her guilt, thanks to a spell by Amy, manifests itself by turning Willow into the murdered Warren. The spell is eventually broken, and the incident leaves Willow able to enter a new love relationship, but she remains uncertain about her control over magic. She says, "If I let myself go, I could just go" ("Touched"). Willow obviously fears she will lose her ability to make sacrifices for the betterment of others. In other words she doubts her ability to make good moral choices when she is under the power of magic. She fears that the power of her magic will once again isolate her from her connection to the group and its guiding influence.

But her friends need her, so with the confidence of Buffy, and with Kennedy by her side to keep her grounded, she connects to the power of the ancient Guardian women so that all the Potentials can share Willow's (and Buffy's) deep-rooted power. Instead of "scary veiny Willow" we see glowy-white Willow ("Chosen"). The glowing white Willow signifies that Willow understands the beatitude of great power: sharing power controls power. As Farah Mendlesohn in "Surpassing the Love of Vampires" points out, "the writers have constructed a matrix of interdependence and control that rests on relationships rather than rules" (48). The strong social bond of the group has allowed Willow to tap into great power and still hold on to Willow and, of course with the help of the group (thanks, Spike), save the world. In the end Willow gets what

Willow wants: a strong emotional connection to a morally-strong group which gives her the power to make positive moral choices in the *Buffy* style.

In *Why Buffy Matters* Rhonda Wilcox claims that *Buffy* "is both magic and ultimately real" (1). On many levels, the character Willow certainly fits Wilcox's definition of magic; and, because Willow's struggles with moral choices are familiar to all, her struggle is the magic hook that provides the viewer with the connection needed to learn from Willow's choices: a strong connection to a group that is grounded in an altruistic moral code will help the individual to channel the emotional "decider" part of the brain into making positive moral choices.

To test the relevancy of the connection claim, a look at real-world findings is in order. Kristen Monroe discusses the driving forces behind moral choices. Monroe claims that a careful study of the brave rescuers of Jews during the Holocaust finds that it was not logical contemplations or membership in a specific religion that drove these uncommon heroes to risk their own lives for the safety of the Jews. She says, "a particular view of self in relation to others" exemplifies why the rescuers found the moral courage to act (405). In essence, it was a deep connection to others that motivated the bravest of the brave to act: the connection to the group "trigger[ed] a sense of moral salience" (Monroe 405).

Sociologist Dr. Frank Elwell is in agreement on the need for the individual's commitment or connection to a morally functioning group. He discusses the decline of morality due to what the nineteenth century sociologist Emile Durkheim called "the weakening of the social bond" (Elwell). Elwell points out that, once the social bonds are broken and the individual loses the connection to a morally-functioning group, the individual loses a "coherent, consistent or insistent moral guidance." Elwell again refers to Durkheim's claim that, when the social bonds are broken, the individual makes moral choices that "will tend to satisfy his [or her] own appetites with little thought on the possible impact of his action on others." In other words, the individual will act in an "all about me" manner.

In addition to the "all about me" moral choices category, the real world is replete with examples of what could be called *doppelgangers* to the Scooby Gang's connections. Such groups, as morally challenged as they may be, provide further proof of the connection claim. One recent group that exemplifies this connection is the 9/11 hijackers. It is common knowledge that the nineteen hijackers had strong connections to their group. Probably there would be little argument to the claim that the hijackers were acting in agreement with the moral code of their group, and there can be little doubt that the hijackers' emotional sections of their brains were overriding the cognitive sections of their brains when they made the choice to kill — and die — for their cause. This doppelganger effect is analogous to many of the forces of evil on *Buffy*: Spike and Druscilla's gang; the Trio; the Initiative; and the Master, Glory, Harmony, and all their minions. Obviously, a strong connection to a group affects an individual's moral choices, but it is also obvious (the "duh" factor) that for the individual to make a positive moral choice the moral code of the group must be — moral.

Franz Kafka once said, "A book must be the axe for the frozen sea within us" (Barnstorff 162). Now, "gentle reader" (Andrew, in "Storyteller"), please substitute the word fiction for book in Kafka's quote and let us sharpen the axe by returning to the *Buffy* definition of a moral code: The first tenet is that human life is inviolable and the second tenet is that an individual is willing to risk one's own aspirations for the betterment of others (Stevenson 166). The *Buffy* moral code is simple, and, yes, it comes from a television show, but the code is not new. This simple, beautiful code is as familiar to modern individuals as it was to Confucius, Socrates, Aristotle, and Jesus. This same sentiment can be found in an Ibo (the Nigerian people of the fictional Okonkwo) saying — "I am because we are" (Badaracco 51). What we learn from Willow is that, when she is in strong concert with the Scooby Gang and its moral code, she is able to resist the corruptive isolation of power by sharing power, which leads her to make positive moral choices. And perhaps it is the close relationship to the group that keeps Willow believing the tenets of the code, for Willow must stay connected to the group to continually reinforce the sacredness of each human life.

Moral choices—connected now.

Notes

1. Jean-Paul Sartre was a French existential philosopher.

Is It Art?

The Artful "Hush" of St. Francis and the Gentlemen Blue Meanies

———✠———

GARY MOELLER

What if, during the fourth season of what has become the cult classic *Buffy The Vampire Slayer* and long before the last episode was put to bed, an innocent (evidently living under those proverbial rocks) sits back in his[1] Stratalounger and pushes on the remote? Not terribly caring what is *on* and just needing to relax after a stressful day, he finds a program with at times no dialogue — at least not an audible dialogue, no narration, in an ordinary-looking setting peopled by both *ordinary* folks and strange characters obviously up to no good.

What is really happening here? Why is so much in this show that he stumbled onto so reminiscent of old feelings and images? As he thinks about what he is watching, he finds both subtle and obvious assumptions a viewer can make about this episode titled "Hush."[2]

He postulates that, without the burden of the knowledge of characters' roles, storylines, and the *suspended disbelief* of an avid follower of the series, he can be free to objectively discover the visual clues and integrations that may hold the whole composition together.[3]

Finding possible visual revelations is always fun and relying on pop culture memory is a good place to begin. Our lounge-chair detective is armed with many years of movie and TV watching and a fairly decent background in art history and is therefore ready to employ these tools in the critical dissection of this strange new show.[4]

From the very beginning, he wonders why the college kids in the opening scene are so attentive to what the professor is presenting. Why is the room so golden warm, bathed in the light of the Caravaggesque,[5] and why are two of the students encouraged to participate in a kissing exercise in front of the class? After all, the viewer's experience in college would dictate that in a room that dark we would find at least a third of the class asleep ten minutes into the lecture, although the kissing exhibition may well explain why everyone in the room is so alert.

The room goes suddenly dark and is devoid of all but the two kissing experts, Buffy and Riley: Buffy the student and Riley the teaching assistant. The next odd thing occurs. After the two kissers untangle and as Buffy leaves the classroom, she makes a turn into a long hallway. In the background there appears in a flash, for a flash, the image of a statue, apparently that of St. Francis. There, just for a second or two, in a niche at the apex of the turn in the hall is this almost-subliminal image. Is this the image of the saint who speaks for those who cannot, the one that cares for those who suffer, and the one who receives the bloody stigmata? The viewer is left looking for more confirmation, but instead the next shot is of some little blond girl saying a verse at the end of the hall.

She is holding a box. What could the box be? It could be a smaller version of so many mythical boxes. Boxes play a part in many a story and myth. We remember the Ark of the Covenant and Pandora's (which in the original Greek version is a vase) (*Women's Belly Book*).

This whole sequence turns out to be a dream. Ah ha! Someone did fall asleep in class! Not only is it a dream; it is the *teaser* before the intro, credits, theme-music, and action montage all so common on television action series.

After the flashy opening, the plot thickens. Another strange thing happens. Soon all the college students and towns folk are asleep — at the same time. Weird. Weirder still is what is happening in the bell tower of an abandoned church. (An abandoned church is unlikely in Sunnydale — an abandoned church. Think about it. Considering the fact that the possibility of a grisly death in this particular town seems fairly high, the need for prayer is equally high. Spiritual paranoia, soul searching, and getting right with God should be a fairly high priority, one would imagine: churches are in demand.) Or maybe the bell tower is on some old civic building. This seems reasonable since it has a big clock. Whatever the building's original purpose, here is a new purpose, a house of the up-to-no-good. Here in this tower, odd, perpetually-smiling, silvery-blue tall fellows with sort of short little minions in straitjackets are cooking up a curse. Or are they? This activity is centered on the above-mentioned magic box, which is apparently designed to suck the very ability to speak from every Sunnydaleon. After every good citizen's voice is in fact spirited into the box, chaos, frightful circumstances, and some hilarity ensue.

The viewer may be haunted by all this, but not necessarily in a frightening way, although that certainly seems to be the intent. The haunting may actually come from memories of pop culture and religious icons and how eerily similar they are to certain aspects of this episode.

Blue Meanies and The Yellow Submarine

Even though the casual viewer may assume that the majority of *Buffy* enthusiasts may be too young to know much about *The Yellow Submarine*, the popularity of the *Buffy* show would allow for at least some mature followers. Those elders (excluding any Young Republicans of the time or, on the other side, those people who took the whole drug-culture thing too seriously and may not remember much anyway) should be able to recall the 1968 animated film driven by the Beatles's psychedelic period of pop music and inspired by the art of Heinz Edelmann and Milton Glaser (and maybe Peter Max), and from that recollection understand the comparisons that abound between the happenings in Pepperland and those in Sunnydale.

Basically, the plot of *The Yellow Submarine* is simple. Everything is wonderful in Pepperland. Music, dancing, and colorful people experiencing the *joie de vivre* are everywhere. Sgt. Pepper's Lonely Hearts Club Band plays regularly and the character Old Fred Pepper himself acts as sort of a protector of the town. (Actually, he seems totally bewildered and stumbles around town most of the time, mumbling to himself.) The whole place is attacked by Blue Meanies who, through various methods, steal the sound and color from everything and everyone. In the end, the Beatles save the day, and Pepperland and its inhabitants are restored to all its previous psychedelic glory and the Meanies are magically made friends of Pepperland.

There appear to be no actual vampires operating in the wonderful, colorful, and musical place called Pepperland, other than occasional rainbow-colored butterfly floating about and landing on the heads of the citizens. (We might think of those butterflies as vampiric because, in reality, several species of butterflies like to suck the salt and oils from the sweaty pores of people. They apparently need more salt than they get from nectar — or at least they like it) (Scoble).

There is, however, as the story proceeds, a great amount of draining of human essentials (you know those essentials — joy, love, souls — things of that nature) from those same citizens by the over-the-top grinning hoard of Blue Meanies and their minions.

The Blue Meanies are perpetually-smiling, plump, mostly blue anthropomorphs, with sharp teeth, claws for fingers, and large upturned noses. They wear hats that look like the black film carriers from the old-time hand-crank motion picture cameras and black bandit masks over their eyes. The main Meanie, the boss, has a headdress that resembles the long, slightly out-of-control ears of a jackrabbit, only black. These blue characters do not float menacingly through the town as do the Gentlemen, the creepy bad guys of "Hush," but their hired help is certainly capable of such.

Backing up the Blue Meanies is a strange army, consisting of an array of characters from clowns with tall pointed hats to Snapping Turks. The Snapping Turks have bodies that actually do the snapping, opening at a toothy belly. Their heads seem nothing but ornaments. There are also odd purple cats with erect tails, black-rimmed glasses, and large orange numbers on their chests and, along with these felines, little bald guys in sunglasses with smiles and lobster-claw hands. As a matter of fact, all these characters are smiling, grinning like frozen toys.

The main weapon, other than a cannon that also wreaks havoc by encapsulating all the music in impenetrable bubbles, is the Glove, a floating large blue-purple hand that flies through the countryside and town and pounds the color out of everything. Everything except the butterfly is bopped colorless. Between the Glove and the cannon, all of Pepperland is made seemingly lifeless; the citizens are reduced to black and white frozen living statues. Music and sound is also drained from the place.

Being Bad

Back in Sunnydale, the now not-so-casual viewer is looking for trouble. He's not looking for trouble in the plotline. He's looking for trouble in the artistic elements of the episode. He has decided there must be one glaring visually-difficult passage in "Hush" that comes at a most critical time in the plot of which he may be able to give a searing and profoundly negative critique. Why there is such a need to give this show a critical drubbing, at least as an exercise in his own mind, must be hidden deep within the results of his upbringing and education. Anything too cute and cheesy grates on him like No. 36 (that means really rough) sandpaper on a chalkboard. This is an anatomic reaction to the sickeningly cute and to the unflinching lies of the gurus of over-the-top sweetness in art and applies to some traditional forms art as well (Norman Rockwell and that hack that does the syrupy landscapes who used to have galleries of his work in all the local shopping malls— and still does in some —come to mind).

To continue — at this point in the "Hush" story, the Gentlemen have somehow found the riddle to opening the box (which is apparently fairly easy) and all the voices in Sunnydale are sucked into the little cube and sealed away, presumably forever. Visually however, are there problems with how this is portrayed?

All the folks of the town, good, bad, and androgynous, are asleep, and the spell is cast. The voices float from all the sleeping mouths and undulate across town, into the box. Is the graphic depiction, the animation of the voices, silly and clumsily done? Is the imagery too obvious and overdone? Are these poorly drawn like lazy S's, or even worse Z's, and so very distracting to anyone not so caught up in the story to the point of turning their soul over to it, that the whole sequence becomes a bit laughable?

Unfortunately for this viewer the answer is no, the sequence is not laughable. The use of an airbrush, warping program, or some such thing to distort the areas where the voices are intended to travel is quite slick and even somewhat believable.

The hope of fulfilling this need to deliver a scathing critique further weakens with the realization that the visual bar the episode has set for itself to this point is fairly high and goes a long way toward suspending disbelief. Surely, this relative quality cannot continue throughout the entire program. Something like poorly-animated voices would therefore destroy the artistic continuity of the piece and he would feel self-satisfied in his suspicion. But no joy is found in this pursuit. Alas, at least to this point the whole *mise en scène* of "Hush" remains visually coherent.

The Yellow Submarine, on the other hand, can at times be weak as it relates to animation, with too many stills and many grainy, jumpy movements. It was done in 1968, so a negative reaction would be a little too easy and no fun at all. We're all spoiled by now by current special effects, CGI, and good animation. Besides, the main visual emphasis of the film is on the pre–MTV music videos of *Sergeant Pepper's Lonely Hearts Club Band* tunes, such as the hallucinogenic "Lucy in the Sky with Diamonds." These musically-driven pieces are fairly strong visually in terms of animation for the time. The colors and shapes reflect the music well by ebbing and flowing with modulated sound, putting the viewer into a trance without the necessity of actual drugs or the side effects of possible future flashbacks.

Oh, well, fun must be found elsewhere for the armchair critic.

Straitjacket Oz

What about those poor pawns of the Gentlemen of "Hush"? What about those hunched-over, straitjacketed creatures scuttling along like dogs with their noses to the ground, their undone jacket sleeves flopping about as they move, bound by gravity and some untold hold their silver-blue masters have on them? Once again, they are so familiar that we have to investigate their possible antecedents.

Could their characters be inspired by the Igor of the Hollywood *Frankenstein* flicks of the 1930's and 40's? Or is it "I"-gor of Mel Brooks's *Young Frankenstein,* or is it Frankensteee-n? Or maybe they are inspired by those extremely-menacing flying monkeys from *The Wizard of Oz*? That seems a better bet. Those monkeys were so incredibly creepy; some aspects of their creepiness relate directly to the Gentlemen's minions.

Are the Gentlemen's minions in that way equal to the flying primates?

At first the fact that the *Oz* monkeys can, in fact, fly may seemingly create a disconnect between the two sets of characters. But what about those flopping sleeves? Are they not flightless wings? Are these partially-restrained assistants subhuman mentally/emotionally, previously capable of flight but now captive with clipped wings?

Visually the straitjacket guys have potential. They could have been so much more interesting as Jack Nicholson-type *One Flew Over the Cuckoo's Nest* crazies. Nicholson did straitjackets proud in that role. The *Buffy* straitjacket guys are just too typical, in terms of script, in the genre of action sequences and Saturday afternoon mid-twentieth century movie serials. The minions are easily defeated with a karate kick or some sort of ray gun (the animation involved with the taser/ray gun was not bad either). Unfortunately, they just turn out to be normal dumb villains—a little laughable and sad—too easily disposed of.

The fact is, whatever the similarities, these straitjacketed characters are nowhere close to the hair-raising monkeys on the fright scale and they really are not even as foreboding as the clowns of *The Yellow Submarine*. Those monkeys had evil human characteristics—like eyes that could make the viewer want to disappear—hide—go away. A flying hoard of monkeys with just enough minds of their own to make things a bit unpredictable will focus most people's attention.

Clowns on the other hand are just inherently weird. They often have exactly the opposite of their intended impact on children. The viewer recalls a recent trip to the State Fair with his two-year-old granddaughter. He saw a clown with bright green hair, an elaborately painted face (with a big smile), and all the other gaudy and oversized garb of the typical clown, sitting at a display for trailer houses. Naturally, he thought his lovely granddaughter would be interested or entertained by this freakishly-attired entity, and he pointed the clown out to her. Instead of running toward the clown, she instead dug her heels into the ground and turned and hid in her grandfather's kneecaps. She saw this guy as a monster, not a friendly fool. (It all turned out to the good, however, because the clown was really just a ploy, an advertising gimmick for a trailer park, in which neither the granddaughter nor grandfather were interested.) The creators of *The Yellow Submarine* obviously recognized the spooky contradiction of clowns and likely used the painted smile of toy clowns as the model for the entire Meanie mob, which may have later been inherited by the Gentlemen.

It also could be that whole idea of toys, such as toy monkeys that can be wound-up and, when released, jump around and play cymbals, is the impetus for the images. Could the windup toy money be what is really behind the concept of the *Oz* monkeys? Something intended to please can become crazy frightening.

The minions look to be escaped maniacs in some ways; so do the *Oz* monkeys.

Apparently, the novelist Stephen King has done a great deal with the subjects of menacing clowns (*It*) and killer toy monkeys (King, "The Monkey"). There is something about King's complaining about Stanley Kubrick's film adaptation of *The Shining* that has always soured for some the appreciation of anything King-ish from that time forward (Sexton). For some, Kubrick is (was) a god. Since the demise of Kubrick, our viewer's reading habits mainly have consisted of historical accounts, historical fiction, or art history works.

Back to the subject of crazies — and returning to one of the initial images in the episode, St. Francis was certainly seen as, if not a maniac, certainly crazy — or disturbed — by his contemporaries after his conversion to the life of purity. Remember, he was transformed from the major young party man in town and slayer of Perugians to someone who cast aside all worldly possessions, including his clothes. How would we react, seeing a naked young man proselytizing about being Christ-like, running through our town? Even in a college town, including those in the Bible Belt, that kind of behavior might seem a little crazy.

Sacred Lonely Hearts Club Canned

Thinking back to the little girl (evocative of a younger *Buffy*?) chanting at the end of the hall in one of the opening sequences, one is curious about the subject of the hearts, (yes, the uninformed viewer has turned up the sound in order to listen more intently to the chant) and what, if anything, it has to do with the images of St. Francis and *The Yellow Submarine*? She says, "Can't even shout / Can't even cry / The gentlemen are coming by.... / They need to take seven." (We find out later that *seven* refers to extracted hearts from living victims, a lovely image.)

St. Francis, protector of those that cannot speak. St. Francis, recipient of the stigmata — to the hands, to the feet, to the heart.

The Blue Meanies, silencers of music, and of beauty, and of sound. The Blue Meanies, capturers of the color and essence of humanity.

As concerns St. Francis, many paintings in the history of art depict him and the stigmata. The stigmata include the piercing of the heart of St. Francis of Assisi, often by a lance. Giovanni Bellini was a more-than-noteworthy painter of St. Francis themes with several important images to his credit. The fifteenth century *Virgin and Child Enthroned with Saints Francis, John the Baptist, Job, Dominic, Sebastian, and Louis of Toulouse* (Stokstad 655) deftly crams all these non-chronologically-concurrent folks, saints, Jesus, Mary, and the main donor (he gave Bellini the money to make the painting) all into the space very similar to that of Masaccio's *Trinita* (Stokstad 636) and reveals telling facts about each character.

In the case of St. Francis, the saint holds open the cut in his tunic, revealing the wound to his heart. Curious. And why is he pierced in the heart as opposed to the standard biblical understanding of being lanced in the side, which is more often replicated to evoke the wounds of the crucifixion? The *With Saints Francis* pose almost seems a Doubting Thomas pose, much like that of the depiction created by Verrocchio in one of the niches of Orsanmichele in Florence. At Orsanmichele, Christ looks down knowingly while Thomas places his finger inside Christ's lance wound, which is below the ribs of the Christ figure.

In the Bellini *With Saints Francis* piece, however, the wound is to the heart. St. Francis does not actually hold the weapon that inflicts the heart part of the stigmata in his right hand as so many mere martyrs might do, but Bellini has subliminally suggested such a symbol through the shapes imposed in the composition. If viewers of this piece step back and focus only on the St. Francis section of the painting, it is possible to see the shape of a sword in the negative space between his tunic and the golden pilaster to the viewer's left. Another important St. Francis piece by Giovanni Bellini, a piece that is even more of an icon, is *Saint Francis in Ecstasy* (Stokstad 656). This one, however, while revealing the stigmata of the hands, shows nothing of the heart wound.

Piero della Francesa, another Italian Renaissance painter, also paints Saint Francis revealing his chest wound in the beautiful altarpiece *Polittico di Sant' Antonio* (found in the National Gallery in Perugia). In the center altarpiece predella, the base, there is also a depiction of St. Francis on one knee (ashamedly, some viewers—okay, I'm one—can only think of Al Jolson while examining the predella piece) while he receives the stigmata. There are hundreds, if not thousands, of images on the subject of Saint Francis, especially throughout central Italy, and many of them reinforce the "Sacred Heart of Jesus" aspect of the stigmata. The Franciscan coat of arms incorporates a seal of symbolic images of both Christ and St. Francis. The banner beneath the seal reads "*In Corde Jesu,*" which means "*in the heart of Jesus.*" This ties the concept of Francis even closer to the life of conversion and to the pursuit of a Christ-like existence ("History").

Curiously enough, there also exists at least one portrait from the Simon Dowsey collection painted by a Japanese artist that shows the heart of St. Francis Xavier (the guy that temporarily or partially converted the Japanese to Christianity in the 16th Century) with his heart out of his chest, a crucifix/lance penetrating it while winged baby-heads rejoice all around in heaven (Vlam). All this Baroque visual fun may be a misinterpretation in that Xavier apparently did not receive the stigmata (although he apparently *was* known for speaking in tongues). It would have been easy for an ill-informed artist from a non-western culture to get the images and stories of the two saints a little mixed-up. Xavier, after all, was known to have a spiritual fire in his heart.

So, maybe there is something to this Saint Francis connection and maybe it extends to the hearts the Gentlemen seem to be preserving in fruit jars. Do they need to save them for their own heartless bodies? They seem only power-ful spirits with more-than-human powers, but not truly human.

It could be that the Blue Meanies have something to do with the hearts in canning jars as well. The idea of the jars could correspond to the big bubble the cannon shoots over Sergeant Pepper's Lonely Heart's Club Band, killing the music and color from Pepperland. Maybe.

We might note that the story goes that Francis was not St. Francis's given name. He apparently had his persona re-branded by his fellow Christian Assisi associates because he read French poetry. He also apparently approved this nominal transformation. If this is truly the case, this may be the only time in the history of the western world where a truly macho man actually chose to change his name *to* Francis (of course that is not true and a bad joke, because there are thousands of Latin men, macho or not, with a *Francis* derivative as their namesake). This saint was no sissy (well, not as it relates to willingness to fight). Before he became a pacifist and a mirror image of Christ, he kicked butt all over Umbria. This is the same guy who was known for his involvement with lavish parties as a young man and the same person that wanted originally to be a knight and to right the wrongs inflicted upon his people by Perugia. Of course, he did become that very thing—fighter against Perugia—for a short while until he was thrown in prison and before he heard from above (Chesterton 38).

Speaking of kicking butt, could all this karate in "Hush" or in the series in general have anything to do with St. Francis?

St. Francis cast the demons out of Arrezzo. Or, was it a giant wolf out of Gubbio?[6] The demons— or the wolf— were apparently the cause of the plague and possibly leprosy in Arrezzo and/or Gubbio, which is another beautiful hill-side town not far from Assisi. Giotto's (or the St. Francis Master's) *St. Francis Cycle* of frescos that traces the life of St. Francis in the Upper Church of St. Francis of Assisi depicts our saint pointing at winged-demons (so similar to the *Oz* monkeys— really similar, *sans* the little hats and vests) as they flee the walled city. He saves the town by figuratively kicking the demons out.

Is It Art?

What have we learned from this happenstance? Did our viewer find this episode artful?

On the surface and without a rather thorough scrutinous viewing of "Hush," the answer from most art aficionados would be, simply, *no*. Now, please note that these critics would be viewing the piece from a "High Art" vantage point and pop-culture would seldom float above the sewage of commercialism in their world. This is the same perspective assumed by our viewer in the "Being Bad" section of this piece.

Then again, we should well realize, from documented time forward, art has been a servant of kings and queens, popes and cardinals, dukes and duchesses, and business executives of all types. It was meant to educate and indoctrinate and to make some institution or some powerful individual stronger.

The great stained-glass windows and frescos of the cathedrals educated the multitudes of the illiterate faithful to the doctrines of the church with state-of-the-art, knock-out images, much like television and the Internet create followers for whatever purpose "the powers" desire by rapid-firing sparkly images at the surface-loving public today. Today's world is almost as visually dependent as the Early Renaissance. Today's art world is much less "High Art"-oriented, even though that orientation is mostly manifested in such places as the Walton Collection in Bentonville, Arkansas[7]; Las Vegas casinos[8]; and vaults in Tokyo (Sterngold).

Money and fame associated with popular acknowledgement of certain artists and movements have fanned the flames of desire for the rich, *nouveau* and otherwise, to possess great art in very public places as well as behind closed doors. Everyone wants the last Van Gogh because his stuff can be almost as pretty as Thomas Kinkade's and worth a whole lot more money, not because Van Gogh's work was revolutionary and insanely gutsy.

It is no wonder the art educated are a bit shy about the reality of pop culture as "High Art," even though pop culture — that's art/culture that is current, of the time — seemingly has dictated the production of what now is seen as "High Art" for over the last hundred years of the modern era. (And, Van Gogh was pop culture — or at least current culture — for the years he was painting.) Richard Hamilton, Andy Warhol, and, before them, the true pop artists, the DADA print and photomontage/assemblage artists Ernst, Duchamp, and Hannah Hoch all mined the actual refuse of industrial and technical societies, the gold of art that washes up as trash (or trashy), and reflects the actual nature of those societies' existences (Hughes 57–364). Their most important goals were to question art and the cultures that produced it.

This also questions the exclusive realm of the rich and powerful as relates to the control and driving force behind art. The powerful often may be the people who buy and commission art, but seldom do they actually create anything progressive or, for that matter, have any sound idea of what any of it actually means. Artists, like the DADA, are champion biters of the very hand that feeds them — for which we should all be thankful.

St. Francis is actually a fine example of this revolting behavior. Not only did he throw all the material finery and secure future provided by his wealthy family into the gutter, he also wanted nothing to do with the gilded monuments and garb of the Catholic Church. For a time he became a recluse and a bohemian. He had a higher and more basic calling to pursue, and nothing was to seduce him from that path. This has been at least the initial direction many artists of all types have taken. Most of them had nowhere close to the resolve of a St. Francis.

Even *The Yellow Submarine* resonates with a basic moral purity that shines through the drug haze. That good is found when people are allowed to be different, to sing, and to be colorful seems to be the moral of the tale (as long as they don't overdose). *Buffy* shares this simple plan of good over evil. The Buffy character may not be a saint, but she always seems to be in the process of kicking demons out.

Serious art, in whatever its form, also is neither meant to be purely decorative nor mindlessly pleasurable (with the noted exception of the above mentioned Thomas Kinkade[9]). What is more likely to stimulate and drive a culture: sameness and false sweetness or the type of stimulation that causes thought and reaction? Do we hide what is fearful and perfume our vision to protect us from ourselves? Most artists will say, "No! That would be counterproductive to the truths art depicts." Or, do we reveal that which is most threatening and, by doing so, create opportunities to react and respond? If the answer is properly "Yes" (since, revealed through art, we do need to know all, even the most frightening), then "Hush" passes this test, at least in terms of intent. It is visually sound and somewhat challenging in terms of not falling too deeply into the pit of TV sameness—to a moderate degree. Whatever its position on the fine art scale, this particular installment certainly brings back memories of important visual pop-culture and religious icons.

As for the other 143 episodes, our viewer may have been sparked enough by "Hush" to investigate *their* merit.

Notes

1. Gary is male so he can say "he."

2. In "Hush," the Gentlemen, grinning, floating, and courteous fairy-tale figures with floppy minions, steal the voices of the people of Sunnydale in order to steal hearts from some of the populace. Only Buffy's scream saves the day.

3. In 2000, Joss Whedon was nominated for an Emmy for Outstanding Writing for a Drama Series for "Hush," and Michael Gershman was nominated for Outstanding Cinematography for a Single Camera Series for "Hush" ("Awards").

4. Most critics have focused on communication, fear, silence, music, power, and community in "Hush" (Hornick).

5. Caravaggio was a Baroque painter famed for the drama of his use of light and shadow.

6. Arrezzo and Gubbio are towns in Italy.

7. See <crystalbridges.org>.

8. See <lasvegasartmuseums.com>.

9. I think you can detect a clear bias here.

Signs, Signs, Everywhere Signs

Brechtian Techniques in *Buffy*

———⊗⊗⊗———

DAVID BLAKELY

Introduction: The Television and Its Audience

Part of the nature of art is its interaction with its audience. Art that does not interact with an audience is art without an audience. Some philosophers might suggest that art without an audience is not art at all. Simple art interacts with its audience in a simple way — it may simply make them feel good, or feel reaffirmed, or feel superior. As the art — or its medium — becomes more sophisticated, it interacts with its audience in more complex ways. A traditional folk tune affects its audience in a less-refined way than a Beethoven symphony. Not that the folk tune is somehow inferior to the symphony, not at all. The folk tune is, perhaps, more direct, more single-minded. The symphony writer has any number of strategies to infiltrate the hearts and minds of its audience. While the writer of the folk tune sees the task set before it and accomplishes that task directly, the symphony is more devious.

Every art form has its folk tunes and symphonies— the Grandma Moseses and the Rembrandts, the limerick and the epic poem, the pup tent and the Taj Mahal. Theatre and performing arts, too, have their share of simple and complex cousins in their genealogy. From simple ritual to complex computer-generated images found in contemporary movies, performing arts have various strategies with which to work on their audiences to affect meaning.

Television is no exception. A laugh track, for example, can be used by situation comedies as a strategy to help the audience laugh along with the show.

But there are more subtle strategies. The popular television show *Buffy the Vampire Slayer* uses techniques similar to ones developed by Bertolt Brecht[1] in getting the audience to see the show in more than one light. Use of Brechtian techniques in *Buffy* to direct the audience's attention to issues in the series creates a more thoughtful audience, and a more complex reaction to the art of television.

Specifically, *Buffy* contains signs to inform its audience of the inner workings of its characters and to comment, for the audience's benefit, on the action. Signs in *Buffy* are a way to create meaning in the television series. Signs help to bring the audience to see the series as more than just a vicarious experience, to make the audience aware of the experience at hand. Signs are everywhere, commenting on the action and on the characters of the series: signs point to what may happen, signs comment on the emotional upheavals of the characters, signs comment on the audience experience.

To follow the signs in *Buffy*, we'll need a roadmap. First, it is necessary to have some information on how audiences perceive a performance. Second, we'll need a little background on Brecht's theory of distancing audiences from performances. It will also be good to know something about the medium of television and the fan base watching *Buffy*. Finally, we'll look at specific examples from the television series to help support the idea that signs are everywhere.[2]

Performance as Perception Shifts

Performative art is viewed through time. This is the essential to understanding how performances are perceived by the audience. The audience starts with little or no information about what they will see. As a performance moves through time, the performance gives information to the audience to process or digest. As the audience gets more information, they start to form perceptions of the performance. For example, viewers see vampires attacking innocent high schoolers and perceive the vampires as bad. They see a small blonde defend the high schoolers by fighting vampires with a combination of martial arts and wooden stakes, and they perceive the blonde as good, perhaps even as a protector or hero. If the blonde continues to fight and kill vampires, the audience will perceive her as a "Vampire Slayer."

If the audience never changes their perception of the blonde, they will soon lose interest in that character, for their job is done. That character has been "perceived" and there is nothing in the performance that changes that perception.

That is why a good film/television series/episode must include perception shifts. The audience must shift their notion of what the character is capable of doing. In the series, Buffy starts fighting villains other than vampires in "Teacher's Pet" of Season One. Eventually, Buffy battles witches, demons, monsters of all shapes and sizes. She falls in love, kills her lover, finds someone new, battles demons inside herself. With each new piece of information, the audience shifts their perception of the character. At the same time, certain aspects of her character remain the same: her physical abilities, her emotional attachment to her friends, her internal struggle to be both the savior of the world and a "normal" person. Enough core characteristics must stay the same to allow the audience to perceive this character as Buffy while, at the same time, enough new information is provided through time to enlighten and inform the audience of the constant change the character is going through.

The techniques a performance through time uses to portray the character of Buffy can translate not only to the other characters, but also to the plot. As the audience receives pieces of information, they form perceptions of what will happen next. They anticipate what will come of the current miscreants to terrorize Sunnydale, knowing that Buffy will probably prevail, but unsure as to how. If there is not enough uncertainty as to the final outcome — if the opponents are not of relative equal power — then the audience will perceive that the threat is minimal and will lose interest in the plot. To keep the audience interested, the performance must mete out enough information to allow the audience to anticipate an outcome — usually a battle of some sort — but balance the information to make the odds appear slightly in favor of their hero's defeat. In a nutshell, this is the nature of dramatic conflict. Each piece of information that allows the audience to perceive that Buffy will prevail must be followed by information that counters that perception. This makes the audience shift their perception back and forth and keeps them emotionally involved.

"Brechtian" Theatre and Television

Brechtian techniques pull the audience out of the emotional connection with the performance. While these techniques can be both visual and performative, visual signs can pull the audience out of the traditional viewing mode and into a more reflective mode. These techniques give the audience an opportunity to think about what they are watching.

What are the Brechtian Techniques? Brechtian techniques have been used for a long time, perhaps as long as there have been signs and actors. But Bertolt Brecht, a playwright and director, in a thoughtful work called *A Short Organum for the Theatre*, laid out a philosophical viewpoint that offered an alternative view (from Aristotle's view[3]) of how plays work. Included in this work were suggestions of techniques that could be used to influence the audience and work against the (at least to Brecht) numbing effects that theatre normally has on an audience.

Brecht was concerned with encouraging audiences to think rather than to become too involved in the story line and to identify with the characters. He developed a form of drama called epic theatre in which ideas — or didactic lessons — are important. In an epic theatre production, everything the audience sees, including the actor, or hears can lend itself to creating a distance between the audience and performance. This distance, sometimes called an aesthetic distance — a knowledge that what the audience is seeing is not actual — prevents the audience from storming the stage every time a friendly character gets in trouble. Audiences know, perhaps a bit below the conscious level, that the person in front of them is not in real danger. This person is not even a person, but a character in a play performed by actors. Nevertheless, audience members will continue to think of the actor as a character and to think of the character as "real" in order to travel the emotional journey. In Brecht's theatre, however, he wants the distance emphasized to encourage, not an emotional attachment, but an intellectual attachment.

Hence, the "epic" (narrative, non-dramatic) theatre is based on distance or detachment, on the alienation — or A-effect, achieved through a number of devices that remind the audience that they are presented with a demonstration of human behavior in scientific spirit rather than with an illusion of reality — or, to put it more simply, that the theatre is only a theatre and not the world itself.

It is essential to understand what happens in the audience when Brechtian techniques are used. The audience becomes involved with the action, yes. But the audience also becomes aware of the significance of the action. When audience members are pulled out of the action they are participating in, i.e., the traditional act of being emotionally involved in a play, and are, instead, made aware of the action itself, distance is created from that action and the object of that action. The play becomes an object to consider rather than an object to be experienced.

Specific Brechtian Devices

Brecht believed that devices could be used pull the audience out of the vicarious experience of living through the character. He believed that, specifically, the use of signs could distance the audience.

Signs can function in a number of ways. Signs can comment on the action. They can, for example, tell us what happens in the scene we are watching so that the dramatic tension deflates. Knowing who wins the race takes a lot of the emotional attachment out of the running of the race. Or the signs can comment on audience behavior. For example, we might see a sign revealed during a particularly emotional death scene, or good-bye scene, in which the audience is crying and carrying on. A sign during such a scene could say something like, "Why are you crying? This is only a play." A sign like this would bring the audience into the present moment — leaving behind the imaginative moment in which they are immersed in the action of the play — and allow the audience to reflect and evaluate why indeed they are crying. Such a moment would move them out of the emotive line of the play and into the theme or thought or argument of the play. Signs serve to distance the audience from the performance emotionally to allow them to think about and analyze what it is they are experiencing.

It is one thing to create a world that is strange and different in order to alienate the audience (something Brecht also believed in) and it is quite another to use a created world similar to a "normal" world to cause that alienation. Arguably, the dichotomy of the supernatural life of vampires and demons and the high school life of English class and study hall could be considered a device to alienate the audience from the characters to make us think. After all, the high school life of *Buffy* has a tendency to interrupt the forward motion of the supernatural story, pulling the audience into the "real" world of high school and out of the "imagined" world of the Slayer. In actuality, the high school world is there to ground the characters in an imagined world similar enough to our own to make them recognizable. The dissonance between Slayer world and high school world is more of a change of focus rather than a device that brings the audience out of direct connection with the story. The high school world is, after all, just as much a fiction as the Slayer world.

Finding Brechtian Devices

After such a lengthy discussion about Brechtian devices, two questions arise. First, what would lead an audience member to think that those devices are used in *Buffy* episodes? And second, if so, where can they be found?

The short answer to the second question is that signs, signs that comment on — and distance the audience from — the action, will, for the most part, be found in the background. These images could be written off as set dressing — posters and images that are put up on the set to create a realistic notion that the sets are actual places and not empty backgrounds. But that does not mean that these signs can be dismissed. Quite the opposite: signs in the medium of television often fulfill several functions, and, in *Buffy*, signs often create very particular effects. Knowing the general use of the sign in television and moving to a specific application of signs in *Buffy*[4] will lead to an understanding of how signs can push the audience away and make them think.

There are three main uses of signs in the television show. These are moments when audience members are expected to look at, read, or somehow process the sign put before them on the screen. These signs can be put into three categories: signs used for plot-related purposes, signs to be looked at because of the nature of the shot, and signs used for non-plot use.

First, there are signs — often in the background — that are used for plot-related purposes. These signs somehow indicate to the audience what may be happening in a particular episode. Each episode is a blank slate on which to write the scene; the audience discovers what things create meaning in their minds. The signs are clues as to what will be important to the plot of the particular episode.

Signs can, and often do, announce events happening around Sunnydale High. Signs announce special events, such as Career Day, Spring Fling, or the Sadie Hawkins Dance, to both the students and the audience, within the context of the plot. A large banner that says "Career Day" indicates to the audience the event that students are going to be involved in during this episode. It also announces to the students—i.e., the characters within the context of the plot—that an event is taking place. That the signs are there is logical; they announce that the event will be taking place in the high school. High schools put up signs announcing the Spring Fling, or Sadie Hawkins Day, or Homecoming. That is part of what high schoolers (and high schools) do. These signs make sense to the audience because they belong in the episode as much as character lines that establish the same events: "Have you got a date to the dance?" or "What are you doing at Career Day, Buffy? Don't you already, uh, have a, uh, career?" The set creators intend the audience members to look at and process signs in order to create context and support the lines. The important thing is that the audience is supposed to look at them. It gives them practice.

Signs can also be used in a logical, plot-oriented way to express the inner life of a character. Most often this kind of sign manifests itself in the interiors of individual characters' lockers and rooms. When the location of a scene takes place at the school, a great deal of the action of each episode happens outside the classroom and in front of lockers.[5] As the characters change classes, they move to their lockers for books, jackets, whatever is needed for the next place they are headed. As characters open their lockers, the audience sees the pictures and posters and flags that are on the inside, or back, of the locker door. Now, logically, those signs are put up by the characters themselves to decorate their lockers. The inside of the lockers have a tendency to be private places— lockers have locks on them after all—for personal expression. These locker signs can help the audience to see inside the characters.

For example, when Xander and Cordelia are having an on-going, secret physical affair, Cordelia makes no overt indication that she has any emotional attachment to Xander. In fact, in the face of his obvious affection for her, she treats him just the opposite: she tells him that she does not like him; she hides the relationship from her friends; and, instead, she talks trash about him to friends, often in his presence. It is, however, her locker that gives away her true feelings. When her locker opens, there are pictures of Xander and her together as a couple. Other characters discover these pictures—that is part of a plot episode—but they are not the first to see inside Cordelia's locker. The audience gets access first.

A quick flip book of the signage on Willow's locker reveals her growing interest in Wiccan arts, even as she starts to explore those arts as a character. The audience is invited into the inner world of a character each time one opens his or her locker. And those signs are there for the audience to see.

The same holds true of the rooms they live in. As high school students, the only places at home where they can express themselves are their bedrooms. The audience discovers a bit more about the characters when those characters are at home in their rooms. The audience, in effect, read the walls. The soft lighting and peaceful posters of Buffy's room are a stark contrast to the rock 'n' roll posters of Xander's room and an equal contrast to Willow's room of cork boards, science posters, and a prominent computer. The point here is that there ARE differences, that the differences in the rooms help reveal inner character just as the lockers do, and that the audience actively looks at the room to come to conclusions about the characters. The audience reads the room. The room is as much a sign to the inner life of a character as the Sadie Hawkins Dance sign is an indicator of the inner life of a high school.

But there are other ways, more mechanical ways, that an audience can be drawn in to read a sign. The second use of signs comes from the medium itself, television. Television has certain mechanics to tell a story, such as establishing shots and two shots that direct an audience's focus to a particular thing. And in directing the audience's attention, the audience sees what is in the shot and is influenced by how the shot is made.

A quick example of signs in action can come from an establishing shot. It is the opening shot or sequence of shots used to set the scene. Frequently an exterior shot is used to "establish" where the scene is taking place. In the case of *Buffy*, before we see any hall shots of Sunnydale High, there is an exterior shot of the building itself, letting the audience know that it is in this building where the next scene will take place. Often, the establishing shot is a series or sequence of shots that helps create this context quickly. For example: Shot of exterior of Sunnydale High, followed by shot of interior hallway with medium shot of "Career Day" banner strung between two columns, followed by a wide shot of a common area in the schools with many tables set up and many students milling from table to table. Within the "establishing shot" sequence, the "Career Day" banner is a sign that the audience is meant to read in order to understand why students are milling around tables ("What's My Line, Part One").

It helps to think of the television mechanics in their totality. There is, actually, a term for this: *mise en scène*. The *mise en scène* is the staging of the action for the camera: the physical objects, the arrangement of those objects, the costumes, lighting, and actor movement. All of this is the *mise en scène*.

In creating a particular shot, the director considers all the elements. For example, if two characters are talking, the director might want to frame those two characters in a medium shot. This is called a two shot. Two characters are in the frame together interacting. There are many ways to set up such a shot, and how the shot is set up directs the audience to look at different things. What the audience sees will depend, often, on how the characters get into, and out of, the shot, and what is in the background. If the shot is first established and the characters walk into the frame, then whatever was in the frame to begin with has a moment of focus. Similarly, if the characters walk out of the frame and the shot lingers a moment on the background, then that background has temporary focus. Finally, if two characters are in the shot, facing each other with a bit of space between them, then whatever might be in the shot between them also has focus. For example, the action is that two characters walk down the hallway talking. One stops to confront the other, to say something important. To capture the action, the camera points to a part of the hallway that has a poster; the two characters walk into the frame, have their say, and one walks out. The other character is left, alone and sighing, next to the wall with the poster. The second character leaves the shot, leaving only the poster on the wall.

In this example, the poster has focus in three different ways. First, it is in the shot before any character is and therefore is sitting before the audience. Second, it sits in the background for the duration of the scene, sitting between the two characters as they confront each other. Third, when the last character leaves the shot, the camera lingers on it for a brief moment.

To extend this imaginary example further: these two characters are somehow knowledgeable about vampire Slaying. One is good at it; the other is not. In fact the other who is not a good Slayer is, in fact, a very bad Slayer. The confrontation is about the good Slayer telling the bad Slayer not to go out alone looking for vampires. No good will come of it. The no-good Slayer will hear none of this; he/she is going to go out and Slay the evil ones. The good Slayer storms off; the bad Slayer sighs and walks off.

A blank wall creates both mechanical and psychological problems for television production: it causes light to bounce (mechanical) and the audience doesn't see the blank wall as a "real" place (psychological). So, something must be on the wall. If the invented poster is an inspirational message — something like "Carpe Diem: Seize the Day"— the scene might have a different effect on the audience than if the poster were one of the many Red Cross Blood Drive ("I'm Giving Blood Today") signs littered across the halls of Sunnydale.

A scene such as the one above allows the audience to pull away from the plot and character-driven argument and, if only for a brief moment, instead to focus on a process or technique of television production. Television has a name for this non-narrative method of drawing attention to the making of a television show: it is called the reflexive mode.

Finally, there is one last category of signs which are intended to be seen but are not part of the narrative plot structure, or — as I said before — not for plot use. Often the background signs will reflect a non-plot related message, though one appropriate for high schoolers. These signs are often considered set decoration, i.e., they create a realistic environment rather than blank walls to set the scene in. Driver safety signs, stay in school signs or — in an ironic twist — signs that encourage students to give blood. But these signs need not be posters. Often in Sunnydale classrooms, chalkboards will be rife with lesson plans and quotations from the particular text being studied. These signs might have nothing to do with the particular plot, though they may illuminate it a bit.

There is one particular sign worth mentioning. It may appear to be only as a sidebar, in that the sign itself has no bearing or commentary on the plot.[6] It is seen all over Sunnydale, not just the high school or the students' rooms. It is a sign advertising a particular band (a band from the "real world," not the *Buffy*verse) called Widespread Panic. Setting aside for the moment the irony of the band's name and focusing instead on the placement of signs that advertise the band, something interesting emerges. The signs themselves are small, oval signs with two capital letters on them: WP. The signs are small, unobtrusive, black letters on a white background, and they are in almost every scene. They appear on lockers, on a bulletin board, on the bathroom wall, stuck to the wall in the Bronze — literally anywhere.

Considered in isolation, the WP stickers do not give us much to discuss in terms of Brechtian techniques. Their placement may be simply an inside joke by a set designer or member of the production team whose favorite band is Widespread Panic. But the placement of these stickers has sparked websites that tally the WP sightings. A Widespread Panic (the band) blog had a trivia question on its web site asking, "Which popular TV show featured Widespread Panic's Black and White Oval WP sticker in at least 13 episodes?" (*Nothing*). Those audience members clued in to seeing the WP signs find enjoyment not just from the episode, but also from stepping out of the episode when they notice one of these stickers. This puts at least some of the audience members into the "Where's Waldo?" frame of mind — looking at the background for signs that might be there.

Buffy *Episodes*

Looking at episodes even from only the first two seasons of *Buffy*, we can see fine examples that shed light on the way signs can point up the action in some way and give the audience an opportunity to step back and look at the show in a more objective manner. These moments ask the audience to remove themselves from the emotional involvement of the performance and instead ask the audience to analyze the significance of the moment.

The first example is from the very first episodes: "Welcome to the Hellmouth/The Harvest." The season premiere from 1997 was a two-hour event in which the first two episodes played back-to-back. In these episodes, Angel appears as an enigmatic figure, as a figure who knows both of vampires and of Slayers, but is not in either camp. He seems to be very knowledgeable on the subject of Slayers and vampires and on the particular event that is happening: the Harvest. Though a suspicious character, always appearing in the wrong place at the wrong time, he does not (by his own admittance) appear to bite.

At the end of the episode, Buffy has succeeded in staving off the vampires and in killing the Master's lead vampire, Luke. She turns to two lesser vampires. The vampires panic and run. Outside, the vampires run down the alley and past Angel who stands in a doorway behind some crates stacked against a wall. He watches the vampires run, then looks back the other way. He says, "She did it! I'll be damned!" He walks off camera. The camera lingers on the door which displays the words, "Watch Your Step."

What exactly "watch your step" may mean is open to discussion. It could mean nothing. The sign certainly works within the logical framework of the episode and works as set dressing, nothing more. It is simply a sign on a door that leads to a rickety staircase that requires users to pay attention to their footing. But the sign is associated by the shot to a character who has yet to be fully defined. Perhaps the sign means something about Angel. Or the sign may be associated with the line, "She did it! I'll be damned!" Perhaps Buffy, who seemed to dispatch the villains handily in this instance, needs to watch her step in future episodes. Maybe Angel needs to watch his step with Buffy: she is the Slayer. Maybe Buffy needs to watch her step with Angel: he is a vampire. Maybe.... The sign is there. It lingers in the shot for the audience to view as a character lurking in the shadows runs off. The sign does not read "Employee Entrance" or "Staff Only" or nothing at all. So the question arises, why is it there?

It comes to mind that such signs on doors might be considered happy coincidence: the production team just happened to find an alleyway that contains a door with the words "Watch Your Step." It is good to point out here that television sets are expensive to build and are often used over and over again. It is certainly true of this particular alley. This alley is seen in many of, if not all of, the first few episodes of *Buffy*. It is often redecorated with crates and boxes and cars and trashcans, but it is the "lurking alleyway" set for Buffy. It may, indeed have been happy coincidence that someone decided to put "Watch Your Step" on the door of the vampire show set, but in framing the shot to include the sign, the director (for this episode, John Kretchmer) chooses to put the sign in the shot. In doing so, happy accident is swept aside in favor of the artistic decisions of the production team.

The second example comes from the very end of Season One in "Prophecy Girl." One of the sub-plots of the season is Xander's romantic feelings toward Buffy. He speaks of this with his best friend, Willow, though never to Buffy herself. He is afraid of being shot down, and this fear in part keeps him from getting too close to Buffy. His romantic feelings, however, keep him moving closer and closer to her as he (and the audience) know more about her. In the final episode of Season One, Xander gathers his courage and asks her out, revealing his feelings. Buffy gently lets him down, telling him that she does not feel the same way about him, and she does not want to spoil their friendship with complicated relationships. In his fragile state, Xander escapes to an empty classroom. Willow follows him to console him.

On the open door to the classroom is a poster. It is a "Just Say No" poster — similar to those that suggest that taking drugs is wrong. This poster, however, is not a poster about drugs; its image, just below the lettering, has nothing to do with drugs. It is, instead, a picture of two people, a boy and a girl, embracing and kissing. As Willow and Xander talk, the poster is sitting between them.

This sign acts as commentary on an event from the (immediate) past. This poster points to the immediate past event and, perhaps, its emotional impact on Xander. The poster is also, perhaps, humorous, though the scene is a rather dramatic one. Buffy just said no to Xander; Xander has to say no to his aspirations; Willow is continuing to say no to her (unexpressed) feelings for Xander.[7] Everyone is just saying, "No." This sign might work in a similar way to the sign mentioned earlier that Brecht might have used: "Why are you crying? This is only television."

The third example is of a sign that comments, not on future or past events of the characters, but on the audience itself. There is no doubt that *Buffy* built a following during Season One. Its anticipated second season opener attracted attention from its loyal viewers. The beginning of the first episode of that second season, "When She Was Bad," offers us a comment on that loyal viewership.

The scene takes place in the school lounge. Buffy, Xander, and Willow are eating lunch. They are talking about dreams, specifically Buffy's dreams, and appear to be enjoying themselves, though Buffy, as is often the case, seems a bit distracted. We get a shot of Willow, sitting on the couch alone. Over her shoulder, on the wall behind, is a poster. It says, "Do you arrange your schedule around this habit?" and shows a cartoonish picture of people sitting around watching television.

Even if this does not directly point up the audience's habit of, indeed, arranging their schedule around *Buffy*, it does point up the idea of people watching television to an audience that is watching television: it is putting the audience who notices the poster into a "reflexive mode." Die-hard fans who see the poster would probably laugh, recognizing their own habit.

In the same episode is an example of a sign helping us with an emotive moment for a particular character. At the very end of the episode, Buffy is talking to Giles and walking to class. She is feeling bad and, according to Giles and by her own admission, is punishing herself for her bad behavior. She does not know whether she can face her friends. She did, after all, put them in mortal danger, nearly getting their throats slit. When she gets to the classroom, Giles leaves her, and she takes a moment to gird herself to face her friends. She slowly walks into the room. As she does, the shot moves inside the room. The camera focuses on the book assignment for the month: a book of essays about peace. The word "peace" and a dove figure prominently on the cover of the book. Buffy walks into frame, pausing directly in front of the book, takes a breath, walks to her friends, and makes peace with them.

This example points up several factors involved in this discussion of signs. First, the sign is an outward sign of an inward feeling, Buffy's feeling and her friends' feelings. Second, the sign comes from an assignment put up on the wall and is, thus, a different kind of sign. Certainly it is set dressing, but it is not a poster or words on a door, but an academic plan that was put up specifically for this classroom.

The final example comes from the Valentine's Day episode of the second season, "Bewitched, Bothered, and Bewildered." In it, all the women of Sunnydale fall for Xander, including Buffy. At one point in the action, Xander has the opportunity to experience what he has always wanted: a romantic interlude with Buffy. She throws herself at him — and he refuses her. At the end of the episode, they talk of this: how he really would like to have a throw at her, so to speak, how he had a chance and he declined, and how she appreciated his reserve. In the background is a poster with one big word on it: "OPPORTUNITY."

This is a good example of the audience seeing the topic of the scene without ever hearing it mentioned. Interestingly, turning down opportunity is actually the topic.

Signs to Be Read

These examples should whet the appetite of the *Buffy* fan and encourage potential audience members to examine the episodes for visual cues to the significance of moments in *Buffy*. For the most part, these signs offer an interruption of the usual way audience members view a performance. As I said at the beginning, audiences receive information from the performance and — based on the information — create perceptions, perceptions of what characters are like and of what might happen next. These perceptions shift, depending on what new information audience members may receive from the performance they are viewing. These perceptions and shifts flow together to create both a dramatic tension in, and an emotional connection with, the performance. Brechtian signs interrupt that flow and, if even for a moment, pull the audience out of their emotional connection with a performance. In removing the audience from the spell of emotional connection, these signs ask them to consider thoughtfully what they are watching. In doing so the audience may consider the significance of the moment, or question their attachment to the moment, or even recognize that they — as an audience — are part of the moment and its significance.

This kind of audience-performance interaction makes for a more-complex relationship between the art form and the audience than simply passive viewing. *Buffy* takes full advantage of the medium of television and the conventions and strategies used therein in order to offer the audience a multifaceted experience. *Buffy* is no simple folk tune, and, while it might not be a symphony either, its relationship with its audience is made richer by the use of these Brechtian devices.

Notes

1. For further reading on Brecht: *Brecht: A Choice of Evils* by M. Esslin (1959); *Brecht: The Man and His Work* by M. Esslin (1959); *Bertolt Brecht* by R. Gray (1961); *The Art of Bertolt Brecht* by W. Weideli (1963); *Bertolt Brecht* by F. Ewen (1967); *Bertolt Brecht* by W. Haas (1968); *Understanding Brecht* by W. Benjamin (1973); *Brecht as They Knew Him*, ed. by H. Witt (1975); *Bertolt Brecht in America* by James K. Lyon (1981); *Brecht in Exile* by Bruce Cook (1983); *Brecht* by R. Hayman (1983); *Bertolt Brecht* by J.Speirs (1987); *The Poetry of Brecht*, by P.J. Thompson (1989); *Postmodern Brecht* by E. Wright (1989); *Brecht* by Hans Mayer (1996); *Brecht & Co.* by John Fuegi (1997); *Brecht-Chronik* by Klaus Völker (1997); *Bertolt Brecht* by G. Berg (1998).

2. This short chapter will only use examples from the first two seasons in order to restrict the massive scope of the topic.

3. Aristotle said that a theatre experience should be a cathartic one, one in which an audience is so caught up in and so empathetic to the "hero" that the audience feels as if the events are happening to them.

4. *Buffy* made it to seven seasons. That's a lot of signs. So, as I said, for the purpose of this argument and to contain that argument in space shorter than from New York to San Francisco, I'm going to concentrate on only two seasons: One and Two.

5. In the commentary for "Welcome to the Hellmouth," Whedon says the Buffy production took place in a warehouse in Santa Monica on a very tight budget. He said that the school hall was only the "one hall, so we use it over and over again."

6. Or we can say that there is irony in the signage: if the "regular" student of Sunnydale High School knew the extent — or even the existence — of the monster population in Sunnydale, there would be widespread panic.

7. In recognizing what will come of the ephemeral boyfriend/girlfriend relations between Xander and Willow in future episodes, we can see foreshadowing here — and an unheeded warning.

"The Ants Go Marching"

Effective Lyrics in Buffy *Episodes*

~~~

Lori M. Butler

Much has been written about the musical themes and scores pertaining to this long running series;[1] however, few have discussed the lyrics of the songs. Music is an asset to the episodes, but the lyrics are the subliminal narrative. Lyrics play many diverse roles in *Buffy*: lyrics explain how the characters feel, they describe the mood of the scene, and they even foreshadow what will happen later. Just as the Greek chorus in ancient drama, the lyrics tell the audience significant pieces of information, if only they listen. The lyrics echo mood and feelings and add humor, however grim or dark.

The music in each episode of *Buffy* directly correlates with the issues the young Slayer and her gang must face. The lyrics themselves often take the same role as the Greek chorus in drama, offering "comment on the action of the antagonists" and expressing the "judgment of objective bystanders, compassionate and intelligent, representative of the best morality of the community" (Frye). The chorus gives background information to help the audience follow the performance, comments on main themes, and expresses feelings that the actors themselves cannot. Furthermore, the chorus draws in the audience and makes it feel a part of the play, much as the song lyrics in *Buffy*.

Rhonda Wilcox, in *Why Buffy Matters*, states that *Buffy* "is a work of music and sound" (13). Katy Stephens calls the music "an ethereal piece, complete with siren song," in part of a larger discussion of the significance of sound in *Buffy* (qtd. in Wilcox); S. Renee Dechert states, "Music is almost omnipresent on Buffy, appearing either in the background to enhance a scene, such as the song 'No Heroes' when Joyce drops Buffy off at school on her first day, or as an essential component of the plot, like the Flamingoes' 'I Only Have Eyes for You' in an episode named for the song" (218).

Listeners and critics alike find a union between the lyrics chosen and the issues in each episode: "Simply put, music is at the heart of the Scooby Gang and Buffy. Indeed, it functions as a form of rhetorical discourse every bit as important as the lines the characters speak" (Dechert 219). The song lyrics themselves add that extra something to help us understand the significance of each event.

Considering the quality of the series, all of the songs must be intentional. The music, or lack of music, emphasizes what we are seeing. It is, in effect, allowing us to hear as well as see what is important. The lyrics come sometimes as background and at other times from bands performing at the Bronze. However presented, one important element is always the lyrics.

The lyrics, in addition, give us a closer look at our own reality, tying us to the series because the songs exist in the "real" world as well as the *Buffy*-verse. By adding a human quality, the lyrics pull us in so that we find ourselves relating to the storyline on a personal level.

Humor/Irony

Lyrics often inject humor into otherwise grim situations. In *Buffy*, in Season Six, for example, the main characters have forgotten who they are because of one of Willow's spells. As Xander, Willow, Tara, and Dawn trek through the sewers to escape vampires, Dawn sings, "The ants go marching one by one, hurrah, hurrah," which makes a serious situation rather comical. Also, the lyrics comment on the scene being played out ("Tabula Rasa"). Dawn and the others, much like ants, are oblivious to reality and live in the miniscule world of *Buffy*dom (the kingdom of the Slayer), just as we might find ourselves marching like ants through our own lives in mindless routine.

In Season Seven, events make for an intense, serious season, but lyrics tend to lighten the situations at times. In "Same Time, Same Place," Willow returns to Sunnydale but no one can see her because she has inadvertently cast an invisibility spell on herself by worrying about what her friends think. A sing-song, skin-eating demon captures her, and, since Buffy and Xander cannot see and rescue her, the demon begins to eat Willow's flesh, as he sings about Willow being "locked away in nice, white skin." Gross, yes, but he chants those words in a childlike singsong. Dark humor may offer a brief respite from the horror of watching someone being eaten alive.

In "Him," when Dawn, Buffy, and later, Anya and Willow gaze upon R.J., the letter-jacketed boy of whom they are all ardently enamored, the "Theme to *A Summer Place*" by Max Steiner[2] plays. Each is convinced that the boy loves her — and only her. Squabbles occur, and the spell is broken when Xander destroys the bespelled letter jacket.

With *Buffy*, the lyrics function not only as ironic humor but also as commentary. Season Three begins with a quest. In the first episode, the band at the Bronze plays Bellylove's "Back to Freedom," a song about finding a way back to freedom after being confined. The Scooby Gang wonders where Buffy is and if she will return. These lyrics are almost ironic: if Buffy returns, Sunnydale offers anything but freedom to her. However, the gang will have more freedom and security once the Slayer returns because they will not have to patrol anymore. They can return that job to the Slayer herself.

Another ironic twist in lyrics is in "Faith, Hope, and Trick," when the band sings Third Eye Blind's "The Background," about the quiet. Things are anything but quiet as Buffy dreams she is at the Bronze, dancing with Angel. Quiet is not a word that would be congruent with Buffy's life. Once again, our modern pop Greek chorus, or song lyrics, helps us make sense of what is happening.

In "Homecoming," lyrics paired with actions set up the ironic twist. Romantic music plays as Willow and Xander discuss Oz and Cordelia, their respective "significant others," and then they end up kissing one another. The lyrics of Lisa Loeb's "How" echo what we feel, asking how hearts feel and how someone can continue to breathe when so involved. Willow and Xander are confused because they have just betrayed the people they loved, but they feel something for one another at the same time. How can they know what to feel? How can they even breathe with this revelation of love in their hearts and on their minds?

Twists and turns continue. In "Revelations," the Dingoes Ate My Baby sing Four Star Mary's "Run," about walking together, and, later, Buffy tells Faith she can trust Buffy. It is as though the music reinforces the idea that Buffy will walk at Faith's side if Faith will let her. Yet another twist occurs in "Lover's Walk" when we see each of the characters suffering from love lost because of Spike's actions: Angel tells Buffy she should go away; Cordelia tells Xander to stay away from her; and Willow and Oz are left alone thinking of each other. The twist presents itself at the close of the episode when Spike drives out of town, singing Sinatra's "I Did It My Way!" at the top of his lungs in a spectacular twist. Spike destroys every person's life in this episode and turns out to be the only one happy in the end.

In "The Prom," several instances of musical irony and dark humor present themselves. Buffy tells the Scooby Gang, "You'll have a normal prom even if I have to kill everyone in Sunnydale." This same dark humor and irony can be found in the Kool & the Gang's song "Celebrate" as Buffy battles the Hellhounds trained to attack people in formal wear. Yes indeed, these are good times to celebrate. However, we also hear "Praise You" by Fat Boy Slim.[3] Although Buffy has not known that the class is even aware that she has helped them keep down the body count, they praise her and she ends up winning "Class Protector" at the end of the prom.

Foreshadowing

In addition to adding humor, lyrics in *Buffy* often foreshadow crucial events. Beginning in the first episode of Season One, "Welcome to the Hellmouth," listeners at the Bronze hear Sprung Monkey's "Believe" about finding the way and being lost. In fact, the lyrics foreshadow the quest that we will watch Buffy undertake: she spends the next seven seasons trying to find her way. Buffy is constantly questioning where she fits and what she is supposed to do. In the next episode, "The Harvest," Dashboard Prophets' "Wearing Me Down," about fighting and wearing someone down, is in the background. Buffy is fighting the good fight against evil, and she might prevail. To some extent, Buffy is wearing down evil as a whole, even as she herself is worn by battle. In "Reptile Boy," Angel asks Buffy out for coffee sometime and the listener hears the background song, Louie Say's "She," about a girl who loves but then takes that love away, which foreshadows not only one but several long torturous relationships in which Buffy cannot fully give what she receives.

In "The Harsh Light of Day," Buffy seems to be in two separate relationships: one with Parker, a potential boyfriend, and the other with Spike, a definite enemy at this point. At the beginning of the episode, Buffy and Parker run into Spike with Harmony (his off and on girlfriend) at a fraternity party. The music offers a couple of comments on the situation. As Bif Naked's "Moment of Weakness," about being taken for granted, plays, the possibilities are endless. Spike obviously takes Harmony for granted and simply uses her. At the same time, Spike also takes Buffy for granted because he dismisses her strength and duties. In addition, Parker takes Buffy for granted and leaves her because he takes all women for granted.

In another episode, "All the Way," a new relationship almost arises as an old relationship falls apart; we have intimations of this early in the episode. Dawn and her friend sneak out of the house to spend Halloween night with a couple of boys. As they are playing teenage pranks on the neighborhood, Nikka Costa's song "Everybody Got Their Something" plays in the background. The "something" these boys have is a secret: they are vampires. Dawn's attempt at a relationship ends with her literally putting a stake through the guy's heart. At the same time, it seems that Tara and Willow are falling apart because Willow is overusing her powers. As Tara and Willow look around the Bronze through the help of magic, Man of the Year's "Just as Nice" echoes what each of them feels: "you just simply don't understand."[4] Tara does not understand why Willow must use magic for everything, and Willow does not understand why Tara is so opposed.

The concept of being wrong is reiterated and prefigured in "Wrecked," in which Willow makes some bad choices. Amy takes Willow to see Rack, a dark magic practitioner. (He's like a drug dealer offering a quick "fix" to his customers, who all seem too strung out to notice the effects of his nasty little drug.)

The background "Black Cat Bone" by Laika emphasizes the evil of the situation and warns about what's coming. Something is coming: major withdrawal after addiction for Willow. And this is only the beginning of the bad things to come.

In Season Six's "Seeing Red," Willow becomes enraged and vengeful when Warren shoots Buffy and a stray bullet also hits and kills Tara. Azure Ray's "Displaced" echoes exactly what Willow is feeling: nothing survives, someone falls, someone else still stands. Each word penetrates the heart, reinforcing what we know Willow feels, that she will not survive when she is left standing alone. Her true love has been ripped from her, her best friend may be dying, and all that is left is hatred. This hatred rages through the next episodes and does not end until the last episode of Season Six.

Later on, in Season Seven's "The Killer in Me," some resolution comes for Willow. Kennedy, one of the potential Slayers, finds herself attracted to Willow and feigns an illness to spend alone time with Willow. Kennedy convinces Willow to go to the Bronze with her. As Kennedy is putting the moves on Willow and Willow lets down her guard, the song in the background echoes these words: "I can be happy again" (Aberdeen, "Cities and Buses").[5] Up to this point, Willow has not thought of looking for anyone else; she has been content to wallow in her loss of Tara. Finally, a turning point has emerged, and Willow will try for happiness once more, lyrics again both prophetic and reflective.

In "Touched," bonds form as impending doom lurks in Sunnydale. Faith and Robin Woods (the principal of Sunnydale High) come together to share an intimate moment before the apocalypse just as Willow and Kennedy, Xander and Anya, and even Buffy and Spike share some quality time (just of a different nature from the others). Lyrics from Heather Nova's "It's Only Love" about losing the feeling of love and about all eternity play in the background, reflecting the moment and presaging what is to come. Yes, the characters feel the love at that point, and, in the end, love will save the day. Spike gives his life, or his inner light, to save them all because of his love for Buffy. But, even so, he knows Buffy does not love him (he has lost love). Still, the events will resonate through eternity. And, speaking of the grand finale, what better way to end our vision of Spike than to see the light coming from him and hear his parting words to Buffy about school being out for the summer, which are lyrics he is quoting from a heavy metal song, "School's Out," by Alice Cooper. School, or life, is out, or over, but there's no moan from Spike, only a joyous — and slightly Spike-ish sardonic — paean. Again, lyrics, an integral part of *Buffy the Vampire Slayer*, reflect, reinforce, and foreshadow.

Commentary

In *Buffy*, lyrics also often comment on and/or reinforce the situation or characterization. Music and lyrics become two separate entities when listeners distinguish between the level and roles each plays. Music is significant and does set mood. However, lyrics are what give us the words that reinforce the meaning of scenes. One episode, in particular, emphasizes music and lyrics which show how characters feel: "Once More, With Feeling." In that episode, the characters must sing about their feelings and the secrets they have been keeping. Xander and Anya sing about the nasty little quirks that each has and that never get mentioned because "God knows I'll never tell." Tara sings of being under Willow's spell. Giles sings of being in the way. More significantly, Buffy sings that she needs "something to sing about," and, later, she tells the Scooby Gang in song that she thinks she was in heaven (on a minor chord) but was yanked from paradise when they resurrect her. Every song in this episode reveals another secret, and the closing song asks, "Where do we go from here?" The question becomes pertinent as the characters wonder how to move on from knowing the now-exposed secrets. It is too bad this episode does not come until Season Six because then we can truly realize the significance of lyrics in the series itself: this episode might be the first time that we pay attention to the words of the songs. The words, emphasized in this particular episode, are also present in many episodes in which they seemingly go unnoticed.

Aside from the one musical episode, other episodes directly link song lyrics and the event of the scene. In "Prophecy Girl," the listener hears "I Fall to Pieces" by Patsy Cline as Xander wallows in his rejection by Buffy. He even comments that country music is "the music of pain." Buffy may have rejected Xander's advances, but it is the lyrics to the song that increase our sadness and reveal to us how bad we are supposed to feel about this sad situation.

In "Bargaining, Parts One and Two," a vampire in a Hanson shirt fights the Buffybot, a robot version of Buffy which is substituting for her after she dies at the end of Season Five. The Buffybot malfunctions during the fight. Later, that particular vampire enters a monster bar where Static X's "Permanence," about the extremes of and conflict between ice and fire, reflects the chaos of life in Sunnydale without Buffy. Everything is mixed up and not quite right with Buffy gone. The monsters create more chaos in Sunnydale even as the resurrected Buffy is fighting the chaos that has overtaken her mind as a result of being torn from heaven.

In "Tabula Rasa," the episode ends with Buffy sitting at the Bronze alone, hearing Michelle Branch's "Goodbye to You." Tara is packing and moving out because she and Willow have broken up. Giles is on a plane going back to England. Our chorus tells us this is a sad story, a story in which everything means goodbye.

Some lyrics reflect the loneliness and separation that the characters experience. In "Conversations with Dead People," the First Evil (the really bad guy in Season Seven) plays the role of different people (people who have died) to make each character feel alone and separated from the group. The First takes on the shape of Cassie, a girl who dies of a heart attack after being rescued from a demon, and pretends to be speaking for Tara. Willow almost buys into the act. Dawn is alone at home when the First pretends to be her mother who tells her to be careful of Buffy because Buffy won't take care of her. Buffy is alone at the cemetery. Lyrics of "Blue" by Angie Hart and Joss Whedon resonate with the isolation each group member experiences. Everyone seems to stand alone, just as in the story of the man in the moon: no one around, no united front, just each individual to fend for him/her self.

In the following episode, "Sleeper," the focus turns to Spike, who is being controlled by a song. Spike's mother, when Spike was the human William, used to sing the English folksong "Early One Morning" to him. The song asks, "How could you use a poor maiden so?" This song is a trigger for the First Evil to make Spike do evil things that he does not remember. The lyrics not only change Spike to pure evil but also exemplify the actions taken. Spike kills and destroys souls without remembering it: how can he "use a poor maiden so?" At the same time, he tears apart his own soul as bits of memories come flying back. He even attempts to retrace his steps and show Buffy what he has done so that she can help him correct what is wrong. Pieces of two other songs echo the sentiment of the now soul-possessing Spike: we hear a line about shame from Aimee Mann's "This Is How It Goes"[6] as Spike tries to remember what he has done. Later Aimee Mann sings again: "we can't talk about it" (Aimee Mann, "Pavlov's Bell").[7] Can Spike talk to Buffy, or anyone for that matter, about what is happening to him? Can he ask for help? The lyrics assert uncertainty; Spike is uncertain of his future.

Audience Voice

Buffy, because of its premise, does not reveal the consensus of the people of Sunnydale, which, in any case, would involve mistaking vampires for gangs on drugs ("The Harvest"), but it does contain lyrics that represent the consensus of large numbers, such as the entire Scooby Gang. Season Two's "Surprise" allows us a deeper insight into Buffy and Angel's relationship. Buffy dreams of Drusilla killing Angel and Cari Howe's "Anything" in the background is about finding love. With Buffy, the audience hopes that this is true, that Buffy will find love and Angel will not be killed.

Disappointed in Angel because he has left her to go to Los Angeles (and the *Angel* series), Buffy rejects others. In "I Only Have Eyes for You," the band sings Splendid's "Charge," about a girl who loves in a way that cannot be understood as Buffy rejects a guy from her math class. Further into the same episode, the background song is "I Only Have Eyes for You" by the Flamingoes. We watch Buffy and Angel play out the roles of two star-crossed lovers. We know that, like the two lovers, Buffy and Angel are at odds, but have had eyes for each other before. At the end of Season Two, after Buffy has stabbed Angel to close the mouth of hell, Sarah McLachlan's "Full of Grace" in the background proclaims words of strength and courage, yet also says the current place is not the right place. Buffy leaves Sunnydale and her friends and family behind. Her mother has told her not to come back if she leaves the house, not really meaning it. Buffy leaves because she feels unwanted and also because she desperately needs a change. It would take more courage than she has at this point to stay and face everyone after all of the secrets and lies. The audience wants her to have more courage, to face the "demons" that are her non-vampire-killing life.

Other strange relationship twists happen when werewolf Veruca[8] begins to hit on Oz. In "Beer Bad," a female singer, Veruca, makes eyes at Oz as she wails about flesh and its realities in THC's "Overfire." The words not only seem to foreshadow an affair between these two characters (which they do), but they also make the point that there are other places with other realities. Two episodes later in "Wild at Heart," Veruca sings about attachment in THC's "Dip." Oz, Xander, and Giles are entranced by her. She will twist their feelings—and challenge their morals. The audience sees that is happening—and its inevitability. And later, Oz is shown trying to twist away from her—as well as from his guilt—for what he is doing to Willow when he liaises with Veruca. Still later, as Oz talks to Veruca, THC's "Need to Destroy" lyrics are about not being caught or encircled. We might question: Who won't be encircled? Oz? Veruca? Or both of them? But we see that all are caught in a net (a circular net) of circumstance. We find out that Veruca is a werewolf like Oz, and the two of them end up physical together. This affair is an awful twist which leaves Willow outside the circle, and Oz trying to straighten everything out.

As a result of this horrible act, sadness consumes Willow. In "Something Blue," Willow attempts to forget Oz by drowning her sorrows with beer. In the background, Blink-182's "All the Small Things" proclaims the lights should go out, someone should go home, but that someone does not want to go. The lyrics emphasize the most significant part of the scene: Willow wants someone to say it's not true, that her love with Oz is not going away; she wants someone to take her home and turn the lights off so she can forget what happened. We want that too. We want this relationship to work; it is a good one.

In "Doomed," which is the next episode, the Hellacopters' "Hey" asks about someone wanting to help. Willow is at a fraternity party feeling a little lost. She is trying to forget Oz when she sees Percy, a guy she tutored in high school. She tries to talk to him to forget how bad she feels and only ends up feeling worse when Percy tells his girlfriend Willow is a loser, which Willow overhears. She has helped Percy out, but he will not help her out in her time of need. We, the audience, are in tune with those background words; we want to help our favorite geek.

In "Lie to Me," in the background, we hear the band croon the song (and episode) title (by Shawn Clement and Sean Murray), "Lie to Me," as Angel tells

Buffy he stayed in all night and read. We — and Buffy — know otherwise. We, the audience, are aware, as Buffy is aware that all is not right. In "The Yoko Factor," Giles sings the infamous "Free Bird" by Lynyrd Skynyrd. The lyrics are significant. Riley finds out about Buffy and Angel's "moment of happiness" (in which they love and he turns into the evil Angelus) and will leave soon because he knows there is nothing to his relationship with Buffy. Also, Giles will leave Buffy soon and return to England. The lyrics seem to ask the questions that Giles wants answered by Buffy. Will she remember him and everything he has taught her? Giles continues questioning what will happen even when he is ready to leave; he is still concerned with how Buffy will do without him. We worry about that too.

In Season Five, new relationships emerge, and again lyrics emphasize the feelings of the characters involved — and of the audience. In "Family," Melanie Doane's "I Can't Take My Eyes Off You" is about obsession as Willow and Tara float above the dance floor in a slow dance at Tara's birthday party. The lyrics proclaim what is seen in the scene: Willow is falling in love with Tara. Love has consumed her, and she cannot look away from Tara. We also are fascinated.

Another relationship that evolves is that of Spike and his love for Buffy. In "Crush," the band at the Bronze sings Summercamp's "Thing of the Past" about love, confusion, and anxiety as we see Buffy and Spike sitting at a table where Spike is attempting to carry on a conversation. The episode closes with another band singing Devics's "Key," about staying around as Spike takes Drusilla to the Bronze in hopes of making Buffy jealous. He has no intentions of staying with Dru, but he will stay in Sunnydale for Buffy. Lyrics help the audience empathize with the love, confusion, anxiety, and ambivalence.

Yet another bizarre relationship that is never truly realized is that of Joyce, Buffy's mom, and Giles, Buffy's Watcher. In "Forever," Giles mourns the death of Joyce as Cream sings "Songs of Brave Ulysses" being tormented by the sirens. In other circumstances (like "Band Candy"), Joyce could have been Giles's siren, but she's gone. She saw Giles not only as the stuffy librarian but also as Ripper, the young rebellious guy he used to be. Of course, he still is rebellious, but only Joyce understood him well enough to know that — after Jenny (Giles's girlfriend) was gone. Again the lyrics help the audience mourn the lost possibilities.

In "Smashed," Willow sits at a table alone at the Bronze watching Amy (who has been a rat, literally, for the last couple of years) dance with some boys. The song (Virgil's "Vermillion Borders") echoes her isolation and loneliness. She is caught in the corner because she feels she should stay (she feels guilty for Amy being a rat for so long), but she really wants to be at home. She is also cornered by magic. The lyrics facilitate the audience's recognition of her capture — in both senses.

"Grave" concludes Season Six with a look into anger created from loss and the love that triumphs over such a bad feeling. Sarah McLachlan's "The Prayer of St. Francis" sets the mood, as it gives us hope in the place of despair, light in the place of darkness, joy for sadness, and life for death. The words, simple and direct, state exactly what is in the episode. Willow feels hate; Xander brings her love. What Willow is doing is wrong; Xander brings her forgiveness. She is in despair; Xander offers her hope. Willow is consumed by shadows of what happened to Tara; he brings her back into the light with his friendship. He comforts her, understands her, and loves her. No words better set the mood than these lyrics. We see redemption and echo the prayer.

Conclusion

Humor, foreshadowing, irony, commentary, and mood are all displayed for us by both actions on screen and lyrics that tell us about what we are seeing. The lyrics demonstrate and reinforce what is significant. As we watch, we become absorbed in a world full of literal demons, relating them to our everyday figurative demons. Through the trials and tribulations of the Slayer and her friends, we find countless storylines and situations that we ourselves can relate to and learn from. Fiction then becomes the Greek chorus to our own reality.

Lyrics are much more prevalent in the episodes than most notice at first viewing. So much goes into each episode, and the action and characters are so intense, that the words to the lyrics can become a subliminal message that goes generally unacknowledged. We may hear the music, just as we acknowledge the lighting or the setting, but we may not pay much homage to the incredible job that producers did in choosing the music. The words reiterate what is happening to the characters, how they are feeling, what the mood of the scene is, what will happen next, and even how we are feeling — or supposed to feel. The lyrics go as far to provide some humor, be it dark or not, to alleviate otherwise horrific events in the scenes. The song lyrics even help us analyze our own reality. What a great tool for something that many consider just a television show. *Buffy* is anything but an ordinary television show with all of the underlying meaning: few shows have such intertwining layers. And without knowledge of the wide field of the humanities, we might miss some of those layers.

Notes

1. See Bach's chapter.
2. *A Summer Place* (1959) is a film about love, love triangles, and sex.
3. "Praise You" from *Praise You*, Fat Boy Slim (Astralwerks/EMD, 1999). Reprinted by permission of Maat Music Co.
4. "Just as Nice" from *The Future is Not Now*, Man of the Year (Loveless Records, 2000). Reprinted by permission of Tod Morisey/Man of the Year Music.

5. "Cities and Buses" from *Homesick and Happy to be Here*, Aberdeen (Better Looking, 2002). Reprinted by permission of Tremelo Users Arm Club ASCAP.

6. "This is How It Goes" from *Lost in Space*, Aimee Mann (Superego Records, 2002). Reprinted by permission of Michael Howsman Artist Management.

7. "Pavlov's Bell," from *Lost in Space*, Aimee Mann (Superego Records, 2002). Reprinted by permission of Michael Howsman Artist Management.

8. Just as a side note, a *verruca* is a kind of wart.

"Love the One You're With"

Developing Xander

J. MICHAEL MCKEON

One of the truly remarkable aspects of the television series *Buffy the Vampire Slayer* is generosity. While the prologue reminds us of Buffy's unique importance as "*the* Slayer," subsidiary characters also have opportunities to grow and develop before us—a tricky line for a series to walk. But the mark of talented writing, directing, and producing is *not* to diminish the central importance of the protagonist at the expense of digressions and explorations into supporting characters. *Buffy* is quite successful in sharing Buffy's spotlight with other characters, and the first episode dedicated to an understanding of character besides Buffy is Xander from Season One's episode "Teacher's Pet." "Teacher's Pet" chronicles Xander's initial love interests with Buffy, his adolescent insecurities, and finally his near fatal attraction to Ms. Natalie French, Sunnydale High's new science teacher.

What follows is an attempt to understand some of the development of Xander's character within the world of televised fiction, with the aid of Greek ethics, Freudian psychoanalysis, and the Hollywood horror film genre. What emerges is a complex though comic character of psychological depth, whose choices are the product of puberty with which most adolescents may identify and sensitive adults may empathize.

Horror in film and television is an optimal venue for exploring issues of teenage sexuality, and it is in the context of horror that we can understand Xander's sexual coming-of-age. During puberty, teenagers find themselves going through a number of unwilled physical and psychological changes that are, according to Walter Evans, "strangely" fascinating events that they have

131

reason to fear (465), for instance, a youth's shock over a rapidly-changing body.

Emotional development as a product of these unwilled physiological changes casts the opposite sex in an entirely new light as well. Sexual attraction and the desire for intimacy between the sexes give new force to the meanings of acceptance and rejection. In adolescence, sexual intimacy can be the most immediate, reassuring acknowledgement of acceptance whereas fear of rejection can also become a major source of anxiety and insecurity. Indeed the need for acceptance can lead to certain types of obsessively-compulsive behavior, such as Xander's constant fawning over Ms. French. His need to feel sexually acceptable drives much of the plot and leads the episode to a moral crisis: Xander's knowledge of the fear brought on by the life-threatening and life-affirming powers of Eros.

Xander and Eros

Xander's callow recklessness is hinted at early in the series. Introduced as a youth literally out of control, Xander precariously weaves and winds his way between students on his skateboard as he makes his way to Sunnydale High. Once he sees Buffy, her sexual allure comically disorients him. Momentarily distracted, Xander is creased in two by a metal handrail, and at the groin region no less. What ought to be a painful lesson to Xander, that is, "don't think from the waist down," becomes the ideal premise for Episode Four, a lesson learned in the context of Greek Eros and horror.

Why "Teacher's Pet" entertains resides in a conceptual tension between Eros and horror. Eros was the Greek god of sexual desire, lust, and intercourse, and, although many mythic narratives differ as to his origins, most are in general agreement concerning his power and authority. Among humans, as well as all animate nature, Eros is the power that draws individuals together for sexual purposes—but not merely to satisfy the demands of lust. Sexual urge is channeled toward consummation largely because of what nature has designed us and all animate nature to do—perpetuate life within a given order of species (Calame).[1]

Thus, the continued existence of nature and its inherent order is the result of Eros's power. Eros is the power that draws the sperm to the egg; it causes the seed to burgeon forth from the earth; it is what causes all plant and animal life to riot upon it (Calame). Horror, on the other hand, is a confounding of natural processes and order, and our enjoyment of it in art stems from the delight we take in reading or watching natural processes violated, whether in the form of bestiality (e.g., King Kong, or Beauty and the Beast), unnatural metamorphoses (e.g., the Wolf Man or Dracula), or in the unnatural creation of human life (Frankenstein's monster). Xander's erotic desire for

Ms. French is natural enough and understandable, but that she is in reality an insect makes Xander's erotic attraction something unnatural, indeed horrific.

In Dreams

Except for two minor jump cuts, the structure of "Teacher's Pet" is charmingly simple. At the beginning, we see Xander's daydream, which at first does not appear to be a dream. We are at the Bronze, a veritable bacchanal of youthful dancing, loud music, singing, instrument playing, intoxication, flirtation, making out, necking, and heavy petting, not to mention other nightly ritual goings-on.

Immediately we see and hear Buffy on the receiving end of a vampire attack. The agile vampire has quickly subdued her; their coital positioning suggestive of violent rape, dominance, and the hoped for destruction of the Slayer. Then something happens that clearly stretches belief into incredulity.

Xander, as if cast in the role of St. George, the saint who slays the dragon, knocks unconscious the would-be vampire assassin. Once liberated, Buffy runs to him. Buffy swoons as Xander touches her. She attends to Xander's hand, wounded in the defense of her virtue. He masks the pain, then jumps to center stage, and, with all eyes upon him, starts rhythmically stroking the neck and plucking the strings of a Les Paul Custom Three Pick-up. There the daydream ends. We are suddenly summoned back to reality through Buffy's whispering, "You're drooling.... Xander, you're drooling."

What are we to make of Xander's reverie? In Freudian terms,[2] the demands of Xander's id upon his conscious ego during sleep arise from an unconscious instinct or, in Xander's case, his pre-conscious love for Buffy and his desire to possess her sexually. The reconciliation of the id and the ego takes the form of a wish-fulfilling dream that remedies personally-embarrassing limitations (Freud, *An Outline*).

Xander, for instance, lacks experience with women, but, in a dream, he becomes the dashing hero and brave protector of feminine virtue. In reality Xander lacks musical talent, but, in a dream, he can become a rock-god. Buffy is continuously saving Xander from deadly vampires, but, in a dream, *he* becomes the Slayer. But in the end all is still a dream. Much like Willow's perception of Xander's character, the dream is something sweet, comical, cute, and whimsical. As we investigate the dream symbols, we uncover and ultimately understand their deeper, more layered meanings.

Guitar Solos

One of the dominant themes in classic horror films is the unholy search for the "secret of life" (Evans 469). Dr. Frankenstein nearly goes mad channeling all of his time, energy, talent, and resources into discovering life's greatest secret: its regenerative animating properties (Shelley). The pursuit becomes unholy once it threatens, in the form of the monster, Dr. Frankenstein's impending marriage, that divinely sanctioned institution where the secret of life can only be discovered legitimately (Evans 471–472).

Like Dr. Frankenstein, teenagers cannot seem to resist searching for, tampering with, or feeling insecure about the secrets of life. The relationship between Blayne, one of the "popular guys"; Xander, our hero for this episode; and Angel, the vampire with a soul and Buffy's love interest (but not until later in the series) illustrates this point. We find Blayne down at the Bronze boasting of his many seductions and conquests, and, as Xander listens in, his sense of sexual inadequacy is palpable. The feeling is compounded when Xander later notices the "buff" Angel interacting with Buffy. On two fronts then Xander's masculinity is threatened. Xander's drive to remedy the matter of his sexual inexperience plays perfectly into the hands of Ms. French, the science instructor replacement for Dr. Gregory who has mysteriously disappeared.

Our first impressions of Ms. French are that she is siren-like. Her power lies in her beauty. She seductively explains insect reproduction and pollination processes in science class. She even elicits a response from the bookish, asexual Giles. In addition to her physical beauty, she is a passionate creature whose cattiness with Buffy over the non-sociable aspects of praying mantis life foreshadows their ultimate physical fracas. The ending of the episode pits both women in a fight to the death, deciding if one will sexually possess and destroy Xander or the other will protect him from such a fate.

Ms. French is something of an enigma as well. Her beauty belies a hideous reality. She is a giant female praying mantis who preys upon unsuspecting male virgins for the purposes of copulation and fertilization. Her true nature whiffs of earthy, matriarchal religions, where women exercised greater authority in the social and religious life of a culture. Prehistoric female figurines, such as the *Venus of Willendorf* (20,000–18,000 B.C.E.) are archaeological evidence of societies that center on women and procreation. Within such societies, women were elevated to positions of power, status, and pride, depending on their fertility (Ehrenberg 74–76).

Ms. French proudly describes the female praying mantis as being larger and much more sexually aggressive than the male. Dr. Gregory's decapitation resembles the mating habits of the female praying mantis, but the decapitation, its sexual component, and their connection with Ms. French, are not readily apparent to either Blayne or Xander, the chief rivals for her affection. She welcomes and encourages the young boys' ardor. But how is it that Blayne and Xander are so easily deceived by her?

In Greek mythical terms, Blayne and Xander's overt sexual behavior is ruled by Eros, a creative power that brings men and women together for procreative purposes. When erotic desire leads to the possibility for sexual intercourse, the power is all-consuming, and this is most evident in the teenage boys' unanimous vote to help Ms. French create model eggs after school for the upcoming science fair. When Xander shows up at school lunch break to help Ms. French, they share a comically-intimate moment when he reveals his middle name to her; secrets are shared.

Eventually Ms. French invites him to her house later that evening, but the invitation surprises and excites Xander, for the very thought of possible (even if he suspects it might be imaginary because she is so far out of his league — an adult woman with experience) sexual activity with her, and in a matter of hours, is maddening to the young lad. In the presence of Ms. French, Xander is more driven than driving and the eroticism is playfully suggested in the episode's first jump cut back to the original daydream sequence. Referencing the guitar solo, the once-veiled sexual metaphor is revealed and made explicit. The male orgasm is roughly approximated.

The audible imagery is equally compelling and illustrative. The transition from musical form to greater degrees of formlessness in the brief seconds of the cut expresses Xander's inward ecstasy and loss of control to Eros. The sudden upward thrust of the guitar, combined with the sound of screeching notes, plucked and reverberated over and over again, is a hint of hoped-for earthly delight and an affirmation of Freud's pleasure principle (*An Outline*). Nature designed us to seek pleasure, and, as we do so at every opportunity, we ensure the survival of our own species.

Dramatic Irony

Classic horror movies often depend on the principle of dramatic irony. We, along with wiser characters in the movie — whoever they happen to be, know a key bit of information the unsuspecting victims do not. How does this create heightened anxiety in the audience? Prior to every slashing, decapitation, strangling or murder, we say to ourselves and the victim, "Don't open that door" or "Don't let him in" or "Don't go into the basement!"

A particularly key scene from "Teacher's Pet" does much to forward the plot and offer us insights into Xander's erotic states of mind, and it works on the principle of dramatic irony. Buffy (as do we) knows Ms. French's true identity and also knows she is preying on Xander's sexual weakness. Buffy wishes to warn Xander, but he is particularly dubious at this moment. Sexually threatened by Blayne and Angel and naturally aroused by the physical beauty of Ms. French, Xander thinks Buffy's warning is nothing more than veiled jealousy because of all the attention Ms. French has shown him lately. He thinks he loves Buffy, however, and would certainly forsake any amorous interests in Ms. French if only she would come around; but Buffy isn't interested, and this pains him. So he strikes back at her by insulting Angel (as having a "girlie" name) and considering Buffy's warnings to be worthless. Because of his feelings for Buffy and his attraction for Ms. French, we know, as does Buffy, that Xander is walking into a trap. Eros defines him at this moment and is guiding him unwittingly to a destiny of his own making.

Xander's Great Folly

The climax of "Teacher's Pet" takes place at the residence nest of Ms. French. A seductively-clad Ms. French welcomes Xander into her apartment where the fire glows and crackles. The lighting is soft, the music romantic. The scene reeks with sexuality. To break the tension, Ms. French and Xander imbibe martinis, but she slips Xander a mickey. He is looking to score, and all the Freudian slips and references are delivered in so blatant a fashion as if to seem trite and clichéd, e.g., "chest" confused with "dress."

After minimal wheedling, Ms. French finally extracts Xander's most guarded secret: the truth of his virginity. We know about this fact in an earlier colloquy between Giles and Buffy, but there is something sheepishly comical in Xander's confession to Ms. French. Immediately she assuages his embarrassment by confessing her "need" for a virgin. She slyly reaches for and touches Xander's hands, but her touch triggers remembrances of the dream he had at the beginning of the episode, especially the caring and attentive way in which Buffy held his hands. Utterly beside himself, Xander declares his love for Buffy, yet Ms. French, unfazed and undaunted, still encourages him to touch her, whereupon the drugged martini kicks in. "Your hands are sooo ... serrated," Xander says. But it is too late for Xander to effect an escape, and success is hers. Xander, like Blayne and countless others before, has become a victim to Ms. French and his own erotic desires.

In every way Ms. French becomes the focus of Xander's erotic passion, and yet the mere mention of "hands" diverts his attention away from her to the true object of his desire. What are we to make of this? First, the drugged martini has the effect somewhat akin to truth serum, and his declared love for Buffy apparently brings the plot to a moral crisis. Should Xander continue to pursue Ms. French even after he remembers his true love? Is it right that, even as he loves Buffy, he channels his erotic desires toward Ms. French, an object of mere gratification and of passing fancy?

There isn't much here to allay these moral concerns since the hastening dénouement requires the physical destruction of Ms. French rather than moral contemplation. Why? Because it would seem inconsistent, given the generally comic tone of "Teacher's Pet," for Xander to suddenly pose as Lord Hamlet and recite a soliloquy on the folly of man. It is enough to know of Xander's hopeless love for Buffy, that she is the object of his sexual fantasy, and that it is on her whom he will rely in an ironic reversal of the daydream at episode's end. It is Buffy who in *reality*, and not a dream, saves Xander from death and prevents him from committing an unholy act that seeks to violate nature in the sexual confounding of species: humans and insects.

Intuition, Imagination, and Challenges

There is another device of horror that makes "Teacher's Pet" a fascinating case study in teenage sexuality. It is a variation on what Walter Evans identifies as the constant struggle between reason and intuition. In many horror movies, the supernatural always trumps the limits and powers of human reason. For example, we often scoff at ignorant characters who doubt the existence of werewolves, witches, ghosts, or other superstitious entities. The smug certainties of individuals who place their faith in reason are no match, however, for the deep emotional truths known only through the irrational, the highly imaginative, or the largely intuitive (Evans 469). Silver bullets, stakes through hearts, the use of garlic, and the wearing of a crucifix are protective measures the faithful employ against potentially-destructive vampires, and yet all these tactics fly in the face of reason. To the believer, even without evidence, however, they are grace-saving, life-preserving tactics.

In "Teacher's Pet," reason, logic, and academic training get Buffy and Giles to a point where the supernatural takes over. Buffy first researches the preying and mating habits of praying mantises. She hopes to build a case that convinces Giles of the true identity of Ms. French, which Buffy has already intuited. Giles is naturally inclined to the supernatural, but he still uses logic and academic training to ascertain facts about the she-mantis, or *kleptis-virges*. Only once authority is consulted in the form of Carlyle, Giles's old chum from college, does he see the truth in Buffy's intuitions as they set off to find and destroy Ms. French. However, Buffy must subdue and question a vampire before she and her team come to know the true location of Xander's imprisonment: Ms. French's basement. Reason, logic, and academic training are essential in combating evil, but in the end we discover that it is necessary to enlist the vampires's intuitive knowledge of evil to defeat evil, the she-mantis.

Hastening Dénouement

The final scenes are notable for their spectacle. Ms. French, the *kleptis virges*, she-mantis and shape shifter, is a perception distorter. However, the waxing and waning of that power, most noticeable in the basement scenes, now reveals her true reality in all its glorious horror. A giant bug, she seems to leap right off the pages of Franz Kafka's *The Metamorphosis*.

In the closing scenes, Xander's dream becomes a reality, albeit with a number of interesting reversals. What Xander can only be in a dream (a savior) is a role Buffy now assumes in saving him. In Xander's dream the vampire's bite originally sought, metaphorically speaking, sexual contact through attack and penetration, but in reality the she-mantis's attempt to sexually unite with Xander is thwarted through Buffy's adept use of bug spray, martial arts, recorded bat sonar, and the skillful wielding of a machete. As the duel between females ensues, Xander tries to insinuate himself into the fight, but this is no dream: it's reality. Buffy shoves Xander aside for his own safety; Xander is out; this is her fight. The she-mantis is destroyed, and all thanks to Buffy.

In the final remaining seconds, Willow tenderly acknowledges the truth of matters. The boys are still virgins. In defiance, Blayne threatens a lawsuit if the facts are ever made public. Xander tells Blayne to "shut-up," and in ruthless bravado wields the machete, clearly phallic, raising it upward in the same pose as the dream-guitar. Armed with the machete, Xander proceeds to hack to pieces the evil spawn of the she-mantis. The image of phallic power as destroyer is now complete and coherent. Xander's "perverted compulsion" for sex with an insect is a dream returned to the earth. Saved by Buffy to live another day, he is nonetheless wiser because of his experience.

Xander and Ancient Greece

When Xander gives free reign to his erotic compulsions, common sense fails him miserably, and he fails to measures up to the self-restrained beauty indicative of ancient Greek ethics. Why? The Greeks believed man was a composite being. On the one hand, he possessed limitless passions and desires, and seemingly uncontrollable diametrically-opposed emotions, such as love and hate, repulsion and desire. On the other hand, to live a beautiful life was to moderate and check such potentially-intractable forces inherent in man's being. The key was exercising reason over passion, common sense over desire, and restraint against food, money, sex, and power. But, according to the Greeks, what sorts of activities activated and enlivened the mind as opposed to the body? The very things that Xander shuns: the study of geometry, science, and biology (Copleston).

We may judge the choices Xander makes as morally blameworthy according to contemporary ethical standards derived from Greek ethics. Yes, Xander should have wisely considered Buffy's revelation of Ms. French's true identity. When dealing with his own sexual desires, he could have exercised greater moderation and temperance, especially when placed in physically-intimate circumstances with Ms. French. Moral condemnations such as these, however, are based on the timeless struggle between reason and the darker angels of our nature. But, for Xander, reason and emotion are just two among many other self-defining characteristics. Were Xander to limit his choices to them we would fail to appreciate other personality traits that inexorably lead to the actions in "Teacher's Pet," and in the end we would be presented with an altogether different character from Xander. Yes, Xander is blameworthy according to Greek ethical standards, but his failings make him a much richer and more lively character to watch.

Greek virtue ethics is one way of understanding character decisions and action. What about biological determinism? Like the unwilled physical changes that every adolescent, including Xander, undergoes, teenage behavior is consistent with, if not the product of, those physiological changes. Like the Wolfman whose predatory habits are entirely predicated on his physical transformation, we are a witness to changes in Xander's emotional behavior, given his physical reaction to Ms. French. In the daydream, Xander amorously fixates on Buffy but in reality shifts his amorous attention to Ms. French. This shifting in no way substitutes Ms. French for Xander's true love but merely suggests a new reaction and motivation of character not yet given expression. Once placed in a sexually-compromising set of circumstances, Xander's behavior is entirely predictable, comic, and determined. With Ms. French, we are a witness to Xander acting out the daydream, however falsely, since if he can't be with the one he loves, Buffy, then he must love the one who will allow him full sexual expression.

Horror and the Great Chain

A popular medieval metaphor that helps to explain the inherent order of the world, one which was popular among eighteenth-century natural philosophers, was the Great Chain of Being. Such a theory positioned all animate and inanimate nature on a *scala naturae* (natural scale or ladder) (Lovejoy 58). A hierarchical arrangement, starting with God at the top, determined the subsequent positioning of all things, according to varying degrees of privation. Humans possessed reason but animals did not, so humans were placed higher on the scale than animals. God is at the top since he lacks nothing; rocks and other inanimate objects are at the bottom since in their mere existence they barely escape non-being.

A hierarchically-arranged world no doubt comforted the eighteenth-century psyche. Confident and certain, the enlightened individual knew a divinely-sanctioned order guided the shape and trajectory of natural history. They knew, according to the book of Genesis in the Bible, that all animals and plants were divinely created and possessed the power to procreate within their sphere of existence; moreover, any potentially-disruptive act in that ordered chain of existence was a threat to God's intended purpose in nature and was therefore aptly described as evil, or even horrific. Indeed, Christian hell is often depicted as a horrific confounding of species, and the works of Heironymous Bosch are evidence of this (Eco 102).

Nor was the Great Chain of Being at odds with Greek mythic notions of Eros either. Eros aptly described the creative urge that drew men and women together for procreative purposes. Freud eventually called this creative drive the "pleasure principle," but its mythic appellations are just as valid and compelling a story as psychoanalysis, perhaps even more so, since human nature is easily inclined toward art. Nature, in other words, has genetically-structured human individuality such that we seek out pleasing human activities. Is it any coincidence then that the two most pleasurable activities humans would most assent to, that is, eating and sexual intercourse, are life-sustaining for the purposes of life-creating?

While contemporary culture largely does away with cosmological frameworks of this sort, we still are fascinated and titillated by the implications entailed in such theories. To be sure, Western artistic notions of horror are still aptly based on a perspective of Christian metaphysical realism (that is, the belief that God and angels really do in fact exist). No other film better illustrates this point than the 1931 version of *Frankenstein*. The film's horror is derivative of the creationist account found in Genesis. Man sins as he reaches for what is denied to him: knowledge. "Now I *know* what it is like to be God!" shouts Dr. Frankenstein at the creation of his monster. The blasphemous nature of his utterance resides in an implicit understanding of the reason for man's expulsion from the garden: his overreaching. It is not necessary that a culturally-literate audience buy into the Edenic myth, just that it understands how it functions as sub-text essential to the horror of the work. In other words, even atheists can still take delight in the underlying horror of the film, just as they can take delight in the music of J.S. Bach without believing in the God he dedicated it to.

Xander, like Dr. Frankenstein, is driven by a desire for knowledge that awakens him erotically. In form and feature, Ms French elicits his affections but most importantly elicits in him a desire to *know* things originally forbidden. Just being around her enlivens and animates Xander in ways that seem to make his former life a counterfeit. For all intents and purposes then, Xander has lost his psychological virginity, thus heightening the dramatic irony even more, given the facts about Ms. French's true identity.

Usually such misunderstanding makes for great comedy, but in this case the outcome is potentially horrific. Something deep inside us, perhaps culturally induced, knows it is simply wrong for Xander, and for us, to try and copulate with insects, or any other life form that doesn't seem to resemble us to some degree. (She does originally resemble us—and it's when she doesn't that

Xander is appalled.) Bestiality is its name, and a sin, according to some, that is explicitly proscribed in the Old Testament. For Freud it was simply sexual perversion and deviancy. What art reveals in the form of "Teacher's Pet" is a delightful, though distanced, rendering and retelling of the ancient taboos that are constantly a part of the human drama.

Notes

1. Understanding Eros assumes some understanding of the mythology of which it is a part. Today we speak of a perceived order in nature using biology, e.g., "genetic history," "biological species," and "human sexuality," terms describing nature according to our own contemporary mythology.

2. Sigmund Freud (*The Ego*) believes the human psyche is divided into three essential parts, namely the id, the ego, and the super-ego. The id consists of two unconscious drives: the sexual and the destructive. The super-ego socializes the id by imposing limits that regulate the appropriate use and expression of its drives in society. The ego mediates between the two, deciding when it is and when it is not appropriate to express the demands of the id (*The Ego*).

Texting Buffy
Allusions of Many Kinds

—∞∞—

EMILY DIAL-DRIVER
AND JESSE STALLINGS

Buffy the Vampire Slayer, self-aware and self-referential series, has what is possibly the largest cache of literate and literary references in television — or any other medium. From Dr. Seuss to Milton, from *Star Wars* to *Star Trek*, Joss Whedon and his stable of writers (where does that come from anyway, the idea that a writer can be trotted out at need like a pony for rent?) have mined pop culture and literature — and elsewhere — and broadened the viewer appeal. But, far from being derivative, *Buffy* has become an influential work in genre television. The audience's referential awareness, and the corresponding feeling of being "in the know," of knowing "what's up," makes Buffy a "smart" series.

Some time ago, students in introductory philosophy class (required) were resistant. They could not determine — and didn't want to determine — why anyone would be interested in, much less be required to *read*, material about old, stuffy philosophies— and, according to the group, no matter how current the philosophies, they were all old and useless. One day an especially resistant student came into class, threw his book onto the table, and, with the greatest of surprise — and satisfaction, told the class, "I know why we have to study philosophy. It's so we can understand *The Simpsons*." It was a breakthrough. From that time on, philosophy was important. Those students didn't need a philosophy of life; they needed a philosophy of *The Simpsons*.

The Simpsons is similar to *Buffy* in sheer number and quality of allusions, philosophical and otherwise. So many allusions, so little time: one needs to learn about the entirety of western culture in order to fully understand and appreciate the series and its crafting. Recognizing allusions and references can also increase resonance because those allusions evoke psychological, rational, and emotional connections of which the viewer may not even be fully conscious.

What is an allusion? What is a reference? Starting with reference: a reference is an allusion (no, no, this cannot be!). To straighten this out, we mulled over a number of definitions. Harmon and Holman's *A Handbook to Literature* says an allusion is "A figure of speech that makes brief reference to a historical or literary figure, event, or object" (14). And Abrams's *A Glossary of Literary Terms* says an allusion is "a passing reference, without explicit identification, to a literary or historical person, place, or event, or to another literary work or passage" (10).

So we can conclude that an allusion is a particular kind of reference, one related to history or literature, right? Well, but, Frye's (et al.) *The Harper Handbook to Literature* says an allusion is "A meaningful reference, direct or indirect..." (15). And Murfin and Ray's *The Bedford Glossary of Critical and Literary Terms* says an allusion is "An indirect reference to a person, event, statement, or theme found in literature, the other arts, history, myths, religion, or popular culture" (11). So we can use the more lenient, the more inclusive definitions and conclude that an allusion is a reference to something outside the element with which we are engaged; it is a reference to something outside the text, the episode, etc. Thus, an allusion is a reference to "something" that is not internal to *Buffy*. Therefore, we will use *reference* and *allusion* as synonyms.

An astute reader might notice that some of the definitions distinguish between direct and indirect references. A direct reference is on the order of a character saying, "What would Spider-Man do?" (nobody in *Buffy* says that), directly alluding to the Spider-Man character. An indirect reference is on the order of a character saying, "My Spidey sense is tingling," which Buffy does say in "I Robot You Jane," indirectly alluding to Spider-Man. So there is a distinction between the two types of references. Perhaps a viewer feels a frisson more knowledgeable in recognizing an indirect reference. Perhaps an indirect reference is more "tasty" or shows more accomplishment in handling language. Perhaps. However, we have determined that, direct or indirect, an allusion is a reference is an allusion — and we have "counted" both indirect and direct in the same way.

When we were deciding how to deal with allusions, we made some determinations.[1] We decided not to deal with visual allusions. We also decided not to deal with allusions that were internal to *Buffy*. That is, we decided that, if in one episode a reference is made to an event, character, etc., from a previous episode, we would not "count" that as an allusion. We also decided not to include allusions appearing in music, unless a character was singing. Thus, lyrics are not included in the allusion tally.

Allusions are interesting from several viewpoints. One is how allusions function in context. We deal with that and with some statistics that seem important or interesting. First, we look at how an allusion actually functions.

Allusions, Literary and Otherwise

From Season One to Season Seven, characters make clever statements and, in addition, evoke life outside the series, leading to a more universal experience for viewers. Not only Sunnydale exists in our minds; the real world exists as well. The allusions in *Buffy* have more than one function: they comment on the situation at hand; they connect the episode, the situation, to the outside, keeping the episode, however fantastic, grounded in "the real world"; they add humor, lightening a situation or just making the viewer smile; they add drama to the situation, heightening the tension (raising the stakes), allying Buffy to the grand cosmic conflict of good and evil that exists on large and small scales in all our lives; and they illustrate character, revealing by type and style what kind of person each character is.

Sometimes allusions are commentary on the situation. Season Two's "I Only Have Eyes for You" has Xander saying, "The quality of mercy is not Buffy." This, of course, is a reference to the "mercy speech" from Shakespeare's *The Merchant of Venice* in which Portia asks Shylock, the money lender, to show mercy to borrower Antonio, saying, "The quality of mercy is not strain'd, / It droppeth as the gentle rain from heaven / Upon the place beneath: it is twice blest; / It blesseth him that gives and him that takes..." (Shakespeare, *The Merchant of Venice* 4.1.2125–28). Portia maintains that mercy is better than justice, giving blessing to both granter and grantee.

However, in "I Only Have Eyes for You," Buffy is not feeling merciful. Learning of the story of James and Grace (characters who appear in only that episode), that James shot Grace before killing himself, she decides that James should be punished severely. There is no mercy in her decision. There is instead vengeance and revenge and maybe a little justice, which may be a projection of her own history onto the other couple's situation. Buffy then goes through the experience of "becoming" James, feeling the angst of his rejected love, and realizing that he had not actually been rejected and that his shooting Grace, his teacher and the woman he loved, was an accident. After learning the full story, and being forgiven — as James — by Grace, Buffy both can and cannot understand Grace's forgiveness. She still reserves a corner for her need not to forgive. Forgiveness and mercy seem to go hand in hand, yet the distinction can be significant in the mind of those scorned, especially in the young. But in that forgiveness is Portia's mercy, maybe not Buffy's.

Allusions grounding the situation in the real world occur often in the series. For example, in "Fool for Love," Buffy and Giles research terminations of Slayers (that means they died, were killed by vampires), but there's little information. Buffy is perturbed by this, saying that she understands that every Slayer comes with an end date but that she wants her end date to be like the end date on a package of Cheetos, which have a notoriously long shelf-life. In this allusion, the Slayer, a mythically-strong woman who fights evil, in a situation in which she is researching other mythical women, refers to a very solidly-grounded item, Cheetos. Almost everyone can relate to the long-lived Cheeto, orange-dusty, finger-crusted, cheesy-residued, comfort food extraordinaire.

Dawn's comment in "No Place like Home" also helps ground the situation. Buffy is making breakfast for her mother, who is suffering from headaches. In typical sisterly fashion, Dawn and Buffy bicker. Buffy tells Dawn not to touch the breakfast tray, at which Dawn asks, "When did you become the Iron Chef?" The Iron Chef, in the Japanese television program of the same name, is the winner of a fierce cook-off competition. Here we have a food-related reference and a battle reference, both to the extremely competitive nature of the television show. (*Iron Chef* is a weekly series: the battle goes on, with each contestant striving to be the weekly winner. The show seems to echo sibling rivalry: the continuous battle to be on top, number one, the favorite, the best. The statement is also ironic and unexpected. Buffy has never been known as a cook. For her to qualify as a chef, lots of chefs would have to disappear or die.)

Humor, of course, is a prime motive for allusion. When Andrew says he is bored in "Showtime" and continues, "*Episode One* bored," it's funny. Even of those people who are obsessed with *Star Wars*, many complained that *Episode One* of the second trilogy was not their favorite. For Andrew to characterize boredom in this way brings a chuckle to the geek in us.

When Spike, in a basement full of bodies, tells Buffy, "Scream Montressor all you like," that also, in a sad, "black humor," ironic way, is funny. Montressor is the man who walls Fortunato up in the catacombs in Edgar Allan Poe's "The Cask of Amontillado." Fortunato spends his last moments, before falling silent, screaming, "Montressor." However, both Fortunato in the catacomb and Buffy in the basement are in places where it really doesn't matter. "Laugh and the world laughs with you" (Wheeler 131); scream and no one cares — or something like that. Or maybe it's something like "In the basement no one can hear you scream."

One of the most interesting functions of allusion in *Buffy* is to heighten the drama or increase the significance of the situation. One instance occurs in "The Harvest." The Master (who is an ancient vampire and the "Big Bad" of Season One) misquotes Milton, saying, "And the stars themselves will hide." The lines from *Paradise Lost* are actually, "like the God / Of this new world; at whose sight all the stars / Hide their diminished heads" (Milton 4.34–36), in which Satan is thinking about his power. Of course, the Master is also thinking about power. He is anticipating release from his imprisonment and his rise to so much power that the stars will be ashamed to show themselves. (Not to worry; Buffy prevails.)

Another instance of raising the stakes occurs in "Becoming." In this episode, Spike is willing to ally himself with Buffy to defeat Angel and regain the fidelity (so to speak) of girlfriend Drusilla. In his speech to Buffy about why he, the badass vampire, will collaborate with the enemy Slayer, he says he likes the world the way it is, with humans just "[McDonald's] Happy Meals on legs." If the world ends, as is likely if Angel awakes Acathla (the demon who will destroy the world), then, according to Spike, he will have to say farewell to both Piccadilly and Leicester Square. This is a direct reference to the song "It's a Long Way to Tipperary," popular in the early twentieth century and sung by soldiers during World War I (Duffy). Spike is expecting a war, at least on a small scale, and if he loses, that is to say, if Buffy loses, it would be the end of the world, which really would be the war to end all wars.

In addition to situational commentary, grounding, humor, and increasing resonance, allusions can reveal character. In "Enemies," Buffy says of Faith, another Slayer, "That girl makes Godot look punctual." The irony in Samuel Beckett's *Waiting for Godot* is that Godot never arrives. And Faith has a habit of not showing up when she's expected/needed. In this case, Buffy needs the books a demon has for sale. Wesley, the new Watcher, thinks Buffy needs to wait for Faith before Buffy makes her approach to the demon. Faith is unavailable, because Faith is out killing that same demon and rescuing the books for the evil Mayor. This allusion reveals Faith's character—and shows that Buffy is better read (or capable of picking up allusions and using them correctly) than we expect from her attendance and interest in high school.

More of Faith is revealed in "Bad Girls." When she is unable to follow Buffy's direction in a fight (Buffy had suggested something like "one-two-three-let's fight the vampires"; Faith ignores this, leaping on "two"), Faith says that battle is not like a Tupperware party and that one cannot plan a fight. Buffy replies to Faith that counting to three is "not a plan. It's *Sesame Street*."

The conversation tells us several things. Faith is all emotion and little rationality. In addition, this allusion reveals that Faith is familiar on some level with the "normal," "middle-class" joy of Tupperware parties—and that she scorns them and the culture from which they spring. Buffy would, having a mother in her life and being more immersed in the ordinary world, know about Tupperware parties and the bonding that they imply. Faith's comment diminishes the import of that "normal" world from which she feels so alienated.

Faith does not respond well to another's direction, even in counting to three. Faith has not progressed even to the level of *Sesame Street* in her ability to play well with others. *Sesame Street* highlights basic toddler play: playing together is one of the first concepts normal children learn. (Perhaps the key word is "normal" and that is why Faith doesn't comprehend that concept.) She is still the needy, greedy child. This also tells us that Buffy is aware of Faith's immaturity and that Buffy herself is past the *Sesame Street* stage.

In another character revelation, Buffy refers to her new college roommate Kathy as the *Titanic* ("Living Conditions"). She is convinced that Kathy is affecting her ability as a Slayer because Kathy is so irritating, to the point of metaphorically sinking Buffy's life (actually making Kathy the iceberg). We viewers are expected to think of Buffy as over-reacting to a normal situation. We are expected to see an only child trying to adjust to living with a roommate. Of course, as it turns out, Kathy is a demon and wants to take Buffy's soul so Kathy can escape her family and keepers and live as she wishes in the world of Buffy, which would be without Buffy. (It wouldn't be the exact world, but perhaps the world of the 1980's, since we hear Cher's "Believe" at least a dozen times during this particular episode. Re the *Titanic* connection, Cher's song is the rough waters, and Buffy is finally the iceberg that takes out Kathy. And, ironically, it is Kathy who sinks into the floor, being sucked into a portal to her home dimension opened by her father's minions.) With the *Titanic* reference, we have a comment on Kathy, a characterization which turns out to be true-ish, and find an overstated, almost irrational, but ultimately correct, characterization made by Buffy.

Xander reveals his character with his comment about moving out of his parent's basement into an apartment in "Replacement." Suave Xander (Xander has been split into a suave Xander and a scruffy Xander by a demon) and Anya, his girlfriend, are inspecting an apartment, and he's deciding whether to sign the lease. He says there comes a time either to move out of the parental abode or just give up and buy a Klingon costume (*Star Trek*), implying that with that purchase he would have to accept the fact he is a geek and a "loser"—and will always be. Complete Xander has had doubts about signing the lease; he's afraid that he will not be able to afford the apartment. Suave Xander does not have many doubts. Scruffy Xander would buy a costume — and live in the basement, in costume, in fear. What would complete Xander do? It turns out that he would move into the apartment, after the two halves are reunited. No Klingon costume in his future! (No costumes, only a vengeance demon.)

Some allusions serve more than one function. For example, in Season One's "Never Kill a Boy on the First Date," "militia man" sings lines from "At the River," known to most as "Shall We Gather at the River," written by Robert Lowry. The militia guy implies that his head is filled with the song because the Master has put it there. The familiar hymn grounds the situation in the real world. In addition, this hymn raises the significance of the situation. The words are meant to suggest that the believer can find communion, fellowship, and God by the river. Seemingly, the Master wants to call in his minions for fellowship of the demented kind. However, the hymn has other resonances. Since militia guy only sings the lines in the hymn about the river, the viewer might think of other rivers, the river Styx, for example. And, through contrast, it recalls us to the fact that the Master is far from being a god, however much he would like to be one.

In "This Year's Girl," Buffy's comparison of Adam, her opponent in Season Four, to the Terminator, only not so charming or bashful, shows us that she sees Adam as more dangerous than one of the most dangerous film villain/heroes—here Buffy is referring to the original Terminator who is the epitome of bad, making a comment on the situation, and reinforcing the badness of the season's Big Bad. The allusion is also humorous because, while we might vest many attributes in the Terminator, charm and, especially, bashfulness are probably not too far up the list.

A reference to *The Cat in the Hat* (Dr. Seuss) in "Triangle" serves more than one purpose as well. Willow refers to Anya as being like the fish (the rule keeper, the spoilsport) in the classic children's book. Anya is disturbed, not by the comparison, but by the fact that the comparison must be explained, which reveals her lack of knowledge about the culture in which she is living. This exposes Anya's character and placement (out of placement) in time, as it shows Willow's increasing lack of moral compass, which will lead ultimately to her downfall. Like the cat, Willow is "playing" while the "mother" (Giles) is away. The comment also reinforces the situation because Willow is plundering the Magic Box, just as the cat would do. And after all that import, the comment is humorous because the viewer recalls the amusing cat/fish/thing situation and, well, it's just funny.

Humor and grounding occur in another allusion, Buffy's reference to *Sleepless in Seattle* when she sees the chicken and the cow meat (meet?) experience mincing and become one in the Doublemeat Palace patty. The idea that the two main characters in *Sleepless* (the ones played by Meg Ryan and Tom Hanks) become one in the same manner as the Doublemeat burger ingredients has a "gross out factor" at the same time as it is very funny. Then too, that same "gross out factor" grounds the episode. In the real world, many people turn to the fast food industry for employment when all else fails. Minced parts ("parts is parts," says the '80s Wendy's commercial) are a fact in ground beef and many other fast-food patties. Gross, but the image allows us grounding.

An allusion to filmmaker David Lynch is commentary, humor, grounding, and drama-increasing. In "Dead Things," Warren kills his ex-girlfriend and sets Buffy up to take the fall by importing a demon that causes time to warp and people to hallucinate. Buffy, under the demon's influence, thinks she is the killer and goes to confess. Spike tries to stop her, to no avail. However, she discovers the truth inadvertently and comments, "That's why time went all David Lynch."

This allusion serves three purposes. First, it is funny. David Lynch films tend to play with time, as in *Mulholland Drive*, so this is an apt, amusing comparison. Second, it grounds the moment in real life. David Lynch is a real filmmaker who makes real films about "real" life. Third, at the same time that the reference grounds the moment, it both comments on the situation and heightens the drama because Lynch films often feature abused women, just as Katrina is abused, first emotionally and psychologically (by being spelled to be obedient and concubine-ish) and then physically (by being killed).

Numbers and Meaning

We've looked at some functions of allusions, which have a number of roles in a literary sense. Statistical (numerical) analysis allows us to look at allusions in different ways. What does statistical analysis tell us?

Statistics can give us some basic tools to investigate allusions. In order to use those tools we had to find the allusions. After listing all the allusions several of us individually could find, we combined the lists into a master document. The list, however extensive, is not exhaust*ive* (although it was exhaust-*ing*). Still, as it stands, the list provides some interesting insights into the authors and characters of each episode.

We start with the total number of references we gathered, approximately 4,231 (plus or minus however many mistakes we made).[2] However, because there are multiple writers on some episodes, sometimes the reference has to be counted twice — or even three times (but not for the total, only counted as one allusion for each of the writers).[3]

So we trot those writers out of their stable and we look at who put allusions in the scripts to illuminate situations and characters. It might be easier to see these figures in a table, with the writers listed in alphabetical order.

Writer	Total Number of References Writer Makes	Number of Episodes Written	Percentage of Total Series References	Average Number of References per Episode
Batali	106	20	2.5%	7
DeKnight	171	5	4%	34
Des Hotel	106	5	2.5%	29
Ellsworth	32	1	below 1%	32
Espenson	758	23	18%	33
Forbes	80	3	2%	26
Fury	526	17	12%	31
Gable	36	2	almost 1%	18
Goddard	157	5	4%	31
Gordon	64	1	1.5%	64
Greenwalt	200	5	4%	34
Gutierrez	11	1	below 1%	11
Hampton	38	1	almost 1%	38
Kiene	1	2	below 1%	below 1
King	56	2	1%	28
Kirshner	231	8	5%	29
Noxon	729	23	17%	32
Petrie	506	17	12%	30
Reinkemeyer	52	2	1%	29
Reston	23	1	below 1%	23
Swyden	36	2	below 1%	28
Vebber	62	2	1%	31
Whedon[4]	647	22	15%	29

Crediting allusions is not totally fair — and we don't want to imply there's any competition here or that an episode with more allusions is "better" than one with fewer. For example, "Hush," which has limited dialogue, should not count "against" a writer simply because the number of allusions would be necessarily restricted by the limited amount of total dialogue. And the two-part "Becoming" at the end of Season Two is filled with fighting, running from the police, dying, and other action. In those two episodes, the average number of allusions drops from around thirty-three to four. Still, we might conclude that some writers are more likely to use allusions than others. Maybe. What we can determine is that, depending on the type of episode and the writer, allusions can vary. That's not a very earthshaking conclusion.

We can also make conclusions about seasonal allusions.

Seasons differ in the number of allusions, perhaps due to the factors noted above — writer and subject of episode/type of episode/events in episode. The seasons come in the following order from most to least allusions: Three (858 allusions), Two (662), Five (648), Four (629), Six (613), Seven (612), and One (209), which, adjusting for the decreased number of episodes in the seasons, would be 418 (if there had been twice as many episodes). What significance this has is unclear. If a researcher would look at the types of episodes and the story arc(s) in each season, then perhaps we could draw conclusions about writing dialogue and making allusions based on the story, the narrative arc, the types of episodes, the events of the seasons and the individual episodes, or other items.

However, the types of allusions *are* significant. Seventy-six percent of the allusions (over three thousand) are to general pop culture. For example, Spike makes a reference to Big Blue in "Innocence," referencing both Acathla and IBM. Buffy, in "Out of My Mind," wants Giles to drive faster, saying disparagingly of his BMW, "Ultimate driving machine, my ass." Six percent of allusions are to film, which could count as a literary reference, which we do, but we broke down the literary allusions into sub-groups as well. Dawn calls Zander "double-o" ("Lessons"), a reference to the "double-o" designation of those with a license to kill in Ian Fleming's works; and Buffy talks about doing the "time warp" ("Band Candy"), a reference to the *Rocky Horror Picture Show*. Adding another five percent of "regular" literary references, such as to printed material, to the six percent for cinema takes us to eleven percent.

Some of the allusions could fall in more than one category (and we had to make a decision into which category to place them). One of the allusions which we credited to a "regular" literary allusion could well be to film: Buffy says, of the scythe she takes from the stone, that she "King Arthured it out" ("End of Days"), which could just as likely be a reference to Disney's *Sword in the Stone* as Thomas Mallory's *Morte d'Arthur* — or both. "Purer" references come from Spike in "Lies My Parents Told Me" when he says, as Shakespeare's Hamlet does, "There's the rub," and in "Primeval" when he talks of Alice and the rabbit hole of Lewis Carroll's *Alice's Adventures in Wonderland.* (Oops, both of those are also movies. Hmmm.)

Only two percent of the references come from history. Willow and Buffy discuss the Nazi-esque characteristics of Amy's mother ("The Witch") and Oz says, "As Willow goes, so goes my nation" ("Homecoming"), a variant of which has been used by Pope John Paul II ("As the family goes, so goes the nation....") and by many political pundits ("As California/Ohio/pick a state/pick an issue goes, so goes the nation").

Less than one percent each comes from religion, science, mythology, and philosophy. In terms of religion, Mrs. Holt refers to Jezebel ("Where the Wild Things Are") and Giles refers to Christ as a carpenter ("The Replacement"). In the realm of science, natural selection ("Teacher's Pet") and quantum mechanics ("Out of Mind, Out of Sight") are referenced by Blayne and Giles respectively. From mythology, the Fates ("Wild at Heart"), referred to by Spike, and the river Styx ("The Replacement"), referred to by Anya, appear. Spike says he never figured Drusilla for "existential thought. I mean, you hated Paris" ("Bring on the Night"). Mike talks of the social construction of reality, a melding of philosophies that became Peter L. Berger and Thomas Luckmann's *The Social Construction of Reality.* We can see that many fields are mined for allusion.

What research on allusions can really tell us is about character. We start once more with the total number of references we gathered, 4,231 (again, with a reliability rate of plus or minus "some"). Of that total we determined how many references each major character makes. Not so oddly, Buffy makes the most[5]; Xander makes the next number; Willow and Spike come in next; Giles, Cordelia, Andrew, and Oz follow. "Minor" characters make 1,481 references (thirty-five percent).

What can we determine from this? Buffy, as hero, and as a character who is in every episode, we would naturally think would have the highest percentage. She is the main character; she has the most screen time; she has the most dialogue; she should be granted most allusive dialogue. And the numbers bear this thinking out.

After Buffy, some interesting patterns emerge. We might have speculated that Giles would be the character who would emerge as second in the allusion race. Giles is a librarian; Giles is stuck in the world of books; he is defined as a Watcher, not as a doer. Thus, Giles *should* have the next most allusions. But he doesn't. He is beaten out by Xander, Willow, and Spike. Spike! Spike is not even in every episode. Well, neither is Giles, who runs away to England and abandons Buffy (one reading) in order to teach her to stand on her own two feet and not to rely on him for support (another reading).

Why then is Giles not accorded more allusive dialogue? He does refer often to historical facts, discussing the ducking stool, used on witches ("The Witch"), and even music of his era, using a chorus line from the Crystals about rebels not being any good ("Amends"). Is his lack of allusion because he is stuck in the world of books and thus not able to access all the pop culture and shop culture and teen culture references that other characters would use? But Spike is more than a century old. He has—more or less—kept up with the world, not being stuck in the era of his teens, as so many are.

For instance, if we look at the favorite music of teens and those in their early twenties, favorite music is usually what is current — and popular with the people they group with or admire. If we look at the favorite music of those in their forties, it is the music that was current in their teens and early twenties, as if music taste is solidified and permanent by age thirty. Not Spike. He listens to the Sex Pistols ("The Initiative"), popular years after he was turned, and he knows about Happy Meals ("Becoming, Part Two"). Giles doesn't even know about monster trucks ("Lie to Me"). And his musical taste petrified in his youth in the 1970s, with Pete Townshend and the Who ("Where the Wild Things Are") and Cream ("Band Candy").

Perhaps then Giles loses out in the allusion race because of his character, which is typical of the middle-aged person who sowed his wild oats in wild youth and then becomes "respectable." He looks back on his youth with regret for the things he has done, yet longing for the youth he was, and filled with sadness that opportunities taken should have been shunned and opportunities missed will never come again. This is reminiscent of those who think the best years of their lives were in high school. Some even grow up far enough to think the best years of their lives were in college. This might freeze their musical taste in the groups who were popular with them during the "best years of their lives." Or maybe that music flavor sticks because so many new experiences are overlaid by music and the music later is capable of psychologically evoking the feeling of that newness.

Is that the explanation for Giles's musical oeuvre — and of his inability to absorb, respond to, and allude to pop culture? Yet another view of Giles may be that all of Giles's book smarts (and immense recall of esoteric texts) have pushed the "trivial" information (popular culture) from his brain. There is simply not enough room for it all, as Sherlock Holmes would maintain (Doyle). And there's not enough time to absorb everything: looking into dusty tomes takes time that might be spent, oh, say, watching television. So, since Giles can remember — and find — an obscure reference to an arcane demon, showing that he has immense mental libraries of knowledge at his command, the trivial (for that, read "current" in Giles's psyche) is swept aside.

Spike, however, is never one to look back, not at lost opportunities, anyway; he pretty much took them all. It is not until he realizes how short he comes of Buffy's expectations, and his own ("Seeing Red"), that he seeks and finds a soul ("Grave"), feeling all the remorse of a person with a conscience who has killed and killed and killed ("Lessons"). But during all his six seasons on *Buffy* (he appears first in Season Two), Spike is *au courant* with the culture in which he lives—at any decade. He is not culturally stuck in his teen/early twenties years, perhaps because much of that era was a period of rejection for him ("Fool for Love"). So Spike can be granted allusive dialogue that includes references from today and yesterday — lots and lots of yesterdays!

Coming in before Spike are Xander, who has second most allusions (ten percent), and Willow, with third most (six percent). These two major characters are in almost every episode. They are major Scoobies, in fact, the original two members who "sign on" in the first two episodes, "Welcome to the Hellmouth" and "The Harvest." Willow, as the bookish nerd, might be expected to use more allusions than Xander, who has to continually go to her for school help. However, it is Xander who has more. Xander is the person who takes every opportunity to allude to something outside himself, perhaps in both self-deprecation and self-protection. When he loses an eye, he says the advantage is that he will not have to watch 3-D *Jaws* ("Empty Places"). Pity is an emotion he would like to avoid, and he uses his ability to connect his life to life outside himself, life "other," to distance himself from that pity.

Xander also has the tendency to over- and under-state the situation in which he finds himself: when the cheerleaders of Sunnydale High are experiencing difficulties, like catching on fire, Willow and Xander volunteer to help Buffy, who is reluctant to endanger them. Xander says, "I laugh in the face of danger. Then I hide until it goes away" ("The Witch"). Here he makes it clear he will help Buffy, that he recognizes the danger, and that he will still help. He doesn't make this clear by saying it but by using a line from *The Lion King*— and adding his own take.

Willow gives us allusions to witchcraft, of course, but she is not restricted to witchy references. She also alludes to various political stances, decrying *Mr. Rogers' Neighborhood* as patriarchal ("Gingerbread"). She tries to defuse situations, even reassuring Spike when he is unable to bite her because of the pain caused by chip the Initiative placed in his head, telling Spike that surely inability to bite (vampire impotence) happens to other vampires ("The Initiative").

Through the first five seasons, Willow's allusions generally center on politics, witchcraft, and making situations smooth and people contented. When she turns to the dark in Big Bad of Season Six, she chooses different types of allusions, turning to denigration, as in calling Giles "Jeeves," and to irony, as in saying, "Fly, my pretty" to the fireball she sends to destroy the remaining members of the evil Trio (the Duo?), Jonathan and Andrew ("Grave"). "Fly, my pretty" is a conflated misquote from the film *The Wizard of Oz,* in which the Wicked Witch of the West sends flying monkeys to kill the Scarecrow and Tin Woodman and capture Dorothy. The Witch calls Dorothy "my pretty" on several occasions and tells her monkeys to "fly." Willow is the wicked witch in this situation, and she wants to kill Andrew and Jonathan and perhaps also Dawn and Buffy, or she wants to at least distract Buffy. This allusion may seem humorous but it adds to the malevolent aura surrounding evil, veiny Willow.

Cordelia trails Willow, Spike, and Giles, using almost four percent of the allusions. This is especially interesting because Cordelia leaves the series after Season Three. So in three seasons, catty Cordelia has almost as many allusions as Giles in seven. What kinds of allusions does Cordelia throw around? A nasty jab is probably one of Cordelia's best-known and most-quoted. In the very first episode, "Welcome to the Hellmouth," Cordelia says Willow has "seen the softer side of Sears."[6] This introduces both Willow, the ill-dressed nerd, and Cordelia, the well-dressed popular master of the magnificent putdown.

Cordelia is also the master of the brand name, citing Todd Oldham (in "Angel") and Laura Ashley (in "Out of Mind, Out of Sight"), and using those brands as judgments on her peers. Cordelia also twists allusions, revealing her own twisty character. She defends Marie Antoinette by saying that Antoinette would have let the peasants eat cake ("Lie to Me"); she says Shylock is whiny for saying people look down on him and that Shylock should think of the pain of others ("Out of Sight, Out of Mind"), describing how, when she ran over a girl on a bicycle, it was Cordelia's trauma that was most important in the incident. Both of these allusions point to Cordelia, the queen bitch, the self-centered, the narcissist.

As Cordelia begins to enter the Scooby Gang, she keeps the cutting edge of wit, to the point that, when called upon to help and to drive Buffy home, she simply tells Giles, "If the world doesn't end, I'm going to need a note" ("Helpless"). She even begins to use her wit to overcome evil, telling vampire Lyle Gorch that Buffy is only runner up, that Cordelia herself is the queen ("Homecoming"), playing on her race against Buffy for homecoming queen and implying that she can out–Slay Buffy as well. Cordelia is the queen of the quip, as evidenced by the number of clever remarks she makes.

After Cordelia, Andrew, Oz and the Master qualify for placement in the allusion stakes. Oz is only sporadically in the first half of Season Two, making short appearances in "Halloween" and "Inca Mummy Girl" before becoming a regular, and Willow's boyfriend ("What's My Line?"). He stays a regular until Season Four, leaving in order to learn how to control his inner wolf. He returns later in the season, only to leave again permanently when he discovers controlling his inner wolf is difficult when he is jealous. In the few episodes he is a Scooby, his tone is of gentle ironic humor, telling Willow that the only animal cookie to wear clothes is the monkey ("What's My Line, Part Two") and turning her advances down despite the fact she has "the Barry [White] working" for her ("Amends"). Oz is often the calm voice of reason in the midst of chaos, at least until he morphs and tries to eat people.

Trailing Oz in allusion numbers, the Master, Buffy's first opponent, uses perverted religious references, talking of final days ("Prophecy Girl") and of finding the Anointed One ("Never Kill a Boy on the First Date"). His allusions function to make him seem even more evil than his snarled visage. In addition, they make the situation of his impending release upon the "upper" world itself more ominous.

Andrew, with more references than Oz or the Master, is an interesting case. He appears in only two seasons, Six and Seven. In Season Six, he is companioned by Jonathan and Warren, who do not place in the allusion stakes. Andrew appears (mostly) without Jonathan and Warren in Season Seven. His dialogue is peppered (actually, salted, since there are so many) with allusions, mostly to pop culture, such as his statement, "Scully wants me so bad" (*The X Files*) in Season Six's "Life Serial" and his references to Pinhead and Hellraiser in Season Seven's "Conversations with Dead People." Andrew does throw in a few science references (for example, to the Bronsted-Debye-Huckel equation,[7] in "Storyteller"), although it is Warren who is supposed to be the engineer. However, pop culture references define Andrew, the definitive geek/nerd, who is immersed in film and television and who lives his life through a lens of make-believe.

Other characters, those who appear less often, account for thirty-five percent of the allusions. They make reference to everything from Baskin Robbins ("Get It Done") to hamster habitats ("Wild at Heart"). Kennedy, a Potential Slayer and Willow's new interest, encourages Willow to try all flavors of magic, despite Willow's fear, revealing both her support of Willow and her disinclination to see harm in what Willow might do. Veruca, a werewolf interested in Oz, comments on hamster habitats to taunt Oz for locking himself up during his werewolf phase, revealing her disdain for his worry about consequences of his actions as a wolf.

The use of allusions in these cases is to illuminate character. Each of the above character-enhancing examples shows us that an apt allusion can expose character traits in ways that other dialogue might have to struggle to illuminate. An allusion can be characterization shorthand. Cordelia illuminates her own snarky character when she "disses" a previous date and his car by saying "my Barbie dream car had nicer seats" ("Halloween"). We know something more about Cordelia, her past, her actions, her personality, her wants and needs. Cordelia is moneyed, dismissive of those less favored, needing to be "best," wanting to be "top."

Allusions come from various venues, leading to an enhancement of the situation and the series. They are a result of writer and situation. They enhance and illuminate characters as they evoke a world inside and outside the situation on the screen. They serve multiple purposes: characterization, grounding, humor, increase in effect (and affect). Other purposes are intellectual illumination and just plain fun.

"My egg just went postal on me" ("Bad Eggs"), "You think they left his [actual] heart in San Francisco?" ("Surprise"), "I'll take the Smurf" ("Innocence"), "Masks? They're here to exfoliate?" ("Dead Man's Party"), "Ritual sacrifice. With pie" ("Pangs"), "Yeah, back when Bond was Connery and movies were decent" ("All the Way"): all repeatable lines that add magic to the moment, in the real world and in Sunnydale.

Notes

1. We want to thank some other people who helped with this article: Frances E. Morris and Jim Ford helped conceptualize, and Debbie Hendryx did some of the interminable typing of quotations.

2. For those who want to know how we managed to come up with the numbers, here's a quick run-down. We knew there were lots of allusions. Emily Dial-Driver read scripts and highlighted allusions. Jesse Stallings watched each episode (again), in order to look for allusions, and wrote them down. Thus, we acted as a check for each other. Jesse created a database that sorted by character, episode, writer, season, type of allusion, etc. Then he did the magic database thing and sorted the allusions so we could use them as we analyzed and wrote.

3. If you're not a number person, you can skip down some. The essay gets character-driven again and loses much of its number emphasis.

4. It is hard to categorize Whedon, who is listed as writer on each of the episodes by the Internet Movie Database and has creative oversight of each. Since he is the "writer" of all of the episodes, we could credit him with all of the allusions, the more than 4000 of them, or we could simply credit him with the allusions in the episodes in which he is listed as the "first" writer, making him follow only Jane Espenson and Marti Noxon. However, even creative oversight does not mean he wrote the words of the script. Thus, we "credit" him with the 647 allusions in the scripts on which he shows up as author, according to the various episode guides and DVD screen credits.

Except for Joss Whedon, we used the number of episodes credited to each writer by the Internet Movie Database (imdb.com) and information on the DVDs. As we said, some of these initial figures are skewed by the fact that some writers worked on more than one episode each. But Jane Espenson (23 episodes), Marty Noxon (23 episodes), and Joss Whedon (credited as writer on all 144 episodes by the Internet Movie Database, but actually writing 22, with additional credit for story creation on three episodes, according to various episode guides on-line) lead the pack with eighteen (758 references), seventeen (729 references), and fifteen percent (647 references) of the percentage of total references made respectively.

Following them are David Fury and Douglas Petrie, each writing seventeen episodes and scoring twelve percent of total references. Rebecca Rand Kirschner and David Greenwalt each wrote eight episodes and score five percent of total references. Steven S. DeKnight and Drew Goddard wrote five episodes each and make four percent of total references each. Rob Des Hotel wrote five episodes, using three percent of total references. Dean Batali wrote twenty episodes, making three percent of total references while Tracy Forbes wrote three episodes, using almost two percent of total references. Howard Gordon, writing one episode, uses one and one-half percent of total references (and that's a lot).

Dan Vebber and David Tyrone King each wrote two episodes, each using one percent of total references. Joe Reinkemeyer, writer of two episodes, made one percent of total references. Scoring fewer than one percent of the total number of references are Carl Ellsworth (one episode), Ashley Gable (two episodes), Diego Gutierrez (one episode), Elin Hampton (one episode), Matt Kiene (two episodes), Dana Reston (one episode), and Thomas A. Swyden (two episodes).

Averaging the number of allusions per episode puts Gordon in the lead at sixty-four allusions in one episode (and he only wrote one episode). Then we see Hampton at thirty-eight per episode; DeKnight with thirty-four; Ellsworth and Noxon with thirty-two; Goddard, Fury, and Vebber with thirty-one; and Petrie with an average of thirty. Whedon, Des Hotel, Kirschner, and Reinkemeyer come in next with twenty-nine per episode, followed by King with twenty-eight per episode, Forbes twenty-six, Greenwalt twenty-five, and Reston twenty-three. Gable and Swyden follow with an average of eighteen per episode. Gutierrez has eleven; Batali comes next to last with an average of seven allusions per episode. Kiene is last with less than one allusion per episode.

5. Here are the figures:

Character	Number of References	Percentage of References
Buffy	799	19%
Xander	689	16%
Willow	399	10%
Spike	240	6%
Giles	217	5%
Cordelia	147	4%
Andrew	134	3%
Oz	61	1%
Master	17	less than 1%
Other Minor Characters	1,481	35%

6. The "softer side of Sears" is a line from a 1993 commercial about Sears clothing.

7. Brondted-Debye-Hucket is a scientific equation that expresses how ion content (that is, the kinds of ions present and the concentrations, or amounts, of ions present) in a solution affects the reaction rates in protein/protein reactions or in protein/small ion reactions.

"What Shall Cordelia Say?"

Buffy as Morality Play for the Twenty-first Century's Therapeutic Ethos

GREGORY J. THOMPSON AND
SALLY EMMONS-FEATHERSTON

"Tact is just another way of not saying the truth. I'll pass," states Cordelia in Season Two of *Buffy the Vampire Slayer*, indicating she is neither concerned with what others think of her brazenness nor is she interested in the feelings of the others present at this moment ("Killed by Death"). Instead, her concern is more with herself and her perception of herself. The line speaks volumes for a character who has not garnered much attention in the writing on *Buffy the Vampire Slayer*.

Cordelia seems like a vapid, cartoon-like projection of American, materialistic, narcissistic, teenage superficiality. Closer examination of Cordelia, however, reveals a number of larger issues brought up in her reflection of contemporary American culture. Even more interesting, Cordelia's connection to her literary predecessor and namesake from *King Lear* suggests that Joss Whedon selected the name because it places us within the realm of Shakespearean morality plays.

Would Shakespeare be pleased to find his work, and his character names, referenced beside *Scooby-Doo*, vampires, and a teenager named Buffy? The juxtaposition of cultural references is just one way in which *Buffy* uses pastiche to create new genres, meaning, and significance while unfolding its narrative. This clever incorporation of ideas and styles allows the show to move beyond the realm of television entertainment and enter the panoply of serious scholarly cultural debate.

Like Shakespeare, Joss Whedon's *Buffy the Vampire Slayer* incorporates a number of cultural references and cultural re-interpretations in order to create a particular type of drama that is both entertaining and edifying. In this capacity, *Buffy* is a morality play for the twenty-first century, incorporating elements of the traditional medieval drama to tell its contemporary audiences a new tale regarding the struggle for one's humanity. More importantly, the morality play enacted in the series evidences a shift in the hegemonic, or predominant, placement of the moral authority.

Like many of Shakespeare's plays, *Buffy the Vampire Slayer* is grounded in the tradition of morality plays dating back to the fourteenth century. *Buffy*, Shakespeare, and medieval morality dramas all incorporate allegorical characters, supernatural elements, a journey on the part of its central character that includes a struggle for the soul, a de-historicized time and place, and the forces of good and evil. Interestingly, *Buffy*, Shakespeare, and morality plays all include an acknowledgement of or a knowledge of the world in which they exist. They each reveal the primary cultural authority of their time. For the medieval morality play, the Catholic Church was the hegemonic, or central, force; for Shakespeare, a significant change brought about by, among other things, the Protestant Reformation created a new destabilized, but still Christian, moral hegemony. The morality plays of the medieval and Elizabethan world were firmly grounded in the traditions of Augustinian and Aquinian dichotomies of good and evil, right and wrong, the material and the spiritual based in Judeo-Christian concepts of sin and salvation (Boyce).[1]

In its contemporary incarnation, however, *Buffy* as morality play speaks not to traditional medieval Christian morality but to twentieth century moral authority grounded in what historian Philip Reiff coined the "therapeutic ethos" or "therapeutic culture." As early as 1966, Reiff, in his book *The Triumph of the Therapeutic*, identified the therapeutic ethos as a worldview characterized by an obsessive concern with psychic and physical health defined in broad terms. It manifests itself in contemporary American culture in everything from religious and political arenas, to economics, to entertainment, and more. Due to its dominance in virtually every institution in American life and the dominance of supporting structure of ideas, in "From Salvation to Self Realization" historian J.J. Jackson Lears implies that the therapeutic ethos in some instances goes largely unobserved.

Buffy's Cordelia functions in a number of important ways related to the creation of the morality play of the therapeutic ethos. First, as a stereotype, Cordelia fits the mold of the allegorical character who represents more than she appears. Second, as a character who invites reference to Shakespeare's famous Cordelia, *Buffy's* Cordelia displaces the historical setting and time frames of the television series. Third, as Cordelia Chase, "Queen C," she speaks to the therapeutic ethos of self-valuation in twentieth century American culture.

Buffy's Cordelia clearly encourages an association with the character of the same name from Shakespeare's *King Lear*. *Buffy*'s Cordelia is not an exact replica intended to evoke memories of King Lear's daughter. In fact, there are many discrepancies between the two characters. Why go to so much trouble to choose such an unusual name for a character, especially one that will evoke comparisons with Shakespeare? Doing so constructs a world that has just enough reference to make it appear real but simultaneously to bring into question that reality. In this very important sense, Cordelia helps to dislodge the *Buffy the Vampire Slayer* series from any position of reality. Additionally, in choosing the name "Cordelia" a larger importance and meaning is created, taking the character from the realm of human to the realm of allegory. It can hardly be a coincidence — especially given the care put into other elements of the series — that the name Cordelia was chosen simply by happenstance. It is an unusual name and one that points clearly to the Shakespearean character of the same name.

The name Cordelia has many resonances. It evokes an association or image of the Latin word "heart" (Wells 101). Another possible interpretation of Cordelia Chase's name relates to the Latin "corpus" or body. Cordelia Chase = chasing bodies. Of course, this can be understood in two ways, both of which fit with many of the themes in *Buffy the Vampire Slayer*. In addition to Cordelia as a Scooby who chases vampires, men of the series — some of whom are vampires — enjoy "chasing" the beauties in the show, and characters like Cordelia are a clear magnet for the male gaze.

For Shakespeare, "The symbolic name of Cordelia ... focuses not on her situation but her character; she is all 'heart,' a woman of prescience, compassion, and courage" (Hamilton 151). This hardly sounds like the Cordelia of Sunnydale High School, but perhaps that is part of the creative process of the writers of the *Buffy*verse. In the *Buffy*verse, Cordelia, at least originally, appears to be a narcissistic character concerned with her own well-being and image. Is it possible that Shakespeare's character can also be viewed in the same light?

Shakespeare's Cordelia is viewed most frequently as virtuous in her denial to speak or play her father's game of favoritism. Cordelia muses to herself, "What shall Cordelia speak? Love and be silent," when her sisters are overstating their feelings for their father King Lear (1.1.68). While this moment can be seen as a virtuous act of truth and bravery on Cordelia's part, there are some who point to it as an act of hubris, a stubborn act that helps to set in motion the tragedy of the play. McGinn asserts that "She must have known, knowing her father, what impact her initial silence would have on him touchy and imperious as he was. Yet she was unwilling to bend to his— no doubt unreasonable — request. She refused to act the part demanded of her, resolutely so" (McGinn 128). McGinn goes on to say that Cordelia "refuses to accept the superior virtue of the white lie, as if not wanting to taint herself.... She is more concerned with preserving her integrity than in protecting her father's feelings" (McGinn 128).

Likewise, *Buffy the Vampire Slayer*'s Cordelia is far more concerned with her own integrity, however skewed that integrity may be, than she is in protecting the feelings of those around her. Tact is not a common denominator of either Cordelia's personality.

Shakespeare's Cordelia, while perhaps positioned as a source of virtue is, no doubt, the beginning of the play's conflict. Cordelia's admission that she is unable to participate in the favoritism game that her two sisters, Goneril and Regan, willingly play with their father, is what sets Cordelia's father off. When her father turns to her, after listening to her two sisters, expecting Cordelia to top them in the "I love you the most" competition, Cordelia asserts, "Unhappy that I am, I cannot heave / My heart into my mouth. I love your majesty / According to my bond, no more no less" (1.1.100–03). Lear's crushing disappointment leads to his irrational response. He disowns his daughter, an action which will end in his downfall. He tells all gathered, "Here I disclaim all my paternal care, / Propinquity, and property of blood / And as a stranger to my heart and me / Hold thee from this forever" (1.1.125–28).

Cordelia's disappearance following the first scene in Act I leads to a situation in which the character is nearly forgotten, except through the second-hand reminders from characters such as Kent. The reunion between father and daughter in the seventh scene of Act IV appears to restore Lear's mental capacity, but his kingdom and regal authority have long been stripped by Regan and Goneril (and their husbands). Lear sees Cordelia and, remembering what events have transpired, what he has lost, and how he has treated her, tells Cordelia, "I know you do not love me, for your sisters / Have, as I do remember, done me wrong: / You have some cause; they have not" (4.7.83–85).

Cordelia's role in Lear's restoration is only tangential. She does nothing more than show up and Lear is restored. However, Cordelia serves a vital role in the play. Like *Hamlet*'s Fortinbras she is rarely onstage but is constantly referred to by the other characters and is ever present in the audience's minds. Cordelia's relationship with Lear colors every event in the play whether she is actually at hand or not. Cordelia's lack of presence draws attention to the failure of human interaction in the play's tragic universe (Boyce 129).

Buffy's Cordelia can be seen allegorically as a figure of abundance in American culture. On the surface, she appears to be a spoiled rich girl; in reality, she has far more depth. According to Jackson Lears's *No Place of Grace*, displacement of the Protestant ethic in the twentieth century helped usher in the therapeutic culture. The commercial profusion present in America led to a two-fold need for restraint and reassurance. The wide-open opportunity for advancement which was initially set up by a seemingly-unlimited frontier was followed by the copious production of material; this ultimately helped to create a sense of alienation from the work ethic in those who experienced the plenty. This culture of economic abundance was a new mode of thought in America in which the values of the nation shifted from one of a producer-valued Puritan ethic of hard work and character to one of consumer-based self-realization and personality. Consumerism necessitates both restraint, in order not to over-commit one's own resources, and reassurance, that one's consumerism is right and proper.

Cordelia's role as abundance allegory gradually emerges in her stint on *Buffy*. Ironically, Cordelia, the spoiled rich girl, is the only character who ends up with a job in the first three seasons of the series ("Choices"). This is because Cordy's father loses everything due to income tax evasion. Thus, she loses her economic/consumerist identity and finds herself hiding, disguising her new identity as a member of the working class from her friends. It is only through the good graces of Xander (and unbeknownst to her at first) that her identity is restored — or at least seems to be restored by her appearance in a pricey gown — when Xander pays for the prom dress Cordelia placed on layaway ("The Prom").

Buffy's Cordelia plays an important role. In a world in which the women are physically powerful (Buffy) and intellectually powerful (Willow), Cordelia functions as the foil. She is not imbued with superhuman powers (at least, not until *Angel* when she becomes a higher being), and she does not usually participate in one-on-one combat with vampires. (She does, however, use her "Cordelia strength" to overcome villains in several episodes, the most striking of which is "Homecoming," in which she vanquishes Lyle Gorch, a vampire, by telling him, when he taunts her and tells her he's going to kill her, "In the end, Buffy's just the runner-up. *I'm* the queen. You get me mad, what do you think I'm going to do to you?" After thinking it over, Gorch flees.)

However, the perception is that Cordelia is "just ordinary": "In *Buffy*, Cordelia is as close as it gets to a normal girl," states Lorna Jowett. "She is often represented as powerless in the other side of Sunnydale, but her power is that of a soap queen, the (limited) power to play the 'real' world" (Jowett 33). *Buffy's* Cordelia constantly strives for power; ironically, the other characters see her as already possessing power because she is wealthy, beautiful, and popular.

Interestingly, while Shakespeare's Cordelia refuses to "play the game" her father and sisters play, *Buffy the Vampire Slayer's* Cordelia is a master of the game. According to Jowett, "From a feminist point of view, Cordelia's power is entrenched in patriarchy; her power is privilege based on her father's wealth and the ability to manipulate her own image to gain (sexual) power over males" (30). Jowett further asserts that Cordelia "seems independent and strong-minded, but her hyperfeminine appearance and behavior undercut this. Cordelia is successful because she adheres to social norms..." (30).

The social norms of Sunnydale (and most of the rest of the U.S.) require Cordelia to be pretty, popular, and perfect. These are superficial qualities that are undermined by the end of Season Three; however, they are never fully explored, only explained away, when Cordy fails to return in Season Four. When Cordelia's world is shattered by her father's income tax evasion, she loses her moneyed status and therefore her symbolic power. She is no longer the person she believed she was, and, rather than admit this economic failure (no failure on her part), she hides what she perceives to be a shameful new persona. Throughout the series, Cordelia bases her identity on consumerism: Does she carry the right purse? Drive the right car? Wear the right clothes? When these consumer "successes" are removed, Cordelia views herself as a flawed personality. It is through Cordelia as allegorical character that we can begin to see *Buffy the Vampire Slayer* not only as cautionary moral tale but as evidence of the changing grounding for moral authority being performed for twentieth century audiences as a morality play.

Morality plays were a popular form of drama that flourished in Western Europe during the fifteenth and sixteenth centuries. According to Charles Boyce, the genre grew out of the biblically-based mystery or miracle plays[2] of the Middle Ages, and they represented a shift towards a more secular dramatic form for European theatre (443). Most often they are a combination of religious sermon and festive entertainment. At their heart, both mystery plays and morality plays deal with issues concerning the fate of the human soul. While mystery plays depict biblical stories and significant stories from sacred history, the morality play dramatizes the spiritual struggle of human beings. The morality play is filled with allegorical characters who face and overcome personified moral problems or temptations. As part of their entertaining nature, the plays are constructed with alternating serious and comic scenes that are intended to entertain while they instruct. The English plays *The Castle of Perseverance*, *Everyman*, and *Mankind* are excellent examples of the genre. The characters in the morality play are usually personifications of good and evil involved in a struggle for humankind's soul. The form is generally static, but it contributed significantly to the secularization of European drama. Locations in the plays are also fairly standardized and more often represent larger ideas than simply geographic locations. One of the most common locations in the medieval morality is "The Hellmouth" (Wertz 452), a location, similarly, near and dear in the *Buffy*verse.

The characters in morality plays are generally one or two dimensional and allegorical, with names like Charity, Understanding, Perseverance, Hope, Vice, Agape, Everyman, and Humankind. Being allegorical, the characters represent larger ideas rather individuals. Charles Boyce says, "Morality plays are a type of theatrical allegory in which the protagonist is met by personifications of various moral attributes who try to prompt him to choose a Godly life over one of evil" (443). The allegorical characters in the play are based on well-known models that medieval audiences would have quickly and easily recognized. They are a collection of ideas or representations and are often a pastiche of figures and thoughts from various sources, including the Bible, saints' stories, and Christian stories.

Medieval morality plays are not concerned with historical accuracy and depictions of the past, present, or future. The plot and characters are displaced from history, yet simultaneously clearly couched within the material world of human history. They do not concern themselves with past or future on earth but the everlasting future following death. Time is not an issue in the play, other than to say that the plays take place, generally, over the span of a human lifetime. But the specific when and where that lifetime takes place are irrelevant. It can be any time and any place. Similarly, Shakespeare's morality plays are often not dependent on time, which helps their universality, leading to (appropriate) staging in a variety of historical contexts.

The locations of the medieval morality plays are largely displaced and, in a sense, enchanted realms where the allegorical figures can live and breathe in contexts that reality cannot allow. Although placed in the material realm and therefore human history, locations were frequently viewed as allegorical. For example, in the *Castle of Perseverance*,[3] a literal separation between the real world and the theatrical world is achieved through the construction of a circular moat and earthen embankment around the playing area. Through the use of these allegorical locations, the enchanted realm created in the play is removed from the "reality" of everyday life. In *Enchanting a Disenchanted World*, sociologist George Ritzer talks about the creation of enchanted locations that remove humans from the dreariness and worries of "reality" through controlled environments or fictional(ized) locations.

In *Buffy* the enchanted is created through the realms of vampires and demons in Sunnydale. The audience does not believe that they are seeing reality (or we hope not). Rather, an enchanted space is created so the dis-enchanted twentieth century can be removed, or at least pushed aside, in order to explore questions of philosophical and spiritual concern.

It is possible, easy even, to equate the series as a straightforward morality play replete with Christian imagery and messages of self sacrifice and salvation; yet *Buffy the Vampire Slayer* is not merely a series of episodes loosely bound together by similar characters. Instead, the show is a continuous narrative that unfolds over the course of seven seasons, encompassing some seven years of the characters' lives, from teen angst to early adulthood. The issues confronting the characters are seldom mundane or even based in the material world. Because the show investigates realms of living (including "after living," i.e., the afterlife), *Buffy* raises serious existential and deterministic questions: How did the world originate? Is there any purpose to its existence? Is nature intelligible? Why are we here? These are metaphysical, cosmological, and existential questions, questions as old as human cognitive existence.

In "The Door Theologian of the Year," Skippy R, a fan of the series, writes, "Hidden among the stupid sitcoms, copycat dramas and reality shows of broadcast TV, *Buffy the Vampire Slayer* has been acting out a modern-day morality play for seven seasons ... dealing with topics like evil, redemption, resurrection, sex, guilt, existential angst, selflessness and sacrifice, religion and the occult, often all before the first commercial break." Like the characters in morality plays, *Buffy's* characters confront situations in which they are forced to make decisions, often between gradients of good and evil, in order to survive. Many times good and evil are clearly delineated — the humans are good whereas the vampires are evil — but, as the seasons progress, the show increasingly questions these distinctions.

The construction of the "Scooby Gang" during the high school years of the series is one example of allegorical characterization. The gang initially is made up of outsiders who do not fit into other socially-accepted groups on the high school campus. In this capacity, the Scoobies become an even greater collection of allegorical figures representing larger ideas beyond Sunnydale: Giles symbolizes reason and rationality and typically enlightens the Scoobies in each episode as they battle a new evil; Tara McClay and Willow Rosenberg, names evoking references to the land and nature, are witches who represent earth, nature, woman, the pagan world. Xander is the only human of the group endowed with no particular talent or superhuman ability; his greatest asset to the group is his unconditional love, or agape. Xander is humanity — and love. Anya is a former vengeance demon who, in human form, represents materialism: she is concerned with money, capitalism, and "living the American dream." Like Cordelia, Anya is greed, but she is also the character who speaks the unadorned truth. Spike, a vampire who has lost his capacity to hunt humans because of a chip in his brain, also functions as the voice of truth and efficiency, cutting through to the truth more quickly than others, saying what is on his mind regardless of the feelings of those around him. Dawn is the "Key," an ethereal essence whose powers could unlock the boundaries that separate time and space dimensions. And Buffy? Buffy is the center of the story and is symbolic of the morality play's Everyman. Buffy's soul and life are constantly in jeopardy, and her trials ultimately represent the "lesson" for the series. Though Buffy possesses superhuman physical powers unlike typical Everyman characters, she is the central figure of this morality play. She is the quintessential Everyman figure recast in the form of a young adult woman.

In the morality play, and in the *Buffy*verse, these allegorical characters live and act in a world that is historical and chronologically grounded, yet is not completely dependent upon accurate depictions of time and space to create their world. Indeed, space and time, along with narrative, action, and spectacle are often allegorical and therefore can be altered in order to convey lessons. The series illustrates this in "The Wish," when Cordelia wishes an alternate world, one without Buffy in Sunnydale, into existence. The resulting events prove to the viewer (but not Cordelia, because in that world she dies) that Sunnydale is better off with its Everywoman Buffy right in place where she's needed.

Locations and history are displaced in *Buffy* for didactic purposes, in order to make points. *Buffy* demonstrates then the hegemonic construct, the central emphasis, of the contemporary world. *Buffy the Vampire Slayer* illustrates a changed moral authority in culture. There is also a didactic element to the Buffy "play" as well; we, the viewers, are to be both entertained and taught during the course of an episode. By using the medieval morality play genre, writers such as Shakespeare and Joss Whedon are able to identify shifts in their cultures including shifts in moral authority.

According to Matthew Pateman, "Buffy's particular anxiety stems from trying to keep her job secret in a de-mythologized age and to that extent conflicting historical perspectives create significant tension" (64–65). The intentional confounding of history helps to create the larger sense of the morality play inherent in the show. In "Doppelgangland," once again a wish/spell goes awry and Willow's alternate self appears in Sunnydale, wreaking havoc, making it clear that wishes may not be the best thing to come true and that circumstances often change people — and vice versa. Without the ability to play with time and place and with insistence on too many references to a specific history, the series would only become a pedestrian romp through evil-filled cemeteries.

Like the morality play, *Buffy* is not concerned with the historical environment in which the show is set. Although it is clear that the setting is Southern California of the late twentieth and early twenty-first centuries, that time and place is in many ways inconsequential to the story as it unfolds. Additionally, larger world events taking place during the course of the show rarely make it into the *Buffy*verse. A case in point is lack of any direct reference to the attacks of September 11, 2001. While other shows with continuous narratives, such as NBC's *The West Wing*, disrupted their narrative arcs momentarily to address the attacks, *Buffy* did not. The entire show has been built upon attacks, the "other," and saving the world. By not specifically addressing a contemporary historic event, the narrative is able to continually de-historicize and displace itself from the realm of ordinary existence.

Ordinary existence does creep into the series. Pateman argues that the consumer-oriented individual is a "historical quirk" and that the instinct of a person to need a group and the other needs of characters overwhelm narcissistic individualism in favor of a collective good. We disagree. Even in the coalescence of the collective, the individual and his/her material and psychological desires lead to a therapeutic process that is often viewed as the means to the necessary end. It is here that we can see how the morality play of the *Buffy the Vampire Slayer* world is evidence of the changed ethos in American culture. We are no longer living in a world dominated by the Christian ethos of sin and salvation epitomized by the medieval morality play; rather we are living in the world of sin and salvation that is given in therapeutic terms.

Many of Shakespeare's plays, not far removed from the medieval world of the morality play tradition, demonstrate the changing hegemony of Shakespeare's world: a shift from religious hegemony to secular, nationalistic hegemony. If we take the model of the fifteenth and sixteenth century morality play and examine Shakespeare as example of a playwright on the cusp of a changing world, influenced by the past and influencing the future, then we can see evidences of morality plays in the Elizabethan dramas of Shakespeare and Christopher Marlowe, but we must keep in mind that both these playwrights strove to create new genres out of the old.

Marlowe's *Dr. Faustus* for example, often considered a great morality play of the Elizabethan stage, challenged the genre by allowing the Vice character to win in the end. Shakespeare uses the same character type, Vice, in many of his plays in the form of Aaron from *Titus Andronicus*, Richard III from *Richard III*, Edmund from *King Lear*, and Iago from *Othello*. These characters do not "find" their evil through some connection with a religious understanding of evil. Rather they are evil because they were born that way. The destruction of the evil and the salvation of the central characters in Shakespeare's morality plays does not come at the hands of religious salvation but through individuals who are able to recognize their faults, however late, and repent for their misdeeds. Ultimately, their sacrifice has a lasting effect on the government/nation/political power of their world: Othello to Venice, Romeo and Juliet to Verona, Macbeth to Scotland, Titus (Andronicus) to Rome, and so on.

Shakespeare also frequently used direct references to medieval morality plays by incorporating obvious allegorical characters and portrayals of abstractions in his plays, such as the chorus in *Henry V* and *Romeo and Juliet*, Time in *The Winter's Tale*, and disguised characters of Tamara and sons as Revenge, Murder, and Rape in *Titus Andronicus*. Shakespeare correctly identified and brilliantly articulated major shifts in the intellectual culture of his world during the sixteenth and early seventeenth centuries: economic, political, religious, scientific, and philosophical. By incorporating aspects of the changing world in his dramas and poetry, Shakespeare created and left an important record of these changes.

Much like the era in which Shakespeare wrote, the late twentieth and early twenty-first centuries were a period of *fin de cycle*—end of cycle—ambivalence. It was a paradoxical time of simultaneous optimism and dread for the upcoming new century. In the most recent transition perhaps, it was largely based simply on the changing of the calendar, the millennial change from years that began in the one-thousands to ones that begin in the two thousands. One hundred years before, in the transition from the nineteenth to twentieth centuries, historians such as Henry Adams observed and noted a similar change.

In the *Buffy* world, we also see a shift to a worldview in which consumerism and personality are elements that dominate the social and cultural landscape. The disenchanted, rationalized world of Sunnydale is constantly confronted, because of its location on the Hellmouth, by the enchanted world of hell, demons, and vampires. To combat these forces, the realm of superstition is accessed through the use of religious symbols and supernatural magic, but in most instances the symbols are dislodged from their original religious connotation. Although religious iconography, such as crosses and holy water, frequently play an important role in controlling these forces of evil, the church (and its original grounding in Christianity) is not what gives these weapons power. The objects are displaced, disconnected, and de-enchanted from their original location and symbolism. In essence, the religious iconography in the show is secularized. Inwardly, characters (especially Buffy) are confronted with ethical, emotional, and sociological questions that force a consideration of feelings and a need for a decision-making process. Those considerations are most frequently approached and solved via the world of psychological explorations of feelings and emotions.

In this way the series speaks to the new voice of moral authority. According to some who espouse the therapeutic ethos, no longer is the church and the culture of character the hegemonic force in society, at least in American culture; instead, the touchstone for moral authority lies in therapeutic responses to personal and social questions. For example, characters must make decisions based on their personal experiences and not based in an Augustinian black and white world. In "The Gift," Giles kills Ben, the human face of Glory, the hell-god, because Giles sees the need to expunge the possibility of continuing evil emanating from a still-living Glory.

Buffy cannot kill Ben; she is the hero who bases her morals in an absolute: good people do not kill humans. However, in "Becoming, Part Two," she kills her love — and first lover — Angel (a "good" vampire who goes bad and then back to good) because she must save the world — and this is her curse, her gift, and her destiny. This experience leads her to vow *not* to kill the Key, her sister Dawn, even if Dawn is originally not human and even if this will save the world from destruction ("The Gift").

Since she has used magic so dangerously and had to give it up, Willow refuses to use magic to save the group both in "Older and Far Away" (the group is held hostage in Buffy's house by Dawn's wish) and in "As You Were" (the group needs help in finding and eliminating a demon). However, in spite of the danger, she chooses to use magic in "Chosen" when she potentiates all the possible Slayers, sharing power with many girls.

Each of the characters makes a moral decision, based on personal experiences and personal knowledge. *Buffy* is not conveying a new moral message; rather, it uses a new position to ground the moral message.

Drawing on the insecurities and fears of people about their lives and their relations to others, the "therapeutic ethos" pushed the concept of gratification, fulfillment, and peace-of-mind through the consumption of commodities, according to Lasch and Lears, and the necessity for development of personhood. The therapeutic ideology created an environment in which consumption was not only acceptable and necessary but also fulfilled the soul of the individual. However, religion and morality are not dismissed (nor are they in *Buffy*, despite any real grounding in "the church"). Although Philip Rieff maintained that personal psychology replaced religion (Loss), Eva S. Moskowitz's *In Therapy We Trust: America's Obsession with Self-Fulfillment* maintains that religion is only transmuted in the light of the therapeutic ethos. Religion acts to reconcile God and person, aiding in attaining happiness and not deleting belief in God: Sin is "alienation from God" and salvation is "personal 'wholeness' achieved through a reunion with God manifest in a 'Beloved Community'" (Loss). Therefore, a morality based in the person and in the community exists. One of the elements of "becoming" a "whole" person is understanding self. The need to be fulfilled, complete, and satisfied is best exemplified in consumerist behaviors but is even more completely understood in the realm of feelings.

In the twenty-first century the fundamental question changes from the earlier philosphical question of "Why am I?" to the existential question of "Who am I?" The epistomological, or knowledge-based, construct of meaning has changed from one in which intellectual exploration can lead to self-awareness to one in which psychological explorations will lead to self-realization. In the *Buffy*verse there are frequent references to "I'm nobody" ("Anne") and "What if I'm nobody?" (Anya, "Selfless"). Each of the characters has to become "somebody" to be fulfilled.

Much of the fandom literature refers to the psychological nature of the show. "Buffy has played out in the same setting, an eruption of good and evil, Christian and pagan, crosses and spells, books and computers, crude stakes and high-tech taser blasters," states Paul McDonald: "Buffy herself has been repeatedly split down the middle, her life divided by her desire to be a teenage girl and her destiny to be the Chosen One. Yet instead of embracing all of one and ignoring the other, she strives to bring the fragmented pieces of her psyche together." McDonald concludes this thought: "Ultimately, this may be the central theme of the show as well as our lives, her struggle to reclaim a sense of wholeness a mirror reflection of our own."

For some of the characters on *Buffy*, the consumer personality becomes the main focus for understanding the self. For example, Cordelia is, at the outset of *Buffy*, obsessed with consumerism. She is not interested in Willow, dressed by her mother in the "softer side of Sears" ("Welcome to the Hellmouth"); she is interested in the better-dressed Buffy from the magical land of Neiman Marcus until Buffy extends friendship to the high school "losers" Xander and Willow ("The Harvest").

However, through circumstance and because she has her life saved *so* many times by Buffy,[4] Cordelia becomes one of the Scooby Gang, albeit reluctantly. She further evolves as she loses her moneyed status and realizes that her worth is not based in her past privilege. (As noted before, in "The Prom," Xander, even after she has left him, buys her the prom dress she covets.) She begins to become a "real" person, developing a personality divorced from consumerism. The personality becomes the focus of differentiations. The personality is dependent upon understanding the self. In order to avoid the superficiality of being only a personality that is surface level, depth is achieved by exploring emotions. Cordelia, through her three seasons on *Buffy* and her five seasons on *Angel*, explores a myriad of events, emotions, and development — to become a "higher being."

In the first seasons of the *Buffy*verse, the "sameness" of society is marked by the traditional high school groups: the jocks, the popular girls, the geeks, and the freaks. Characters who appear the same — in appearance and lifestyle (Cordelia and Harmony) — are viewed as the norm because they adhere to society's established consumerist rules. The other group, the Scooby Gang, is marked by its differences. Their personalities are not constructed through consumerism because they recognize their own individuality, even as they are members of the group. They also recognize that their differences make explorations of emotions and inner feelings necessary in order to fully complete themselves as human beings.

Harold Bloom's contention that Shakespeare invented the human may still leave much to be debated, but this sense of personality plays an important role in the therapeutic ethos. Henry Laurent's discussion of the realization of the self in the world, appearing in *Personality: How to Build It* (New York, 1915), is the primary focus of Warren Susman's chapter on "Personality and the Making of Twentieth Century Culture." At the heart of Susman's understanding of the importance of self in the twentieth century is the emphasis placed on the individual standing out from the crowd. In the twentieth century the self is identified through personality, and, according to Susman, "Personality is the quality of being somebody" (277). This is a recurring theme throughout *Buffy*. All the characters, starting from their liminal states as teenagers, are constantly on a quest for self-realization. More often than not, especially in the world of therapeutic responses to problems, the self is revealed through feelings and emotions. Understanding and controlling those emotions helps lead the self to become a more fully-realized human being.

Throughout the series, the feelings of characters are at the center of things: Spike's feelings for Buffy, Buffy's feelings for Angel, Tara and Willow's feelings for each other, Xander's feelings of inadequacy compared to other members of the Scooby Gang, Giles's conflicted feelings as pseudo-father figure to Buffy, Buffy's desires to be "just a girl." The psychological conflict of the show is based in the constant struggle for characters who examine and re-examine and discover their inner emotional problems. In Season Six's "Villains," Warren, just before his death, says to Willow, "Don't you want to talk about my feelings?" In the same season's "Conversations with Dead People," Buffy is psychoanalyzed by a recently-turned vampire high school friend who was a psychology major in college. The Freudian tenants of restraint versus release (*An Outline*) are frequently at the center of episode storylines and actions. Which action will the character take? What consequence will ensue? In "I Only Have Eyes for You" the consequence of release — the untrammeled lust and then accidental killing of a lover — leads to disorder in the halls of Sunnydale High, disorder that must be ordered by the Scooby Gang's resolution of the lust/death. In "Teacher's Pet," Xander is almost mated with and eaten by a human-preying praying mantis substitute teacher because of his desire for release.

Shakespeare did not invent the self as moral-agent. What Shakespeare did was to create depth of character through personality traits that sometimes contradict and confound themselves. Harold Bloom writes, "insofar as we ourselves value, and deplore, our own personalities, we are the heirs of Falstaff and of Hamlet, and of all the persons who throng Shakespeare's theatre of what might be called the colors of the spirit" (4). Moral agency is not at the heart of understanding representations of the self in the twentieth and twenty-first centuries; instead, it is the desire to assert and to achieve a personality, a sense of a fully-realized self in a society that values sameness. In the late capitalist world of the twentieth century the "self" is what individuals are left to create, having moved from fulfilling roles in a community to becoming individuals in communitarian groups.

Ironically, the self-realization and achievement of understanding a "higher self" in the therapeutic ethos harkens back to early theologies that were first in competition with and then persecuted by early Christian thought and believers. This hints of a "Manichean" mode of thinking, a theory that specifies human beings have a dualistic nature: a soul (the realm of the spiritual) and a body (the realm of the material). In this dichotomy, the soul defines the person and is incorruptible, but it is under the domination of a foreign power. Humans are said to be able to be saved from this power (matter) if they come to know who they are and identify themselves with their soul. The person is seen as a battleground for these powers: the good part is the soul, which is composed of light, and the bad part is the body, composed of dark earth (Wilson 150). Similarly the therapeutic ethos enourages attention to the self through explorations of the inner self, emotions, or feelings. In a therapeutic society humans have two natures, not a single free will, from which to choose.

For the Manichean, the higher self only emerges after great internal — and maybe external — struggle. In the therapeutic ethos, a therapist helps the individual to discover his or her feelings. The therapist encourages individuals to tend to their self interests and focus on emotional needs and feelings. In this process the therapist defends the individual's feelings as a source for self-validation (Dworkin). However, in the *Buffy*verse, characters do not need a therapist to defend their feelings — or search for self-validation; they have the Scoobies for that.

Buffy the Vampire Slayer finds its therapeutic responses and strength not just in the individuals but also in the collective group.[5] This presents a new way of viewing the therapeutic model. The narcissism that therapeutic ethos theorists Rieff and Lasch speak of and complain about in their description of therapeutic ethos is replaced by a collective working to solve the problems facing the individual and the world. The most obvious example is the joining together of the Scooby Gang and Giles to overcome Adam, the evil opponent of Season Four. In a spell, Xander, Giles, and Willow join themselves as heart, mind, and spirit in order to actuate the "hand" (supernatural super–Buffy) so Buffy is able to defeat Adam ("Primevel").

The responses are still therapeutic — the realm of feelings and the inner mind — but it is only through working together to overcome the evil inherent in the *Buffy*verse, that the whole Scooby Gang, not just Buffy, is able to save the world ... a lot.

Notes

1. Augustine and Aquinas were writers and philosophers who heavily influenced Christian church philosophy and theology. Both are considered seminal thinkers who codified certain elements of church thought. Both believed in a dichotomous world in which good and evil are totally separate from each other (and that every action falls into one of the two categories) and that the material world and the spiritual world are also totally separate.

2. A miracle play is a drama that dealt with religious subjects and is based on Bible stories or the stories of saint's lives. A mystery play is a drama also based on a Bible story, but one that deals with Christ's life, death and resurrection. A morality play is a drama that personifies abstract elements, such as lust, pride, etc.

3. In *The Castle of Perseverance*, the life of the "everyman" is seen as a child, a youth, and a old man. As a youth he sins but is led to the Castle by Penitence and Confession. Vices cannot prevail against the Castle. As an old man, he sins again but is rescued from hell by Pity and Peace.

4. "Out of Sight, Out of Mind," "The Witch," "Some Assembly Required," etc.

5. See Frances E. Morris's chapter.

Witchy Women

Witchcraft in Buffy the Vampire Slayer and in Contemporary African Culture

Juliet Evusa

When I first started watching *Buffy the Vampire Slayer*, I began toying with the idea of offering an "outsider"[1] interpretation of the meanings and roles of witchcraft. I feel that contrasting the representation of witchcraft between geographic and cultural areas is important because it demonstrates that, even though witchcraft is diverse in its cultural appearances, the dynamic of power it presumes operates in a similar fashion globally. Highlighting major similarities (and differences) on the meanings, roles, and practices of the representation of witchcraft in *Buffy* and in the contemporary African community allows us to look at the uses of power in different contexts and to investigate how similar uses of power can be, even in the face of cultural differences.

As we think about *Buffy the Vampire Slayer* and witchcraft practice in Africa, we see that, in both scenarios, first, the location of magic has been changed; second, witchcraft is symbolic of female empowerment; third, we can distinguish between the utilization of positive and negative witchcraft, and its moral evaluation; fourth, witches also function as a metaphor for social outcasts, subjected to public persecution when exposed; and, last, witchcraft is abhorred by established churches.

The Location of Magic in a Contemporary World

Anthropological scholars have come up with various definitions of witchcraft, such as "local beliefs about good, evil, causation, divination and healing that provided a coherent ideology for daily living" (Fortes, as quoted in Moore and Sanders 3); "the use of supernatural power by one person to damage others" (Austen 90); or an "illegitimate action engaging capacities of human persons to cause harm or accumulate wealth and power by mysterious means" (Ashforth 206). Moore and Sanders's reference to the terms "local" and "daily living" insinuates that witchcraft has to be understood within a particular period as well as cultural context; hence, they imply the term may lose meaning if transferred to different circumstances. Their broad definition also provides a more-contextualized approach to witchcraft, including the notion that there are both positive and negative uses of witchcraft. Although Austen's definition pays particular attention to the use of magic to harm others, Ashforth's introduces a contemporary aspect of the practice linked to the new forms of consumption — the "comodification" of witchcraft for purposes of amassing wealth. Therefore, these definitions attest to the complex nature of this practice — first, that it is historical; second, that it is specific to local contexts; third, that it represents both negative and positive purposes; and finally, that it has evolved and changed over time, hence, is specifically tied to different forms of modernity. This is the case with the depictions of the role and the practice of witchcraft in *Buffy* and in the contemporary African community.

Witchcraft is not only specific to local contexts; it also is tied to forms of modernity. Both cases, *Buffy* and Africa, present an opportunity for explaining the different meanings of magic. In *Buffy*, for example, magic and witchcraft are open to a broader and more diverse set of meanings than those portrayed in the traditional occult where witches, according to Krzywinska, "seduced men, disrupted patrilinear dynasties, caused storms, danced under the moonlight with the devil, captured and baked small children, and summoned the spirits of the dead to see the future" (186). This traditional portrayal of magic is parallel to assumptions in traditional African communities in which witches were associated with certain traits. For example, they were believed to stare fiercely at others; possess powers that cause death, infertility, diseases, miscarriages, crop failures; and dance, as well as roam at night, stark naked or sometimes in animal form. In the sixteenth and seventeenth centuries, witchcraft was disapproved as a pagan practice in Western Europe and in North America; those accused of practicing witchcraft were executed after a legal trial. In Salem, Massachusetts, for example, the witch hunting incidence of 1692 resulted in the death of twenty suspected witches and the trials of thousands of people (Klaits 4).

In both Africa and *Buffy* we witness the intermingling of traditionalist modes of presenting witchcraft with contemporary notions. This is clearly displayed in *Buffy* when we are first introduced to Jenny Calendar in "I Robot You Jane." Jenny is the high school computer teacher and her computer skills are instrumental in updating the concepts of magic in the show. With the help of her computer knowledge and network, Jenny gets rid of a medieval demon, Moloch the Corrupter, from the web. Moloch is unintentionally uploaded into the school's library computer system during a book scanning session. By storing her magic on disk as well as performing magic over the Internet, Jenny invokes a modern aspect of magic — "techno-magic" — that is notably different from the conventional practice involving casting spells and dabbling.

On the other hand, as the high school librarian and Buffy's Watcher, Giles's knowledge of books and his suspicion of computers is representative of old knowledge. Giles is adamant that he will survive the modern world without being slave to the "idiot box," which he misnames the computer. (As Jenny, his girlfriend to be, points out in "I Robot You Jane," this is a term applied by "normal" people to the television and not the computer.)

Another example of the mingling of the traditional modes of presenting witchcraft with contemporary ones is displayed in *Buffy* by the main witch character Willow. The episode "Hush" introduces us to a group of UC Sunnydale's Wiccan members whom Willow calls "a bunch of wanna-be's." Despite their invoking concepts associated with the "contemporary" feminist spirituality movement, Willow accuses them of failing to practice the "conventional" prehistoric magic, complete with spells. Therefore, Willow rejects the contemporary feminist movement and insists that she practices "old-agey" witchcraft ("Show Time"). We, however, witness her regularly employing the Internet as a source in the fight against evil. By using Jenny Calendar's "techno-pagan" skills (computer disks containing "cyber-magical" research) and occasionally borrowing Giles's books, Willow merges what she terms as old-agey witchcraft with modern technology.

We also see this contemporary practice of witchcraft in *Buffy* when Amy Madison's ex-cheerleader witch mother exploits youth and beauty as means to power to serve her own egotistic desires. In "The Witch," we first encounter Amy's mother in her attic using, amongst other magical objects, a Barbie doll that she converts into a voodoo doll to perform a spell. The use of contemporary artifacts—in *Buffy's* case Barbie dolls—as a substitute for conventional ones is another prime example of the postmodern practice of magic.

This is also the case with contemporary African magicians who have been known to use modern artifacts or ingredients in place of traditional objects once used by spiritual specialists. Historians have attributed this "comodification"— or mass production of magical objects— to modern influences brought about as a result of migration. Carolyn Long's exploration of the historical roots of magical objects in African religion reveals that most objects consisted of natural items, including roots, herbs, handmade dolls, shells, animal horns, and stones that were selected according to their "natural" principle of imitative magic (99). What makes traditional voodoo dolls more authentic is the fact that, during the making process, their creators performed rituals to ensure their resemblance to their intended "target."

Likewise, witchcraft within the African community operates as an important aspect of modernity. Recent works on witchcraft suggest that the success

of some elites—civil servants (also known as state officials) and politicians—
is connected, in one way or another, to the occult. Todd Sanders's article highlights accounts of "materialized witchcraft" involving the sale of human body
parts—human skins, vaginas, and penises—that are said to be in high demand
by sorcerers who create powerful concoctions believed to make the "rich richer,
and the mighty mightier" (160). It is also not uncommon to hear rumors and
stories from local communities accusing elites of utilizing illicit means to amass
"evil" wealth, as well as attain new positions and roles. Although it is impossible to draw the line between the legitimization of prosperity brought about
by the presence of "good" and "evil" wealth, the latter has been associated with
"materialized" witchcraft.

Examples of postmodern ways of accumulating private and economic gains
through witchcraft activities include reports from the Tanzania media that the
authorities arrested people for the alleged murder of six school boys, purport-
edly found skinned (Sanders 160). The report adds that the alleged murderers
were attempting to sell the skins for private economic and political gain. Other
examples include rumored stories from Nigeria involving the trading of relatives to cannibals who "consume" their life-force in order to get rich and, from
Sierra Leone, where witches are suspected of performing human sacrifices in
order to obtain medicines of power and enrichment for their patrons. What is
common amongst these rumored accounts and stories is the (old) belief that
concoctions derived from vital human body parts (especially children and
women's reproductive organs) provide patrons access to the products and priv-
ileges of globalized modernity in the form of western consumer goods and
international mobility (Shaw 66).

Accounts invoking modern forms of accumulating wealth linked to the
occult forces are not confined to the African continent. Media reports from the
Netherlands indicate that authorities cracked down on a crime ring that
allegedly used voodoo to gain hold of children before smuggling them abroad
to work as sex slaves in France, Italy and Spain (Little). A similar story comes
from Haiti, where witches owe their success to the exploitation of "zombie"
laborers. These witches are rumored to transform people (especially children
and the youth) into zombies and put them to work on "invisible plantations"
(Geschiere 139). Cultural anthropologists attribute this obsession with the
occult as a way of making sense of ideas and experiences that are current in
different times and socioeconomic contexts (Shaw 51), ideas and experiences
that confuse or frighten.

Witchcraft as a Cultural Metaphor for Women's Power

Witchcraft is also metaphoric. Witchcraft is "known" as the domain of
women. Stevenson (129) and Krzywinska (186) both assert that the idea of

witchcraft in *Buffy* symbolizes a cultural metaphor for women's power. These writers contend that, throughout the show, the audience witnesses Willow's growth in magical expertise from an introverted and unconfident girl with no experience in magic to a more-confident, empowered woman.

Likewise, in African communities, witchcraft is associated with female empowerment. Although the practice of witchcraft can be acquired through learning, it can also pass from mother to daughter. In *Buffy*, for example, Amy inherits her mother's powers. In "Bewitched, Bothered and Bewildered," Amy, upon Xander's persistence, attempts to perform a spell to help him regain Cordelia's love. Xander witnesses Amy cast an invisible spell on a teacher who accepts Amy's practice of witchcraft is transmitted from one generation to another, and given the fact that her mother was a witch, it is inevitable that she is capable of performing a spell.

The idea of the use of witchcraft for cultural empowerment is also similar within the African community where it is common for female witches to transmit their powers to their daughters.[2] Findings from an ethnographic study of witchcraft conducted by Middleton and Winter attest to the fact that the practice of witchcraft is transmitted matrilineally (5). These ethnographers discovered that among the Tallensi of Ghana, women alone can pass their powers to their daughters whereas the power of male witches dies with them (Middleton and Winter 5). Witchdoctors, on the other hand, who tend to be male, can pass their powers to their sons. This is true with the majority of African communities in which magic is practiced.

Willow's power is displayed in early seasons. Not only is she scientifically as well as technologically inclined, she also gains feminine empowerment by becoming a powerful witch. It is through her innate magic powers that Willow acquires a position of power, thus, challenging the traditional roles that females hold in society. As a practicing witch, Willow holds the capability of performing astounding things that are beyond ordinary human beings' control. As the series progresses, her powers become so frightening that Buffy remarks, "I need you, Will. You're my big gun, the strongest person here" ("The Gift"). Although Willow does not use her magic for selfish ends at the beginning, she later on discovers that "magic is all that is left to possibly satisfy her desire for power, dominance, control, recognition, and self-image, a desire that really can never be satisfied" (Richardson and Rabb 100).

When we are first introduced to Willow in "Welcome to the Hellmouth," Xander implores Willow to assist him with his math assignment. Willow's knowledge of advanced academics and computer proficiency earns her a reputation of being the class "geek." In the same episode we learn of Willow's insecurity with boys and her inability to engage in meaningful conversation with them. Her conversation with Buffy reveals that "Well, when I'm with a boy I like ... it's hard for me to say anything cool, or witty — or at all" ("Welcome to the Hellmouth"). She does get over this fear by the time she starts dating Oz, but it is in her relationship with Tara that she occasionally uses the power of magic to exert control over the relationship. For instance, in "Tabula Rasa," Willow uses magic to make Tara forget that they have been quarreling.

In the last three seasons of the series, we watch Willow making the transition from "seeking dominance and power in academia and computers to seeking it in magic and witchcraft" (Richardson and Rabb 100–01). It is though her preoccupation with witchcraft that Willow gains confidence, or rather, "sexual empowerment." Not only does witchcraft enable her to reveal the extent of her crush on Xander ("Bewitched, Bothered and Bewildered"), it may also function to allow her to realize her sexual identity—lesbianism ("Halloween").

Willow, however, also uses her power to ease her pain and ends up hurting her friends. When she thinks her boyfriend Oz is interested in fellow-werewolf Verucca, Willow tries to invoke evil spirits to break their dishonest hearts, but she is stopped ("Wild at Heart"). She ends up blaming herself for failing to make him stay. She turns to her power to ease her broken heart, an action which backfires and leads to Giles's blindness and Buffy's and Spike's engagement ("Something Blue"). We see Willow's transition and the increase in her powers which enable her to utilize her witchcraft to dominate in a masculine way.

In African communities, witchcraft is set up as the domain of women. Since most African women lack opportunities for leadership, as well as collective self-expression, the practice of witchcraft becomes a form of empowerment. It is also a means for elderly women to attain social status. Some African communities are, however, experiencing an emerging trend involving the use of witchcraft for sexual and economic empowerment. This relatively modern trend presents a new threat to the status quo—that of challenging patriarchal boundaries. In Nigeria, for example, youthful witches are believed to support themselves through the commodification of their bodies or what locals believe to be alliances with the "wild spiritual forces" (Bastian 82). These forces perform the important task of protecting as well as introducing the women to their "prey"— in this case, rich and powerful males. Rumored accounts reveal that young urban women acquire occult powers to challenge patriarchal boundaries by using the power of their profuse sexuality (Bastian 88). This emerging trend goes against societal expectations in most African communities for a variety of reasons. First, these young urban females are living outside the lineage of control; second, these women are participating in modern social lives—including sexuality not tied to marriage; and third, they are failing to fulfill, amongst other roles, child-bearing and -rearing roles. Unlike the typical female sex trader, these Nigerian witches claim revenge—rather than material gain—as their goal. This, according to accounts by Bastian, is accomplished by using "powers residing in their vagina" to destroy rich and powerful men by making them impotent and useless—to the point that their business fails to prosper and their families are destroyed (82).

This idea behind challenging patriarchal boundaries also appears in *Buffy*. In both cases, witchcraft is credited with the power to "take away male organs," thus threatening male sexuality. This introduces the notion that witchcraft is a metaphor for female defiance (Bodger 8). Some argue that sexuality has always been central to the representation of the witch in history. In both Western and African traditional societies, those practicing witchcraft — mainly females — were feared to possess supernatural powers threatening to men and, by extension, the patriarchal order. *Buffy* offers a depiction of this metaphor of female defiance in various ways. First, envisioning Willow and Tara in a lesbian relationship is, according to Bodger, an updated view of the "defiant" woman threatening male sexuality (8). By dating a female, Willow defies male patriarchy; she is no longer in need of sexual, as well as emotional, fulfillment from the opposite sex — thus, marginalizing men. This view sends a message, on behalf of the patriarchal order, that "defiant women are a threat" and must therefore be brought under control.

Second, Willow's growing reliance on magic in Seasons Five and Six displays her inability to handle power. Whenever she encounters rejections in her relationships, Willow becomes more absorbed in witchcraft to deal with her heartaches. For instance, in "Something Blue" and "Doppelgangland," witchcraft becomes an outlet for her emotions, a way to deal with stress and hardships, a way to escape her problem with rejection. She, therefore, uses magic, at times beyond her competency, to solve minor issues that could otherwise have been taken care of without magical spells.

Willow also uses her power to dominate in a masculine way. By doing so, Jowett points out, Willow's empowerment goes against patriarchal structures that keep power exclusively for men and are also designed to keep women under control (40–42). We see this in "Flooded" when Giles is disappointed with Willow for using powers beyond her understanding to resurrect Buffy. He refers to her magical skills as "amateur." Willow angrily replies, "I am very powerful and maybe it is not a good idea for you to piss me off." Her reaction demonstrates that, unlike Buffy, who is under Giles's "Watch," she does not need masculine approval for her decisions.

Buffy initially represents the persistence of male domination over women by sending the message that female power is acceptable only when authorized by men. It can be argued that, unlike Willow, Buffy is assigned a "Watcher" who is supposed to keep her use of power in check. This argument supports the notion that strong femininity is usually only permissible when governed by a stronger masculinity. Although Willow becomes almost as powerful as Buffy, unlike Buffy, she has no controlling patriarchal figure to guide her; as a result, Bodger argues, she uses her powers for evil (6). However, the series breaks with this concept when Buffy defies the Watcher's Council and removes herself from their control ("Checkpoint") and when Buffy breaks with Giles, telling him she's learned all she can from him ("Lies My Parents Told Me").

Similarly, in contemporary Nigerian communities, Bastian notes, while feared, urban teen witches who "demonstrate the tendency to move beyond normalized gender boundaries" through the commodification of their bodies are ultimately tamed by "money magicians" and brought under the scrutiny and control by masculine forces (86). The "money magicians" take up the role of their watchers, protectors, or "spiritual husbands" who empower them with magic that traps and eventually destroys rich men. Findings from Bastian's ethnographic study in urban Nigerian also reveal that, apart from submitting to the masculine authority of "money magicians," teenage witches also yield to the power of evangelical Christianity (88). Therefore, by submitting to money magicians as well as the Christian religion, these witches are firmly put back into their place: that of the "properly fertile, properly submissive, no longer magical girl" (Bastian 88). We witness something of the same trend in *Buffy* when Willow agrees to temporarily lay off her magic and attend the "witch rehabilitation" school with Giles in England, although she is certainly strong enough to resist.

The Moral Evaluation of Witchcraft

In *Buffy the Vampire Slayer* and in modern Africa, we see a distinction between negative and positive witchcraft; its moral evaluation depends upon the community of the victims of misfortune. Although local terms associated with witchcraft, magic, and powers are very specific in their meanings, as is the case in our earlier definition of witchcraft,[3] not all of these terms are associated with harmful activities. Witchcraft historiography reveals that the "same technique may be moral and approved in one context and immoral and outlawed in another" (Moore and Sanders 4). As a result, anthropologists have experienced difficulties while attempting to distinguish between witchcraft and sorcery. In Kenya, for instance, there are two kinds of witches: *mganga* (a Swahili word for a traditional medicine person) who uses supernatural powers to perform good deeds and *mchawi* (a Swahili word for sorcerer), who uses evil magic to harm others. While a *mganga* holds supernatural power that is instinctive, a *mchawi* practices evil magic learned intentionally to harm others. In Francophone Africa (western African region), on the other hand, the French translation for the word "witchcraft," according to Moore and Sanders, means *sorcellerie* (3). In other African societies, the terms witchcraft, sorcery, and juju (another word for voodoo) are used interchangeably.

A number of studies have noted a distinction between female witches, who are stigmatized, and men, who are recognized as "healers" and legitimate figures of political and ritual authority (Austen 91). In many parts of Africa, while negative (harmful) witchcraft is associated with women (and children to some extent), men are known to possess the harmless or positive witchcraft and are, therefore, referred to as "witchdoctors." Using the term "doctor" at the end of the epithet associates it with positive, as well as modern connotations. While witches uncover the hidden supernatural misfortunes, witchdoctors are believed to treat "external symptoms" associated with diseases, such as malaria, tuberculosis, and HIV/AIDS. In many parts of Africa, prominent leaders, especially those seeking to be elected in office, are believed to seek the services of witchdoctors who specialize in both healing (witchdoctor) and supernatural (witchcraft) powers. Therefore, a public position held by a male witch makes witchcraft somehow more tolerable, and even in some cases celebrated.

In *Buffy*, for example, Gregory Stevenson notes that "magic used for selfish ends ultimately results in destruction or pain, while on the other hand, when used for noble ends is a valuable asset" (129). In earlier episodes, Willow starts to experiment with witchcraft out of curiosity. She begins by using her power in the service of others. For instance, in "Primeval," she casts a spell that allows Buffy to overcome her enemy. On the other hand, she also indulges in magic for purely selfish reasons. We see this in "Villains," "Grave," and "Two to Go," which depict Willow's use of magic driven by her own selfish desires and passions. In addition, in "Wild at Heart," Willow uses magic to try to escape from her pain at losing Oz. Finally, she uses magic, at the risk of great personal loss, to help overcome the First Evil in "Chosen."

Despite choosing to situate Sunnydale right on top of the Hellmouth — an opening straight into hell — Whedon does all he can to present most witchcraft as a positive, harmless, and empowering force. As a result, witchcraft in *Buffy* is not represented as necessarily evil; witchcraft practiced with evil or individualist purposes, on the other hand, invites evil.

This is also true within the African communities. Magic in Africa's precolonial era involved an entire community and aimed to maintain a subtle harmony between people and the natural world. For instance, magic was used to invoke the spirits of the rain gods during severe droughts, as well as cure any epidemics sweeping across a community. Conventional witchcraft was also responsible for the fertility of the community, livestock, and harvest. Modern magic, on the other hand, is about the individual and tends to be commodified. Magic permeates modern African society, where students resort to it before sitting for exams, politicians use it to defeat their rivals, soccer teams use it before a game, business men use it to destroy their competitors, and women use it to "tame" their promiscuous husbands.

Witchcraft and Religion

Finally, in both *Buffy* and Africa, we see witchcraft abhorred by established churches. Modern Christianity, however, has not displaced ideas about witchcraft and the occult; it has provided a new context in which they make perfect sense. In Africa, for instance, although witchcraft is an integral part of Africa's traditional religious heritage and permeates modern African society, it was declared "satanic" and therefore illegal with the coming of missionaries during the colonial era. However, modern day Africa is beginning to witness a radically different approach dealing with this phenomena. Onyinah's study of ministry in Africa revealed a current trend undertaken by most churches to include exorcist activities in their programs (332). In Kenya, for instance, the Pentecostal Church chooses to convert, heal, reconcile, as well as reintegrate witches into the community, as opposed to punishing them. By doing so, witches avoid public persecution. This approach is based on the Christian belief that witchcraft is caused by a particular kind of ancestral evil spirit which can be removed by exorcism. It is, therefore, not uncommon to witness suspected witches yielding to the power of evangelical Christians or diviners who ward off the power of the evil spirits by invoking the Holy Spirit.

Buffy's frequent depiction of witchcraft has been a center of controversy among many Christians who believe that the show exalts satanism (Stevenson 128). Yet, the producer of the show, Joss Whedon, does not set out to offer either a positive nor negative representation of modern witchcraft. On the contrary, use of positive magic on *Buffy* restores social order and reflects the moral judgment of the practitioner.

Witches as Representation of Social Outcasts

In *Buffy the Vampire Slayer* and modern Africa, witches can be social outcasts. By portraying witches as social outcasts, it appears that *Buffy* acknowledges the feminist perspective throughout history that patriarchy used accusations of witchcraft to control women who threaten societal norms (Bodger 10). This is true in both cases where the elimination of the "defiant" woman becomes an essential theme. In Africa, for example, witch hunting was controlled during pre-colonial and colonial Africa. This has not been the case during the postcolonial era. Scholarly studies on witchcraft and modernity contend that "witchcraft findings, cleansing and accusations increased with breakdown in social stability, negative effects of colonialism, wage labor, migration, Christianity and urbanization" (Moore and Sanders 8). This is especially true in societies that have declared witch hunting illegal and yet lack mechanisms for addressing this phenomena.

The *Buffy* episode "Gingerbread" provides a novel take on witch persecutions and burnings (Krzywinska 187). The audience is surprised by what seems to be a fierce battle between mothers and daughters, resulting in Amy, Willow, and Buffy nearly being burned. The episode opens with a shocking revelation of what seems to be the ritual murder of two children, and the community begins to suspect witches or Satanists of committing the act. Mothers Opposed to the Occult, an action group, led by Buffy's and Willow's mothers, suspects Willow, Amy, and Michael (a Goth boy), who all turn out to be innocent.

Similarly in Africa, female witches are believed to hide exotic animals, shells, feathers, and other unusual possessions in their homes. When exposed, these witches are subjected to public persecution, ranging from relocation and banishment from the community to public executions. In Kenya there have been reported incidents of arson and murder in the recent past. The worst incident was reported in 1993 when youths attacked and burnt eight elderly women on suspicion that they practiced witchcraft ("Youth"). Similar reports from South Africa reveal that members of a youth organization burnt to death forty-three alleged witches (Niehaus 184). The report adds that, between 1985 and 1995, the execution of suspected witches is estimated to have exceeded 389. In Tanzania, approximately 400 alleged witches were killed between 1997 and 2000 ("Yes, Belief in Witchcraft Is Widespread in Africa"). The rise in the numbers of executions by angry mobs raises crucial questions about what African governments are doing to end the violence against alleged witches.

After independence, most African nations retained the British Witchcraft Act that was designed to punish those who practiced or consulted witchcraft, yet implemented hardly any official laws to apprehend witch killers. However, in the absence of institutional support, villages resort to witch killings. Many African states, as a result, attempted to introduce legislative changes to end "witch hunting." South Africa recently proposed a Witchcraft Control Act to stem witchcraft accusations. However, this attempt to outlaw witchcraft accusations often results in the law taking action against those accused of killing witches (Niehaus 196). The villagers view this as an indication of modern state apparatuses aligning themselves on the side of evil (Moore and Sanders 1). Some village members believe these measures are designed to protect witches and sorceresses against retaliation by their innocent victims.

Conclusion

The central notion guiding this essay confirms the notion that, even though witchcraft is diverse in its cultural appearances, the dynamic of power it presumes operates in a similar fashion globally. Modern witchcraft, despite being shaped by tradition, is brought to life by men and women as they seek to make their current world manageable and meaningful. The writers of *Buffy* use creative, imaginative, and entirely twentieth-century transformations to depict witchcraft as a cultural metaphor for women's empowerment; to distinguish positive and negative witchcraft, and its moral evaluation; to address threats faced by those suspected of practicing witchcraft; and, last, to address the fact that modern Christianity has not displaced ideas about witchcraft and the occult but has provided a new context for them. What is interesting is that these depictions are also reflective of the urban Africa society, in which communities are threatened by newly-empowered women who evoke the image of the witch; where positive witchcraft involves an entire community and aims to maintain a subtle harmony between man and the natural world; and finally, where this practice was declared illegal, but not wiped out, with the coming of missionaries during the colonial era. The role and representation of witchcraft in *Buffy* and the African communities have a lot in common.

Notes

1. I was born in Kenya, schooled in India, and experienced higher education in the United States. Thus, I'm both outsider *and* insider. Okay, I'm cross-cultured.

2. This does not deny rare instances of the transmission of such powers patrilineally from a man to his children.

3. Moore and Sanders broadly define witchcraft as "local beliefs about good, evil, causation, divination and healing that provided a coherent ideology for daily living" (3).

"I'm Cookie Dough"

Exploring Buffy Iconography

───❦───

KENNETH S. HICKS
AND CAROLYN ANNE TAYLOR

Many have argued that *Buffy* contains powerful and positive feminine themes and that Buffy is a kind of feminist icon (Daughtey, Vint, Culp). However, others have criticized the show, claiming that the show recreates a patriarchal environment that further encourages violence against women (Bodger). Similarly, many group-identity activists initially cheered some of the more daring story lines, but protested when favored characters died or were portrayed in a negative light (Greenman). A more positive but less explicitly "feminist" interpretation seems justified. We are less interested in criticizing the current state of "Buffy as feminist" literature than to present an affirmative defense of a "post-feminist" interpretation of Buffy.

While there is little current consensus about what constitutes "feminism" and "post feminism," "many views of feminism derive from what is often described as the 'second wave' of feminism of the 1960s and 1970s" (Jowett 4). According to Joanne Hollows, recent thought assumes that "even within specific historical contexts, there is no single feminine identity, but multiple feminine identities," and that "feminine identities are also cross-cut by class, sexual, 'racial,' ethnic, generational and regional identities" (Jowett 4). For the most part, feminists seeking to appropriate *Buffy* as an explicitly-feminist hero appear to appropriate a specific aspect of *Buffy* that fits into a particular interpretation of feminism. However, the fact that the show enjoys ironic juxtapositions does not reliably translate into any explicit feminist narrative. This collapsing of boundaries is characteristic of post-modern thinking, which raises the possibility that Buffy's character should probably be conceived as "post-modern," and to some extent "post-feminine," rather than as an explicitly "feminist" narrative.

Much of feminist literature centers on practical problems that the women's movement brought to the public's attention, such as sexual harassment, economic discrimination, and domestic violence, among others. Several *Buffy* episodes deal with these topics, but the series struggles to avoid reducing women (or Buffy, for that matter) to the status of "mere victims," and therefore (at least potentially) advances a feminist perspective. Although much of the power of the *Buffy* narrative revolves around Buffy receiving help in need, Buffy is rarely portrayed as a damsel in distress. At the same time, in some areas of intense interest to feminists (e.g. reproductive issues, equal pay for equal work, the glass ceiling etc.), *Buffy* has little to nothing to say.

At various points *Buffy* employs archetypes to explore important political and social themes. The most obvious theme — "Buffy as Savior" — offers insight into the challenges of constructing a believable heroic character by exposing character flaws that render Buffy and other feminine characters more believable. A second important archetype — "Buffy as Oppressed Other" — offers insight into the subtle coercion of gender roles that place even heroic women like Buffy at a disadvantage in contemporary society. In many ways, *Buffy* directly challenges the way we think about gender roles in society, but at the same time is silent on issues that are often of central importance to feminists. Whether these lacunae are calculated or simply omissions driven by the imperatives of the storyline is for Joss Whedon and his writers to clarify; in any event, *Buffy* is less interested in advancing an explicitly-feminist narrative than in defending a post-feminist reality in which gender roles have blurred.

Buffy as Savior

From its genesis, *Buffy* was intended as a celebration of the idea of feminine power. While Buffy appears to be a typical California teenager, her status as a "Slayer" provides her with the strength, stamina, reflexes, and healing power to combat superhuman vampires and demons. The origin of the Slayers' powers — first explored in the Season Four finale "Restless" — lies in a prehistoric decision by a group of village shaman to magically substitute the heart of a demon for that of a young girl, who becomes the first Slayer. A number of important implications emerge from this legendary moment.

First, the creation of the role of Slayer was imposed by powerful men on a young, presumably weak, woman. Like every other Slayer before her, Buffy does not choose to become a Slayer, but rather through some mysterious means becomes a Slayer, and she spends quite a bit of time in Seasons One and Two rebelling against this imposition, such as when she runs away after killing Angel at the end of Season Two.[1] This appears to be one reason that many critics have argued that *Buffy* is simply recreating an essentially patriarchal political order (Bodger). That loss of autonomy is offset by what Buffy does with her power. She neither slavishly follows the dictates of the Watcher's Council — who are described as the "descendents" of the first shamans who created the Slayer — nor does she (for the most part) use her power impulsively to advance her own interests. With occasional lapses,[2] Buffy consistently attempts to use power responsibly, and rarely, if ever, resorts to over manipulation to get her way.

Second, the notion that the Slayer's power has its origins in evil[3] becomes an important source of moral ambiguity in *Buffy*. The distinction between good and evil is often blurred, as if power inevitably relates to the capacity for violence, and violence is always evil. The origin of the Slayer's powers in evil may at least partially explain why Buffy is attracted to vampires like Angel and Spike and offers an intriguing window into the show's complicated and ambivalent portrayal of power. In contrast to most vampire-based shows, the writers of *Buffy* clearly rejected a flattened "good-evil" landscape with nothing in-between, and that rejection becomes more pronounced after the high school years. There is a wealth of "gray" explored in an otherwise traditional horror narrative.

Aside from her physical strength and combat skills, Buffy also struggles emotionally to reconcile the horrors of being a Slayer with her "normal" life as a teenager and young adult, sometimes by making morally dubious choices. Especially in the early seasons, the burden of responsibility triggers flight impulses, and Seasons Two and Three begin with Buffy *en absentia*, with her friends discussing their concerns over Buffy's capacity to cope with her latest Slayer-related trauma. At various points in the show, Buffy aggressively uses sex and sexuality to cope with the traumas of being "the Chosen One." For example, in Season Two's "When She Was Bad," Buffy somewhat cruelly taunts her friend Xander (who at the time is nursing a serious crush on Buffy) on the dance floor, which is later revealed as a coping mechanism for her brief death at the end of Season One.

In later seasons, Buffy increasingly experiences difficulty communicating her emotions. She actually goes into a catatonic state in Season Five's "Weight of the World" when her sister Dawn is taken by the demon-god Glory, and Willow is compelled to work a complicated spell to pull her out. This remoteness is frequently conveyed in scenes in which Buffy is looking on while her friends enjoy themselves dancing or partying. In Season Six's "Dead Things," Buffy and Spike have sex on the balcony of the Bronze, with Spike whispering, "You try to be with them ... but you always end up in the dark ... with me." Throughout, Buffy is not portrayed as a cardboard, stoic, Beowulf-like figure, but is rather depicted as a very human young woman struggling to deal with enormous responsibility.[4]

The apocalyptical nature of *Buffy* means that the world periodically requires saving. More often than not, Buffy is the savior, frequently through extraordinary acts of courage and self-sacrifice. Twice, Buffy dies in her confrontations with antagonists, and is on the verge of death at the end of Season Six when Willow magically heals her from a gunshot to the chest in "Two to Go." Buffy frequently faces seemingly-certain death, and is often confronted with seemingly-insurmountable odds against seemingly-unbeatable foes. What is remarkable about her triumphs is less her heroism and martial skill than her humanity in identifying the problems and utilizing all the assets available to her.

Buffy's heroism lies less in super powers than in her ability to make command decisions, sacrificing where necessary, correctly perceiving what needs to be done, and in marshalling all of the resources at her command. Frequently, the actions of another member of the Scooby Gang are instrumental to Buffy's survival and success. In war, even flawed assets (e.g. Angel, Anya, Spike, Andrew, etc.) can make valuable contributions to victory. In Seasons Three and Seven, Buffy occupies the role of military leader, organizing defenses and constructing a military strategy. Buffy consistently searches for alternative solutions when it appears that a conventional approach might yield success with unacceptable consequences.[5] The fact that someone named Buffy can occupy so many heroic roles is both iconic and subversive, eroding the notion that women are unable to lead, that men will not follow a woman, and that women lack the ruthlessness necessary to succeed in matters of war.

Buffy as Oppressed Other

Many storylines in *Buffy* effectively explore the nature of female powerlessness. Aside from the fact that as "the Slayer" Buffy is the object of a great deal of malevolent intent, she frequently finds herself suffering the slights of being a relatively-poor middle-class female in contemporary America. In numerous episodes, Buffy is either robbed of her strength or appears insufficiently powerful to confront a particular threat.[6]

Initially, Buffy is portrayed as a child of affluence, complete with designer *ensemble*. However, Slaying is a full-time gig, and, over time, she finds that her most marketable skills are distinctly working class. In Season Five, after the sudden death of her mother, Buffy must drop out of college, unable to afford tuition. In Season Six's "Flooded," when the cost of keeping her mother's house begins to mount and Buffy is compelled to seek a loan, the loan officer treats her with the cold efficiency of a man calculating the earning potential of a young, uneducated woman. Even after Buffy saves his life from a bank-robbing demon, the officer is completely unsympathetic to her needs. In this sense, being a Slayer contrasts completely with Angel's role as sort of a "Travis McGee"–type private investigator (*Angel*). Where charging a fee to clients is feasible for Angel, no one is rushing forward to pay Buffy for the nightly grind of patrolling and killing vampires. What Buffy does is a uniquely "public good"; thus, like so many forms of employment that society labels as "women's work," Slaying simply doesn't pay.

Season Six also sees Buffy reduced to working at a fast food restaurant, the Doublemeat Palace, to make ends meet.[7] There she suffers the indignities of the polyester uniforms, the oppression of being covered in grease, and the mortification of being fed the ideology of fast food by her typically strange manager: "You wanna get something out of this, Buffy?" he asks with the weird intensity that anyone who has put in time at that kind of job can identify, "You put the work in, and ten years from now, you'll be where I am," pointing to a button on his shirt with "10 years" on it ("Doublemeat Palace"). The scene is designed to cause the audience to want Buffy to run screaming from such a fate, but the need for money is stronger than the atavistic terror of a dead-end job. While her friends visit her at work and treat her with pity, a visit by Spike characteristically strikes to the heart of the matter, with Spike arguing that Buffy is engaging in an act of self-deception: "A normal job for a normal girl," as he describes it. There's just one problem: Buffy's not normal. He scoffs at her being reduced to menial labor: "You're not happy here. You're something.... You're better than this" ("Doublemeat Palace"). Still, the need for money is too great to provoke Buffy to leave. It takes old flame Riley Finn coming back to the Doublemeat Palace in "As You Were" to enlist her aid in fighting a demon to escape the poverty-wage job. The power of this episode is somewhat robbed by the fact that poverty issues seem suddenly to fall away. It's as if Whedon and the writers didn't want to scare away an audience with a more sustained look at how Buffy would resolve her money woes. Poverty is too big a demon to Slay.

Buffy's choice of love interests is often suggestive of dysfunctional or self-destructive impulses. Her first lover and principal love interest is Angel, a 242–year old vampire "cursed" with a soul (and, hence, conscience), and whose curse is lifted when Angel experiences a moment of perfect happiness, which happens when he and Buffy have sex. The two spend the rest of Season Two trying to kill one another; and, despite Willow's curse successfully reuniting Angel with his soul, Buffy must kill him to prevent the demon he is calling forth from destroying the world. Angel returns in Season Three, soul intact, but the relationship is doomed by the fact that sex with Buffy creates the "perfect happiness" that causes Angel to revert to the demon Angelus.

In Season Four's "Harsh Light of Day," Buffy is attracted to a fellow student named Parker, who seduces her but is ultimately just interested in a one-night stand when she is in a vulnerable state (having had a resurrected Angel break up with her at the end of Season Three and not yet feeling comfortable in her new surroundings at college). When Buffy asks if she did something wrong, Parker demonstrates how little value he places in sex, saying, "Of course not. It was fun. Didn't you have fun?" His whole approach is that of a serial seducer with no interest in an emotionally-committed relationship. Buffy's awkward response captures the fullness of feeling that come when a person thinks she has made a connection with another person and finds out that person is stuck in "hunting" mode, unable to move into a trusting and caring relationship.

Willow's confrontation with Parker exposes his casual shallowness when she asserts to Parker that "People like Buffy and me assume that intimacy means friendship and respect." When Parker begins to pull the moves on Willow in Season Four's "Beer Bad," Willow — still in a relationship with Oz, but who has spent time on the sidelines observing — knows precisely what he is up to. "Just how gullible do you think I am?" she asks after leading him to think that he has her under his sway, "This isn't sharing. This isn't connecting.... I mean, you men! It's all about the sex. You find a woman, drag her to your den, do whatever's necessary as long as you get the sex."

Buffy's love interest of Season's Four and Five, Riley Finn, is portrayed as a decent, normal guy, the classic kind of "good guy" that girls *should* want, and the kind of normal guy for whom Buffy claims to yearn. Unfortunately, their mutual inability to communicate erodes the trust between them, leading Riley to despair. Their problems emerge in Season Four's "The Yoko Factor," when Xander exposes Buffy's prior romantic relationship with Angel just as Buffy is rushing to L.A. to confront Faith for her attempted framing of Buffy for her crimes, and, more importantly, for her seduction of Riley in Season Four's "Who Are You?" Riley's anxiety is heightened when she is enthralled by Dracula in Season Five's "Buffy vs. Dracula."

Riley's insecurities are brought out into the open in Season Five's "The Replacement" when Riley confides to Xander about how crazy he is about Buffy and the feelings she provokes in him. Then he looks at Xander and says, "But she doesn't love me." Despite frequent reassurances that she loves him, the fatal flaw in their relationship is Buffy's own power. For a time, Riley's augmented "Initiative" strength gives him greater-than-human capabilities. However, in Season Five's "Into the Woods," he is confronted with the reality that if he does not have surgery that will save his life but leave him with mere human strength, he will die. Riley confides his reluctance to have the surgery, telling Buffy, "You're getting stronger every day, more powerful. I can't touch you. Every day, you're just ... a little further out of my reach." The juxtaposition of a woman growing too strong for a man ironically plays on the realities of many relationships in which one member outgrows the relationship through his/her success at work. Riley feels as if, because he is weaker than Buffy, he is not as "important" as she is and that she will ultimately reject him for his weakness.

Eventually, lacking superpowers of his own, and fearful that his own "normality" will not be enough to hold Buffy's interest, Riley begins experimenting with "vampire sucking" in Season Five's "Into the Woods." A rather clever melding of intravenous drug use and prostitution metaphors, a human "John" pays a female vampire to suck blood from his arm. This is another sort of inversion, in which a woman's power is such that the male is overshadowed, minimized, and ultimately emasculated. Ultimately, Riley recognizes that he is miscast as "husband to a Slayer," and Buffy is unable to reach him in time to persuade him otherwise. Unable to bridge the communication gap, Riley leaves Buffy to return to government service, fighting demons in his own way.

Perhaps the most primordial illustration of oppression and helplessness is rape, which for some feminists stands as an archetype of gender relationships. While the very notion of vampirism is suggestive of the violence of rape, *Buffy* explores the problem of rape in several interesting formats. In Season One's "The Pack," Xander is possessed by a demon hyena and attempts to rape Buffy. The language he uses captures the mentality of a rapist perfectly: "We both know what you really want, don't cha?" Xander/Hyena asks, "You like your men dangerous." When Buffy tells Xander that he is infected by "some hyena thing," Xander conflates his own attraction for Buffy as mutual, dismissing Willow as a poor second for a sexual mate, and moves in the for the kill, breathlessly telling Buffy, "I like when you're scared. The more I scare you, the better you smell." The linkage of fear with scent and that the smell of fear excites the rapist captures the predatory sadism that appears to motivate most rapists (Freund 23–25).

Buffy's manipulative sexual relationship with Spike in Season Six — and his attempted rape of Buffy — powerfully encapsulates the death spiral that ensnares so many women in violent relationships. Initially, Buffy is drawn to Spike in Season Five for utilitarian reasons: he is a tool that can be used, and his insights in Season Five's "Fool for Love" help Buffy understand a fundamental weakness of all Slayers: "Death is your art.... Part of you is desperate to know: What is it like? Where does it lead you?... Every Slayer has a death wish.... The only reason you've lasted as long as you have is you've got ties to the world." In Season Six's "Afterlife," Spike intuitively understands the depths of Buffy's distress at having to claw her way out of her coffin when the Scooby Gang magically resurrects her. That insight, combined with their natural attraction, creates the basis for their romantic attraction.

Buffy's motivation is tragically manipulative. Taken from a peaceful afterlife, Buffy throws herself into Spike's willing embrace in order to feel something, and is clearly aware throughout that she is playing with fire. Spike's motivation is hardly noble, either. Spike is obsessed with Buffy. With the military chip implanted in his head, Spike is unable to act out violently, which was his *modus operandi* as a primary antagonist in earlier seasons. When Buffy returns from the dead, the chip doesn't react when he hits her, but by then he is neither fully evil nor fully rehabilitated. Their first sexual consummation is preceded by extremely violent foreplay in which a building is almost completely destroyed. Spike's lack of humanity is captured when he says to Buffy the next morning, "I knew the only thing better than killing a Slayer would be f....," a sentence Buffy cuts off (this is "family programming," after all). Buffy recognizes the mutual use between them, muttering, "You were just convenient." She wants to limit the affair to a one-night "mistake," but Spike will have none of it. "I may be dirt," Spike says, "but you're the one who likes to roll in it, Slayer" ("Wrecked").

The events that lead to the attempted rape present a plausible context. Two people are trapped in a mutually-abusive relationship that one wants to end and the other addictively and selfishly wants to continue. After Buffy breaks off the relationship, Spike, looking to ease the pain, seeks a spell from Anya, who has just been left at the altar by Xander. The two get drunk and have sex, which the Scooby Gang inadvertently witnesses through cameras that the "Evil Trio" planted in the Magic Box. A drunken Spike seeks out Buffy to apologize, but the situation spins out of control, resulting in Spike attempting to "reawaken" the passion in Buffy, and with Buffy finally physically stopping his advances.

Why does Spike attempt to rape Buffy? First, that Spike drinks heavily that night is a common element of most rape scenarios. Second, one can doubt whether Spike can differentiate appropriate from inappropriate sexual behavior. To say that the two had a complicated relationship, where violence and sex freely intermingle, is to make an understatement of considerable magnitude. Spike does not have a soul and, based on the show's equivalence of soul with conscience, is indifferent to moral niceties like consent. He is reduced to a kind of pseudo-constraint based on pain, and Buffy's death and resurrection lift that burden from him where Buffy is concerned. Third, we learn from various sources that Spike was a painfully-sensitive mortal, a bad poet, and a "mama's boy" who was repeatedly rejected by women ("Fool for Love"). Fourth, Spike's romanticist understanding of love probably blinds him to the dysfunctional nature of the relationship. When Buffy admits that she has feelings for Spike, but that "I could never trust you enough for it to be love," Spike scoffs, "Trust is for old marrieds, Buffy. Great love is wild and passionate and dangerous. It burns and consumes." Buffy counters, "Until there's nothing left; love like that doesn't last" ("Seeing Red"). Buffy understands that sex without love and love without respect is ultimately self-destructive, and her ending the relationship triggers Spike's desperate, drunken violence.

Another effective portrayal of Buffy powerless occurs in her relationship with Faith, the "Slayer from the wrong side of the tracks." As Faith steadily succumbs to the temptations of exploiting her powers as a Slayer to selfish ends, she repeatedly manipulates and hurts Buffy. She attempts to seduce Angel in Season Three's "Enemies," and, then in Season Four's "Who Are You?" masquerades as Buffy by using a magical spell that switches their identities. While acting as Buffy, she has sex with Buffy's boyfriend Riley, asking him, "What do want to do with this body?" Buffy's confrontation with Faith over her seduction of Riley and attempt to have Buffy pay for Faith's crimes occurs on the first season of the *Buffy* spinoff *Angel*, in the episode "Sanctuary."

Faith, after attempting "Death by Angel,"[8] takes refuge with Angel. Buffy comes to L.A. to confront Faith, who is finally recognizing how lost she is and wants to reform. Buffy, on the other hand, is determined to provoke a confrontation. When Faith attempts to run away to the roof of Angel's apartment, with Buffy pursuing, Faith complains that "Angel said there was no way you were gonna give me a chance." Buffy replies, "I gave you *every* chance! I tried *so* hard to help you, and you *spat* on me.... Angel, Riley, anything you could take from me, you took. I've lost battles before, but no one has *ever* made me a victim." Her anger with Faith is justified, but she is unwilling to act on it, perhaps because intuitively she knows that Faith will one day be a useful weapon against some future foe, and perhaps because she sees some truth in Faith's rejoinder that Buffy is "always about control. You have no idea what it's like to be on the other side! When nothing's in control! Nothing makes sense!" By setting aside her anger and helping prevent Faith's assassination by some (apparently) rogue agents of the Watcher's Council, Buffy enables Faith to make amends as Faith confesses her crimes to the police and voluntarily goes to jail (*Angel*, "Sanctuary"). Although vengeance might have been more satisfying, Buffy does the responsible thing and is rewarded by Faith's return to help fight the First Evil in Season Seven.

One disappointing aspect of the show's portrayal of female helplessness is the absence of discussion of how having children can disadvantage women. While the show's writers "magic up" a sister for Buffy in Season Five, the only person to explicitly fill the role of mother is Buffy's mother Joyce. Her role as a single mother is likewise explored in such a superficial manner as to completely elide the challenges confronting single mothers. Buffy's struggles to play the role of care giver in parts of Seasons Five, Six, and Seven feel like an opportunity not fully explored. This absence of consideration of how women's reproductive roles can create obstacles to women's success in society strikes us as a serious omission and leads to speculation as to why Whedon and the writers avoided the topic.[9]

As with the superficial portrayal of Buffy's financial challenges, perhaps this lacuna is calculated to avoid the charge of being an explicitly "feminist" show, recognizing that the world viewers must inhabit must be somewhat similar to the world in which they live, but not so similar as to be prosaic or formulaically "feminist." As Whedon has stated, it's better to make teenaged boys comfortable with assertive women than to try selling them on feminism (Bellafonte 82–84).

Nevertheless, while these portrayals of helplessness and powerlessness could be viewed as reinforcing gender roles and women's inability to overcome, that seems a deeply uncharitable reading. A more positive interpretation is that human beings find themselves in adverse situations, and, in nearly every instance mentioned, *Buffy*'s writers conceive of imaginative ways of overcoming.

Buffy Challenging Tradition

While *Buffy* is premised on the view that old knowledge and received wisdom are important, the show also repeatedly challenges the notion that tradition is to be uncritically accepted. One of the clearest challenges to traditional mores is Willow's lesbianism, which emerges rather suddenly in Season Four after her breakup with Oz. Religious groups found Willow's relationship with Tara as another reason to denounce the show, while gay rights groups initially applauded the relationship. Amber Benson, who played Willow's lover, Tara, has publicly commented that she has received numerous letters from young gay people who found inspiration in the insertion of a believable gay relationship into the show.[10] After Tara is killed in Season Six's "Seeing Red," however, many gay activists criticized the show, accusing Whedon of deploying what has been described as the "dead/evil lesbian cliché" of introducing a minority into the show simply for dramatic effect, and then killing her off (Tabron). Many gay and lesbian viewers felt betrayed by Tara's death and Willow's subsequent insanity and (brief) turn toward evil (Black).

That reading of the Willow-Tara relationship seems flawed for a number of reasons. First, the depiction of Willow and Tara's relationship is more positive than just about any other character bonds in the show, and their relationship is central to many of the show's most important narratives. In Season Five's "Tough Love" Willow tenderly cares for Tara after her "brain-sucking" at the hands of the demon-god Glory, saying, "She's my girl.... Do you hear that, baby? You're my always." Her tenderness and willingness to sacrifice is starkly contrasted in Season Six's "Villains," in which Willow demands from the gods or the spirit world that Tara be brought back and then leaves her body unattended to seek vengeance against Warren and the Trio. Her humanity is stripped away by her addiction to dark magic, which justifies all manner of sins, which includes killing (human) enemies and even attacking her closest friends. Dawn's reaction to finding Tara's body, staying with her for hours until Buffy and Xander return home, is a telling contrast to Willow's purposeful inhumanity. The contrast between "the softer side of Sears" Willow of Season One[11] and the "evil, veiny Willow" of Season Six illustrates how far Willow's dependence on dark magic has deranged her character and fed her insanity.

Second, the more critical interpretation of Tara and Willow's relationship ignores the fundamentally dystopian nature of *Buffy*. The writers at Mutant Enemy were not creating a just world; they were creating, within the horror genre, a *dangerous* world where bad things happen to good people. Both Giles and Xander lose loved ones, and Buffy is forever denied her one true love, Angel, because physical intimacy would banish his soul and turn him into the evil Angelus. Tragedy strikes heterosexuals and homosexuals alike, and Tara's death is one tragedy among many. Unlike Xander's love life, which is pretty much treated as an opportunity for comedy, Willow and Tara's relationship is for the most part portrayed with reality and care. A third reason to doubt the motivations of the writers of *Buffy* is that they didn't treat Willow's lesbianism as some kind of "phase." Had the show's writers decided in Season Seven to have Willow stop practicing magic altogether, hook up with Xander, and become a loving housewife, then critics could legitimately question whether the show employed "queerness" as a way of ginning up controversy. That doesn't seem to be the case. Indeed, in Season Seven's "The Killer in Me," Willow finds herself courted by Kennedy, one of the "Potentials" drawn to Sunnydale.

Buffy also contains an implicit critique of traditions that oppress women. For example, in Season Five's "Family," the centerpiece of the show is Tara, who throughout Season Four is more Willow's companion than a full-fledged Scooby. The explanation for Tara's shyness and low self-esteem emerges when she is confronted with her family's sudden appearance and demand that she returns home with them. The reason, according to her father, is that Tara is part-demon, and that on her twentieth birthday she will be transformed physically into a demon. When Tara refuses to go, her cousin Beth calls her a "selfish bitch" and launches into a guilt-trip inducing diatribe: "You don't care the slightest bitty bit about your family, so you?" Beth storms, "Your dad's been worried sick about you every day since you've been gone. There's a house that needs taking care of...." Implicit in Beth's tirade is that Tara's going to college is an irresponsible shirking of her "duty" as housekeeper and body servant to her male relatives.

Tara's insecurity causes her to cast a spell that causes the Scooby Gang to be blind to demons, which naturally creates a problem when a gang of demons attacks the group at the Magic Box. The final confrontation at the Magic Box pits Tara's natural family against her adopted family, the Scoobies. Spike proves that Tara is not a demon in typical Spike style, punching her in the nose, which triggers his government-implanted anti-violence chip. "That's just a family legend, am I right?" Spike needles Tara's father, "Just a little bit of spin to keep the ladies in line." When Tara's father explodes, "This is insane! You people have no right to interfere with Tara's affairs. We are her blood kin! Who the hell are you?" Buffy responds, "We're family." Despite their anger at being on the working end of Tara's spell, the gang unites to defend Tara.

The episode's title, "Family," is clearly an ironic play on the contrast between the family of relations and the family we create through our voluntary relationships, and the question is which is more important. Tara's family and blood ties in general are portrayed as nothing more than oppression and constraint on feminine autonomy. Beyond that, however, Tara's family stands as a kind of caricature of moral conservatism. No legitimate rationale for the family's sudden appearance is forthcoming — other than the "men folk" wanting a woman in the house to cook and clean — and even assuming that the "demon myth" is a little platonic "white lie," the episode ultimately fails to construct a credible picture of a rural, morally-conservative family. In a show that prides itself on its depth of character development, that lack of depth stands out.

In contrast, in *Angel*, the *Buffy* spinoff series, Whedon and the writers at Mutant Enemy manage to portray Fred's (Fred is one of Angel's investigative partners) parents in a completely human and sympathetic manner. In "Fred-less," an episode from Season Three of *Angel*, Angel and the other characters have difficulty understanding Fred's clearly rural parents when they come searching for her after not hearing from her for five years.[12] Fred's parents are portrayed as commonsensical — if decidedly un-cosmopolitan — people, and even Fred's mother's vocation as a bus driver comes in handy when she hijacks a bus to run over a particularly dangerous bug-demon. Certainly, families like Tara's exist, but presenting such a family creates a kind of archetype-*cum*-stereotype that seems to paint all of Middle America with the same bigoted brush.

Buffy's relationship with her "Watcher," Rupert Giles, offers another implicit challenge to conventional relationships between an older man and a young woman. From one perspective, Giles can be viewed as a paternal figure who controls Buffy's actions, a reading which reinforces a patriarchal world view. A more discerning analysis yields a more complex relationship. Certainly, Giles is a father-figure to Buffy, whose biological father is both geographically and emotionally unavailable. However, the relationship evolves considerably over the arc of seven seasons, and Giles's ability to "command" Buffy is never particularly authoritative.[13] By Season Seven, the Buffy-Giles relationship has evolved toward one of equals, and in Season Six's famous musical episode "Once More, With Feeling," Giles sings of his longing to act like a father to Buffy but recognizes that he would be holding her back, saying, "You're not going to trust [what you have learned] until you are forced to stand alone." Giles's departure — and his frequent return when needed — is hardly the actions of a paternalistic manipulator.

Two events from Season Seven help to illustrate the evolution of the Buffy/Giles relationship. In Season Seven's "Lies My Parents Told Me," Giles reaches the conclusion that Spike is a threat and, with Principal Wood, hatches a plan to kill Spike, against whom Wood is nursing a personal grudge. Giles takes Buffy out for a training session, where he attempts to occupy Buffy while Wood attempts to kill Spike. Early in the dialogue, when Buffy questions the utility of a training session, Giles asserts that "I'm still your teacher" and that "It's time you looked at the big picture." Giles attempts to persuade Buffy that Spike is an unacceptable threat and that good leaders are sometimes required to be ruthless. Buffy refuses to allow Spike to be killed, for reasons similar to those for which she rejected sacrificing Dawn to forestall a demon-god's plan to merge demon and human worlds: she believes that Spike will be instrumental in defeating the First Evil — and she doesn't want to lose another being important to her and the killing itself would be wrong. Buffy eventually realizes Giles is stalling, and later, when the plot fails, Giles attempts to justify his actions. Signifying the loss of trust, Buffy closes the door in Giles's face, saying, "No, I think you've taught me everything I need to know."

A further evolution occurs in Season Seven's "Empty Places," when Buffy proposes another attack on headquarters of the First Evil's priest. When Faith demurs, suggesting that they need more information before attacking, Giles agrees, suggesting that acting on Buffy's intuition might be reckless. Whether he is acting out of resentment of Buffy's rejection of his moral authority or simply believes that the assault is unwise is unclear. Buffy accuses Giles of having sent Spike on a mission to sandbag her and further claims, "I wish this could be a democracy.... Democracy doesn't win battles. It's a hard truth, but there has to be a single voice. You need someone to issue orders and be reckless sometimes and not take your feelings into account. You need someone to lead you." Giles points out that Buffy has not done the work leaders must sometimes do: persuade followers that a risk is worth taking. Despite Buffy's claim that the group is not a democracy, the group votes Buffy "off the island," and Buffy goes but gives the *de facto* leader Faith some advice, "Don't be afraid to lead them."

A couple of insights emerge from these Giles-Buffy exchanges. First, the paternalistic nature of the Giles-Buffy relationship — never particularly strong even in Season One — has eroded; if Giles is a father-figure in earlier seasons, by Season Seven he is an increasingly estranged father-figure, partly by his own actions and partly by the nature of Buffy's growing leadership. Second, Giles's manipulation harms their relationship, but not irreparably. Forgiveness and redemption are such elemental components of the show that irreparable breaks among the original four Scooby Gang are inconceivable. Later, when the First Evil inadvertently reveals to Buffy what she must do to defeat the threat, Giles responds to her proposed solution by noting that it "flies in the face of what every generation has done in the fight against evil" but that it's "bloody brilliant." Their relationship has not been harmed to the point that they cannot communicate, respect, and value one another's opinions.

From one perspective, Buffy's role as a martial leader may seem like a female figure head of a largely masculine narrative, putting a feminine face over a largely-patriarchal social structure (Buttsworth 185–99). One response to such a criticism might be, "so what?" Politics will always involve the distribution of power and, to some extent, the application of violence when political solutions fail. The premise of a female organizing and leading a paramilitary organization comprised of both men and women in response to an external threat can also be interpreted as empowering (Showalter). Perhaps the biggest indicator of strong character development is Buffy's determination to offer advice to Faith *after* she has been repudiated by the group. That Buffy could retain sufficient resilience to "soldier on" in the face of her group's rejection likewise is essential to final success, as she goes by herself to find the magical scythe that will prove to be a key to defeating the First Evil. Buffy may make mistakes, but her missteps are credible and "human." Perhaps the most important inversion is that Giles and the other masculine characters are defined through their relationships with Buffy, not *vice versa*.

Conclusion

Ultimately, the creators of *Buffy* attempted what great literary authors, such as Dickens, Shakespeare, and Alexie, attempted: to provoke and teach without becoming pedantic. In Whedon's world, every tragic flaw and bad decision and miscalculation bring with it consequences, although usually not those the audience might expect. Is Buffy a conventional feminist portrayal? Whether or not Buffy should be seen as a feminist icon or simply as an action hero is a matter of perspective. However, a number of elements of the show's basic narrative suggest that some interpretations may be more defensible than others. Clearly, Buffy is heroic, and her heroism is frequently manifested in complex — dare we say "feminine?" — resolutions to difficult challenges. Although she has enormous power, she frequently avoids brute force as a means of winning. As Spike — Buffy's nemesis-turned-lover — observes in Season Four's "The Yoko Factor," Buffy's willingness to surround herself with friends is unique to Slayers, and makes her a particularly effective problem-solver. Both Spike and Riley echo the same note of admiration, "You're a hell of a woman," which is the kind of "gendered praise" that may not sit well with most second wave feminists.

One alternative interpretation can be drawn from Season Seven's "Chosen," as Buffy tells Angel to stay out of the coming fight in Sunnydale. Angel learns of Buffy's relationship with Spike and is somewhat jealous. Buffy acknowledges her lack of success in romance and wonders if there was something wrong with her, and why she has not been able to make any of her relationships work. Angel offers her Slayer status as an excuse, but Buffy is not so sure. As she ruminates on the future, she suggests a possible answer: "I'm cookie dough. I'm not done baking. I make it through this and the next thing and the next thing and maybe one day I turn around and realize I'm ready. I'm cookies. And then, you know, if I want someone to ... enjoy delicious cookie-me, then that's fine. That'll be then, when I'm done." The metaphor guiding Buffy's statement is revealingly un-feminist — and painfully awkward — but also circles back to the malleable nature of identity that is always central to *Buffy*; in the early years, the characters are teenagers, a transitional phase of life. To the very end of the show, Whedon appeared determined not to lock his principal character into any particular fate, and certainly not into any conventional roles, feminist or otherwise.

Buffy is not ready to have romantic success because that would involve a husband and children to protect and might make her a less effective Slayer. To some extent, then, Buffy remains trapped in the limiting roles that society has created: Slaying is a career, and she is a career girl. However, her smile at the end of "Chosen" when Dawn asks her, "What do we do now?" as Sunnydale collapses into the now-destroyed Hellmouth, is suggestive of a different future than any previous future she dared to hope for, one in which she is no longer "cookie dough" alone, but has thousands of super powerful "sisters" with whom to share the burdens of fighting evil.

The show repeatedly explores interesting juxtapositions and inversions of stereotypes of how we should think and what we should assume about gender roles, but whether this playful impulse gives rise to a genuinely-feminist sensibility seems questionable. Whedon's relentless shattering of stereotypes means that Buffy could never be a stereotypically-feminist show, and the show's unwillingness to explore many core gender issues in any depth suggests something less than feminist aspirations.[14] As *Slate's* Tim Appelo notes, *Buffy* "boasts the least stupid shows ever done on date rape, teen suicide, and seducer teachers." Part of *Buffy's* allure as a show lies in its unpredictability and its unwillingness to compromise a story line to any notions of political correctness. Keeping people interested and perhaps afraid appears to have mattered more to the show's creators than other elements (Gross).

One of the show's actors, Danny Strong,[15] who played Jonathan,[16] suggested that Buffy is not a *feminist* icon *per se*, but rather should be perceived as a *humanist* icon. In that sense, Buffy is a post-feminist show. Buffy, a petite young woman, is a powerful leader, and her leadership is not resented by the men or women she leads. Moreover, Buffy is a believable character with believable flaws. She makes mistakes and deals with the consequences of those mistakes. In this sense, *Buffy* is not so much seeking to shatter stereotypes as to nudge them in a less settled direction. Thus, forcing Buffy into a purely feminist mold would probably be viewed as confining to the people who created and sustained her — and watched her — for seven seasons. She is a hell of a woman.

Notes

1. Season Three begins, as did Season Two, with Buffy having left town. The difference is that, instead of going to stay with her dad, before Season Three Buffy runs away from home, and works as a waitress, presumably in Los Angeles.

2. In Season Six's "Gone," for example, Buffy is rendered invisible by the "Evil Trio." Her behavior is mischievous, and bordering on mean-spirited, but her motivations may be more complex. Season Six finds Buffy struggling to reconcile being wrenched out of heaven and returned to the world of the living. Additionally, that she would act out — rather impishly — in a moment of anonymity plays into one of Buffy's primary character flaws; already burdened with being the "Chosen One," she also finds herself the primary care-giver to Dawn, having to feed, clothe, and keep a roof over their heads at a rather tender age.

3. We find out that Slayer power comes from the imposition of a demon's essence by a council of men ("Get It Done").

4. Some have suggested that Buffy is a "Christ-like" heroine, who willingly goes to her death in Seasons One and Five. See, for example, Anderson.

5. For example, Buffy refuses to accept that her magically created Dawn must be killed to thwart the plans of the demon-god Glory in Season Five's "The Gift."

6. In Season Three's "Helpless," Buffy is robbed of her powers by the Council of Watchers in a birthday "test."

7. Buffy also takes a job as a waitress in the Season Three opening episode, "Anne."

8. "Death by Angel" is analogous to "death by cop," an attempt by a person to commit suicide by threatening aggression and provoking the police to shoot them, a phenomenon that has increasingly been reported on.

9. The exception to this is that, when forced into caregiver role by her mother's death, she tries to reject that role and force Giles into it, partly a reason for Giles leaving her ("Tabula Rasa").

10. In an interview for the companion disk "The Chosen Collection" to the collector's box set, Benson comments that numerous people wrote to say that they hadn't committed suicide "because of a fricken TV show."

11. In Season One's "Welcome to the Hellmouth," Cordelia condescendingly greets a clearly shy and nerdy Willow by commenting on her dress, saying "Good to know you've seen the softer side of Sears."

12. Fred has been pulled into the same demon dimension as Cordelia at the end of Season Two.

13. Season One provides numerous instances in which Giles begs Buffy not to do anything "rash" and Buffy calmly disregards his admonitions. For example, in Season One's "The Witch," Giles plaintively asks Buffy, "Do you ignore everything I say as a rule?" Also, in "Teacher's Pet," Giles chides Buffy for hunting despite his extracting her promise not to, and she replies, "Yes. I lied. I'm a bad person. Let's move on."

14. Perhaps ironically, the *Buffy* spinoff *Angel* deals with many feminist issues much more straightforwardly, despite its seeming intent as an action show.

15. A.K.A. "Jonathan," of Season Six's "Evil Trio." He makes this observation in "The Chosen Collection," the collector's set of the complete seven seasons of *Buffy* issued in 2005.

16. A member of Season Six's "Evil Trio," he also appeared in Season Three's "Earshot" as a suicidal classmate, and, in Season Four's "Superstar," he casts a spell that makes everyone in Sunnydale think he's an improbably versatile Slayer/athlete/musician/international man of mystery.

A Life Well-Lived

Buffy and the Pursuit of Happiness

—————⊸⊛⊶—————

JIM FORD

"The hardest thing in this world is to live in it."
— *Buffy, "The Gift"*

From its inception, *Buffy* has been a rich ethical resource. Even in the first season, the obvious contrast of "humans good, vampires evil" is balanced by the inclusion of virtuous vampires like Angel and vicious humans too numerous to delineate. As the series progresses, each of the characters becomes more nuanced and complex, which is to say more human. The on-going narrative that develops suggests a number of intriguing philosophical issues.

One leading theorist suggests that "popular philosophy" is "a genre that makes philosophy accessible by leaving out the arguments—that is, the philosophy."[1] The charge is understandable, if not always accurate. Much writing on popular culture *is* superficial, and some popular philosophy does neglect the kind of rigorous argumentation that philosophy requires. At its best, though, popular philosophy uses the raw material of popular culture as the entry to deep and significant philosophical arguments. A close examination of Buffy's life illuminates two crucial ethical concepts: the difference between an admirable life and a desirable life,[2] on the one hand, and the complexities of human happiness, on the other.

The two concepts are related in key ways. In the context of her world, Buffy certainly leads an admirable life. She is the heroine of the series and repeatedly prevents the apocalypse. In the words of her headstone, at the end of Season Five (obviously she isn't "all dead," since she comes back for two more seasons), "She saved the world / A lot" ("The Gift"). Without her, that world literally could not have gone on. So while one should be glad that Buffy

201

is the Slayer and lives the life that she does, it is not at all clear that one would want to be Buffy, or live that kind of life. She leads an admirable life but not necessarily a desirable one; the sacrifices necessary to be the Slayer drastically undermine her overall happiness. Is Buffy happy?

It is a truism that happiness means different things to different people, so much so that some philosophers despair of ever reaching a precise account of the concept. A clear and convincing definition of happiness is not forthcoming. The contemporary philosopher Nicholas White suggests that, rather than a clear concept that guides our thought, the better way to think of happiness is as a "regulative concept," something that identifies the problem of human happiness rather than a supposed solution. For White, that problem is how to reconcile the multiple and often conflicting aims that every individual human being has (164). A regulative concept of happiness "sets before us a certain *task* for our thinking, but without making clear to us how to fulfill it, or even assuring us that in the end it can be fulfilled at all" (White 166). A number of philosophers have offered their accounts of happiness, but the first systematic account is still the most useful: that of Aristotle. Aristotle's catalog of moral virtues provides a helpful framework for analyzing Buffy's own virtues. Aristotle also takes seriously the role of fortune in human happiness, the fact that, in the wrong circumstances, even the best of us will have trouble being happy, and he recognizes the number of goods necessary for full happiness, such as health, wealth, friendships, freedom, and at least some sort of pleasure.

It was the Athenian statesman Solon who said, "Call no man happy until he is dead" (Aristotle 1.10). Buffy's life is particularly ready for evaluation on that account. She has died twice (in "Prophecy Girl" and "The Gift"), and her television series has long finished its run. Reflecting on Buffy's life as a whole, her pursuit of happiness in a world beset by evil is a constant battle. Buffy struggles (often unsuccessfully) to balance the various goods in her life: individual character, career, family, friendships, and romantic relationships. All of which is to say, for a television character, she lives a pretty typical human life. There is no one right formula for how to balance these various goods; as Freud observed, "There is no golden rule which applies to everyone: every man must find out for himself in what particular fashion he can be saved" (*Civilization* 34). Buffy excels in some areas of her life (personal character, family relationships, friendships, and a clear sense of calling in her career), less so in others (particularly her romantic relationships, all of which are ultimately unsuccessful). The question of whether her life is a desirable one, and whether she is happy overall, depends on the relative weight one gives to those goods. Is a life of rich friendships, a noble calling, and superhuman heroics worth a series of failed romances, meager finances, and constant danger? Such is the plight of Buffy, the Vampire Slayer.

Buffy's Virtues

"You have the power to do real good, Angel, to make amends."
— *Buffy, "Amends"*

Even a cursory glance at *Buffy* reveals a number of admirable qualities evident in the way Buffy lives her life.[3] For Aristotle, happiness is "an activity of the soul in conformity with excellence or virtue" (Aristotle 1.7). Buffy displays a wide range of Aristotelian moral virtues. She is courageous, facing mortal danger in nearly every episode, but is rarely foolhardy; she is generally temperate in regard to pleasures (although she does lose control a bit in Season Six — more on this later); and she is just to her friends and loved ones, caring for them as she should, while protecting the innocent and giving vampires what they usually deserve (which is a stake). While practical wisdom — the ability to discern the proper means to the virtuous goal — is sometimes less evident, this is due in part to Buffy's youth (she is a high school student the first three seasons, so still in her early twenties by the end of the series). As the series progresses, she repeatedly demonstrates her ability to plan, make wise choices, and, in general, to pursue her virtuous goals in an appropriate manner. Other virtues are visible in her life as well; she is quite rightly proud of her abilities as the Slayer, appropriately valuing the excellence that is the product both of her calling and her training. Even less-prominent virtues, like friendliness and righteous indignation, are present in the appropriate amounts. In the context of her universe, Buffy is undeniably virtuous.

Pleasure

"I mean if you're looking for fun, there's death, there's glory, and sod all else."
— *Spike, "Fool for Love"*

Pleasure is certainly not the whole of happiness, but it is an important part. Most philosophers have followed Aristotle in dismissing the "vulgar view" that maximizing pleasure is the path to happiness, but a life without pleasure holds little attraction for even the most sophisticated observer. Pleasures for Buffy and her friends generally fall into one of three categories: the mild pleasure of the quip ("Or is this like one of your little pop culture references I don't get?" — Anya, "Selfless"), the relief of the triumph over evil (from the satisfaction of staking a vampire to the exhaustion of averting another apocalypse), and the true joy of what the series calls "moments of happiness." Humorous jokes, asides, and allusions are a staple of the show, and the pleasure they yield for both the characters and the audience is considerable.[4] So too, the pleasures of a job well done are also worth noting, although they are often mitigated by the unending nature of the struggle against evil (a new vampire or apocalypse always awaits). Most important, though, are the show's recurring "moments of happiness."

The phrase is first used by a gypsy named Enyos, to describe the curse placed on the vampire Angel. After a long history of murderous evil, Angel's soul is restored to him through a curse, so that he is conscious of (and anguished over) every one of the many horrible deeds he has committed. But the curse is such that "one moment of true happiness, of contentment, one moment where the soul that we restored no longer plagues his thoughts, and that soul is taken from him" (Enyos, "Innocence"). Angel experiences his moment of happiness shortly after he and Buffy make love for the first time, costing Angel his soul, and returning him to his malevolent ways. Their passionate expression of true love produces the briefest moment of true happiness, which is followed by agony all around. Buffy is confused but quickly realizes that the man who was her first lover has become a monster.

This pattern of happiness followed by horror is repeated at key points throughout the series. While it is Angel's true happiness that is the focus of the curse, it is Buffy who will find her happiness shadowed by trauma over the course of her life. She sleeps with Angel for the first time, Angel turns evil and murders Buffy's teacher (and Giles's lover) Jenny Calendar ("Passion"). Ultimately Buffy has to sacrifice Angel to save the world and stabs him just as his soul is returned to his body, forcing them both to feel the pain once more ("Becoming, Part Two"). Two years later, Buffy makes love with her boyfriend Riley in a particularly romantic setting, enjoying a moment of true happiness after her mother's seemingly-successful brain surgery; just a few minutes later she sees the same Riley letting a vampire bite him, and Riley blames Buffy for it, leaving town before they can reconcile ("Into the Woods"). In fact, the way the series handles Buffy's sexuality — Buffy has sex, crazed evil follows — is a little too melodramatic. As Dawn says in another context, "Don't get all movie-of-the-week" ("Blood Ties"). But the larger point about true happiness, about sustained, deep, joyful happiness, as opposed to simple pleasure or post-apocalyptic triumph, remains; happiness is a constant struggle for Buffy and her friends in their fight against evil.

Work

"Vampires are vampires, and my job description is pretty clear."
— *Buffy, "Into the Woods"*

Buffy's calling as the Slayer is not exactly a traditional job. Perhaps most importantly, the salary stinks. As she explains to one vampire, "I don't get paid; it's more like a calling" ("Conversations with Dead People"). As jobs go, this is a pretty serious drawback. On the other hand, while her daily encounters with vampires sometimes grow routine, her work does involve a great deal of excitement, while improving the world around her. On a surface level, this does not require careful thought or analysis. As Buffy herself says, "If I have to kill demons because it makes the world a better place, then I kill demons" ("Intervention"). Sometimes the moral reality can be much more complicated; Buffy distinguishes between the vampires who deserve staking and the ones who do not (first Angel, later Spike), much to the chagrin of other Slayers (such as Kendra, the Slayer who is called after Buffy's first death). The good news is that the work is available for as long as Buffy can handle it. As she notes at her first high school Career Day, "unless hell freezes over and every vamp in Sunnydale puts in for early retirement, I'd say my future is pretty much a non-issue" ("What's My Line? Part One"). At the same time she does sometimes long for a "normal life," the kind she had before becoming the Slayer.

She tries to maintain a somewhat-normal life in addition to her Slayer work, partly by staying in school — not that she had that much choice the first three years, until her graduation from high school at the end of Season Three. Although she longs to leave Sunnydale behind, she decides instead to enter the University of California at Sunnydale — joining Willow, who passes up Oxford, Harvard, and the like so that she can fight the "good fight" with Buffy ("Choices"). Buffy spends about twenty-five episodes in college (a little more than one season), but her commitments to her family and her Slaying increasingly encroach on her studies, and ultimately she withdraws from college. After her mother's death (and her own return from the grave), the financial pressures of being the Slayer become pressing. Working full-time at a job that pays nothing makes it impossible for Buffy to support herself and her sister, so she takes a series of day-jobs: working construction ("Life Serial"), an endless hour at the magic shop ("Life Serial"), a fast-food restaurant ("Doublemeat Palace"), before finally settling in as a sort of paid mentor to high school students ("Lessons"). Ultimately, even that job (her most lasting one, as it turns out — roughly fifteen episodes before she is fired) turns out to be based on her being the Slayer ("Get It Done"). All of which is to say that Buffy's calling makes it nearly impossible for to hold a regular job (i.e., one that pays).

The pay may be bad, but the work is pretty good. Most of the time Buffy seems to genuinely enjoy fighting evil, which is important. While it is nice to think about the noble sacrifices one makes sometimes, in reality it is difficult to be happy when one does not enjoy the work that occupies the majority of one's time. Buffy likes fighting vampires, particularly when her friends are by her side. But this ebbs and flows throughout her career — again, a pattern that is typical of most careers.

The fact that Slaying is a calling, rather than a job freely chosen, contributes to that ambivalence. Of course, for many people their jobs are not freely chosen, and people often feel trapped in a particular job or career. In a bizarre high school reunion-type moment, Buffy explains her predicament to the newly raised vampire Holden, whom she has not seen since high school. Holden has been at Dartmouth, majoring in psychology and pursuing the kind of normal life that eludes Buffy. She feels "superior" to those around her, because only she is the Slayer and no one else can relate; but at the same time she feels guilty about her superiority. Holden tries to explain to her that "everybody feels alone. Everybody is, 'til they die" ("Conversations with Dead People"). The truth is that despite her status as the Slayer, Buffy is not alone; she is connected to her friends and family in deep and significant ways. But her career constantly threatens to isolate her from those deep connections, to alienate her from those she loves.

Ties to the World

"The only reason you've lasted as long as you have is, you've got ties to the world. Your mom. Brat kid sister. Scoobies. They tie you here but you're just putting off the inevitable."
                                            — *Spike, "Fool for Love"*

What distinguishes Buffy from the traditional Slayer is her deep connection to those around her. The Slayer normally works alone, as Buffy tries to explain when she first discusses it with Xander; "There's no 'we.' Okay? I'm the Slayer, and you're not" ("The Harvest"). Xander refuses to accept this, however, and soon he and Willow are fighting by her side. They form a sort of "Scooby Gang," and the three remain best friends for the full seven seasons of the series. Together with Giles, who departs briefly in Seasons Six and Seven but otherwise is also a constant presence, the four central characters form a particularly tight-knit group. Angel and Cordelia are secondary members in the first three seasons, as are Spike and Anya for much of the last four seasons. The Scoobies clearly function as a second family for Buffy. She has the typical teen-age tension with her mother early in the series (understandable given the fact that Buffy was kicked out of her previous school for burning down the gym and that she keeps sneaking out of her house), culminating in a confrontation in which Buffy confesses that she is the Slayer ("Becoming, Part Two"). Although she runs away from her family and friends after being forced to Slay Angel, after her return to Sunnydale, she and her mother gradually grow closer ("Anne"). The addition of a sister in Season Five (Dawn) further enriches Buffy's family, and, after her mother's particularly sudden death, Buffy grows even closer to her sister and friends.

This bare summary of Buffy's non-traditional family can hardly convey how central her friends and family are to her happiness. These connections to the world make her a better Slayer, and, while Buffy does the bulk of the actual fighting, her friends are always a crucial part of her effort. One of the major story-arcs for the series is the tension between the individuality of being the Slayer and her close ties to her loved ones. In Season Four, this tension becomes explicit, first as Buffy works increasingly with members of the Initiative (a government unit dedicated to investigating, researching, and fighting the forces of evil), but then the tension continues to deepen after the Initiative turns against her ("The I in Team").

Spike keenly perceives the tension within the Scooby group and exploits it to weaken them. Just as the Beatles grew apart and everyone blamed Yoko, he explains, the Scooby Gang has grown apart as well: "You know how it is with kids—they go to college, they grow apart. Way of the world" ("The Yoko Factor"). The Scoobies do grow apart, and their frustrations with each other soon reach fever pitch. As Buffy states, "I'm starting to get why there's no ancient prophecy about a Chosen One and Friends" ("The Yoko Factor"). The revealing fact about Buffy and her friends, however, is how quickly they come back together. Despite the forces that threaten to pull them apart, they repeatedly come together to help each other, saving the world in the process. Just a few hours after their Yoko moment, they realize how much they need each other, and Willow, Xander, and Giles cast a spell to let Buffy draw on a combined power much greater than her own ("Primeval"). The moral of the story could not be clearer—despite Buffy's status as the Chosen One, her success depends on the four of them working in harmony.

How the Slayer can stay close to her loved ones remains uncertain, however, and in Season Five Buffy begins to doubt whether her calling is compatible with her human love. She laments to Giles, "I'm starting to feel like being the Slayer is turning me into stone" ("Intervention"). Her doubts are prompted by the break-down of her relationship with her boyfriend Riley, but the problem runs much deeper. The sudden death of her mother, in one of the most poignant television episodes ever, only furthers Buffy's isolation ("The Body"). This is also the occasion for the most disturbing vampire attack of the series, as a naked vampire rises from the dead to attack Dawn while she stands over her mother's corpse. Buffy enters just in time, but her silent struggle with this vampire to a grim ending illustrates the true horror of Buffy's existence. For the first time, humorous quips and Slayer skills are not enough. The vampire is dusted, but the horrible isolation remains.

Giles suggests a sort of vision-quest as a way for Buffy to reconnect, to find meaning in being the Slayer. On her quest, the First Slayer appears to guide Buffy and articulates her problem, saying, "You're afraid that being the Slayer means you're losing your humanity" ("Intervention"). The First Slayer's response—"Death is your gift"—is hardly comforting. It only confirms to Buffy that Slaying is all about death, having little to do with real human life. When Season Five's "Big Bad," Glory, kidnaps Dawn, Buffy breaks down completely, falling into a catatonic state. Once again her friends step in, and Willow is able to bring Buffy back to reality, but her breakdown just illustrates how traumatic her life has been. She is increasingly unable to relate to things she cannot stake. She fights Glory, and, with the help of the Scoobies, Buffy is able to defeat Glory, but not before a ritual begins that must end in Dawn's death. Buffy finds redemption when she is able to sacrifice her life to save Dawn in the season's final episode ("The Gift"). Had her life truly ended at this point, it would have been a fitting ending. Dying at twenty-one would have been tragic, but the sense that Buffy had fulfilled her life's purpose and sacrificed herself for her loved ones would be some consolation. She goes to the grave with a clear understanding that she has lived her life well, and Buffy dies happy.

Romantic Relationships

"We can love quite well, if not wisely."
— Drusilla, "The Crush"

Buffy goes to the grave, but she does not stay there long. Her friends, worried that she might be "trapped in some hell dimension ... suffering some eternal torment," but also just feeling the hole in their lives, raise her from the dead ("Bargaining, Part One"). The clear and decisive end to Buffy's life is short-lived, as Willow, Tara, Xander, and Anya resurrect Buffy. Her first words on her return — "Is this hell?" she asks twice — suggest that Buffy has not been rescued from some hell dimension at all, but dragged into one ("Bargaining, Part Two"). She soon confirms this, confiding to Spike that she was "happy" and "at peace," "knowing that everyone I cared about was all right" ("Afterlife"). She tells him that she knew her life "was finished," implying she lived and died in the way that it was meant to be. In fact, she reveals, "I think I was in heaven" ("Afterlife"). Her friends have ripped her out of heaven into this world that feels like a hell, and Buffy falls into a nihilistic depression. Knowing that she has lost heaven, nothing else seems to matter.

All of which raises the question of what is accomplished by Buffy's return. What more does it add to her life's story? The truth is that the nihilism she feels after her resurrection is just the culmination of the doubts and uncertainty she feels before her death. The one area of her life incomplete before her death is her romantic relationships. Angel is her first love. Given that she is the Vampire Slayer and he is a vampire, that there is a two-hundred year age difference between them, and that he is cursed to lose his soul whenever he experiences true happiness, it is not completely surprising that their romance does not work out.

But when her second romance falters as well, Buffy doubts whether she can ever truly love. Riley says that she has always held something back, that she has never really let him get close. But she thinks that his problem is with her being the Slayer. She tells him, "And that's really what this is about. You can't handle that I'm stronger than you" ("Into the Woods"). She says that she has given him everything, but he responds that he does not feel it and gives her an ultimatum. Surprisingly, Xander confirms Riley's view of things. He tells her that she shut down after Angel left and that Riley may be her chance at happiness. Deciding that Xander is right, Buffy runs to tell Riley how she feels, but it is too late. Having missed twice, she begins to doubt whether the Slayer can ever find true love, lamenting, "Maybe being the perfect Slayer means being too hard to love at all" ("Intervention"). If not for Buffy's resurrection in Season Six, this would be the last word on Buffy's romantic loves.

It is Spike's love for Buffy that saves her life and ultimately draws her out of her depression. Spike's infatuation for her is a source of great humor in Season Five, but by the time of her death it is clear he truly loves her. He feels responsible for her death, having promised her that he would protect Dawn and then proving unable to do so ("The Gift"). When Buffy returns from the grave, Spike has a second chance at happiness.[5] He is drawn to Buffy, and, when she confides her secret in him, he is only drawn closer. When she is consumed by her nihilism, Spike gives her a reason to live. In one of the series's best episodes, a dancing demon comes to Sunnydale, causing the residents to sing their deepest secrets and feelings. Even musical demons have their dark sides, and, in this case, it is that victims dance until they spontaneously combust. In Buffy's first song, she wonders whether she will "stay this way forever / Sleepwalk through my life's endeavor," an apt description of her life post-resurrection ("Once More, With Feeling"). For Buffy, nothing matters in this world, and she has trouble even summoning the energy to look for the demon or to rescue Dawn (who yet again is in trouble). Confronting the demon, Buffy begins to sing. She tries to put on a happy face, but her song quickly reveals that she has little left to sing about. She concludes, "I live in hell / 'cause I was expelled from heaven" ("Once More, With Feeling").

With nothing left to sing about, she dances faster and faster, and she begins to smoke as her death-dance continues. But Spike breaks in, and his singing calls her back to the world: "Life isn't bliss / Life is just this / It's living" ("Once More, With Feeling"). Life is not bliss, but it can be happy despite the struggles and the anguish. Spike's words call her back to reality, and, when her sister Dawn follows with Buffy's own words of comfort from "The Gift"—"The hardest thing in this world is to live in it," Buffy begins the long slow healing process ("Once More, With Feeling"). When Buffy and Spike close the episode with a passionate kiss, the hope of true love and new happiness reigns supreme.

Not that Buffy's and Spike's relationship necessarily leads to another happy ending or is ultimately successful (what constitutes a successful romance, anyway?). I wouldn't want to gloss over the problems Buffy and Spike have throughout their romance. The relationship soon turns abusive, as the two blend fighting and sex in some truly disturbing ways, culminating in Spike's trying to force himself on her after she breaks up with him ("Seeing Red"). After the murder of Tara, Willow falls into the same sort of all-encompassing nihilism that gripped Buffy, and Willow draws on all her powers as a witch to try to end the world's suffering ("Grave").

But life does go on. Willow is finally stopped when confronted with her friend Xander's love for her, and Spike and Buffy reach a sort of peace in the show's final season. He sacrifices himself to save the world, and she tells him she loves him. He thinks she is just saying that because he is dying, but I think he's wrong. Buffy really does love him, and their parting just confirms that ("Chosen"). She finds happiness again in her romance with Spike, in her love for her friends and her sister, in her work as a Slayer, and in the little joys that she finds in daily life. The series ends with her smiling at the new possibilities for her life, a life that is truly well-lived.

Notes

1. Jeffrey Stout, *Democracy and Tradition*, p. 5. Although Stout is dismissive of "popular philosophy," he also highlights the ethical value of focusing on rich narratives rather than thin moral dilemmas. Great novels and films can provide that sort of rich narrative, but so too can a great television series— such as *Buffy*.

2. Framing the contrast in this way was first suggested to me by the title of an unpublished lecture by Linda Zagzebski, "The Admirable Life and the Desirable Life."

3. For an account of whether one should consider Buffy a moral exemplar, see Jason Kawal's "Should We Do What Buffy Would Do?" in James B. South's *Buffy the Vampire Slayer and Philosophy*. Jana Reiss takes the question in another direction in her book, *What Would Buffy Do?*, showing how the series as a whole does justice to a number of significant moral issues.

4. See Dial-Driver's chapter.

5. This is an essay on Buffy's happiness rather than Spike's, but his story is fascinating as well. I find it particularly noteworthy that he makes the same sort of sacrifice for Buffy at the end of the series that she made for Dawn in Season Five. Like Buffy, he has the same sense of completeness and happiness as he sacrifices himself ("Chosen"). Finally, like Buffy, he too is dragged back, although this time into the *Angel* series rather than Buffy's own.

Appendix

Buffy the Vampire Slayer Episodes

Shows are listed alphabetically (and show season + episode number)

After Life 6.3
All the Way 6.6
Amends 3.10
Angel 1.7
Anne 3.1
As You Were 6.15

Bad Eggs 2.12
Bad Girls 3.14
Band Candy 3.6
Bargaining, Part One 6.1
Bargaining, Part Two 6.2
Beauty and the Beasts 3.4
Becoming, Part 1 2.21
Becoming, Part 2 2.22
Beer Bad 4.5
Beneath You 7.2
Bewitched, Bothered, and Bewildered 2.16
Blood Ties 5.13
Body, The 5.16
Bring on the Night 7.10
Buffy vs. Dracula 5.1

Checkpoint 5.12
Choices 3.19
Chosen 7.22
Consequences 3.15

Conversations with Dead People 7.7
The Crush 5.14
The Dark Age 2.8
Dead Man's Party 3.2
Dead Things 6.13
Dirty Girls 7.18
Doomed 4.11
Doppelgangland 3.16
Doublemeat Palace 6.12

Earshot 3.18
Empty Places 7.19
End of Days 7.21
Enemies 3.17
Entropy 6.18

Faith, Hope and Trick 3.3
Family 5.6
Fear, Itself 4.4
First Date 7.14
Flooded 6.4
Fool for Love 5.7
Forever 5.17
The Freshman 4.1

Get It Done 7.15
The Gift 5.22
Gingerbread 3.11

Go Fish 2.20
Gone 6.11
Goodbye Iowa 4.14
Graduation Day (1) 3.21
Graduation Day (2) 3.22
Grave 6.22

Halloween 2.6
The Harsh Light of Day 4.3
The Harvest 1.2
Hell's Bells 6.16
Help 7.4
Helpless 3.12
Him 7.6
Homecoming 3.5
Hush 4.10

The I in Team 4.13
I Only Have Eyes for You 2.19
I Was Made to Love You 5.15
I Robot, You Jane 1.8
Inca Mummy Girl 2.4
The Initiative 4.7
Innocence 2.14
Intervention 5.18
Into the Woods 5.10

Killed by Death 2.18
The Killer in Me 7.13

Lessons 7.1
Lie to Me 2.7
Lies My Parents Told Me
   7.17
Life Serial 6.5
Listening to Fear 5.9
Living Conditions 4.2
Lover's Walk 3.8

Never Kill a Boy on the
   First Date 1.5
Never Leave Me 7.9
A New Man 4.12
New Moon Rising 4.19
Nightmares 1.10
No Place like Home 5.5
Normal Again 6.17

Older and Far Away 6.14
Once More, with Feeling
   6.7
Out of Mind, Out of
   Sight 1.11
Out of My Mind 5.4

The Pack 1.6
Pangs 4.8
Passion 2.17
Phases 2.15

Potential 7.12
Primeval 4.21
The Prom 3.20
Prophecy Girl 1.12
The Puppet Show 1.9

Real Me 5.2
The Replacement 5.3
Reptile Boy 2.5
Restless 4.22
Revelations 3.7

Same Time, Same Place
   7.3
School Hard 2.3
Seeing Red 6.19
Selfless 7.5
Shadow 5.8
Showtime 7.11
Sleeper 7.8
Smashed 6.9
Some Assembly Required
   2.2
Something Blue 4.9
Spiral 5.20
Storyteller 7.16
Superstar 4.17
Surprise 2.13

Tabula Rasa 6.8
Teacher's Pet 1.4
Ted 2.11

This Year's Girl 4.15
Touched 7.20
Tough Love 5.19
Triangle 5.11
Two to Go 6.21

Villains 6.20

The Weight of the World
   5.21
Welcome to the Hell-
   mouth 1.1
What's My Line? Part
   One 2.9
What's My Line? Part
   Two 2.10
When She Was Bad 2.1
Where the Wild Things
   Are 4.18
Who Are You? 4.16
Wild at Heart 4.6
The Wish 3.9
The Witch 1.3
Wrecked 6.10

The Yoko Factor 4.20

The Zeppo 3.13

Works Cited

Aberdeen. "Cities and Buses." *Homesick and Happy to Be Here*. Better Looking, 2002.

Abrams, M.H., with Geoffrey Galt Harpham. *A Glossary of Literary Terms*. 8th ed. Boston: Thomson, 2005.

Achebe, Chinua. *Things Fall Apart*. Chicago: Penguin, 2006.

Adams, Henry. *The Education of Henry Adams*. Boston: Houghton Mifflin, 1918.

"Adolescent." *Dictionary.com*. 28 August 2007. <http://dictionary.reference.com/browse/adolescent>.

Alessio, Dominic. "Things Are Different Now? A Postcolonial Analysis of *Buffy the Vampire Slayer*." *The European Legacy* 6.6 (2001): 731–40.

Alexie, Sherman. "How to Write the Great American Indian Novel." *Nothing but the Truth: An Anthology of Native American Literature*. Ed. John L. Purdy and James Ruppert. Upper Saddle River, NJ: Prentice, 2001. 425–27.

Ali, Asim. "Religion in *Buffy the Vampire Slayer*, *Buffy* as Religion: The Bronze as a Global Religious Community." The *Slayage* Conference on the Whedonverse. Barnesville, GA. 26–28 May 2006.

Anderson, John. "Television Stereotyping of the Chumash." 2 February 2003. 6 September 2007 <www.expage.com>.

Anderson, Wendy. "What Would Buffy Do?" *Christian Century* 17 (May 2003): 43.

Angel. Seasons 1–5. DVD. 20th Century–Fox, 2007.

Appelo, Tim. "Buffy Slays: Now What?" *Slate* 5 November 2001. 1 October 2007 <http://www.slate.com/id/2058066/>.

Aristotle. *Nicomachean Ethics*. Tr. Martin Ostwald. New York: Macmillan, 1962.

Arnett, Jeffrey. "Adolescent Storm and Stress, Reconsidered." *American Psychologist* 54.5 (1999): 317–26.

_____. *Emerging Adulthood: The Winding Road from the Late Teens through the Twenties*. New York: Oxford University Press, 2004.

Ashforth, Adam. "On Living in a World with Witches: Everyday Epistemology and Spiritual Insecurity in a Modern African City (Soweto)" *Magical Interpretations, Material Realities: Modernity, Witchcraft and the Occult in Postcolonial Africa*. Ed. Henrietta L. Moore and Todd Sanders. London: Routledge, 2002. 206–25.

"At the River." *Lied and Art Songs Text Page*. 19 Sep. 2005. 5 November 2007 <http://www.recmusic.org/lieder/get_text.html?TextId=25706>.

Austen, Ralph A. "The Moral Economy of Witchcraft: An Essay in Comparative History." *Modernity and its Malcontents: Ritual and Power in Postcolonial Africa*. Ed. Jean Comaroff and John L. Comaroff. Chicago: University of Chicago Press, 1993. 89–110.

"Awards for 'Buffy the Vampire Slayer.'" *The Internet Movie Database*. 2007. 18 September 2007 <www.imdb.com>.

Azure Ray. "Displaced." *Azure Ray*. Warm, 2001.

Badaracco, Joseph L. *Questions of Character*. Boston: Harvard Business, 2006.

Barnstorff, Hermann. Rev. of *The Frozen Sea: A Study of Franz Kafka*, by Charles Neider. *The Modern Language Journal* 33.2 (February 1949). 22 October 2007.

Bastian, Misty L. "Vulture Men, Campus Cultists, and Teenaged Witches: Modern Magics in Nigerian Popular Media." *Magical Interpretations, Material Realities: Modernity, Witchcraft and the Occult in Postcolonial Africa*. Ed. Henrietta L. Moore and Todd Sanders. London: Routledge, 2002. 71–96.

Battis, Jes. Blood *Relations: Chosen Families in* Buffy the Vampire Slayer *and* Angel. Jefferson, NC: McFarland, 2005.

Beckett, Samuel. *Waiting for Godot*. London: Faber, 1998.

Bellafonte, Ginia. "Bewitching Teen Heroines." *Time*. 5 May 1997: 82–84.

Bellylove. "Back to Freedom." *Bellylove*. Black/Valenta, 1998.

Berger, Peter L., and Thomas Luckmann. *The Social Construction of Reality: A Treatise in the Sociology of Knowledge*. New York: Anchor, 1967.

Berkhofer, Robert F. *The White Man's Indian*. New York: Vintage, 1978.

Bif Naked. "Moment of Weakness." *I Bificus*. Lava, 1999.

Billson, Anne. Buffy the Vampire Slayer: *A Critical Reading of the Series*. London: British Film Institute, 2005.

Black, Robert A. "It's Not Homophobia, But That Doesn't Make It Right." *Dykesvision* 2002. 15 Oct. 2007 <http://www.dykesvision.com/en/articles/homophobia.html>.

Blink-182. "All the Small Things." *Enema of the State*. MCA, 1999.

Bloom, Harold. *Shakespeare: The Invention of the Human*. New York: Riverhead, 1998.

Bodger, Gwyneth. "Buffy the Feminist Slayer? Constructions of Femininity in *Buffy the Vampire Slayer*." *Refractory: A Journal of Entertainment Media* 2 (2003). 16 Aug. 2007 <http://www.refractory.unimelb.edu.au/journalissues/vol2/gBodger.pdf>.

Boyce, Charles. *Shakespeare A to Z: The Essential Reference to His Plays, His Poems, His Life and Times, and More*. New York: Delta, 1990.

"Brain Imaging Study Sheds Light on Moral Decision-Making." *Science Daily* 14 September 2001. 10 February 2007 <www.sciencedaily.com/releases/2001/09/010914074303.htm>.

Branch, Michelle. "Goodbye to You." *The Spirit Room*. Maverick, 2001.

Brecht, Bertolt. 1949. "A Short Organum for the Theatre." *Brecht on Theatre: The Development of an Aesthetic*. Ed. and trans. John Willett. London: Methuen, 1964. 179–205.

Brooks, Mel, director. *Young Frankenstein*. 1974. 20th Century–Fox, 2006

Buffy the Vampire Slayer. Seasons 1–7. DVD. 20th Century–Fox, 2006.

Buttsworth, Sara. "Bite Me: Buffy and the Penetration of the Gendered Warrior-Hero." *Continuum: Journal of Media and Cultural Studies* 16.2 (2002): 185–99.

Calame, Claude. *The Poetics of Eros in Ancient Greece*. Trans. Janet Lloyd. Princeton, NJ: Princeton University Press, 1999.

Canetti, Elias. *Crowds and Power*. Trans. Carol Stewart. New York: Farrar, 1984.

Carroll, Lewis. *Alice in Wonderland and Through the Looking Glass*. New York: Signet, 2000.

"The Castle of Perseverance." *The Castle of Perseverance, Wisdom, Mankind*. Ed. Mark Eccles. Oxford, England: Oxford, 1968.

Cher. "Believe." *Believe*. Warner, 1998.

Chesterton, G.K. *Saint Francis of Assisi*. New York: Doubleday, 1951.

Chrystos. *Dream On.* Vancouver, BC: Press Gang, 1991.
_____. *Not Vanishing.* Vancouver, BC: Press Gang, 1988.
Clarke, Jamie. "Affective Entertainment in 'Once More with Feeling': A Manifesto for Fandom." 2003. *Refractory: A Journal of Entertainment Media* 2 (27 August 2007) <http://www.refractory.unimelb.edu.au/journalissues/vol2/jClarke.pdf>.
Clement, Shawn, and Sean Murray. "Lie to Me." *Buffy the Vampire Slayer:* "Lie to Me." Season Two DVD. 20th Century–Fox, 2006.
Cline, Patsy. "I Fall to Pieces." *The Patsy Cline Story.* MCA Nashville, 1963.
Conan Doyle, Arthur. *A Study in Scarlet.* Lawrence, KS: Digireads.com, 2005.
Cooper, Alice. "School's Out." *School's Out.* Warner/WEA, 2002.
Copleston, Frederick Charles. *A History of Philosophy* Vol. 1. Westminster, MD: Newman, 1959.
Costa, Nikka. "Everybody Got Their Something." *Everybody Got Their Something.* Virgin Records, 2001.
Cream. "Tales of Brave Ulysses." *The Very Best of Cream.* Polydor/UMGD, 1995.
Crystals. "He's a Rebel." Abkco, 1992.
Culp, Christopher M. "'But ... You're Just a Girl.' The Feminine Mystique of Season Five." *Watcher Junior* 2 (July 2006). 31 Aug. 2007 <http://www.watcherjunior.tv/02/culp.php>.
Dahlberg-Acton, John. "Lord Acton's Dictum." *The New Dictionary of Cultural Literacy.* Ed. E.D. Hirsh, Jr., Joseph F. Kett, and James Trefil. Boston, MA: Houghton, Mifflin, 2002.
Dashboard Prophets. "Wearing Me Down." *Burning Out the Inside.* WEA, 1996.
Daughtey, Anne Millard. ""Just a Girl: Buffy as Icon." *Reading the Slayer: An Unofficial Critical Companion to Buffy and Angel.* Ed. Roy Kaverney. New York: Taurus, 2002. 148–65.
"David Lynch." *Internet Movie Database.* 12 September 2007. <http://www.imdb.com>.
Dechert, S. Renee. "'My Boyfriend's in the Band!' Buffy and the Rhetoric of Music." *Fighting the Forces: What's at Stake in* Buffy the Vampire Slayer. Eds. Rhonda V. Wilcox and David Lavery. Lanham, MD: Rowman & Littlefield, 2002. 218–26.
DeKelf-Rittenhouse, Diane. "Sex and the Single Vampire: The Evolution of the Vampire Lothario and Its Representation in *Buffy.*" *Fighting the Forces: What's at Stake in* Buffy the Vampire Slayer. Ed. Rhonda V. Wilcox and David Lavery. New York: Rowman, 2002. 143–52.
Devics. "Key." *If You Forget Me.* Splinter Records, 1998.
Doane, Melanie. "I Can't Take My Eyes Off You." *Adam's Rib.* Sony, 1999.
Dr. Seuss. *The Cat in the Hat.* New York: Random, 1957.
Duffy, Michael. "Vintage Media: Vintage Audio: 'It's a Long Way to Tipperary.'" *Vintage Media. First World War.Com* 19 July 2003. 18 September 2007. <http://www.firstworldwar.com/audio/index.htm>.
Dworkin, Andrea. *Letters from a War Zone: Writings, 1976–1989.* New York: E.P. Dutton, 1989.
Dylan, Bob. Quoted in David Barker's *33 1/3 Greatest Hits.* New York: Continuum, 2006. 182.
"Early One Morning." English Folk Song.
Eco, Umberto. *On Ugliness.* Trans. Alastair MacEwan. New York: Rizzoli, 2007.
Ehrenberg, Margaret R. *Women in Prehistory.* Norman: University of Oklahoma, 1989.
Elwell, Frank. *The Erosion of Commitment.* Murray State. July 1997. 2 February 2007 <http://campus.murraystate.edu>.
Erikson, Erik. *Identity: Youth and Crisis.* New York: W.W. Norton, 1968.
_____. *The Life Cycle Completed: A Review.* New York: W.W. Norton, 1985.

Evans, Walter. "Monster Movies: A Sexual Theory." *Popular Culture: An Introductory Text.* Ed. Jack Nachbar and Kevin Lause. Bowling Green, OH: Bowling Green State University, 1992.

Everyman. Ed. A.C. Cawley. London: Dent, 1993.

Fat Boy Slim. "Praise You." *Praise You.* Astralwerks/EMD, 1999.

Fenn, Elizabeth A. "Biological Warfare in Eighteenth Century North America: Beyond Jeffery Amherst." *The Journal of American History* 86.4 (March 2000): 1552–80.

The Flamingoes. "I Only Have Eyes for You." *The Best of the Flamingoes.* Rhino/WEA, 1990.

Fleming, Ian. *Ian Fleming Center.* Ian Fleming Publications. 4 August 2007. 2006. <http://www.ianflemingcentre.com/>.

Folks, Jeffrey. "'Memory Believes before Knowing Remembers': Faulkner, Canetti and Survival." *Language and Literature.* Summer 2003. Findarticles.com Summer 2003. 8 July 2007.

Forrest Gump. DVD. Phillips, 1995.

Four Star Mary. "Run." *Thrown to the Wolves.* MSG Records, 1999.

Fowler, Heather. "Messages about Sex and Violence in the Buffy/Spike Relationship on *Buffy the Vampire Slayer.*" Associated Content. 1 June 2006. 8 September 2007 <http://www.associatedcontent.com>.

Frankenstein. 1931. *Frankenstein: 75th Anniversary Edition (Universal Legacy Series).* DVD. Universal Studios, 2006.

Frankl, Viktor E. *Man's Search for Meaning.* New York: Pocket Books, 1984.

Freud, Sigmund. *Civilization and Its Discontents.* Ed. James Strachey. New York: Norton, 1961.

_____. *The Ego and the Id: The Standard Edition of the Complete Psychological Works of Sigmund Freud.* New York: Norton, 1989.

_____. *An Outline of Psycho-Analysis.* Trans. James Strachey. New York: New York: Norton, 1969.

Freund, Kurt, Hal Scher, I.G. Racansky, Kent Campbell, and Gerald Heasman. "Males Disposed to Commit Rape." *Archives of Sexual Behavior* 15.1 (February 1986): 23–25.

Fritts, David. "Warrior Heroes: Buffy the Vampire Slayer and Beowulf." *Slayage* 17 5.1 (June 2005). Collins College. 15 April 2006 <http://www.slayage.tv/>.

Frye, Northrup, Sheridan Baker, George Perkins, and Barbara M. Perkins. *The Harper Handbook to Literature.* 2nd ed. New York: Longman, 1997.

Geschiere, Peter. *The Modernity of Witchcraft: Politics and the Occult in Postcolonial Africa.* Charlottesville: University of Virginia, 1997.

Goddard, Drew, and David Solomon. "Commentary: 'Selfless.'" *Buffy the Vampire Slayer.* Season Seven DVD. 20th Century–Fox Home Entertainment, 2006.

Gorbman, Claudia. *Unheard Melodies: Narrative Film Music.* Bloomington, IN: Indiana University Press, 1987.

Grassian, Daniel. *Understanding Sherman Alexie.* Columbia: University of South Carolina, 2005.

Greene, Joshua. "From Neural 'Is' to Moral 'Ought': What Are the Moral Implications of Neuroscientific Moral Psychology?" *Nature Reviews: Neuroscience* 4 (October 2003). 10 February 2007 <www.nature.com/reviews/neuro>.

Greene, Richard, and Wayne Yuen. "Morality on Television." *Buffy the Vampire Slayer and Philosoophy: Fear and Trembling in Sunnydale.* Ed. James B. South. Popular Culture and Philosophy. Series Editor William Irwin. Chicago: Open Court, 2003. 271–81.

Greenman, Jennifer. "Witch Love Spells Death: Was the Killing of Tara on *Buffy the Vampire Slayer* a Bold Plot Move or Just Another Dead Lesbian on TV?" *Sacramento*

News and Review 6 June 2002. 16 September 2007 <http://www.newsreview.com/sacramento/Content?oid=oid%3A12342>.

Gross, Terri. "Interview with Joss Whedon." *Fresh Air* 9 May 2000. 8 September 2007 <http://www.npr.org/templates/story/story.php?storyId=835108>.

Halfyard, Janet K. "Love, Death, Curses and Reverses (in F Minor): Music, Gender, and Identity in *Buffy the Vampire Slayer* and *Angel*." 2001. *Slayage: the Online International Journal of Buffy Studies* 4 (27 August 2007) <http://slayageonline.com/essays/slayage4/halfyard.htm>.

_____. "Singing Their Hearts Out: The Problem of Performance in *Buffy the Vampire Slayer* and *Angel* " 2005. *Slayage: the Online International Journal of Buffy Studies* 17 (27 August 2007) <http://slayageonline.com/essays/slayage17/Halfyard.htm>.

Hamilton, Sharon. *Shakespeare's Daughters*. Jefferson, NC: McFarland, 2003.

Harmon, William, and C. Hugh Holman. "Allusion." *A Handbook to Literature*. 8th ed. Upper Saddle River, NJ: Prentice Hall, 2000. 14.

Hart, Angie, and Joss Whedon. "Blue." *Buffy the Vampire Slayer: Radio Sunnydale*. Virgin Records (US), 2003.

Head, John O. *Working with Adolescents: Constructing Identity*. London: Falmer, 2002. Taylor and Francis eLibrary ed.

Heizer, Robert F. *The Destruction of California Indians*. Lincoln: University of Nebraska, 1974.

The Hellacopters. "Hey." *Payin' the Dues*. White Jazz, 1999.

Hill, Kathryn. "Music, Subtexts and Foreshadowings: Contextual Roles of Popular Music in *Buffy the Vampire Slayer*, 1997–2003." Slayage Conference on *Buffy the Vampire Slayer*. Nashville, TN, May 2004. 27 August 2007 <http://slayageonline.com/SCBtVS_Archive/Talks/KHill.pdf>.

"History." *Franciscan Friars, T.O.R.: Province of the Most Sacred Heart of Jesus* 2 August 1990. 18 September 2007 <http://www.franciscanstor.org/history.htm>.

Hobbes, Thomas. *Leviathan*. Ed. Karl Schuhmann and G.A.J. Rogers. New York: Continuum, 2003.

Hofstede, Geert H. *Culture's Consequences: Comparing Values, Behaviors, Institutions, and Organisation across Nations*. 2nd ed. Thousand Oaks, CA: Sage, 2001.

Hollows, Joanne. *Feminism, Femininity, and Popular Culture*. Manchester: Manchester University Press, 2000.

Hornick, Alysa. *Buffyology: An Academic Buffy Studies and Whedonverse Bibliography*. 2005. 18 September 2007 <http://www.alysa316.com/Buffyology>.

Howe, Cari. "Anything." (Written and produced by Shawn Clement and Sean Murray.) *Cari Howe*. Cari Howe, 2004.

Hughes, Robert. *The Shock of the New*. 2^d ed. New York: McGraw-Hill, 1991.

Jagodzinski, Jan. *Music in Youth Culture: A Lacanian Approach*. New York: Palgrave Macmillan, 2005.

Jaws. 1975. DVD. Universal Studios, 2005.

John Paul II. *Thinkexist.com*. 12 Sep. 2007. <http://thinkexist.com/quotation/ as_the_family_goes-so_goes_the_nation_and_so_goes/150797.html>.

Jowett, L. *Sex and the Slayer: A Gender Studies Primer for the Buffy Fan*. Middletown, CT: Wesleyan University Press, 2005.

K's Choice. "Virgin State of Mind." Unreleased CD.

Kafka, Franz. *The Metamorphosis*. West Valley City, UT: Waking Lion, 2006.

Kawal, Jason. "Should We Do What Buffy Would Do?" *Buffy the Vampire Slayer and Philosophy: Fear and Trembling in Sunnydale*. Ed. James B. South. Chicago: Open Court, 2003. 149–59.

Kemerling, Garth. "Aristotle: Ethics and Virtues." *Philosophy Pages*. 27 October 2001. 2 February 2007 <http://www.philosophpages.com/hy/2s.htm>.

King, Stephen. *It*. (1990). DVD. Warner, 2002.

———. "The Monkey." *Skeleton Crew*. New York: Montcalm, 1980.

King, Thomas. *The Truth about Stories*. Minneapolis: University of Minnesota Press, 2005.

Kirkland, Bruce. "Creator Lets Us in on His Hidden Message." *The Toronto Sun* 4 January 2006: 67. *Academic Search Premier*. EBSCO. Rogers State University. Stratton Taylor Library. 2 April 2006 <http://www.epnet.com/>.

Klaits, Joseph. *Servants of Satan: The Age of Witch Hunts*. Bloomington, IN: Indiana University, 1985.

Knights, Vanessa. "'Bay City Rollers. Now That's Music': Coolness, Crassness and Characterization on *Buffy the Vampire Slayer*." Sonic Synergies: Creative Cultures Conference. University of South Australia, The Hawke Research Institute and IASPM, July 2003. 27 August 2007 <http://www.ncl.ac.uk/sacs/POP/papers/sonic vkpop.pdf>.

Kool & the Gang. "Celebrate." *The Best of Kool & the Gang 1979–1987*. Island/Mercury, 1994.

Korsmeyer, Carolyn. "Passion and Action: In and Out of Control." Buffy the Vampire Slayer *and Philosophy: Fear and Trembling in Sunnydale*. Ed. James B. South. Popular Culture and Philosophy. Series Editor William Irwin. Chicago: Open Court, 2003. 160–72.

Krzywinska, Tanya. "Hubble-Bubble, Herbs, and Grimoires: Magic, Manichaeanism, and Witchcraft in Buffy." *Fighting the Forces: What's at Stake in* Buffy the Vampire Slayer." Ed. Ronda Wilcox and David Lavery. New York: Rowman, 2001. 178–94.

Lacan, Jacques. "The Agency of the Letter in the Unconscious or Reason since Freud." *The Critical Tradition: Classic Texts and Contemporary Trends*. 2^d ed. Ed. David H. Richter. Boston: Bedford, 1998. 1044–64.

Laika. "Black Cat Bone." *Good Looking Blues*. Too Pure/Beggars, 2000.

Lasch, Christopher. *The Culture of Narcissism: American Life in an Age of Diminishing Expectations*. New York: W.W. Norton & Company, Inc., 1978.

Laurent, Henry. *Personality: How to Build It*. 1915. Trans. Richard Duffy. Whitefish, MT: Kessinger, 2007.

Lears, T. J. Jackson. "From Salvation to Self-Realization: Advertising and the Therapeutic Roots of the Consumer Culture, 1880–1930." *Advertising and Society Review* 1.1 (2000). 2 August 2007 <http://muse.jhu.edu/login?uri=/journals/asr/v001/1.1lears.html>.

———. *No Place of Grace: Antimodernism and the Transformation of American Culture, 1880–1920*. Chicago: University of Chicago, 1994.

Lefkowitz, Eva S., and M.M. Gillen. "'Sex Is Just a Normal Part of Life': Sexuality in Emerging Adulthood." *Emerging Adults in America: Coming of Age in the 21st Century*. Ed. Jeffrey Jensen Arnett and Jennifer Lynn Tanner, Washington, DC: American Psychological Association, 2006. 235–55.

The Lied and Art Song Texts Page. 18 September 2007. <http://www.recmusic.org/lieder/get_text.html?TextId=25706>.

The Lion King. DVD. Disney, 2003.

Little, Allan. "Dutch Smash Voodoo Child Trade." *BBC News* 25 October 2007. 27 October 2007 <http://news.bbc.co.uk/1/hi/world/europe/7061145.stm>.

Loeb, Lisa. "How." *Firecracker*. Geffen Records, 1997.

Long, Carolyn Morrow. *Spiritual Merchants: Religious Magic and Commerce*. Knoxville: University of Tennessee Press, 2001.

Los Cubazteca. "Nicolito." Intersound, 1999.

Loss, Christopher P. "Religion and the Therapeutic Ethos in Twentieth-Century American History." *American Studies International* 40.3 (October 2002): 61. 12 November 2007

Louie Louie: The Very Best of the Kingsmen. Collectables, 1999.

Louie Says. "She." *Gravity, Suffering, Love and Fate.* RCA, 1997.

Lovejoy, Arthur O. *The Great Chain of Being: A Study of the History of an Idea.* New York: Harper and Brothers, 1960.

Lynch, David. *The Universe of David Lynch.* 9 October 2007 <http://www.davidlynch.de/>.

Lynyrd Skynyrd. "Free Bird." *Lynyrd Skynyrd: All Time Greatest Hits.* MCA, 2000.

Malory, Sir Thomas. *Le Morte d'Arthur.* London: Cassell, 2003.

Man of the Year. "Just As Nice." *The Future is Not Now.* Loveless Records, 2000.

"Mankind." *The Castle of Perseverance, Wisdom, Mankind.* Ed. Mark Eccles. Oxford, England: Oxford, 1968.

Mann, Aimee. "Pavlov's Bell." *Lost in Space.* Superego Records, 2002.

_____. "This Is How It Goes." *Lost in Space.* Superego Records, 2002.

Marlowe, Christopher. *Dr. Faustus.* Mineola, NY: Dover, 1994.

Maslow, Abraham H. *The Maslow Business Reader.* Ed. Deborah C. Stephens. New York: John Wiley & Sons, 2000.

McDonald, Paul F. *The Goddess and Her Gift: An Analysis of the Fifth Season of Buffy the Vampire Slayer.* 29 September 2001. 19 August 2007 <http://www.ivyweb.com/btvs/fictionary/essays/010929A_DED.htm>.

McGinn, Colin. *Shakespeare's Philosophy: Discovering the Meaning behind the Plays.* New York: HarperCollins, 2006.

McLachlan, Sarah. "Full of Grace." *Surfacing.* BMG, 1997.

_____. "Prayer of St. Francis." *Surfacing.* BMG, 1997.

McLaren, Scott. "The Evolution of Joss Whedon's Vampire Mythology and the Ontology of the Soul." *Slayage: The Online International Journal of Buffy Studies18* 5.2 (2005). 8 September 2007 <http://www.slayageonline.com/essays/slayage18/McLaren.htm>.

Mendlesohn, Farah. "Surpassing the Love of Vampires." *Fighting the Forces.* Ed. Rhonda V. Wilcox and David Lavery. Lanham, MD: Rowman and Littlefield, 2002. 45–60.

Middleton, John., and E.H. Winter. "Witchcraft and Sorcery In East Africa." *Witchcraft and Sorcery in East Africa.* Ed. John Middleton and E.H. Winters. London: Routledge, 1963.

Miller, Patricia. *Theories of Developmental Psychology,* 2^d ed. New York: W.H. Freeman, 1989.

Milton, John. *Paradise Lost* (Norton Critical Edition). 3^d ed. Ed. Gordon Tesky. New York: Norton, 2004.

Miranda, Deborah A. "Thanksgiving at Soledad and Carmel Missions." E-mail to SAIL Discussion Group. 27 November 2007.

Mr. Rogers' Neighborhood. Family Communications. 12 November 2007 <http://pbskids.org/rogers/>.

Monroe, Kristen. "How Identity and Perspective Constrain Moral Choices." *International Political Science Review/Revue international de science politique* 24.4 (October 2003): 405–25. 3 September 2007

Moore, Henrietta L., and Todd Sanders. "Introduction." *Magical Interpretations, Material Realities: Modernity, Witchcraft and the Occult in Postcolonial Africa.* Ed. Henrietta L. Moore and Todd Sanders. London: Routledge, 2002. 1–27.

Moskowitz, Eva S. *In Therapy We Trust: America's Obsession with Self-Fulfillment.* Baltimore: Johns Hopkins, 2001.

Mulholland Drive. 2001. DVD. Universal Studios, 2002.

Murfin, Ross, and Supryia M. Ray. *The Bedford Glossary of Critical and Literary Terms.* 2d ed. Boston: Bedford, 2003.

Nerf Herder. "*Buffy the Vampire* Slayer Theme." *Buffy the Vampire Slayer.* Seasons 1–7. DVD. 20th Century–Fox, 2006.

Niehaus, Isak. "Witchcraft in New South Africa: From Colonial Superstition to Postcolonial Reality?" *Magical Interpretations, Material Realities: Modernity, Witchcraft and the Occult in Postcolonial Africa.* Ed. Henrietta L. Moore and Todd Sanders. London: Routledge, 2002. 184–205.

Nirvana. "Smells like Teen Spirit." *Nevermind.* Geffen, 1991.

North, Adrian C., and David J. Hargreaves. "Music and Adolescent Identity." *Music Education Research* 1.1 (1999): 75–92.

Nothing but Widespread Panic. 9 September 2006. 17 February 2007. <http://widespread-panic.blogspot.com/2006/09/9906-trivia_09.html>.

Nova, Heather. "It's Only Love." *South.* V2 Ada, 2001.

One Flew Over the Cuckoo's Nest. 1975. DVD. Warner, 1997.

Onyinah, Opoku. "Contemporary 'Witchdemonology' in Africa." *International Review of Mission* 93.370/371 (1 July 2004): 330–45. 18 June 2007.

Packer, George. "The Moderate Martyr: A Radically Peaceful Vision of Islam." *The New Yorker* 61.82 (11 September 2006): 61. *LexisNexis Academic.* 14 September 2007.

Pateman, Matthew. *The Aesthetics of Culture in Buffy the Vampire Slayer.* Jefferson, NC: McFarland, 2006.

Pender, Patricia. "'I'm Buffy, and You're ... History': The Postmodern Politics of *Buffy.*" *Fighting the Forces: What's at Stake in Buffy the Vampire Slayer.* Ed. Rhonda V. Wilcox and David Lavery. Lanham, MD: Rowman and Littlefield, 2002. 35–44.

Pipher, Mary. *Reviving Ophelia: Saving the Selves of Adolescent Girls.* New York: Ballantine, 1994.

Plato. *Plato: Complete Works.* Ed. John M. Cooper and D.H. Hutchinson. Indianapolis, IN: Hackett, 1997.

Poe, Edgar Allan. *The Best of Poe: The Tell-Tale Heart, The Raven, The Cask of Amontillado, and Thirty Others.* Clayton, DE: Prestwick House, 2006. 161–66.

Purdy, John L., and James Ruppert. *Nothing but the Truth: An Anthology of Native American Literature.* Upper Saddle River, NJ: Prentice, 2001.

Ramones. "I Wanna Be Sedated." *Road to Ruin.* Rhino, 2001.

Reiss, Jana. *What Would Buffy Do? The Vampire as Spiritual Guide.* San Francisco: Jossey-Bass, 2004.

Resnick, Laura. "The Good, the Bad, and the Ambivalent." *Seven Seasons of Buffy: Science Fiction and Fantasy Authors Discuss Their Favorite Television Show.* Ed. Glenn Yeffeth. Dallas: Benbella, 2003. 54–64.

Richardson, J. Michael, and J. Douglas Rabb. *The Existential Joss Whedon: Evil and Human Freedom in Buffy the Vampire Slayer, Angel, Firefly and Serenity.* Jefferson, NC.: McFarland, 2007.

Rieff, Philip. *Freud: The Mind of the Moralist.* 3d ed. Chicago: University of Chicago Press, 1979.

_____. *The Triumph of the Therapeutic: Uses of Faith after Freud.* London: Chatto and Windus, 1966.

Ritzer, George. *Enchanting a Disenchanted World: Revolutionizing the Means of Consumption.* Thousand Oaks, CA: Sage, 1999.

The Rocky Horror Picture Show. 1975. DVD. 20th Century–Fox, 2002.

Saint-Saëns, Camille. "Danse Macabre." *Saint-Saëns: Greatest Hits*. Sony, 1995.

Sanders, Todd. "Save Our Skins: Structural Adjustment, Morality and the Occult in Tanzania." *Magical Interpretations, Material Realities: Modernity, Witchcraft and the Occult in Postcolonial Africa*. Ed. Henrietta L. Moore and Todd Sanders. London: Routledge, 2002. 160–83.

Santa Ynez Band of Chumash Indians. 2004. Santa Ynez Band of Chumash Indians. 8 October 2007 <www.santaynexchumash.org/culture>.

Savage Country: American Indian Mascots in Oklahoma High School Football. Prod. Hugh Foley. 2003.

Saxey, Esther. "Staking a Claim: The Series and Its Slash Fan-Fiction." *Reading the Vampire Slayer: An Unofficial Critical Companion to Buffy and Angel*. Ed. Roz Kaveney. New York: Taurus Parke, 2002. 187–210.

Schudt, Karl. "Also Sprach Faith: The Problem of the Happy Rogue Vampire Slayer." *Buffy the Vampire Slayer and Philosophy: Fear and Trembling in Sunnydale*. Ed. James B. South. Popular Culture and Philosophy. Series Editor William Irwin. Chicago: Open Court, 2003. 20–34.

Scoble, M.J. *The Lepidoptera: Form, Function, and Diversity*. Oxford, England: Oxford University Press, 1992.

Scooby Doo, Where Are You! The Complete First and Second Seasons (1969). DVD. Turner Home Entertainment, 2004.

"Secundum Iohannem/The Gospel According to John, Chapter 1." *Novum Testamentum*. English Text: King James Bible; Latin Text: Hieronymi Vulgata. 23 May 2006 <http://faculty.acu.edu/~goebeld/vulgata/newtest/john/vjo1.htm>.

Sesame Street. CTW. PBS. 1969-present.

Sexton, Timothy. "Why Kubrick's *The Shining* Is So Compelling: Stanley Kubrick's Film Actually Reduces Horror of the Book." *Associated Content: The People's Media Company* 31 June 2005. 6 October 2007 <http://www.associatedcontent.com/article/4880/why_kubricks_the_shining_is_so_compelling.html>.

Shakespeare, William. *Henry V*. Folger Shakespeare Library. New York: Washington Square, 2004.

_____. *King Lear*. Folger Shakespeare Library. New York: Washington Square, 2005.

_____. *King Lear*. Ed. Stanton Wells. Folger Shakespeare Library. New York: Washington Square, 1993.

_____. *The Merchant of Venice*. Ed. Barbara A. Mowat and Paul Werstine. New York: Washington Square Press, 2004.

_____. *Othello*. Folger Shakespeare Library. New York: Washington Square, 2004.

_____. *Richard III*. Folger Shakespeare Library. New York: Washington Square, 2004.

_____. *Romeo and Juliet*. Folger Shakespeare Library. New York: Washington Square, 2004.

_____. *Titus Andronicus*. Folger Shakespeare Library. New York: Washington Square, 2005.

_____. *Winter's Tale*. Folger Shakespeare Library. New York: Washington Square, 2004.

Shaw, Rosalind. "Cannibal Transformations: Colonialism and Comodification in Sierra Leon Hinterland." *Magical Interpretations, Material Realities: Modernity, Witchcraft and the Occult in Postcolonial Africa*. Ed. Henrietta L. Moore and Todd Sanders. New York: Routledge, 2001. 50–70.

Shelley, Mary. *Frankenstein*. 1918. Norton Critical Edition. Ed. J. Paul Hunter. New York: Norton, 1996.

Shermer, Michael. "Skeptic: Bad Apples and Bad Barrels." *Scientific American* 297.2 (August 2007): 34–36.

Showalter, Dennis. ""Buffy Goes to War." The *Slayage* Conference on *Buffy the Vampire Slayer*. Nashville, TN. 2004.

Shuttleworth, Ian. "They Always Mistake Me for the Character I Play! Transformation, Identity, and Role-Playing in the *Buffy*verse (and a Defense of Fine Acting)." *Reading the Vampire Slayer: An Unofficial Critical Companion to Buffy and Angel*. Ed. Roz Kaveney. New York: Taurus Parke, 2002. 211–36.

Sid Vicious. "My Way." *Sid Lives*. Jungle UK Singles, 2007.

Sister Sledge. "We Are Family." *We Are Family*. Atlantic, 1995.

Simon, Linda. "The Sleep of Reason." *WorldandI.com*. 2003. 2 October 2007 <http://www.worldandi.com/newhome/public/2004/february/bkpubl.asp>.

Sinatra, Frank. "My Way." *My Way*. Warner, 1990.

Skippy R. "The Door Theologian of the Year." *The Door Magazine* 183 (September/October 2002). 7 August 2007 <http://www.thedoormagazine.com/archives/buffy.html>.

Sleepless in Seattle. 1993. DVD. Sony, 2003.

Sonneborn, Liz. *The Chumash*. Minneapolis: Lerner, 2007.

Sophocles. "Antigone." Trans. Dudley Fitts and Robert Fitzgerald. *Imaginative Literature: Fiction, Drama, Poetry*. 4th ed. Ed. Alton C. Morris, Biron Walker, and Philip Bradshaw. San Diego: HBJ, 1983. 213–59.

South, James. "On the Philosophical Consistency of Season Seven: or, 'It's Not about Right, Not about Wrong." *Slayage 13–14* 4.1–2 (October 2004). Collins College. 3 May 2006 <http://www.slayage.tv/>.

Splendid. "Charge." Unreleased CD.

Sprung Monkey. "Believe." *Swirl*. Surfdog, 1998.

_____. "Saturated." *Swirl*. Surfdog, 1998.

Star Trek the Original Series: The Complete Seasons 1–3. 1966. DVD. Paramount, 2004.

Star Wars, Episode One, The Phantom Menace. 1999. DVD. 20th Century–Fox, 2005.

Star Wars Trilogy. 1980. DVD. 20th Century–Fox, 2004.

Static X. "Permanence." *Machine*. Warner, 2001.

Steiner, Max. "Theme from 'A Summer Place.'" *Gone With the Wind: The Essential Max Steiner Film Music Collection*. Silva America, 2001.

Sterngold, James. "What Price Art? Ask Japanese Collectors." *The New York Times* 8 June 1990. 15 August 2007 <http://query.nytimes.com/gst/fullpage.html?res=9C0CEF D91230F93BA35752C0A966958260>.

Stevenson, Gregory. *Televised Morality: The Case of Buffy the Vampire Slayer*. Dallas: Hamilton, 2003.

Stokes, Mike. "Absolute Power." *Buffy the Vampire Slayer Magazine* 10 (July 2000): 18–19.

Stokstad, Marilyn. *Art History*. 3rd ed. Upper Saddle River, NJ: Pearson-Prentice Hall, 2008.

Stout, Jeffrey. *Democracy and Tradition*. Princeton, NJ: Princeton University Press, 2004.

Stroud, Scott R. "A Kantian Analysis of Moral Judgment in *Buffy the Vampire Slayer*." *Buffy the Vampire Slayer and Philosophy: Fear and Trembling in Sunnydale*. Ed. James B. South. Popular Culture and Philosophy. Series Editor William Irwin. Chicago: Open Court, 2003. 185–94.

A Summer Place. 1959. DVD. Warner, 2007.

Summercamp. "Thing of the Past." *Pure Juice*. Maverick Records, 1997.

Susman, Warren. *Culture as History*. Washington, DC: Smithsonian, 2003.

Sutherland, Kristen. "Featurette: Season Three Overview." *Buffy the Vampire Slayer*. Season Three DVD. 20th Century–Fox Home Entertainment, 2006.

Sutherland, Sharon, and Sarah Swan. "The Rule of Prophecy: Source of Law in the City of *Angel.*" *Reading* Angel: *The TV Spin-Off with a Soul.* Ed. Stacey Abbott. New York: Taurus, 2005. 133–45.

The Sword in the Stone. 1963. DVD. Disney, 2001.

Tabron, Judith. "Girl on Girl Politics: Willow/Tara and New Approaches to Media Fandom." *Slayage* 13–14 (October 2004). 9 September 2007 <http://slayageonline.com/essays/slayage13_14/Tabron.htm>.

Tancredi, Laurence. *Hardwired Behavior: What Neruoscience Reveals About Morality.* Cambridge, England: Cambridge University Press, 2005.

Tanner, Jennifer Lynn. "Recentering During Emerging Adulthood: A Critical Turning Point in Life Span Human Development." *Emerging Adults in America: Coming of Age in the 21st Century.* Ed. Jeffrey Jensen Arnett and Jennifer Lynn Tanner. Washington: American Psychological Association, 2006. 21–55.

The Terminator. 1984. DVD. MGM, 2001.

THC. "Dip." *Adagio.* Red Distribution, 1999.

THC. "Need to Destroy." *Adagio.* Red Distribution, 1999.

THC. "Overfire." *Adagio.* Red Distribution, 1999.

Third Eye Blind. "The Background." *Third Eye Blind.* Elektra/WEA, 1997.

Torrin, Emiliana. "Summerbreeze." *Love in the Time of Science.* Virgin, 2004.

Townsend, Pete. The Who. 2007. 5 November 2007 <http://www.thewho.com/index.php>.

Twain, Mark. *Mark Twain in Eruption: Hitherto Unpublished Pages about Men and Event.* New York: Harper, 1940.

Vedantam, Shankar. "If It Feels Good to Be Good, It Might Be Only Natural." *Washington Post* 28 May 2007: A01. 11 August 2007 <http://www.washingtonpost.com.>.

Vint, Sherryl. "'Killing Us Softly': A Feminist Search for the 'Real Buffy.'" *Slayage* 5 (9 December 2002). 8 August 2007 <http://slayageonline.com/essays/slayage5/vint.htm>.

Virgil. "Vermillion Borders." *Virgil.* unk.

Vlam, Grace A.H. "The Portrait of S. Francis Xavier in Kobe." *Zeitschrift für Kunstgeschichte* 42.1 (1979): 48–60. OK. 1 October 2007

Voltaire. *Candide.* 1758. Trans. John Butts. 1947. Baltimore: Penguin, 1968.

Walters, Anna. *Ghost Singer.* Albuquerque: University of New Mexico, 1994.

Wells, Stanley, ed. *King Lear.* By William Shakespeare. Folger Shakespeare Library. New York: Washington Square, 1993.

Wendy's International, Inc.: Company Profile, Information, Business Description, History, Background Information on Wendy's International, Inc. NetIndustries, LLC. 2007. 9 October 2007. <http://www.referenceforbusiness.com/history2/78/Wendy-S-International-Inc.html>.

Wertz, Dorothy. "Conflict Resolution in the Medieval Morality Plays." *The Journal of Conflict Resolution* 13.4 (Dec. 1969): 438–53.

West, Dave. "Concentrate on the Kicking Moxie: Buffy and East Asian Cinema." *Reading the Vampire Slayer: An Unofficial Critical Companion to Buffy and* Angel. Ed. Roz Kaveney. New York: Taurus Parke, 2002. 166–86.

"What Is Relativism?" *BBC News Magazine.* 20 April 2005. 25 August 2007 <http://news.bbc.co.uk/2/hi/uk_news/magazine/4460673.stm>.

Whedon, Joss. "Commentary: 'Chosen.'" *Buffy the Vampire Slayer.* Season Seven DVD. 20th Century–Fox Home Entertainment, 2006.

_____. "Commentary: 'Hush.'" *Buffy the Vampire Slayer.* Season Four DVD. 20th Century–Fox Home Entertainment, 2006.

_____. "Commentary: 'Once More with Feeling.'" *Buffy the Vampire Slayer.* Season Six DVD. 20th Century–Fox Home Entertainment, 2006.

_____. "Commentary: Welcome to the Hellmouth." *Buffy the Vampire Slayer*. Season One DVD. 20th Century–Fox Home Entertainment, 2006.

_____, Amber Bensen, Jane Espenson, et al. *Tales of the Slayers*. Milwaukie, OR: Dark Horse Comics, 2002.

Wheeler, Ella Wilcox. "Solitude." *Poems of Passion*. 1882. 1911. Kila, MT: Kessinger, 1998. 131–32.

White, Barry. "Can't Get Enough of Your Love, Babe." *Barry White: All-Time Greatest Hits*. Island/Mercury, 1985.

White, Nicholas. *A Brief History of Happiness*. Malden, MA: Blackwell, 2006.

The Who. "Behind Blue Eyes." *The Who: The Ultimate Collection*. MCA, 2002.

Widespread Panic. 2005. 17 February 2007. <http://www.widespreadpanic.com/>.

Wilcox, Rhonda. "There Will Never Be a Very Special *Buffy*: Buffy and the Monsters of Life." *Slayage: The Online International Journal of* Buffy *Studies* 5 (May 2002). 27 August 2007. <http://slayageonline.com/essays/slayage2/wilcox.htm>.

_____. *Why Buffy Matters: The Art of* Buffy the Vampire Slayer. New York: I.B. Taurus, 2005.

Wilson, R.M. "Mani and Manichaeanism." *The Encyclopedia of Philosophy*. Vol. 5. Ed. Paul Edwards. New York: Macmillan, 1967.

The Wizard of Oz. 1939. DVD. Warner, 1999.

Women's Belly Book: Finding Your Treasure Within. 1 November 2007 <http://www.honoringyourbelly.com/book/dialoguewithbelly.html>.

The X-Files: Seasons 1–9. 1993. DVD. 20th Century–Fox, 2006.

Yellow Submarine. 1968. DVD. MGM, 1999.

"Yes, Belief in Witchcraft Is Widespread in Africa." *The East African Standard* 25 September 2006. 16 November 2007.

"Youth Reportedly Burnt Eight Elderly People for Practicing Witchcraft." *Kenya Broadcasting Corporation* 13 January 1993. 16 November 2007

Zagzebski, Linda. "The Admirable Life and the Desirable Life." Unpublished lecture.

About the Contributors

Jacqueline Bach earned her Ph.D. in education at Oklahoma State University and is now an assistant professor in curriculum and instruction at Louisiana State University. Her scholarly work has appeared in *The Journal of Curriculum Theorizing* and *Talking Points*. Her areas of interest are popular culture and young adult literature. She lives with her family in Baton Rouge, Louisiana. Her current scholarship involves the *Thomas the Tank Engine* books for children and the television show *Project Runway*.

David Blakely is an assistant professor at Rogers State University, coordinator of the RSU theatre program and vice-chair of New Plays and Playwriting for Region VI of the American College Theatre Festival. He is a director, designer, actor, musician and playwright. He received his BFA from the University of Oklahoma and his MFA from the Iowa Playwrights Workshop. His directing credits include, among others, *Play It Again, Sam*; *The Rainmaker*; *Ghosts*; *The Meeting*; *Mere Mortals*; *The Taffetas*; *The Fantasticks*; *Oklahoma*; and about twenty new works. His own plays have been produced in Oklahoma, New Mexico, Iowa, North Carolina, Tennessee, Virginia, and Texas. Most notably, *Tales of Shoogilly* was the 2003 winner of the Charles M. Getchell Award; *Laying Felt* was voted "Best of the NeST" in Mockingbird Theatre's 2003 New Southern Theatre Festival; and *Frankenstein: A Modern Prometheus* was performed at the Temple Theatre in October 2004. He was a founding member of the Playwrights Lab at Burning Coal Theatre in Raleigh, North Carolina. He is a member of the Dramatists Guild of America, Inc. He celebrates life with his loving family Lesley, Jessi, Amy, Quinn, and Knox.

Lori M. Butler is an instructor at Rogers State University whose tendencies towards obsessive-compulsive disorder land her in many exciting projects ranging from starting an ambulance service with her husband to working on a *Buffy* book with her dear friends and colleagues. Before Rogers State, she worked for six years at Arkansas State University where she served as an assistant editor for the *Kansas Quarterly/Arkansas Review*. Also, during her time in Arkansas, she was the coordinator for the Safe Jonesboro Coalition — part of the National SAFE KIDS organization. As part of her duties, she wrote grants which funded projects for education and infrastructure improvements in Northeast Arkansas. She is a true Okie from Muskogee who loves spending time with her husband and two young children.

J. Renée Cox earned both her master of arts in English and her bachelor of science in secondary education, history and social studies from Northern Arizona

University. Prior to attending NAU, she completed her associate's degree in liberal arts at Mohave Community College in Kingman, Arizona. Her instructional experience in Arizona includes teaching U.S. history at Kingman Junior High School; teaching English composition, U.S. history and history of western theatre at Mohave Community College; and teaching English composition for the Maricopa Community College district in Phoenix, Arizona. Since moving to Oklahoma, she has become a full-time instructor of English and humanities at Rogers State University in Claremore, Oklahoma, where she lives with her cat, Professor Minerva McGonagall.

Emily Dial-Driver is a professor of English at Rogers State University. She has published textbooks, articles, and poetry; had plays and media produced; and has acted as editor for books, articles, and periodicals. She was reared a traveling Army brat and rancher's kid, served in the U.S. Army Ordnance Corps in Missile Maintenance for four years and as the assistant director of a Girl Scout Camp for one summer, and worked as a dietary interviewer on a national preschool nutrition survey. She serves as fiction editor of RSU's *Cooweescoowee: A Journal of Arts and Letters*. She is the editor (with Carolyn Anne Taylor, Carole Burrage, and Sally Emmons-Featherston) of *Voices from the Heartland* (University of Oklahoma Press, 2007), nominated for the Oklahoma Book Award.

Sally Emmons-Featherston is a self–described "adopted" Oklahoman who now proudly considers Oklahoma home. Of Choctaw and Cherokee descent, she is an associate professor at Rogers State University and teaches a variety of writing and literature courses. When she is not teaching, she serves as managing editor of RSU's literary and artistic journal, the *Cooweescoowee*. In her "free" time she teaches aerobics in spandex, wishes she could kick butt like Buffy, and chases her young son who one day wants to be an airplane pilot, race-car driver, artist, and cook. She is editor (with Emily Dial-Driver and Carole Burrage) of *Voices from the Heartland* (University of Oklahoma Press, 2007), nominated for the Oklahoma Book Award.

Juliet Evusa earned doctoral and master's degrees in telecommunication, a master's in international affairs, and a graduate certificate in women's studies, all from Ohio University. She also earned a bachelor's degree in sociology from the University of Baroda in India. Her area of academic focus is the evaluation, analysis, and diagnosis of modern information communication technologies as tools for socioeconomic development in low-income societies. She has presented extensively on issues related to Africa, including mass media, the Internet, cultural issues, and socioeconomic empowerment. One of her articles, "Women as Victims and Vessels of HIV/AIDS Prevention in East Africa," appeared on the *Communication Initiative* on-line publication. Her article "The Feminization of New Information Communication Technologies (NICTs) for Socioeconomic Development in Africa" appears in *Science and Technology in Africa*, edited by Paul T. Zeleze and Ibulaimu Kakoma. She previously served as adjunct faculty at Ohio University's School of Telecommunications. She is a native of Kenya.

Jim Ford is an associate professor of humanities and philosophy at RSU and director of the honors program at Rogers State University. He is the faculty advisor for the Oklahoma Iota chapter of the Alpha Chi academic honor society. He also serves as the faculty advisor for the university's annual Maurice Meyer Lecture. He received doctoral and master's degrees in religious studies from Princeton University, and a bachelor's degree in religion and philosophy from the University of Tulsa. He participated in an intensive German program at the Goethe Institut in Dresden, Germany, and studied at the London School of Economics. His academic specialties include ethics, philosophy, and religion. He is a member of Phi Beta Kappa. The title of his dissertation is "Nietzsche, Nihilism, and Christian Theodicy." In his spare time, he hosts *The Meaning of Life* on KRSC 91.3 FM.

Kenneth S. Hicks is an associate professor of political science at Rogers State University and heads the Department of History and Political Science. He earned a Ph.D. in political theory and a master's degree in international relations theory from the University of South Carolina and has been at RSU since 1999. He has taught many of the upper division political science courses at RSU and has research interests that transcend the narrow confines of conventional political science, as his two chapters attest. He lives near the RSU campus with his wife, Kelly, and a menagerie of dogs and cats.

J. Michael McKeon is an assistant professor at Rogers State University. He is a faculty member in the Department of Fine Arts where his teaching responsibilities and scholarly interests range from art theory to philosophy and cultural history. He holds a Ph.D. in fine arts from Ohio University where he spent much of his time researching and writing on 20th century German Expressionist art and the Nazi art movement. Since moving to Oklahoma in 2005, he has rediscovered his love for the American west. A lover of Steinbeck's novels and agrarian populist philosophy, Mike is convinced there is much in Oklahoma, in its culture and the values of its people, that redeems America and makes it a worthwhile country in which to live.

Gary Moeller is a professor of art and acting department head in the Department of Fine Arts at Rogers State University. He also served as head of the Department of Communications and Fine Arts (2000–2004) and was the North Central Self-Study Coordinator for RSU (2000–2004). He is teaching two-dimensional studio courses and art history courses, as well as other courses on demand. He has studied rock art extensively in Oklahoma and New Mexico and takes regular art trips to Italy. He exhibits his paintings regionally and internationally.

Frances E. Morris is an instructor at Rogers State University who still claims to be a Beatlemaniac and has recently developed *Buffy*mania. Her manias may be limited, but her occupations have not been. She has been a medical technologist, English bulldog breeder, and cattle rancher. A few years ago she found herself reciting poetry to a rather large, obnoxious bull, so she decided to return to school to study literature and that led her to a master's degree from Northeastern State University and subsequently to her profession of teaching composition at Rogers State University. She was born and reared in Joplin, Missouri, but has enjoyed the prairies of Oklahoma for almost three decades.

Jesse Stallings is a teacher of English at the Tulsa School of Arts and Sciences. He earned his bachelor's degree in liberal arts at Rogers State University.

Carolyn Anne Taylor received a doctoral degree in political science/higher education from Oklahoma State University and a master's degree in political science and a bachelor's degree in history from the University of Oklahoma. Her areas of academic specialty include American federal, state, and local government. She served in the Oklahoma House of Representatives from 1984 to 1992. She is an associate professor of political science at Rogers State University. She is the managing editor (with Emily

Dial-Driver, Carole Burrage, and Sally Emmons-Featherston) of *Voices from the Heartland* (University of Oklahoma Press, 2007), nominated for the Oklahoma Book Award.

Gregory J. Thompson is an assistant professor of interdisciplinary humanities and head of the Department of English and Humanities at Rogers State University. His interests include cultural studies, cinema, theatre, and Shakespeare. Thompson is area chair for Shakespeare and the Early Modern World with the Popular Culture Association and has presented at cultural studies conferences around the United States and internationally. He has published in the *Journal of Popular Culture* and has chapters in books on popular culture in the academy, religion and art, and the American dream. In addition to his teaching duties Thompson directs, acts, and writes for the stage. His productions include *Hamlet, King Lear, Much Ado about Nothing,* and *The Tempest.* Thompson's most recent production is *An Evangelist Drowns,* a one-woman play he wrote based on the life of Aimee McPherson. When not teaching or on stage, he enjoys time at home with his children and dogs.

Index

Aaron 167
Aberdeen 124, 213
Abrams 143, 213
Abu Ghraib 13
Acathla 146, 150
Achebe, Chinua 86, 213
action 10, 11, 12, 13, 14, 15, 16, 18, 19, 23, 30, 31, 34, 39, 42, 49, 59, 76, 77, 89, 92, 94, 97, 99, 101, 108, 110, 111, 112, 113, 114, 115, 118, 120, 122, 126, 129, 139, 150, 155, 161, 165, 171, 172, 174, 178, 183, 188, 196, 197, 198, 200, 218
action hero 198
Acton, Lord vii, 6, 67, 81, 82, 215
Adagio 223
Adam 69, 89, 147, 148, 172
Adams, Henry 167, 213
Adam's Rib 215
Adler, Alfred 10, 12, 19
adolescence 6, 38, 41, 42, 43, 44, 46, 47, 49, 51, 52, 53, 64, 131, 132, 134, 170, 198, 213, 220
"Adolescent Storm and Stress" 213
adult vii, 6, 25, 38, 40, 41, 42, 45, 47, 48, 49, 50, 51, 52, 53, 54, 135, 164, 165, 187, 225
adulthood 38
aesthetic/aesthetics 7, 110
"Afterlife" 17, 191, 208
Africa viii, 8, 34, 35, 43, 50, 173, 174, 175, 176, 177, 178, 179, 180, 181, 182, 183, 184, 213, 214, 216, 219, 220, 221, 224, 226
"After Life" 90, 211
Alessio, Dominic 56, 61, 213
Alexie, Sherman 63, 65, 198, 213, 216
Ali, Asim 21, 213
Alice in Wonderland 214
alienation 7, 90, 110, 111, 161, 169
"All the Small Things" 127, 214
"All the Way" 50, 90, 123, 155, 211
Allan (character) 78
allegory/allegorical 159, 160, 161, 162, 163, 164, 165, 167

allusions 7, 40, 57, 142, 143, 144, 146, 147, 149, 150, 151, 153, 154, 155, 156, 203
"Amends" 20, 151, 154, 203, 211
American dream 165, 228
American Indians 6, 56
American West myth 6
Amy 20, 74, 79, 93, 123, 128, 151, 175, 177, 182, 183, 225
Anderson, Wendy 62, 200, 213
Andrew 15, 16, 51, 52, 53, 95, 145, 151, 153, 154, 155, 157, 188
Angel (character) 14, 16, 17, 19, 20, 22, 23, 25, 28, 29, 30, 34, 43, 44, 45, 46, 47, 48, 52, 66, 71, 72, 73, 74, 75, 76, 77, 78, 79, 82, 115, 116, 122, 123, 126, 127, 128, 134, 135, 136, 146, 154, 162, 168, 170, 186, 187, 188, 189, 190, 192, 193, 194, 196, 198, 200, 201, 203, 204, 205, 206, 208, 209, 210, 211, 213, 214, 215, 217, 220, 221, 222, 223
"Angel" (episode) 29, 30, 154
Angel (series) 14, 16, 17, 20, 22, 23, 73, 74, 82, 126, 162, 170, 188, 192, 193, 196, 200, 210
Angel, "Damage" 16
Angel, "Darla" 73
Angel, "Fredless" 196
Angel, "The Girl in Question" 16
Angel, "Not Fade Away" 23
Angel, "Sanctuary" 17, 192
Angelus 16, 19, 25, 27, 28, 29, 34, 72, 74, 79, 128, 189, 194
"Anne" 45, 169, 200, 206, 211
Anointed One 154
antagonist 69, 82, 120, 188, 191
anthropologist/anthropology 173, 176, 180
anti–Enlightenment 82
Antigone 222
anti-positivists 82
Antonio 144
Anya 14, 15, 37, 39, 49, 50, 51, 60, 121, 124, 125, 147, 148, 151, 165, 169, 188, 192, 203, 206, 208

230   Index

Anyanka 15
"Anything" 126, 217
apocalypse 15, 23, 68, 89, 92, 93, 124, 201,
    203, 204
Appelo, Tim 199, 213
Aquinas, Thomas 159, 172
arc vii, 6, 25, 41, 42, 45, 49, 53, 74, 82, 83,
    150, 166, 196, 207
Arendt, Hannah 18, 23
Aristotle 84, 85, 95, 109, 119, 202, 203, 213, 218
Ark of the Covenant 98
Arnett, Jeffrey 38, 42, 46, 49, 50, 51, 52, 53,
    54, 213, 218, 223
Arrezzo 104, 106
art 5, 7, 56, 96, 98, 99, 102, 104, 105, 106, 107,
    108, 119, 132, 140, 141, 191
"As You Were" 168, 189, 211
Ashforth, Adam 174, 213
Ashley, Laura 154
"At the River" 147, 213
Athens 202
Aud 15
audience 7, 35, 39, 43, 47, 49, 50, 53, 107,
    108, 109, 110, 111, 112, 113, 114, 115, 116, 117,
    118, 119, 120, 126, 127, 128, 135, 140, 142,
    161, 164, 177, 182, 189, 198, 203
Augustine 159, 172
Auschwitz 10, 12, 13, 23
Austen, Jane 5
Austen, Ralph A. 174, 180, 213
"Awards" 106, 214
Azure Ray 124, 214
Azure Ray 214

Bach, Jacqueline 2, 6, 38, 129, 140, 225
Bach, J.S. 140
"Back to Freedom" 122, 214
"The Background" 122, 223
"Bad Eggs" 155, 211
"Bad Girls" 17, 78, 146, 211
Badaracco, Joseph L. 86, 95, 214
"badass" poet 64
Baker, Sheridan 216
Balthazar 78
Band Candy 45, 128, 150, 152, 211
"Bargaining" 10, 17, 20, 21, 80, 90, 125, 208,
    211
Barnstorff, Herman 95, 214
Barbie 155, 175
Baroque 104, 106
Baskin Robbins 155
Bastian, Misty L. 178, 180, 214
Batali, Dean 149, 156
Battis, Jes 15, 214
Bay City Rollers 218
Beatles 5, 38, 98, 207
Beauty and the Beast 132
"Beauty and the Beasts" 211
Beck, Christopher 42, 47
Beckett, Samuel 146, 214

"Becoming" 16, 20, 29, 44, 71, 72, 150, 152,
    168, 204, 206, 211
"Beer Bad" 46, 82, 127, 190, 211
"Behind Blue Eyes" 48, 224
"Believe" 46, 123, 147, 214, 222
Bellafonte, Ginia 193, 214
Bellini, Vincenzo 102, 103
Bellylove 122, 214
Bellylove 214
Ben 15, 18, 168
"Beneath You" 15, 33, 92, 93, 211
Bensen, Amber 194, 200, 224
Beowulf 187, 216
Berger, Peter L. 151, 214
Berkhofer, Robert F. 55, 56, 66, 214
bestiality 132, 141
Beth 195
"Bewitched, Bothered, and Bewildered" 2,
    16, 74, 118, 177, 178, 211
Bible 102, 139, 164, 172, 221
Bible Belt 102
Bif Naked 123, 214
Big Blue 150
Billson, Anne 14, 214
Black, Robert A. 49, 194, 214
"Black Cat Bone" 49, 124, 218
Blakely, David 2, 7, 107, 225
Blayne 134, 135, 136, 138, 151
Blink-182 127, 214
"Blood Ties" 48, 204, 211
Bloom, Harold 170, 171, 214
"Blue" 126, 217, 224
Blue Meanies 7, 96, 98, 99, 101, 102, 104
BMW 150
Bodger, Gwyneth 179, 182, 185, 187, 214
"The Body" 39, 48, 49, 207, 211
bond 93, 94, 124, 146, 161, 194
Bond, James 155
Bosch, Heironymous 140
Boyce, Charles 159, 161, 163, 214
"Brain Imaging" 214
Branch, Michelle 125, 214
Brecht, Bertold vii, 7, 107, 108, 109, 110, 111,
    115, 117, 118, 119, 214
"Bring on the Night" 151, 211
British Witchcraft Act 183
Bronsted-Debye-Huckel equation 155
The Bronze 21, 42, 43, 45, 47, 52, 79, 88, 115,
    121, 122, 123, 124, 125, 128, 133, 134, 187,
    213
Brooks, Mel 100, 214
Buffy the Vampire Slayer: Season One 7, 16,
    30, 42, 53, 68, 70, 74, 80, 108, 116, 117, 123,
    131, 144, 145, 147, 186, 187, 191, 197, 200;
    Season Two 16, 27, 40, 42, 44, 45, 48, 70,
    71, 72, 73, 74, 75, 77, 81, 126, 144, 150, 152,
    154, 158, 186, 187, 189, 199, 215; Season
    Three 44, 45, 53, 69, 71, 75, 79, 82, 122,
    154, 163, 189, 192, 196, 199, 200, 205;
    Season Four 6, 7, 16, 30, 33, 39, 42, 46, 47,

50, 56, 69, 77, 78, 82, 89, 148, 154, 163, 172, 186, 189, 190, 192, 194, 195, 198, 200, 207, 223; Season Five 10, 18, 30, 31, 39, 41, 48, 49, 69, 73, 125, 128, 179, 187, 188, 190, 191, 193, 194, 195, 200, 201, 206, 207, 209, 210, 215; Season Six 11, 15, 18, 20, 21, 30, 39, 47, 49, 50, 51, 53, 71, 79, 80, 90, 121, 124, 125, 128, 153, 155, 170, 179, 187, 188, 189, 191, 193, 194, 196, 199, 200, 203, 206, 209, 223; Season Seven 11, 12, 15, 16, 17, 21, 22, 27, 36, 41, 42, 51, 52, 70, 82, 92, 121, 124, 125, 144, 155, 193, 195, 196, 197, 198, 206, 216, 222, 223
"*Buffy the Vampire Slayer* Theme" 220
"Buffy vs. Dracula" 190, 211
*Buffy*verse 14, 27, 29, 32, 43, 60, 115, 121, 160, 163, 165, 166, 169, 170, 171, 172, 222
bureaucrats 68, 71
Burning Out the Inside 215
Burrage, Carole 2
Butler, Lori 2, 7, 120, 225
Buttsworth, Sara 197, 214

Calame, Claude 132, 214
Caleb 36
California 57, 58, 59, 62, 63, 64, 66, 151, 166, 186, 205, 217
California Mission Period 57, 62, 63
Campbell, Kent 216
Candide 22, 223
Canetti, Elias 31, 214, 216
capitalism 165
Caravaggio 106
Carlyle, Thomas 137
Carmel 64, 219
Carroll, Lewis 151, 214
"Cask of Amontillado" 145
Cassie 125
The Castle of Perseverance 163, 164, 172, 214, 219
The Cat in the Hat 148, 215
Catholic Church 105, 159
Cecily 32
"Celebrate" 122, 218
cello 46
change 10, 11, 14, 17, 18, 20, 32, 33, 38, 43, 49, 53, 61, 63, 77, 109, 111, 112, 126, 127, 159, 166, 167
character 6, 7, 8, 12, 13, 14, 15, 16, 18, 19, 20, 21, 23, 24, 25, 28, 29, 31, 34, 36, 38, 39, 40, 41, 42, 43, 44, 45, 46, 47, 48, 49, 50, 51, 52, 53, 56, 57, 59, 63, 75, 77, 81, 83, 86, 87, 94, 96, 98, 99, 100, 101, 102, 106, 108, 109, 110, 111, 112, 113, 114, 116, 117, 118, 120, 121, 122, 124, 125, 127, 128, 129, 131, 133, 135, 137, 139, 143, 144, 146, 147, 148, 149, 151, 152, 153, 154, 155, 156, 158, 159, 160, 161, 162, 163, 164, 165, 166, 167, 168, 169, 170, 171, 175, 185, 186, 194, 196, 197, 198, 199, 201, 202, 203, 206

"Charge" 126, 222
"Checkpoint" 69, 179, 211
Cheetos 145
Cher 46, 147, 214
Cherokee 56, 65, 66, 226
Chesterton, G.K. 104, 214
Chickasaw 66
Choctaw 65, 66, 226
choices vii, 6, 9, 10, 12, 13, 14, 16, 17, 18, 19, 20, 21, 22, 27, 28, 30, 31, 34, 40, 42, 45, 46, 47, 49, 57, 60, 66, 71, 75, 79, 82, 84, 85, 86, 87, 89, 90, 91, 92, 93, 94, 95, 116, 129, 139, 160, 162, 163, 165, 168, 171, 179, 181, 186, 188, 189, 205, 211, 219
"Choices" 71, 79, 162, 205, 211
Chopin, Kate 86
chorus 120, 122, 125, 129, 151, 167
"Chosen" 12, 16, 17, 19, 22, 52, 62, 87, 93, 168, 169, 181, 198, 199, 210, 211, 223
Chosen One 62, 87, 169, 187, 199, 207, 208
Christ 102, 103, 104, 151, 172, 200
Christianity 22, 29, 64, 66, 81, 85, 86, 103, 104, 140, 159, 164, 166, 168, 169, 171, 172, 180, 181, 182, 183, 213, 227
Chrystos 64, 65, 66, 215
Chumash 57, 58, 59, 61, 62, 63, 64, 66, 213, 221, 222
"Cities and Buses" 124, 130, 213
Civilization and Its Discontents 216
clairvoyance 72
Clarke, Jamie 49, 215
class, social 2, 74, 82, 97, 111, 117, 134, 142, 146, 162, 185, 188
Clem 19, 27, 28, 29
Clement, Shawn 127, 215, 217
Cline, Patsy 39, 125, 215
Coeur d'Alene 63, 65
Coleridge, Samuel 67
colonialism 220
Columbus, Christopher 55, 58
commodification 178, 180, 181
communication 21, 41, 50, 106, 191, 226
communitarianism 171
community 11, 19, 21, 27
Conan Doyle, Arthur 152, 215
concentration camp 10, 19, 22
connection vii, 6, 11, 21, 38, 83
Connery, Sean 155
conscience 6, 28, 30, 34, 35, 36, 37, 71, 72, 81, 152, 189, 192
consequences 13, 15, 75, 79, 90, 155, 188, 198, 199, 211, 217
"Consequences" 211
conservativism 68, 195
consumerism 162, 163, 166, 167, 169, 170, 176, 218
"Conversations with Dead People" 11, 16, 42, 125, 155, 170, 204, 206, 211
Cooper, Alice 124, 215, 220
Copleston, Frederick Charles 138, 215

Cordelia viii, 7, 20, 39, 40, 43, 45, 68, 74, 81,
      88, 112, 122, 151, 153, 154, 155, 157, 158, 159,
      160, 161, 162, 165, 169, 170, 177, 200, 206
Costa, Nikka 123, 215
Council, Watcher's 68, 69, 70, 179, 187, 193,
      200
coven/Coven 80, 92
Cox, Renée 2, 6, 23, 24, 225
Cream 45, 49, 128, 152, 215
creator 7, 14, 24, 25, 31, 36, 58, 67, 101, 112,
      140, 175, 198, 199, 218
Creek 66
Creighton, Bishop Mandell 67, 81
"The Crush" 18, 128, 208, 211
Crystals 151, 215
Culp, Christopher M. 185, 215
cultural pastiche 7
culture 6, 15, 25, 26, 29, 45, 55, 56, 60, 63,
      65, 66, 83, 87, 98, 103, 104, 105, 106, 134,
      140, 142, 146, 148, 152, 155, 158, 159, 160,
      161, 162, 166, 167, 168, 201, 221, 227
curses 15, 72, 73, 77, 78, 80, 82, 97, 168, 189,
      204, 208, 217
Custer, Gen. George Armstrong 61

Dachau 10, 13
DADA 105
Dahlberg-Acton, John 67, 82, 215
"Damage" 16
damnation 16, 25, 26
"Danse Macabre" 47, 221
"The Dark Age" 43, 45, 87, 211
dark side 15, 16, 17, 23, 77, 78, 90, 209
"Darla" 73
Darla 72, 73
Dartmouth 206
Dashboard Prophets 123, 215
Daughtey, Anne Millard 185, 215
Dawn 11, 12, 18, 20, 23, 28, 30, 31, 41, 42, 48,
      50, 51, 52, 82, 121, 123, 126, 145, 150, 153,
      165, 168, 187, 194, 196, 199, 200, 204, 206,
      207, 208, 209, 210
"Dead Man's Party" 155, 211
"Dead Things" 18, 32, 49, 148, 187, 211
death 10, 18, 20, 21, 26, 30, 49, 61, 64, 67, 73,
      75, 77, 79, 84, 87, 90, 97, 110, 128, 129, 134,
      137, 164, 170, 171, 172, 174, 183, 187, 188,
      191, 192, 194, 200, 203, 205, 206, 207, 208,
      209
Dechert, S. Renee 39, 44, 49, 120, 121, 215
DeKelf-Rittenhouse, Diane 16, 215
DeKnight, Steven S. 149, 156
della Francesa, Piero 103
demons 11, 15, 16, 19, 23, 26, 27, 28, 29, 30,
      33, 35, 36, 44, 46, 47, 50, 52, 53, 56, 60, 61,
      62, 63, 69, 71, 72, 73, 74, 76, 78, 79, 82, 89,
      90, 91, 104, 108, 111, 121, 126, 127, 129, 146,
      147, 148, 152, 164, 165, 168, 174, 186, 187,
      188, 189, 191, 194, 195, 196, 200, 205, 209
Des Hotel, Rob 149, 156

Devics 128, 215
Dial-Driver, Emily 1, 6, 7, 9, 142, 156, 210,
      226, 228
Dickens, Charles 86, 88, 198
diegetic 39, 40, 42, 48
Dingoes Ate My Baby 46, 122
"Dip" 127, 223
"Dirty Girls" 14, 21, 36, 211
Disney 150, 218, 223
"Displaced" 124, 214
divine 26, 134, 139
Doane, Melanie 128, 215
Dr. Seuss 142, 148, 215
"Doomed" 127, 211
"Doppelgangland" 15, 83, 85, 166, 179, 211
Dorothy 154
Dostoevski, Fyodor 23
"Doublemeat Palace" 20, 148, 189, 205, 211
Dowsey, Simon 103
Dracula 132, 190
dream 45, 46, 47, 52, 68, 97, 117, 122, 126,
      133, 135, 136, 137, 138, 139, 155, 165, 228
Dream On 64, 215
Drusilla 16, 43, 45, 72, 73, 74, 75, 126, 128,
      146, 151, 208
dual nature/duality 10, 14, 15, 16, 18, 64, 171
Duchamp, Marcel 105
Duffy, Michael 146, 215, 218
Duncan, Robert 52
Durkheim, Emile 94
Dworkin, Andrea 171, 215
Dylan, Bob 5, 215

"Early One Morning" 126, 215
"Earshot" 200, 211
Eco, Umberto 140, 215
Edelmann, Heinz 98
Edmund 167
The Education of Henry Adams 213
ego 29, 37, 133, 141, 216
Ehrenberg, Margaret R. 134, 215
Elizabethan 159, 167
Ellsworth, Carl 149, 156
Elwell, Frank 94, 215
Emerging Adulthood 49, 52, 53, 54, 213, 218,
      223
Emmons-Featherston, Sally 2, 6, 7, 8, 55,
      158, 226, 228
empowerment 177, 178, 179, 183, 226
"Empty Places" 12, 16, 27, 153, 197, 211
"End of Days" 12, 150, 211
Enema of the State 214
"Enemies" 146, 192, 211
Enlightenment 67, 68, 82
"Entropy" 15, 91, 211
Enyos 204
epic 52, 52, 107, 110
epic theatre 109, 110
epistomology 169, 213
Erikson, Erik 41, 51, 215

Ernst, Max 105
Eros 132, 135, 136, 140, 141, 214
Espenson, Jane 24, 30, 36, 56, 149, 156, 224
Esselen 64
ethics 18, 21, 57, 58, 59, 62, 63, 66, 86, 87, 88, 93, 131, 138, 139, 168, 201, 210, 227
Evans, Walter 131, 134, 137, 216
"Everybody Got Their Something" 123, 215
Everyman 163, 165, 216
Everywoman 165
evil 13, 14, 16, 18, 19, 20, 22, 23, 24, 25, 26, 29, 31, 32, 33, 34, 36, 44, 51, 57, 60, 66, 67, 68, 70, 72, 73, 74, 75, 78, 79, 80, 81, 82, 86, 88, 89, 90, 93, 94, 101, 106, 114, 123, 124, 126, 128, 137, 138, 140, 144, 145, 146, 153, 154, 159, 163, 165, 166, 167, 168, 169, 172, 173, 175, 176, 178, 179, 180, 181, 182, 183, 184, 187, 191, 194, 197, 199, 201, 202, 203, 204, 205, 207
Evusa, Juliet 2, 8, 173, 226
existentialism 12, 57, 86, 95, 151, 164, 165, 169, 220
extra-diegetic 39

fairy tale 47, 106
Faith 13, 14, 15, 17, 43, 46, 52, 75, 76, 78, 79, 80, 81, 122, 124, 146, 190, 192, 193, 197, 211, 220, 221
"Faith, Hope, and Trick" 17, 78, 122, 211
"Fall to Pieces" 125, 215
"Family" 46, 128, 195, 211
fan 2, 7, 21, 24, 38, 39, 40, 86, 108, 117, 118, 164
Fat Boy Slim 122, 129, 216
fate/Fates 14, 20, 72, 74, 78, 134, 151, 163, 189, 198, 219
Faustus 167, 219
"Fear, Itself" 211
female empowerment 173, 177
feminism 8, 162, 175, 182, 185, 186, 193, 198, 199, 200, 214, 215, 217
Fenn, Elizabeth A. 66, 216
fiction 5, 7, 8, 95, 102, 111, 131
film 5, 7, 40, 42, 43, 56, 62, 98, 100, 102, 108, 129, 131, 134, 140, 148, 150, 153, 155, 210, 228
Firecracker 218
First Contact 55, 56
"First Date" 93, 211, 212
First Evil 11, 12, 27, 45, 51, 52, 70, 76, 111, 114, 125, 126, 148, 181, 193, 196, 197, 211, 212, 215
First Slayer 207
"Five by Five" 14
Flamingoes 121, 126, 216
Fleming, Ian 150, 216
"Flooded" 17, 71, 90, 179, 188, 211
Florence 103
flute 43, 57
flying monkeys 100, 153

fMRI 84, 85
foil 75, 162
folk tune 107, 119, 126
Folks, Jeffrey 31, 216
"Fool for Love" 16, 30, 32, 73, 74, 144, 153, 191, 192, 203, 206, 211
Forbes, Tracy 149, 156
Ford (character) 18, 75
Ford, Jim 2, 5, 8, 18, 75, 156, 201, 226
foreshadowing 43, 44, 50, 52, 82, 119, 120, 123, 124, 127, 129, 134
"Forever" 30, 128, 211
forgiveness 20, 51, 79, 81, 129, 144
Forrest Gump 28, 216
Fortinbras 161
Fortunato 145
Four Star Mary 122, 216
Fowler, Heather 24, 36, 216
France 176
Franciscan 103, 217
Francophone Africa 180
Frankenstein 6, 67, 69, 100, 132, 134, 140, 214, 216, 221, 225
Frankenstein 67, 100, 140, 214
Frankl, Victor vii, 5, 6, 9, 10, 11, 12, 13, 14, 16, 18, 19, 20, 21, 22, 23, 216
fraternity 15, 74, 123, 127
Fred 196, 200
"Fredless" 196
"Free Bird" 48, 128, 218
free will 27, 171
"The Freshman" 211
French, Ms. 132, 133, 134, 135, 136, 137, 138, 139, 140
Freud, Sigmund 10, 12, 19, 28, 29, 37, 53, 131, 133, 135, 136, 140, 141, 170, 202, 216, 218, 220
Freund, Kurt 191, 216
Fritts, David 14, 216
Frye, Northrup 120, 143, 216
"Full of Grace" 44, 127, 219
Fury, David 24, 149, 156
Future Is Not Now 129, 219

Gable, Ashley 149, 156
gay 194
geeks 51, 53, 59, 87, 127, 145, 147, 155, 170, 177
gender 40, 180, 186, 191, 193, 199, 214, 217
Genesis 139, 140
The Gentlemen vii, 7, 96, 99, 100, 101, 103, 106
Gerhardt, Dr. 57
Gershman, Michael 106
Geschiere, Peter 176, 216
"Get It Done" 11, 34, 155, 200, 205, 211
ghost 81, 90
Ghost Singer 66, 223
"The Gift" 12, 15, 20, 31, 82, 168, 177, 200, 201, 202, 208, 209, 211, 219

Giles 10, 11, 15, 20, 29, 30, 32, 40, 41, 43, 44,
    45, 47, 48, 49, 50, 59, 60, 61, 68, 69, 75, 76,
    80, 81, 82, 89, 90, 91, 92, 93, 117, 125, 127,
    128, 134, 136, 137, 144, 148, 150, 151, 152,
    153, 154, 157, 165, 168, 170, 172, 175, 178,
    179, 180, 194, 196, 197, 198, 200, 204, 206,
    207
Gillen, M.M. 47, 218
"Gingerbread" 20, 82, 153, 182, 211
Giotto di Bondone 104
"The Girl in Question" 16
Gischler, Victor 2, 9, 67
Glarghk Guhl Kushmans'nik 91
Glaser, Milton 98
Glory 15, 16, 18, 31, 94, 168, 187, 194, 200,
    207, 208
"The Glove" 99
"Go Fish" 211
God 25, 26, 77, 125, 139, 140, 145, 147, 163, 169
god 15, 18, 48, 52 , 78, 102, 132, 133, 147, 168,
    181, 187, 194, 196, 200
Goddard, Drew 53, 149, 156, 216
goddesses 87, 88. 99, 219
Godot 146
"Gone" 199, 211
Goneril 161
"Good Looking Blues" 218
"Goodbye Iowa" 211
"Goodbye to You" 125, 214
goodness 6, 13, 14, 15, 16, 17, 18, 19, 21, 22,
    23, 25, 27, 28, 29, 30, 31, 32, 33, 36, 50, 51,
    52, 57, 58, 60, 64, 74, 75, 77, 79, 80, 81, 82,
    83, 87, 86, 87, 89, 90, 91, 92, 93, 96, 97, 99,
    100, 101, 106, 107, 108, 114, 122, 144, 151,
    159, 163, 165, 166, 168, 169, 171, 172, 173,
    176, 180, 184, 187, 189, 190, 194, 196, 201,
    203, 205
Gorbman, Claudia 39, 48, 216
Gorch, Lyle 154, 162
Gordon, Howard 149, 156, 219
Gospel According to John 22, 221
government 55, 58, 62, 68, 69, 70, 167, 191,
    195, 207, 227
Grace 144, 218
"Graduation Day" 17, 46, 71, 76, 211
Grassian, Daniel 56, 63, 216
"Grave" 11, 16, 21, 22, 35, 51, 87, 91, 92, 128,
    152, 153, 181, 210, 211
Gravity, Suffering, Love and Fate 219
Great Chain of Being 139, 140, 219
Greek chorus 120, 122, 129
Greene, Joshua 18, 84, 85, 216
Greenman, Jennifer 185, 216
Greenwalt, David 149, 156
Gregory, Dr. 134
grief 10, 11, 20, 49
Groener, Harry 76
Gross, Terri, 199, 217
grunge 51
Gubbio 104, 106

guitar 45, 47, 135, 138
Gutierrez, Diego 149, 156
gypsy 72, 204

Haiti 176
Hale-Bopp comet 19
Halfrek 39
Halfyard, Janet K. 40, 45, 217
Hall, G.S. 42, 217, 222
Halloween/"Halloween" 123, 154, 155, 178,
    211
Hamilton, Richard 105
Hamilton, Sharon 160, 217, 222
Hamlet 137, 150, 161, 171, 228
Hamlet 137, 150, 161, 171, 228
Hampton, Elin 149, 156
Hanks, Tom 148
happiness viii, 8, 201
Happy Meals 29, 146, 152
Hargreaves, David J. 46, 220
Harmon, William 143, 217
Harmony 94, 123, 170
"Harsh Light of Day" 123, 189, 211
Hart, Angie 126, 217
"The Harvest" 21, 68, 89, 115, 116, 123, 126,
    145, 153, 169, 206, 211
Haydn, Franz Joseph 39
Head, John O. 44, 217
healer 180
Heasman, Gerald 216
heaven 11, 12, 17, 21, 26, 50, 87, 90, 91, 103,
    125, 144, 199, 208, 209
Heaven's Gate 19
hegemony 159, 166, 167, 168
Heizer, Robert F. 66, 217
hell 11, 18, 26, 73, 87, 127, 140, 168, 172, 181,
    195, 205, 208, 209, 211
Hellacopters 127, 217
Hellmouth 2, 21, 52, 71, 74, 87, 88, 92, 115,
    119, 123, 153, 154, 163, 167, 169, 177, 181,
    199, 200
Hellraiser 155
"Hells Bells" 15, 211
"Help" 211
"Helpless" 41, 69, 154, 200, 211
Henry V 167, 221
Henry V 167, 221
heroism 12, 13, 14, 15, 18, 21, 58, 94, 108, 109,
    119, 120, 133, 134, 148, 151, 168, 185, 186,
    188, 200, 201, 202, 214, 216, 219
"He's a Rebel" 215
"Hey" 127, 217
Hicks, Kenneth 2, 6, 8, 67, 185, 227
Hierarchy of Needs 22
high school 44, 45, 46, 59, 65, 68, 70, 71, 74,
    75, 76, 91, 108, 111, 112, 113, 114, 115, 119,
    127, 146, 152, 160, 165, 169, 170, 174, 175,
    187, 203, 205, 206, 221, 226
Hill, Kathryn 39, 40, 217
"Him" 119, 121, 211

Hiroshima 23
history 38, 58, 61, 63, 66, 72, 102, 103, 143, 151, 159, 164, 165, 166, 167, 174, 175, 185, 213, 215, 216, 217, 219, 220, 222, 223, 224, 225, 227
Hitchcock, Alfred 5
Hitler, Adolf 26, 64
Hobbes, Thomas 217
Hoch, Hannah 105
Hofstede, Geert H. 32, 217
Holden 206
Hollows, Joanne 185, 217
Holman, C. Hugh 143, 217
Holmes, Sherlock 152
Holocaust 13, 94
Holt, Mrs. 151
"Homecoming" 43, 75, 122, 151, 154, 162, 211
Homer 86, 88
Homesick and Happy to Be Here 130, 213
homosexuality 59
Hornick, Alysa 106, 217
horror 29, 40, 42, 43, 67, 68, 69, 121, 131, 132, 134, 135, 137, 138, 140, 187, 194, 204, 207
"How" 122, 219
"How to Write the Great American Indian Novel" 65, 213
Howe, Cari 126, 217
Hughes, Robert 105, 217
humanism 199
humanity 10, 11, 14, 16, 24, 67, 68, 80, 81, 82, 84, 92, 102, 159, 165, 188, 191, 194, 207
humility 11
Hus 57, 58, 59, 60, 61, 62, 63, 64, 65, 66
"Hush" vii, 7, 39, 41, 47, 48, 50, 52, 96, 99, 100, 104, 106, 150, 175, 211, 223

I Bificus 214
"I Can't Take My Eyes Off You" 128, 215
"I in Team" 207, 211
"I Only Have Eyes for You" 70, 71, 81, 121, 126, 144, 171, 211, 216
"I Robot, You Jane" 143, 174, 175, 211
"I Wanna Be Sedated" 48, 220
"I Was Made to Love You" 18, 41, 211
Iago 167
IBM 150
Ibo 86, 95
iconography viii, 8, 168, 185, 215
icons 8, 103, 185, 198, 199
id 28, 37, 133, 141, 213, 216
identity 6, 7, 8, 10, 13, 15, 21, 31, 40, 41, 42, 50, 53, 63, 135, 137, 138, 140, 162, 163, 178, 185, 198
"If You Forget Me" 215
Igor 100
In Therapy We Trust 169, 220
"Inca Mummy Girl" 74, 154, 211
India 184, 226
Indian 55, 56, 57, 58, 59, 61, 62, 63, 64, 65, 66, 213, 214, 217, 221

Indian Territory 66
Indigenous 57, 66
Industrial Revolution 82
Initiative 33, 69, 94, 152, 153, 190, 207, 211, 226
"The Initiative" 153
"Innocence" 88, 150, 155, 204, 211
integrity 161
Internet 62, 105, 156, 175, 214, 215
Internet Movie DataBase (IMDb) 156, 214, 215
"Intervention" 16, 31, 205, 207, 209, 211
"Into the Woods" 190, 204, 209, 211
Iron Chef 145
irony 45, 93, 115, 119, 121, 122, 129, 135, 140, 146, 153
Islamic terrorist 19
It 102, 218
Italian Rennaissance 103
Italy 103, 106, 176
"It's a Long Way to Tipperary" 146, 215
"It's Only Love" 124, 220

Jabba the Hut 78
Jagodzinski, Jan 41, 217
James 144
Janus 76
Jaws 153, 217
Jeeves 153
Jenny 44, 128, 174, 175, 204
Jesse viii, 2, 7, 21, 142, 227
Jesus 86, 88, 95, 102, 103, 217
Jezebel 152
Joel, Billy 45
John Paul II, Pope 151, 217
Johnny Rotten 43
Jonathan 16, 47, 51, 52, 153, 155, 199, 200
Jordy 77
Jowett, Lorna 15, 23, 88, 162, 179, 185, 217
Joyce 16, 17, 20, 23, 30, 45, 48, 49, 53, 71, 79, 81, 120, 126, 127, 128, 145, 146, 188, 193, 200, 204, 205, 206, 207
Joyce, James 5
Judeo-Christian 159
juju 180
Juliet 167
"Just as Nice" 123, 129, 219

Kafka, Franz 95, 138, 214, 217
Kant, Immanuel 14, 222
Kathy 46, 147
Katrina 148
Kaveney, Roz 221, 222, 223
Kawal, Jason 210, 217
Kemerling, Garth 84, 218
Kendra 205
Kennedy 93, 124, 155, 195
Kent 161
Kenya 8, 180, 182, 183, 184, 224, 226
Key 128, 165, 168, 215

Kiene, Matt 149, 156
"Killed by Death" 158, 212
"Killer in Me" 124, 195, 212
killing 11, 14, 15, 16, 17, 18, 21, 26, 28, 29, 43,
     46, 57, 58, 59, 60, 61, 62, 69, 70, 72, 73, 74,
     75, 76, 77, 78, 79, 80, 81, 82, 84, 85, 88, 89,
     91, 92, 94, 102, 104, 108, 116, 122, 124, 126,
     127, 144, 146, 147, 148, 150, 152, 153, 154,
     158, 168, 171, 183, 186, 189, 191, 194, 195,
     196, 200, 205, 212, 216, 223
King, David Tyrone 149, 156
King, Jonathan 40
King, Stephen 102, 218
King, Thomas 55, 56, 65, 66, 218
King Arthur 150
King Kong 132
King Lear 8, 158, 160, 167, 221, 223, 228
King Lear 8, 158, 160, 167, 221, 223, 228
Kingsmen 45, 219
Kingsolver, Barbara 86, 88
Kinkade, Thomas 105
Kirkland, Bruce 14, 21, 218
Kirschner, Rebecca Rand 149, 156
Klaits, Joseph 174, 218
kleptis-virges 137
Klingon 147
Knights, Vanessa 39, 40, 44, 218
Kool & the Gang 122, 218
Korsmeyer, Carolyn 91, 218
Krzywinska, Tanya 15, 174, 176, 182, 218
K's Choice 217
Kubrick, Stanley 102, 221

Lacan, Jacques 53, 218
Laika 49, 124, 218
Lange, Michael 56
Lasch, Christopher 168, 172, 218
Laurent, Henry 170, 218
Lavery, David 215, 218, 219, 220
Lears, T.J. Jackson 159, 161, 168, 218
Lee, Spike 5
Lefkowitz, Eva S. 47, 218
lesbianism 178, 179, 194, 195, 216
"Lessons" 92, 150, 152, 205, 212
Leviathan 217
"Lie to Me" 18, 75, 127, 152, 154, 212, 215
Lied and Art Song Texts Page 213, 218
"Lies My Parents Told Me" 16, 34, 150, 179,
     196, 212
"Life Serial" 155, 205, 212
Lion King 153, 218
"Listening to Fear" 42, 212
literature 5, 7, 62, 64, 86, 142, 143, 169, 185,
     186
Little, Allan 176, 218
Little Mermaid 51
"Living Conditions" 147, 212
Loeb, Lisa 122, 218
logotheraphy 10
Long, Carolyn Morrow 175, 218

Los Cubazteca 41, 219
Loss, Christopher P. 169, 219
Lost in Space 130, 219
"Louie Louie" 45, 219
Louie Says 219
love vii, viii, 3, 6, 7, 16, 17, 18, 20, 22, 32, 35,
     36, 38, 39, 40, 41, 46, 47, 48, 51, 54, 69, 72,
     74, 80, 92, 93, 98, 108, 122, 123, 124, 126,
     127, 128, 129, 131, 133, 134, 136, 137, 138,
     139, 144, 160, 161, 165, 168, 177, 189, 190,
     192, 194, 204, 207, 208, 209, 210, 211, 216,
     217, 219, 223, 224, 227
Love in the Time of Science 223
Lovejoy, Arthur O. 139, 219
"Lover's Walk" 45, 122, 212
Lowry, Robert 147
Luckmann, Thomas 151, 214
Luddites 82
Lynch, David 148, 215, 219
Lynyrd Skynyrd 48, 128, 218
lyrics viii, 7, 38, 40, 42, 44, 45, 46, 52, 53,
     120, 121, 122, 123, 124, 125, 126, 127, 128,
     129, 143

Macbeth 168
Macdonald, Andrew 56
Machine 222
magic 10, 11, 17, 21, 41, 47, 49, 56, 59, 74, 79,
     80, 82, 83, 89, 90, 91, 92, 93, 94, 97, 99,
     118, 121, 123, 125, 128, 155, 156, 166, 168,
     172, 173, 174, 175, 177, 178, 179, 180, 181,
     182, 187, 192, 193, 194, 195, 200, 205, 207
Magic Box 80, 148, 192, 195
Magicians 80, 175, 180; *see also* sorcery; war-
     locks; witches
Mallory, Thomas 150, 219
Man of the Year 123, 129, 219
Mandell Creighton, Bishop 67, 81
Manichean 171
"Mankind" 163, 214, 219
Mann, Aimee 126, 130, 219
Man's Search for Meaning 10, 216
Marlowe, Christopher 167, 219
Mary 41, 67, 72, 102, 220
Masaccio 102
Maslow, Abraham 22, 219
Master 94, 104, 116, 145, 147, 154, 155, 157,
     225
materialism 165
maturation 6
Max, Peter 98, 222
McDonald, Paul 169, 219
McGinn, Colin 160, 161, 219
mchawi 180
McKeon, Michael 2, 7, 131, 227
McLachlan, Sarah 44, 47, 51, 127, 128, 219
McLaren, Scott 36, 37, 219
meaning 6, 7, 8, 9, 10, 11, 12, 19, 20, 21, 22,
     23, 70, 107, 108, 112, 125, 127, 129, 158, 160,
     169, 174, 207

medieval drama 159
Mendelssohn, Felix 93, 219
Merchant of Venice 144, 221
messages 9, 14, 47, 50, 51, 64, 114, 129, 164,
  168, 179, 216, 218
metadiegetic 39, 40
"Metamorphosis" 138, 217
metaphor 15, 60, 61, 70, 71, 75, 76, 77, 87, 88,
  135, 139, 173, 176, 177, 179, 183, 198
mganga 180
Michael 183
Middle Ages 163
Middleton, John 177, 219
migration 175, 182
Mike 151
military 61, 66, 69, 188, 191
militia man 147
Miller, Patricia 41, 219
Milton, John 142, 145, 219
minions 97, 100, 101, 106, 147
minority 56, 194
miracle play 172
Miranda, Deborah A. 64, 219
mise en scène 100, 113
Mr. Rogers' Neighborhood 153, 220
Moeller, Gary 2, 7, 96, 227
Moloch the Corrupter 174
"Moment of Weakness" 123, 214
"The Monkey" 102, 218
monkeys 100, 101, 102, 104, 153
Monroe, Kristen 94, 219
Montressor 145
Moonies 19
Moore, Henrietta 174, 180, 182, 183, 184, 213,
  214, 219, 220, 221
moral compass 26, 27, 28, 30, 148
moral relativism 87
morality/moral choice vii, 6, 8, 10, 14, 15, 16,
  17, 18, 21, 22, 25, 26, 27, 28, 29, 30, 31, 32,
  33, 34, 36, 59, 60, 61, 62, 66, 67, 73, 77, 83,
  84, 85, 86, 87, 88, 89, 90, 91, 92, 93, 94, 95,
  106, 120, 132, 136, 138, 139, 148, 158, 159,
  163, 164, 165, 166, 167, 168, 169, 171, 173,
  180, 182, 183, 187, 192, 195, 197, 202, 203,
  205, 207, 210, 213, 214, 216, 219, 221, 222,
  223
morality play viii, 8, 158, 159, 163, 165, 166,
  167, 172
mores 72, 194
Morris, Frances 2, 6, 23, 66, 83, 156, 172,
  227
Morrison, Toni 5
Le Morte d'Arthur 219
Moskowitz, Eva S. 169, 220
MRI 84
Mulholland Drive 148, 220
mummy 74, 154, 211
Murder (character) 167
Murfin, Ross 143, 220
Murray, Sean 127, 215, 217

music vii, 5, 6, 38, 39, 40, 41, 42, 43, 44, 45,
  46, 47, 48, 49, 50, 51, 52, 53, 56, 57, 62, 97,
  98, 99, 100, 102, 104, 106, 120, 121, 122, 123,
  124, 125, 129, 133, 136, 140, 143, 151, 152,
  215, 216, 217, 218, 220, 222
"My Way" 45, 122, 222
mystery play 172
mythology 6, 36, 77, 97, 140, 141, 151, 195,
  219; Western 58, 60, 65, 151

Napoleon 71
narcissism 218
narrative 38, 39, 40, 41, 42, 43, 45, 47, 49,
  50, 53, 67, 68, 71, 77, 80, 87, 110, 114, 120,
  150, 158, 164, 165, 166, 185, 186, 187, 197,
  198, 201, 210
Native Americans 6, 55, 56, 60, 62, 63, 65, 66
Nazism 151, 228
"Need to Destroy" 127, 223
Neiman Marcus 169
Nerf Herder 40, 53, 220
Netherlands 176
"Never Kill a Boy on the First Date" 21, 147,
  154, 212
"Never Leave Me" 36, 70, 212
Nevermind 220
New Age music 48, 53
New Kids on the Block 49
"New Man" 30, 212
"New Moon Rising" 33, 212
"Nicolito" 42, 219
Nicomachean Ethics 213
Niehaus, Isak 183, 220
Nietzsche, Frederick 17, 23, 227
Nigeria 86, 95, 176, 178, 180, 214
"Nightmares" 53, 212
nihilism 14, 208, 209, 210
Nikka Costa 123, 215
Nirvana 51, 220
"No Heroes" 120
"No Place Like Home" 48, 145, 212
noble savage 55
non-diegetic 39
norm 162, 170, 182
"Normal Again" 33, 91, 212
North, Adrian C. 46, 216, 220, 225
"Not Fade Away" 23
Not Vanishing 65, 215
Nothing but Widespread Panic 213, 220
Nova, Heather 124, 220
novels 2, 56, 65, 210, 227
Noxon, Marti 149, 156

occult 165, 174, 176, 178, 181, 183, 213, 214,
  216, 219, 220, 221
Oklahoma 2, 65, 66, 215, 221, 225, 226, 227,
  228
Okonkwo 86, 95
Old Testament 141
"Older and Far Away" 12, 168, 212

Oldham, Todd 154
Olvikon 76
"Once More with Feeling" 39, 47, 49, 50, 53,
    125, 196, 209, 212
One Flew Over the Cuckoo's Nest 101, 220
on-line 24, 36, 39, 156, 226
Onyinah, Opuku 182, 220
orchestral music 50
Orsanmichele 103
Othello 167, 221
Othello 167, 221
"the other" 8, 13, 15, 29, 31, 182
"Out of Mind, Out of Sight" 43, 68, 151, 154,
    172, 212
"Out of My Mind" 150, 212
outsider 8, 59, 173, 184
"Overfire" 127, 223
Oz 10, 14, 15, 40, 46, 77, 79, 80, 82, 122, 127,
    151, 154, 155, 157, 177, 178, 181, 190, 194

"The Pack" 43, 70, 191, 212
Packer, George 19, 220
pan flute 52
Pandora 97
"Pangs" 6, 56, 57, 58, 60, 62, 63, 64, 65, 66,
    155, 212
papal infallibility 81
Parker 47, 123, 189, 190
"Passion" 204, 212, 218, 224
pastiche 7, 8, 158, 163
Pateman, Matthew 14, 17, 18, 40, 59, 166, 220
patriarchy 153, 162, 178, 179, 182, 185, 187,
    196, 197
"Pavlov's Bell" 126, 130, 219
peers/peer pressure 74, 154
Pender, Patricia 40, 220
Pepperland 98, 99, 104
Percy 127
performance 47, 48, 50, 108, 109, 110, 111, 115,
    118, 119, 120
Perkins, George 216
"Permanence" 125, 222
Perugia 103, 104
Petrie, Douglas 149, 156
phallic 138
The Phantom Menace 222
"Phases" 15, 77, 212
philosophy 5, 6, 9, 10, 12, 23, 25, 26, 27, 29,
    30, 31, 32, 33, 34, 36, 53, 78, 84, 86, 87, 95,
    107, 109, 139, 142, 151, 164, 167, 172, 201,
    202, 203, 210, 226, 227
Pinhead 155
Pipher, Mary 41, 48, 220
Plato 84, 220
pleasure principle 19, 135, 140
plot 6, 7, 39, 47, 50, 60, 75, 76, 97, 98, 99,
    109, 111, 112, 114, 115, 121, 132, 135, 136, 164
Poe, Edgar Allan 145, 220
politicians/politics vii, 6, 67, 68, 76, 81, 176,
    181, 197, 216, 220, 223

Politico de Saint' Antonio 103
pop music 7, 46, 78, 83, 96, 98, 104, 105, 106,
    122, 150, 203
Pope John Paul II 151, 217
Pope Pius IX 81
popular culture 7, 55, 56, 96, 105, 142, 143,
    150, 152, 201, 203, 225, 228
Portia 144
postcolonial 61, 213, 214, 216, 219, 220, 221
post-feminism 185, 186, 199
postmodern 39, 40, 119, 220, 175, 176
"Potential" 212
Potential Slayers 11, 12, 21, 51, 52, 82, 93, 124,
    155, 168, 195, 212
poverty 56, 189
power vii, 5, 6, 7, 8, 11, 12, 19, 21, 25, 31, 35,
    59, 67, 68, 70, 71, 73, 74, 76, 77, 78, 79, 80,
    81, 82, 87, 88, 89, 90, 91, 92, 93, 95, 106,
    109, 132, 134, 135, 138, 139, 145, 162, 163,
    167, 168, 171, 173, 174, 175, 176, 177, 178,
    179, 180, 181, 182, 183, 186, 187, 189, 190,
    191, 197, 198, 200, 203, 207
"Praise You" 122, 129, 216
"Prayer of St. Francis" 51, 219
"Primeval" 89, 150, 172, 181, 207, 212
principal 70, 124, 189
prisoners 13
Project 314 69
"The Prom" 122, 162, 169, 212
Prometheus 6, 67, 68
"Prophecy Girl" 116, 125, 154, 202, 212
Protestant Reformation 159
Protestantism 159, 161
psyche 17, 139, 141, 152, 169
psychoanalysis/psychotherapy 10, 216
puberty 131
punishment 14, 17, 26, 29, 35, 58, 73
punk rock 43, 48, 51
"Puppet Show" 212
Purdy, John L. 65, 213, 220
Pure Juice 222
Puritanism 162

Quentin 69, 70

Rabb, J. Douglas 57, 58, 86, 177, 178, 220
Racansky, I.G. 216
Rack 49, 80, 123
Radiohead 5
Ramones 48, 220
Rage (character) 167
rape 23, 24, 34, 133, 191, 192, 199
rationalism 68
Ray, Supryia M. 124, 143, 220
"Real Me" 212
reality 5, 7, 8, 9, 18, 29, 47, 62, 64, 66, 74, 75,
    76, 105, 110, 121, 129, 133, 134, 137, 138, 139,
    148, 151, 160, 161, 164, 186, 190, 195, 205,
    208, 209
reason 137, 218, 222

red devil 55, 57, 60, 62, 64
redemption 14, 16, 17, 19, 21, 22, 25, 26, 30, 34, 36, 79, 81, 129, 165, 197, 208
reflexive mode 114, 117
Regan 161
Reinkemeyer, Joe 149, 156
Reiss, Jana 15, 21, 23, 210, 220
relationships 12, 40, 41, 45, 52, 54, 93, 117, 123, 128, 179, 190, 191, 195, 196, 198, 202, 208
R.E.M. 5
"Replacement" 147, 151, 190, 212
"Reptile Boy" 74, 82, 123, 212
Resnick, Laura 14, 16, 220
"Restless" 47, 186, 212
Reston, Dana 149, 156
resurrection 12, 25, 90, 165, 172, 192, 208, 209
"Revelations" 122, 212
Revenge (character) 167
Richard III 167, 221
Richard III 167, 221
Richardson, J. Michael 57, 58, 86, 88, 177, 178, 220
Rieff, Philip 159, 169, 172, 220
Riley 17, 33, 47, 48, 97, 128, 189, 190, 191, 192, 193, 198, 204, 207, 208, 209
Ripper 128
Ritzer, George 164, 220
R.J. 41, 121
Road to Ruin 220
robot 18, 31, 125, 143, 174, 175, 211, 219
Rocky Horror Picture Show 150, 221
roles 13, 20, 25, 32, 38, 39, 42, 43, 44, 47, 50, 51, 52, 60, 76, 89, 101, 120, 125, 133, 138, 161, 162, 168, 170, 174, 180, 184, 186, 188, 193, 197, 200, 202
Roman Catholic 81
romance 15, 75, 198, 202, 208, 209, 210
Rome 167
Romeo 167
Romeo and Juliet 167, 221
"Run" 122, 216
Ruppert 65, 213, 220
Ryan, Meg 148

sacrifice 10, 12, 17, 18, 19, 20, 21, 30, 52, 88, 155, 164, 165, 167, 188, 194, 204, 208, 210
sadomasochism 72
St. Francis vii, 7, 51, 96, 97, 102, 103, 104, 105, 106, 129, 219, 223
St. Francis Cycle 104
Saint Francis of Assisi 214
St. George 133
Saint-Saëns, Camille 47, 221
saints 10, 13, 14, 21, 97, 102, 103, 104, 106, 133, 164, 172, 214
Salem 174
salvation 14, 16, 159, 164, 166, 167, 169
"Same Time Same Place" 11, 93, 121, 212

"Sanctuary" 17, 192, 193
Sanders, Todd 174, 176, 180, 182, 183, 184, 213, 214, 219, 220, 221
Santa Barabara 58
Santa Ynez 62, 63, 221
Sartre, Jean-Paul 95
satan/satanism 72, 145, 183, 218
"Saturated" 43, 222
Savage Country 221
saving 17, 21, 44, 84, 133, 137, 138, 166, 188, 207, 220
savior 8, 109, 137, 186, 188
Saxey, Esther 23, 221
Scarecrow 35, 153
Scher, Hal 216
"School Hard" 43, 70, 212
"School's Out" 124, 215
Schudt, Karl 17, 221
science 5, 82, 84, 85, 113, 131, 134, 135, 138, 151, 155, 219, 227
Scoble, M.J. 98, 221
Scooby-Doo 158
Scooby Gang 7, 12, 16, 17, 19, 20, 29, 30, 31, 34, 40, 44, 46, 47, 51, 53, 57, 58, 59, 60, 61, 63, 66, 70, 71, 75, 76, 79, 80, 81, 83, 88, 89, 90, 91, 92, 93, 94, 95, 121, 122, 125, 126, 153, 154, 160, 165, 169, 170, 171, 172, 188, 191, 192, 195, 197, 206, 207, 208
scoring 40, 156
Scotland 167
Scully 155
Seals and Croft 45
Sears 87, 154, 157, 169, 194, 200
second wave 185, 198
Secundum Iohannem 22, 221
"Seeing Red" 11, 16, 24, 25, 30, 124, 152, 192, 194, 210, 212
self-actualization 22
self-centeredness 1, 87, 154
"Selfless" 15, 51, 52, 169, 203, 212, 216
self-transcendence 22
Seminole 66
September 11, 2001 166
Sergeant Pepper's Lonely Hearts Club Band 98, 100, 104
Sesame Street 146, 221
Seuss, Dr. 142, 148, 215
Sex Pistols 152
Sexton, Timothy 102, 221
sexuality 32, 41, 47, 52, 131, 136, 137, 141, 178, 179, 187, 204
"Shadow" 212
Shakespeare, William 5, 8, 144, 150, 158, 159, 160, 161, 162, 164, 166, 167, 170, 171, 198, 214, 217, 219, 221, 223, 228
"Shall We Gather at the River" 147
Shaw, George Bernard 176, 221
"She" 123
Shelley 67, 134, 221
she-mantis 137, 138

Shermer, Michael 13, 16, 221
The Shining 102, 221
Showalter, Dennis 197, 222
"Showtime" 145, 175, 212
Shuttleworth, Ian 13, 222
Shylock 144, 154
Sid Lives 222
Sierra Leone 176
signs vii, 5, 7, 107, 108, 109, 110, 111, 112, 113, 114, 115, 116, 118, 119
Simon, Linda 68, 222
Simpsons 142
sin 61, 63, 159, 166, 169
Sinatra, Frank 122, 222
siren 120, 128, 134
Sister Sledge 223
Skeleton Crew 218
Skippy R 164, 222
Slate 199
Slayage 36, 213, 216, 217, 219, 222, 223, 224
Slayage Conference 213, 217, 222
Slayer/Slaying 5, 6, 8, 9, 13, 14, 17, 20, 21, 22, 24, 25, 38, 42, 46, 51, 55, 56, 57, 58, 59, 60, 61, 62, 65, 67, 69, 70, 73, 75, 78, 79, 81, 82, 83, 86, 87, 88, 96, 102, 108, 111, 114, 116, 120, 121, 122, 124, 129, 131, 133, 142, 144, 145, 146, 147, 155, 158, 159, 160, 161, 162, 163, 164, 165, 166, 168, 171, 173, 180, 182, 186, 187, 188, 189, 191, 192, 198, 199, 200, 202, 203, 204, 205, 206, 207, 208, 209, 210, 211, 213, 214, 215, 216, 217, 218, 219, 220, 221, 222, 223, 224
"Sleeper" 126, 212
Sleepless in Seattle 148, 222
"Smashed" 11, 20, 32, 128, 212
"Smells Like Teen Spirit" 51, 220
Smithsonian 66
Smurf 155
Snapping Turks 99
Snyder, Principal 70, 71
Social Construction of Reality 151, 214
social norm 162, 170, 182
Socrates 17, 84, 95
Soledad 64, 219
Solomon, David 53, 216
Solon 202
"Some Assembly Required" 172, 212
"Something Blue" 10, 127, 178, 179, 212
"Songs of Brave Ulysses" 128
Sonneborn, Liz 63, 66, 222
Sophocles 222
sorcery 52, 176, 180, 183, 219; *see also* magicians; warlocks; witches
soul vii, 6, 12, 16, 17, 19, 21, 22, 23, 24, 25, 26, 27, 28, 29, 30, 31, 32, 33, 34, 35, 36, 37, 53, 71, 72, 79, 97, 100, 126, 134, 147, 152, 159, 163, 165, 169, 171, 189, 192, 194, 203, 204, 208
soulless 26, 31, 43
source music 40, 49

South, James 15, 21, 183, 210, 216, 217, 218, 220, 221, 222, 227
South Africa 183
Spain 176
Spider-Man 143
Spike 5, 10, 11, 12, 14, 15, 16, 17, 19, 21, 22, 23, 24, 25, 28, 29, 30, 31, 32, 33, 34, 35, 36, 37, 43, 45, 48, 49, 50, 51, 60, 61, 66, 71, 72, 73, 74, 75, 77, 89, 90, 93, 94, 122, 123, 124, 126, 128, 145, 146, 148, 150, 151, 152, 153, 157, 165, 170, 178, 187, 188, 189, 191, 192, 195, 196, 197, 198, 203, 205, 206, 207, 208, 209, 210, 216
Spinoza, Baruch 23
"Spiral" 212
spirit 17, 25, 51, 57, 59, 60, 64, 66, 89, 103, 110, 171, 172, 174, 178, 181, 182, 194, 214, 220
Spirit Room 214
spiritual 19, 21, 22, 63, 64, 66, 97, 103, 159, 163, 164, 171, 172, 175, 178, 180, 213, 218, 220
Splendid 126, 222
Sprung Monkey 43, 123, 222
Stallings, Jesse 2, 7, 142, 156, 227
Stanford 13
Star Trek 142, 147, 222
Star Wars 51, 142, 145, 222
Static X 125, 222
statistics 149
Steiner, Max 222
stereotypes vii, 6, 8, 20, 55, 56, 57, 58, 64, 65, 66, 199
Sterngold, James 105, 222
Stevenson, Gregory 14, 17, 18, 21, 22, 25, 26, 27, 28, 29, 30, 31, 34, 35, 36, 61, 66, 86, 87, 88, 89, 91, 95, 176, 181, 182, 222
Stokes, Mike 76, 222
Stokstad, Marilyn 102, 103, 222
"Storyteller" 16, 51, 95, 155, 212
Stout, Jeffrey 210, 222
Stowe, Harriet Beecher 86, 88
straitjacket guys 101
Strong, Danny 199
Stroud, Scott R. 14, 222
Styx 147, 151
suffering 10, 11, 12, 23, 80, 91, 122, 145, 188, 208, 210
A Summer Place 41, 121, 129, 222
"Summerbreeze" 48, 223
Summercamp 128, 222
Sunnydale vii, 6, 10, 13, 14, 18, 20, 27, 35, 41, 43, 44, 45, 46, 47, 51, 53, 57, 58, 59, 60, 64, 67, 68, 69, 70, 71, 74, 75, 77, 80, 81, 82, 89, 92, 93, 97, 98, 99, 106, 109, 112, 113, 114, 115, 118, 119, 121, 122, 124, 125, 126, 127, 128, 131, 132, 144, 153, 155, 160, 162, 164, 165, 166, 167, 171, 175, 181, 195, 198, 199, 200, 205, 206, 209, 216, 217, 218, 221, 222
superego 29, 37, 141
superhero 11

"Superstar" 47, 200, 212
Surfacing 219
"Surprise" 126, 155, 212
Susman, Warren 170, 222
Sutherland, Kristen 53, 222
Sutherland, Sharon 17, 222
Swahili 180
Swan, Sarah 17, 222
Sweet 50
Swirl 222
Sword in the Stone 150, 223
Swyden, Thomas A. 149, 156
symphony 107, 119

Tabron, Judith 194, 223
"Tabula Rasa" 91, 121, 125, 178, 200, 212
Tag, Philip 40
"Tales of Brave Ulysses" 45, 49, 215
Tallensi 177
Tamora 167
Tancredi, Laurence 84, 223
Tanner, Jennifer Lynn 51, 218, 223
Tanzania 176, 183, 221
Tara 11, 18, 21, 47, 49, 50, 79, 80, 90, 91, 121,
    123, 124, 125, 126, 128, 129, 165, 170, 178,
    179, 194, 195, 196, 208, 210, 216, 223
Taylor, Carolyn 2, 8, 185, 226
"Teacher's Pet" 7, 74, 108, 131, 132, 133, 135,
    136, 137, 139, 141, 151, 171, 200, 212
techno-magic 175
Ted 81, 212
"Ted" 81, 212
Televised Morality 25, 27, 30, 66, 86, 222
Terminator 148, 223
Thanksgiving 56, 57, 59, 60, 61, 65, 219
THC 127, 223
therapeutic ethos vii, 8, 158, 159, 160, 168,
    169, 170, 171, 172, 219
"Thing of the Past" 128, 222
Third Eye Blind 122, 223
"This Is How It Goes" 126, 130, 219
"This Year's Girl" 147, 212
Thomas 88
Thompson, Gregory 2, 7, 8, 158, 228
Thrown to the Wolves 216
Time (character) 167
Tin Man/Tin Woodman 35, 153
Titanic 147
Titus Andronicus 167, 221
Titus Andronicus 167, 221
Torrin, Emiliana 48, 223
torture 13, 14, 16, 26, 28, 31, 35, 80
"Touched" 12, 93, 124, 212
"Tough Love" 82, 194, 212
Townsend, Pete 152, 223
"Triangle" 148, 212
Trick 17, 75, 79
Trinita 102
Trio, Evil 15, 16, 18, 23, 51, 52, 80, 91, 94,
    153, 192, 194, 199, 200

triumph 20, 21, 22, 32, 129, 188, 203, 204
Triumph of the Therapeutic 159, 221
troll 15
Tupperware 146
Turok-han 52
Twain, Mark 83, 223
two shot 113
"Two to Go" 181, 188, 212

Umbria 104
unconscious 218
undead 82
UPN 24
urge 12, 13, 47, 132, 140

Valentine's Day 74, 118
vampire 13, 14, 16, 17, 18, 19, 20, 21, 26, 27,
    29, 30, 32, 43, 44, 46, 52, 56, 58, 61, 62, 66,
    68, 69, 71, 72, 73, 74, 75, 76, 78, 79, 81, 82,
    88, 89, 93, 98, 108, 111, 114, 116, 121, 123,
    125, 126, 127, 131, 133, 134, 137, 138, 144,
    145, 146, 153, 154, 158, 160, 162, 164, 165,
    168, 170, 186, 187, 189, 190, 191, 201, 202,
    203, 204, 205, 206, 207, 208, 210, 219
Van Gogh, Vincent 105
Vebber, Dan 149, 156
Vedantam, Shankar 85, 223
vengeance 15, 18, 59, 68, 80, 144, 147, 165,
    193, 194
Venice 167
"Vermillion Borders" 128, 223
Verona 167
Verrocchio 104
Veruca 77, 78, 80, 82, 127, 155
Vespucci, Amerigo 55
Vicious, Sid 45, 222
victim 20, 58, 59, 71, 72, 102, 135, 136, 180,
    183, 186, 193, 209, 226
villains 11, 18, 43, 45, 51, 53, 70, 75, 91, 101,
    108, 116, 148, 162, 170, 181, 194, 212
"Villains" 212
Vint, Sherryl 185, 223
Virgil 128, 223
Virgil 223
Virgin and Child Enthroned 102
"Virgin State of Mind" 217
virtue 8, 202, 203
Vlam, Grace A.H. 103, 223
Voltaire 22, 223
voodoo 175, 176, 180, 218

Waiting for Godot 146, 214
Walsh, Maggie 46, 69
Travis McGee 188
Walters, Anna 66, 223
Warhol, Andy 105
warlocks 49, 80; *see also* magicians; sorcery;
    witches
Warren 11, 16, 18, 51, 52, 80, 91, 93, 124, 148,
    155, 170, 194

warriors 214, 216
Watcher/Watcher's Council 1, 16, 68, 69, 79, 89, 90, 93, 128, 146, 151, 175, 179, 187, 193, 196, 215
"We Are Family" 46, 223
We Are Family 223
weakness 16, 17, 135, 190, 191
"Wearing Me Down" 123, 215
"Weight of the World" 18, 187, 212
"Welcome to the Hellmouth" 21, 87, 88, 115, 119, 123, 153, 154, 169, 177, 200, 212, 223
Wells, Orson 5
Wells, Stanley 160, 223
Wendy's 223
werewolf 15, 77, 78, 127, 137, 155, 178
Wertz, Dorothy 163, 223
Wesley 14, 146
West, Dave 14, 217, 223
West Wing 166
"Western" stereotypes 6
"What Is Relativism?" 87, 223
"What's My Line?" 154, 205, 212
Whedon, Joss 2, 5, 10, 14, 21, 23, 25, 27, 28, 10, 34, 36, 41, 42, 47, 49, 50, 52, 53, 57, 58, 71, 72, 74, 76, 83, 86, 87, 88, 106, 119, 126, 142, 156, 158, 159, 166, 182, 186, 217, 219, 220, 223, 224
Wheeler, Ella Wilcox 145, 224
"When She Was Bad" 70, 117, 187, 212
"Where the Wild Things Are" 47, 151, 152, 212
Whistler 19, 27
White, Barry 45, 47, 154, 224
White, Nicholas 202, 224
Who 47, 152, 212, 223, 224
"Who Are You?" 13, 17, 190, 192, 212
Widespread Panic 115, 220, 224
Wilcox, Rhonda 12, 16, 17, 18, 39, 41, 50, 94, 120, 215, 218, 219, 220, 224
"Wild at Heart" 77, 127, 151, 155, 178, 181, 212
Wilkins, Mayor 68, 71, 75, 76, 77, 78, 79, 146
will 12, 19
William 32, 73, 126, 216, 217, 218, 221, 222
Willow vii, 6, 10, 11, 14, 15, 17, 18, 20, 21, 22, 23, 30, 45, 47, 48, 49, 50, 59, 60, 61, 63, 74, 75, 77, 79, 80, 81, 82, 83, 84, 87, 88, 89, 90, 91, 92, 93, 94, 95, 112, 113, 116, 117, 119, 121, 122, 123, 124, 125, 126, 127, 128, 129, 133,

138, 148, 151, 153, 154, 155, 157, 162, 165, 166, 168, 169, 170, 172, 175, 177, 178, 179, 180, 181, 182, 183, 187, 188, 189, 190, 191, 194, 195, 200, 205, 206, 207, 208, 210, 223
Wilson, R.M. 171, 224
"Winter" 64
Winter, E.H. 177, 219
Winter's Tale 167, 221
"The Wish" 15, 165, 212
Witchcraft Control Act 183
witches/witchcraft 8, 56, 59, 74, 79, 80, 82, 89, 108, 137, 151, 153, 172, 173, 174, 175, 176, 177, 178, 179, 180, 181, 182, 183, 184, 200, 210, 212, 213, 214, 216, 218, 219, 220, 221, 224
witchdoctor 177, 180, 181
Wizard of Oz 35, 100, 101, 153, 224
wizards 35, 100, 101, 153, 224
Wolf Man 132, 139
Wolfram and Hart 82
Women's Belly Book 97, 176, 224
Wood, Principal Robin 33, 91, 124, 196
"Wrecked" 49, 79, 91, 123, 192, 212

X-Files 155, 224
Xander viii, 7, 11, 20, 21, 22, 30, 32, 39, 40, 43, 44, 45, 47, 49, 50, 51, 53, 57, 58, 60, 70, 74, 75, 78, 80, 82, 88, 89, 92, 112, 113, 116, 117, 118, 119, 121, 122, 124, 125, 127, 129, 131, 132, 133, 134, 135, 136, 137, 138, 139, 140, 144, 147, 151, 153, 157, 162, 165, 169, 170, 172, 177, 178, 187, 190, 191, 192, 194, 206, 207, 208, 209, 210
Xavier, St. Francis 103, 223

Yellow Submarine 98, 100, 101, 102, 106, 224
"Yes, Belief in Witchcraft Is Widespread" 183, 224
"The Yoko Factor" 48, 89, 128, 190, 198, 207, 212
Young Frankenstein 100, 214
"Youth Reportedly Burnt Eight" 215, 217, 224
Yuen, Wayne 18, 216

Zagzebski, Linda 210, 224
"The Zeppo" 44, 78, 212
Zimbardo, Philip 13, 16
zombie 69, 176